STRATEGIC MANAGEMENT

VALUE CREATION, SUSTAINABILITY, AND PERFORMANCE

G. Page West III

STRATEGIC MANAGEMENT

VALUE CREATION, SUSTAINABILITY, AND PERFORMANCE

Fourth Edition

For permission to use material from this text, submit all requests to:
Riderwood Publishing, 3109 Allerton Lake Drive, Winston Salem, NC, 27106.
Permissions questions can be emailed to strategytext@gmail.com.

ISBN-13: 978-0-9911552-5-5
ISBN-10: 0-9911552-5-5
Paperback version

Riderwood Publishing
3109 Allerton Lake Drive
Winston Salem, North Carolina, 27106
United States of America

RIDERWOOD

About the cover to the 4th Edition

The book's cover design reflects themes discussed throughout the text: new versus old, traditional and new technology industries, and international competition. Images include a 1957 Chevy Belair, 2015 Tesla, 1994 Donkey Kong, 2016 Pokemon Go game, 2016 Tencent logo, 1969 Beatles LP, 2007 iTunes images, and 2016 Spotify logo. The cover was designed by Linda and Page West with helpful input from strategy faculty familiar with this text.

To my best friend and wife of 31 years Linda.
And to my five children – Jennifer, Derek, Brittany, Allison, and GP.

I am fortunate to have been surrounded by many exemplars for my efforts as a business professor. I have never known a teacher more diligent and dedicated to her students than my wife Linda. Nothing stands in the way of ensuring that her students received the very best education. Since beginning this journey to write a textbook some years ago, she has encouraged and supported me in more ways than I could ever recount.

At the same time my five kids have always inspired me with their curiosity, their humor, their intuition, their thoughtful and considered approaches (most of the time!), and especially their hopes for a better world. It is these qualities that I aim to encourage in students through this book.

Preface

If you are a student, you may wonder why your professor has assigned this textbook for your Strategic Management course and asked you to get a copy.

If you are a strategy professor or instructor, you're probably saying to yourself, "There are so many strategic management texts. What makes this textbook unique in a crowded field? And why should I consider giving up the book I already know and going through the effort to prep a new text?" Even as the question of "competitive advantage" is fundamental to the field of Strategic Management, it is also important in the selection of a textbook to use in your strategy class.

So as I developed and edited this text, I carefully considered these questions. I have two sets of responses below: one for students, and one for professors and instructors.

Note for Students

As students, you know the concerns with many textbooks you have been required to read during your time in school.

- Often relatively dry, long-winded, hard to hold your attention.

- Out of touch with your reality, because they often draw upon examples from business that are tough for you to relate to.

- Difficult to put to use practically, because they are often short on how to actually apply the ideas to what you will do after you graduate.

- And unbelievably expensive!

No wonder so many students recommend "get rid of the textbook" in end-of-semester course evaluations! I have been teaching strategy for almost 30 years, and until I wrote and started using this book I never failed to receive this comment at the end of the term. I tried changing textbooks now and then, but the student feedback on the books never really changed.

So what's different here? First, let me start with the last point I made above about expense. I want to save money for students and for parents who pay university bills. Since you're reading this version, you already know it didn't break your college budget. You may have noticed on the dedication page that I have five children. This represented 20 years of college bills for me, and over time I have seen textbook prices getting totally out of control! Printed textbooks can cost over $200 today. Even their digital counterparts through the big publishing companies can cost $75 to "rent" for 4-6 months. This digital book overcomes this huge burden. Another plus: because it is a virtual read, we have not cut down one tree to deliver this book to you!

I'm also trying to solve the other problems. Using a fresh writing style with contemporary examples of companies you're familiar with, useful theory that is proven in management practice, and a step-by-step process to show you how to apply the ideas about strategy, I think you'll appreciate the difference.

I hope you will give me feedback on this new text, so that I can continue to make improvements. Let me know what you like and what you don't like. Tell me where you think something is confusing, tell me when you read something that you enjoyed or gave you new insight. Write your local congressman or congresswoman! (Just kidding.)

Note for Professors and Instructors

While there are opportunities related to students in developing new textbook material, I also wanted to create something special for professors. I wanted to create a text that was sure to enable every instructor to teach strategy more effectively, while at the same time truly engaging students with easily-understood theory and useful examples from practice. To do so I have incorporated several key innovations in this book:

- Integrating content <u>across</u> chapters throughout the book, relying upon important strategy concepts (value chain, resource based advantage) as the primary integrating mechanisms.

- Integrating emerging content <u>within</u> the traditional outline of strategic management, rather than grafting on new chapters.

- Devoting a full chapter to performance.

- Providing guidance on practical use and application of important strategy concepts (e.g., steps to conduct an industry analysis, how to conduct a resources analysis).

- Adopting a writing style that is student-friendly and accessible.

I briefly explore these innovations below.

Integration *Across* Chapters

One of the problems I have encountered over my years in teaching is that we must cover a great deal of material in a typical strategic management course. I have learned that students often view the course as a series of almost stand-alone frameworks – industry analysis, then value chain, generic strategies, etc. – that are not well integrated with each other or with more complicated material later on in the course such as M&A, structuring, or implementation. I'm addressing the integration problem in this book.

First, to lay the groundwork for students, I explicitly introduce two strategic imperatives in Chapter 1. These include the value creation imperative and the opportunity recognition imperative. I position strategic management today as occurring in a constantly changing context, so one real challenge has to do with superior performance both now and in the future. These two imperatives are revisited and touched upon in virtually every chapter.

For you as instructor, the textbook uses "value chain" and "resource based advantage" as core integrating concepts. As you build the foundation for strategic management, the combination of these integrating concepts requires students to consider how firms achieve superior *performance* by creating *value* on a *sustainable* basis. Note that the italicized words here are in the subtitle for the book.

This approach offers several advantages. First, the value chain integration focus enables a broader discussion of organizational stakeholders, corporate social responsibility, and organizational goals. Economic value and social value are each perceived as legitimate organizational goals by students today, and therefore *value* embraces a wide range of organizations including not-for-profits and those with social goals. The relevance of the strategic management course to these sectors, where student interest is rapidly growing, becomes more transparent.

The concept of value also facilitates the discussion of industry entry as well as the discussion of how value is created in different ways at different stages of an industry's or company's evolution. Importantly, the issue of value creation is seen as a critical ongoing strategic challenge in industries characterized by evolutionary and revolutionary change. Therefore, the tension that exists between mandates for change versus the need for continuity can be highlighted.

But these more contemporary ideas cannot exist in isolation from the essential *sustainability* goal of superior performance. I strongly emphasize the importance of coordinating mechanisms across the value chain, routines, and other intangible dimensions. In turn, these help make the discussion of resource-based advantage more practical and more understandable.

Throughout the text you will find occasions where we refer back to the foundational material. Conclusions from industry analysis can be evaluated in the context of value adding activities and resource-based capabilities, as can business level strategies, competitive dynamics, diversification, organizational structuring, and internal control and performance monitoring. I believe that this integrative approach makes the field of strategic management more understandable to students, and it allows instructors to more easily draw on the critical foundations all the way through the semester.

Integrating Emerging Content *Within* Chapters

It always bothered me in my earlier teaching days when the nth edition of an established strategy textbook would be announced and one of its major innovations would be a new stand-alone chapter on something like "international strategy" or "entrepreneurship" or most recently "strategic entrepreneurship." Lately, the 18th edition (!) of a popular strategy text was announced claiming something extraordinary – an entire chapter devoted to ethics. Really? In my view these dimensions have *always* been a part of effective strategic management in the marketplace, and thus always deserving of treatment integrated throughout the text!

In this book "emerging" content in strategic management is thoroughly integrated into existing frameworks. You will not find a separate chapter on International Strategy. Instead, this material is integrated into Chapter 8 on growth and change, since it represents one of many options for firms to pursue in the development of their business. You will not find that Entrepreneurship is separated out in its own chapter, because it is not a separate function or process in any organization. Instead, the dimensions of value creation and opportunity recognition enable the instructor to deal with the ongoing entrepreneurial challenge at any stage of a company or industry. Ethics and principled decision making is often referred to throughout the text, as it actually occurs in business on a day-to-day basis!

Chapter on Performance

This text emphasizes – in fact spotlights – *performance* as a key outcome focus of strategic management by treating this dimension in its own stand-alone chapter. Few other strategy textbooks do this. I encourage the perspective that strategic management demands an ability to move with facility back and forth between the conceptual and the practical, including the performance that results from best laid plans. Students must understand early on that strategic decisions and actions ultimately translate to financial effects. With this understanding, case discussions and other class interactions can easily move deeper than merely "I think the company should do....." to "I think the company should do.....and this is the estimated performance impact."

My observation is that faculty want students to conduct financial analyses of companies for class discussions and projects, yet texts do not usually provide sufficient content to assist in this teaching effort (other than the usual appendix containing financial ratios – we have one of those, too, by the way). By addressing this important topic early in the book in Chapter 2, instructors will have an easier time in drawing upon financial analysis throughout the course and in asking students to consider performance implications in class discussions.

Theory to Practice

This book is strongly grounded in contemporary strategic management theory and thinking, but it also has a very practical bent. Students are increasingly being pushed to translate their education into useful, growth-oriented and value-creating efforts within the companies that recruit them. Today's job search process often involves phone or virtual interviews on the front end. In this environment, to the extent that your students can adeptly apply strategy ideas to real situations and problems they are asked about, they will outperform others.

Many students still go to work for large, diversified companies. Even more so today, these companies are seeking greater proficiency in strategic thinking among new employees. This reality makes it incumbent on courses and textbooks to deliver what students need: an understanding of strategy that they can use immediately after graduating (as well as when they join the ranks of senior management later on), and content that is readily applicable to all businesses.

I want my students to be able to take these ideas and use them, easily. So you will find that most chapters provide guidance on actually putting the ideas to use (e.g., steps to conduct an industry analysis, how to do a resource analysis, how to conduct a value chain analysis) along with examples of how to do so. My classroom tests have found this works!

Engaging Style

Finally, this book overcomes an enduring complaint by students about many textbooks: that they are dry and uninteresting to read. The writing for this book strikes a balance between providing well-explained theory and a style that is engaging for students. I make liberal use of companies and industries that students can relate to in order to provide good translation of ideas to practice (e.g., music industry, Xbox 360 and the gaming industry, PCs, Starbucks, Samsung). In fact, one of the reviewers commented "bang – hits the spot!" when an example from the video game *Call of Duty* illustrated a point about industry analysis. I also use the first person plural "we." I view learning about strategic management as a journey we faculty are embarking on alongside our students, rolling up our sleeves and working hard together to understand this fascinating field.

The manuscript for this book was extensively reviewed by other strategy professors like you (see list which follows), and went through a rigorous "revise and resubmit" process. It received overwhelmingly favorable ratings on both writing style and content.

How do I know this style of writing works? Before the first edition was published I classroom tested this textbook for years. Students responded favorably. In 2016 the book has been adopted in many universities and is being used by thousands of students. Since using this book in my own classes at Wake Forest University, I receive positive comments in the anonymous end-of-semester course surveys about the instructional materials. And it is the honest truth: since using this text I have never again received the student comment "get rid of the text"!

One Last Important Item

In my remarks to students, above, I mentioned the significant cost benefits of using this digital textbook. This is very real for students and their parents. The cost of textbooks has risen 812% in the past 30 years (U.S. Bureau of Labor Statistics; U.S. Census Bureau). That's *more* than increases in healthcare costs, housing prices, and college tuition, all of which have risen faster than the rate of inflation. Now, students are spending an average of $1,200 a year on textbooks and course materials at public four-year colleges. Your adoption of this digital text makes a real difference in more ways than one!

What's New in the 4th Edition?

Below are a few bullet point summaries about the enhancements in this 4th Edition.

- **2016 actually means 2016**. The beauty of the digital-only textbook such as this is that the lag time between finishing the manuscript and publishing the edition is, literally, only days. Printed textbooks are usually dated by the time they come out, because of how long it takes for traditional publishers to do their thing. This 4th edition is copyright 2016. You will find that all the examples of companies used have updated performance numbers through the latest fiscal year and into 2016. Really current events are included, such as the Brexit decision in the material on political risks in international strategy.

- **International Strategy**. Speaking of which, this section in Chapter 8 has been expanded to include a discussion of fit utilizing two additional frameworks. An abbreviated version of Porter's diamond model is presented, and Ghemawat's CAGE Distance model each help qualify decisions about expanding to other countries. I have also included material on modes of entry to foreign markets, as well as material on political and economic risks in doing so.

- **Corporate Strategy Parenting Advantage**. I was hesitant to add material to one of the longer chapters in the text. However, when I attended the Strategic Management Society meeting in St. Gallen I sat in on sessions that focused on the Campbell / Goold "parenting advantage" framework. I found this an interesting and compelling way to help frame the question of diversification, which usually focuses on the relatedness between subsidiaries as the raison d'etre. It is helpful to ask students to consider, too, the relationship between parent and child.

- **Balanced Scorecard**. In Chapter 12 the balanced scorecard is one of three systems discussed as ways to measure and monitor progress on strategy. Since it is difficult in practice to understand how a complete balanced scorecard looks and works, here I have added an additional example and illustration of this method in a non-profit situation.

Acknowledgements

I would like to acknowledge many people who have contributed to this effort through reviewing the text and commenting on material in its various development stages. My thanks to:

Terry R. Adler, New Mexico State University
Brent Allred, The College of William & Mary
Joe S. Anderson, Northern Arizona University
Sonny Ariss, University of Toledo
Charles Bamford, University of Notre Dame
Nachiket Bhawe, North Carolina State University
John Ceneviva, University of North Carolina at Greensboro
Samuel DeMarie, Iowa State University
Pat H. Dickson, Wake Forest University
Thomas J. Douglas, Southern Illinois University, Edwardsville
Scott E. Elston, Iowa State University
Robert E. Ettl, Stony Brook University
Dr. Charles R. Fenner, SUNY – Canton
Robert Gemmell, Georgia Institute of Technology
Debora J. Gilliard, Metropolitan State College
Ari Ginsberg, New York University
Barbara A. Good, Ursuline College
Marcellina Hamilton, SUNY - Canton
Jay J. Janney, University of Dayton
Sal Kukalis, California State University Long Beach
Joseph W. Leonard, Miami University
Paul Mallette, Colorado State University
James Randall Martin, Florida International University
Elouise Mintz, Saint Louis University
Michael L. Monahan, Frostburg State University
J. L. Morrow, Jr., Birmingham - Southern College
Fred P. Newby, Sullivan University
Daewoo Park, Xavier University
Ralph W. Parrish, University of Central Oklahoma
John K. Ross III, Texas State University
Amit Shah, Frostburg State University
Bren Varner, Wake Forest University
Paula S. Weber, Saint Cloud State University

I would also like to acknowledge the tremendous guidance and assistance I have received from my friend and colleague Susan Tague. Without her the production of this digital textbook would never have been possible!

About the Author

Page West, Ph.D.

Dr. Page West is Professor of Strategy and Entrepreneurship and the BB&T Professor of Capitalism and Free Enterprise at Wake Forest University. He earned his B.A. in Economics at Hamilton College, an MBA at The Amos Tuck School of Business Administration at Dartmouth College, and a Ph.D. in Strategic Management at the University of Colorado at Boulder. Prior to earning his Ph.D. he held positions in new business development for 17 years at consumer packaged goods companies including General Mills and Celestial Seasonings, and consulted with Westinghouse and other technology companies. He also started up a food manufacturing company, raised venture capital, and expanded the business to a national level.

At Wake Forest he has taught undergraduate and graduate classes in Strategic Management, Entrepreneurship, International Entrepreneurship, Capitalism and Free Markets, and Shakespeare on Management. He has taught management in London UK and Vienna Austria, and he has been a regular visiting management faculty member of École de Management in Bordeaux, France. He has won awards for innovative teaching three times, and has twice been named as the most influential professor by Wake Forest business school alumni.

His research focuses primarily on strategy and strategic resource evolution in new ventures, and secondarily on the contributions that new business can make to economic development. He has published articles in *Journal of Management, Journal of Management Studies, Journal of Business Venturing, Entrepreneurship Theory and Practice, Academy of Management Learning and Education, Journal of Technology Transfer, Journal of Small Business Management, Management Research Review, Strategic Direction*, and *International Journal of Organizational Analysis*. He has also edited two books, on business education and on challenges presented by the 2008 financial crisis.

Page is married to his college sweetheart Linda. They have five children, and at the latest count have three grandchildren. He enjoys hiking and fishing in the Colorado high country, international travel, and researching his family genealogy.

TABLE OF CONTENTS

SWOT
Value Chain
Value Chain and Competitive Advantage
Conducting a Value Chain Analysis

The Characteristics of Resources
Resources and Capabilities
Conducting a Resource Analysis

Logic of Business-Level Strategies
Low Cost Strategy
Differentiation Strategy
Other Strategic Approaches
Outsourcing, Strategy, and the Value Chain

Industry Life Cycles
Fragmented and Consolidated Industries
Organizational Life Cycles
Strategy Issues in Stages
International Strategy

Competitor Intelligence
Industry Characteristics and Trajectories
Predicting Competitive Moves
Tactical and Strategic Responses
Cooperation

Corporate Strategy Versus Business Strategy
Historical Perspectives

Motivations for Diversification
Types of Diversification
Diversification Performance
Managing the Corporate Portfolio

Aligning Strategy and Structure
Understanding the Structuring Imperative
Key Organizational Components
Coordinating Mechanisms
Types of Organizational Structure

Keys to Implementation Control
Metrics
Developing an Implementation Plan
Strategic Leadership

Section A: Strategy

Look around you. Read the headlines in today's *Wall Street Journal*. Some companies succeed wildly, while others fail miserably, and most fall somewhere in between. Why is this? Why do some companies perform better than others in the same industry, and why do some companies achieve superior performance over the long run? That's what this book is about.

Whatever sort of organization your plan to work for – large company, small company or family business, law firm or accounting firm, not-for-profit, government agency, school – you should be interested in how your organization can excel. It will excel by creating value in unique ways over time, doing this better than its competition, and sustaining that superiority. The sense of accomplishment and personal happiness you will feel by being part of this sort of successful endeavor will likely far outweigh any financial reward you might gain. The principles and ideas in this book should help you succeed in this lifelong agenda!

OK, so here's how we start the journey. This first section of this book covers both the beginning and the ending of Strategy. "Strategy" is a word that used all the time, but in our context it has a very specific meaning. Chapter 1 will tell you about Strategy itself and then provide a roadmap for where the book will take you during the course. Strategy is different in interesting and important ways from other business classes. And the need for strategy has become super-important over the last few years.

Then Chapter 2 drills down into Performance, which is what senior managers (and everyone else in the organization) should be working toward. Superior performance is THE outcome, the end-result of great strategy. I put this ending up front precisely because it is so important. Performance is more than just the numbers, and we'll point this out. But, the numbers have to work, or else all the other desirable performance dimensions are for nothing!

Then in Chapter 3 we go back to the beginning, where you'll read about crafting the strategic vision, the mission, and the principles for how to get where you want to go (hint: Performance).

Each chapter throughout this first section and the rest of the book will begin with two standard dimensions. First is a short list of "Learning Objectives" that outline what the chapter will help you understand. Then a short story about a business is presented to help you see that the subject of the chapter is really relevant and important. After you have finished reading each chapter, the Chapter Summary section provides a review of the learning objectives.

I look forward to working with you collaboratively to better understand Strategy.

Chapter 1: The Need for Strategy

LEARNING OBJECTIVES:

1. Identify and discuss the two strategic imperatives facing every company today.

2. Define the term "Strategy" and describe the five critical questions encompassing what we study in strategy

3. Explain the evolution of the field of strategy and why it is so important today.

4. Connect the concept of strategy with leadership and ethics.

5. Describe the process for developing and implementing strategy.

Sirius XM Satellite Radio Inc.[1]

Today's Sirius XM radio was originally founded as two separate organizations more than twenty years ago. XM Radio began in 1988 as American Mobile Radio Corporation, and Sirius was founded in 1990 as Satellite CD Radio Inc. Both companies were formed to provide broad multichannel, digital, satellite-based radio service for customers in the United States.

In 1997 American Mobile received the first satellite digital audio radio license and contracted with Boeing Satellite Systems to build and launch two satellites. Over the next four years, the company changed its name to XM Satellite Radio, held an initial public offering of its stock, signed licensing agreements with various media providers, and prepared for the March 2001 launch of its first satellite (Rock) followed in May by its second satellite (Roll). In September 2001, XM officially launched its service. Sirius Satellite Radio launched its service in July 2002, and the two companies competed fiercely until their merger in 2008.

For both companies, launching a successful satellite radio business was much more involved than simply competing for customers. New digital signal processing technology was developed. Suppliers of new types of chips had to be identified, and a complete satellite system developed and launched. Consumers could not receive satellite broadcasts on any existing radio, so each company forged receiver technology relationships with electronics manufacturers such as Sony and distribution arrangements with retailers such as Best Buy and Circuit City. XM struck agreements with General Motors and BMW to offer its satellite radio in new vehicles, while Sirius struck deals with Chrysler, Mercedes-Benz, and Freightliner trucks. These were expensive undertakings. By the time its service began, XM had raised over $1.5 billion in debt and equity, while Sirius had raised nearly $2.5 billion.

Each company carefully considered the adoption of different business models – charging subscriptions, selling advertising, or some combination of both. There had never been a business like this before, so there was no telling in advance which model would work best. Allowing advertising would generate revenue faster, but it would then seem more like everyday radio and interfere with the kind of ad-free consumer value that the founders had envisioned. By not allowing advertising each company would need to invest heavily to develop a subscription base, requiring them to compete with other forms of discretionary entertainment spending by consumers.

Neither iPod nor MP3 technology existed at the time of XM's or Sirius's founding. The only way customers could previously listen to the music of their choice was to bring along a selection of CDs or cassette tapes. So-called "free radio" was broadcast locally, using analog technology and continually interrupted by the need to air commercials in order to generate revenue. Then MP3 players were introduced in 1998 and the iPod made its earth-shaking appearance in 2001. The *Wall Street Journal* reported that "many people are simply having iPod adapters installed in their cars and skipping satellite altogether, a concept that was barely on the horizon when the satellite radio industry was young." Internet services like Pandora and Spotify have entered the fray, while smartphones play MP3 files and stream music through wireless networks.

Faced with very slow growth in subscribers because of this unexpected competition, each company made a series of tactical moves to dramatically change their fortunes. In 2004 Sirius announced that shock jock Howard Stern would be moving from CBS radio under an agreement that would potentially cost Sirius over $500 million over five years. This was followed by deals with the National Football League ($220 million over seven years), the National Basketball Association, and the English Premier League. At the same time, XM concluded deals with Major League Baseball ($650 million over eleven years), Oprah Winfrey ($55 million over three years), and the National Hockey League.

After more than six years of frustration through head-to-head competition and cascading technological changes affecting the industry, the two companies merged in 2008 in an effort to create a larger economically viable organization. The proposed merger was carefully examined by both the Federal Communications Commission and the Federal Trade Commission for possible monopolistic practices. Traditional broadcast competitors complained that one company would control 100 percent of satellite radio. XM and Sirius management countered that the definition of the industry and competitors was considerably broader than just "satellite."

When formed, the combined company stock price (SIRI) was $2.50. But with the onset of the financial crisis in 2009 auto sales declined severely, leading to softening in new subscriptions and poor financial performance. Within six months the stock was trading at $0.14. They had to raise cash to cover debt repayments and operations during 2009. Goldman Sachs predicted that the company would lose more than $500 million. Just before being forced to enter bankruptcy in 2009, Liberty Media (owner of DirecTV) scooped up 49% of the company in a last-minute deal, thwarting its longtime opponent who controlled Dish Network from expanding into satellite radio.

With the injection of cash growth resumed even during the recession. By early 2012 it was profitable, generating $700 million annual cash flow. By the end of 2015 the subscriber base had increased to 29.6 million listeners, an increase of 33% since early 2012. These increases have largely been driven by rising new car sales along with increased penetration among leader car manufacturers such as Toyota and Honda. The company's "churn rate" (dropped subscriptions) also declined to only 1.8%. By 2016 its stock price rose to nearly $4 per share, as revenue increased to more than $4.6 billion and EBITDA (earnings before interest, taxes, depreciation and amortization) reached $1.5 billion. In 2014-15 management has used its positive cash flow and additional debt to buy back shares of the company's common stock.

The story of Sirius XM raises many issues and questions that are tied to strategy:

QUESTIONS

1. What elements constitute a "good" strategy?

2. What is the difference between strategy and tactics?

3. What are the appropriate outcomes of an effective strategy?

4. Over what time horizon does strategy play itself out? How does management measure progress toward the accomplishment of outcomes over long periods of time?

5. How do you define your industry? Who is your competition? How do changes in competition and evolving technologies affect strategy?

6. When does it make sense for a company to merge with or acquire another company?

7. What options are available to management to grow the company and improve performance?

8. How should senior management anticipate or respond to government and day-to-day Wall Street scrutiny of its business?

9. Who should be involved in setting strategic direction and making the key strategic decisions for a company?

TODAY'S STRATEGIC IMPERATIVES

Once upon a time, before the 1970s, companies sought to achieve performance amidst fairly stable markets. Back then, markets were fairly well defined (e.g. a phone company provided a telephone and voice telephone service), barriers to entry to many markets were fairly robust, competitors basically understood one another and respected each other's turf, disruptive innovations occurred infrequently, and people in business kept fairly sane work hours.

Today, the game has changed and the rules are very different. Advances in technology occur rapidly and make even the smallest competitor a nuisance to the large, incumbent firm. It's hard to know how to accurately define an industry (e.g. a phone, provided by a company that doesn't even offer telephone service, is a camera is an e-mail device is a portable music player is a web browser). Globalization and the relative ease of forging alliances create situations where even geographically remote firms will compete in your own backyard for your most prized customers. Customers have come to expect more from all companies, pushing out the essential value frontier of more features and greater customization for lower prices. Companies must now account for a wide range of stakeholders affecting many aspects of their business, instead of just stockholders.

The pace of work has escalated because we are now in a global environment. Although the financial markets close in New York at the end of the workday, they are open nearly 24/7 because of the Tokyo, Hong Kong, Johannesburg, London and other exchanges. When you attend a trade show in Chicago, a visitor to your booth uses his cell phone to snap a picture of the new product that your company is proudly displaying. Within forty-eight hours, halfway around the world, a possible competitor has "dummied up" a similar new product in its low-cost manufacturing facility and added the item to its price list. Our colleague Richard D' Aveni coined the term *hypercompetition* to describe today's competitive environment.[2] Jack Welch, former CEO of

General Electric, described the 1980s as "white knuckle" competition but said the next decades would be even worse.

These ideas about intense competition amidst rapidly changing and evolving circumstances have tremendous implications for strategic management today. We believe that every aspect of the practice of strategy today - analysis, formulation, implementation, and evaluation - must embrace two imperatives in light of the new competitive context:

1. *Value creation imperative*

2. *Opportunity recognition imperative*

These two imperatives are the cornerstones of this textbook, and should be the lens through which you examine various aspects of the field and how companies are performing. Creating and maintaining a successful business in the face of ever-changing industry and competitive contexts brings to light the value creation imperative. Successful companies are like machines: once they figure out how to do something well, they refine the process and "institutionalize" it so they become better and better at it. Value creation is a central theme in this book, and we will unpack it more carefully in Chapter 5. As we shall see, however, value creation embraces many stakeholders in a company, not just customers. Therefore, many opportunities are presented to management to create unique value, which is the foundation of sustainably superior performance.

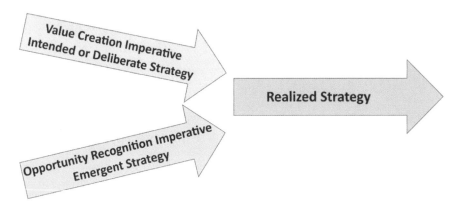

Now along comes a new type of business direction that requires value to be created in fundamentally different ways, challenging the status quo (and likely upsetting a lot of people who made the company so successful under the old way of doing things). Because industries, technology, globalization, and competition evolve so rapidly, every company must also excel at opportunity recognition – the critical need to identify and exploit where the market is heading. In this environment, companies must constantly position themselves to search for, identify, and embrace new opportunities that may ultimately replace their existing business. Rapid change tends to make every new product or service obsolete much faster than in the past. Few companies can rest on the laurels of what they accomplished five years ago or even last year, because hungry new competitors – both small and large – will seek to imitate what made them so successful. Just look at the new, encroaching competitors to Sirius XM in a few short years!

The downside of rapid technological advances, increasing ability to partner with other firms to gain complementary capabilities, and the fluidity of international financial institutions is that competitors now have the tools to go after lethargic companies whose management is rewarding itself for past performance by basking in the sun at a villa on Grand Cayman. The upside is that such change produces many new opportunities that are ripe for pursuit by you and your company. The problem that most successful companies have is that they become set in their ways of doing things and looking at things. The challenge for management, then, is to build an organization and a process that will proactively search out new opportunities, bring them to the table, and embrace experimentation on new products or services. The constant tension that will exist between managing the existing business and supporting new business development efforts will require exceptional management talent.

Companies need to recognize that, as markets change, the process of creating perceived value will also change. Together, this means that every company must become adept at both value creation and opportunity recognition on a sustainable basis. It's not just a one-time shot! Companies today need to understand who their new customers are going to be, what new values these customers will increasingly appreciate, and how to make money creating and delivering those new values.

How Does This Relate to Me?

This is a great question to ask, right here at the beginning of a course in strategy. Soon after you graduate the likelihood that you will immediately become the president of Sirius XM, GE, Netflix, or any of the other companies we will mention throughout this book is slim to none. Yet strategy is not something that is decided upon or occurs at only the very top of the organization. Strategy permeates every aspect of an organization. In fact, every part of an organization is a reflection of its strategy. And people throughout every company are involved essentially in strategy. Take a look again at the Sirius XM story. Research and development, supplier relationships, retail relationships, customer marketing, content providers, finance: both separately and in combination, each of these functional areas is central to the company's effective market entry and successful performance. No matter where you go to work or in what function you work, you will be involved with company strategy.

Perhaps you will not go to work in a large corporation after you have graduated, but instead find employment in a small business or your family's business. After all, more than 99 percent of all business organizations in the United States are small businesses (defined as having fewer than 500 employees), and they employ roughly 50 percent of the U.S. workforce. These types of companies generate most of the job growth in the United States because they are responsible for the lion's share of new technological innovation, export, and GDP.[3] The person who understands strategy in a sophisticated manner is better prepared to succeed in the small business environment.

Who do you think is better able to recognize new opportunities coming along? Who do you think is more flexible to embrace and learn about them as possibilities for new value creation? Young people are far more capable here! This strategy book is for you.

WHAT IS STRATEGY?

Strategy may be one of the most overused and misused terms in society today. Everyone has a "strategy" for so many activities in their lives. These range from those that might truly contain legitimate elements of a strategic decision to those that are fairly mundane and inaccurate uses of the term. Here are a few representative examples of how we see the word strategy used:

- A strategy for getting to work in the morning. Brittany faces a tough commute each day because of the traffic snarls and construction around her house. Each morning she listens to the traffic reports before leaving and uses one of more than a half-dozen routes that she has mapped out to get her to the office.

- A strategy for obtaining a career goal. Realizing that often those individuals with "line" management experience appear to obtain the top spots in the company, Jennifer requests a transfer from her "staff" analyst position into a lower level line position in one of the plants. Her hope is to develop her operational skills and prove her ability to handle mainstream "profit and loss" functions in the company.

- A strategy for waking up on time. Primarily because he has missed his 8:00 class four times this semester, Jesse decided to set two alarm clocks. On his bedside table is a normal buzzer alarm clock. Across the room his Android phone automatically cranks up Daft Punk and wakes him so he can go to class "One More Time."

- A strategy for developing an innovative product. Realizing that their new battery and miniaturization technique for employing GPS technology might have many uses, Derek and Morgan - the founders of FindemNow, Inc. - decide to evaluate each potential market before employing an engineering design firm to adapt the technology into a marketable product configuration.

- A strategy to be #1. Jack Welch, CEO of General Electric for 20 years, had a strategy for every GE division to be #1 or #2 in its industry or to leave it. The ownership of "first place" in an industry (whatever that really means) is actually an outcome, and offers no particular insight about the ways in which the company intends to operate.

A term that describes almost anything can describe nothing very well. Strategy is much more than any simple set of activities designed to obtain some desired end. Let's first talk about what strategy is generally, then we will define it in more specific terms. In general terms you can think of strategy as "the overall concept for how a company organizes itself and all its activities in order to conduct business successfully, outperform competitors, and deliver superior returns to its shareholders." As the Sirius XM story illustrates, a company's strategy has implications for every functional area across a company. That is, the efforts in each functional area (marketing, operations, finance, etc.) should reflect and support the central idea about how a company intends to conduct business and compete. But the concept of strategy is more than just how a business coordinates all its activities; it is also about performing *better* than competitors and delivering superior returns. Some companies may be well-coordinated across their functional areas, but are beat up by competitors in the marketplace and earn only average or below-average returns. We are interested in how to achieve superior performance when we talk about strategy.

Strategic management is the process through which strategy is developed, executed, and evaluated. There are typically four stages of the strategic management process: analysis, formulation, implementation, and evaluation. *Analysis* includes examining and understanding the industry in which you want to compete, and looking carefully inside the company to understand what its unique competitive strengths are and how it organizes its activities to create and deliver value. It is through the analysis process that companies often discover new opportunities or threats, and begin to realize how they can organize or reorganize to create new value. *Formulation* is the stage in which management articulates its vision and mission, outlines its goals and objectives, and decides upon a particular type of strategic approach to take. Of course, formulation depends on good, strong analysis. *Implementation* is where the rubber hits the road. In this stage, the formulated strategy is put into practice through the decisions that companies make about how to allocate resources, how to structure the organization and motivate employees, and which types of tactics, programs, and activities the company actually engages in. Strong implementation efforts call for consistency of effort across all the functional areas of a company. The fourth part of the strategic management process is *evaluation*, an activity that actually occurs throughout each of the first three stages. By creating a system of evaluation that operates continuously, management is able to rethink and respond more rapidly when actual results begin to diverge from what they had expected in the analysis, formulation, and implementation stages. Within each of these four stages are a set of well-grounded approaches and analytical frameworks that can be applied in a variety of business settings.

This general description of strategy and strategic management is helpful only up to a point. We need to get more specific and detailed. So here we define strategy as a field that deals specifically with the following five critical questions:[4]

1. **Why are firms different?** Why do some firms perform better than others? Strategy is about the creation of a position of advantage over other companies in a competitive marketplace, resulting in superior performance.

2. **How are competitive differences sustained?** Strategy is focused on sustaining a superior position in the market and superior performance over an extended period of time.

3. **What is special about strategic decisions?** Strategy deals with types of decisions that rise above specific functional concerns and have a unique character to them.

4. **What is the nature of strategy in a multi-business firm?** Questions 1 and 2 are fundamentally about a *single* line of business. Today, however, many companies are diversified, owning and operating many different kinds of businesses. The top execs at headquarters cannot possibly know every detail about all the different lines. So what kinds of issues do they deal with and what kinds of decisions do they need to make?

5. **How is strategic effectiveness measured?** Examining summary financial performance measures is the most frequently used method of assessing strategy. However, many executives understand that strategy must also consider other stakeholders, and that both qualitative and quantitative measures are required.

Why Are Firms Different? Creating Competitive Advantage

Conventional economic theory about "perfect competition" assumes that any advantage for one firm can be quickly imitated by its competitors and thus neutralized or negated by natural market forces – the result being that all firms in an industry will eventually look and act alike. And yet the reality, that there are many different types of firms in any industry, is obvious to us all. Why are firms different, then, given what we know about economic theory?

Strategy describes the specialized approach a company takes to the market that places it in a superior position relative to its competitors. It is fundamentally about developing a dominant logic for how the company can create value uniquely, focusing its attention and investments on that unique model, and ensuring that all parts of the organization are working consistently in support of that model. A sound strategy is one which creates value appreciated by various stakeholders, and which makes it difficult for competitors to do the same. When companies create value in unique and compelling ways, then markets respond and the results for the company will often include higher market share and profits.

Consider the commercial banking industry and the challenges it underwent during the financial crisis and ensuing recession. Chances are, if your family lives east of the Mississippi or in Texas, you are probably familiar with BB&T. Between 2009 and 2016 this bank grew from 15th to 11th largest bank in the country (now 205 billion in assets), and it outperformed many of its competitors. How? While many financial institutions moved outside their traditional areas of expertise and took on added risk during this period, BB&T stayed focused on its strategy as a community bank lender to local businesses and homeowners. The bank's CEO had for years personally emphasized the company's mission, vision and values to employees at all levels – especially to those out in the branch banks who interfaced on a day-to-day basis with its customers.

Together with strong internal reporting systems and close attention paid to operating practices across its many functional areas, the bank maintained a tight strategic focus in the face of incredible challenges in the financial markets. By 2012 BB&T's performance exceeded nearly all its competitors on net interest margin and return on equity, while maintaining significantly lower volatility (beta).

Excellence in strategic decision making involves several factors. First, to create value uniquely a company must decide not only what it *will* do, but also what it *will not* do. Many banks by 2007 had decided to get involved with exotic new financial innovations, or to broaden out their loan portfolios to higher risk clienteles. BB&T stayed focused on its core mission, practices and customers (even though they were tempted to go for quick profits and higher returns like their competitors!). Second, to create value uniquely requires a systematic approach to developing a set of resources and capabilities that set a company apart from its competitors in a way that is compelling for both its suppliers and customers. One of BB&T's unique resources is its culture and internal practices for ensuring consistency of its strategic approach across all functions, and from the boardroom to the branch lobby. In later chapters we will more carefully discuss these ideas about strategic choice and building resources.

We have already mentioned value creation several times in these first few pages. One of the central concepts of this book is a focus on value creation and the value chain - "a systematic way of examining all the activities a firm performs and how they interact…. " in order to find a basis for competitive advantage.[5] Later on we will also be discussing how to uniquely create value and how this can contribute to superior performance.

How Are Competitive Differences Sustained? Long-Term Orientation

It is nice to get an A on an exam, better yet to earn an A for an entire course, but best of all to graduate with close to a 4.0 GPA after several years of coursework! Strategy is not just about current position and performance; it is also about getting from the present to the future. In business this involves mapping out a direction for the longer term, which takes into account an always-evolving market and smart competitors. When we understand that strategy is about the longer term, we come to realize that many everyday uses of the word strategy are inappropriate, because they often refer only to short-term actions or short-term results.

Strategy is really about the *sustainability* of competitive advantage and superior performance over a period of time. In today's global marketplace we are often witness to rapid changes in technology, economic conditions, and competitive actions. Under these circumstances when so much is constantly in flux, how is it possible to have a long-term orientation? An essential component of strategy is therefore the vision the company develops in the context of all past, present, and anticipated future moves of its competitors, customers, suppliers, and other known and anticipated stakeholders. While today's incredibly competitive global environment might seem to be one in which a longer-term approach is of little value, the simple fact is that the *need for strategy* (the title of this chapter!) is even greater as a consequence of these rapidly evolving marketplace conditions. Otherwise, companies will find themselves bouncing along haphazardly based on decision-making that responds mainly to immediate circumstances. Strategy is the rudder to navigate choppy, even turbulent waters. BB&T bank is a great example of this.

Distinguishing between strategy and tactics is critical. Imagine an NCAA Final Four basketball tournament in which the national championship is decided by only one point at game's end. What enables one team to win at that moment, in that game, is how they and their coach *tactically* deal with the other team's plays and players. Tactics refer to how to match up resources and strengths in the short run with competitive challenges and opportunities. The *strategy* for the winning team, however, was determined much earlier when the coach's vision for how this group of players could compete effectively was put into practice. The combination of years of experience in a

competitive arena, complete knowledge of the competitors, experience in recruiting new high school players, hiring coaches with specific skills and understanding, and thorough training regimens. These strategic dimensions are what puts a team in a position to win.

Figure 1.1 captures the sense of these first two important dimensions of strategy.

Competition in Commercial Aircraft Manufacturing

In 2006, Boeing rolled its last 717 model off the aircraft assembly line in Long Beach, California. The Boeing 717 and its earlier predecessors were 100-seat models designed for regional transportation and routes between cities that did not require large capacity aircraft. The Long Beach factory opened in 1941 and produced almost 10,000 airplanes for the World War II effort, and then converted to commercial airplane construction thereafter. Even though airplanes had only been mass-produced for 34 years by the time this factory opened, Boeing built a factory that lasted 65 years. Do you think Boeing contemplated a 65-year run at that time?

During the same year, Boeing and its chief competitor Airbus Industries both faced critical decisions that would affect their rivalry for decades into the future, their suppliers, the airlines who are their customers and us as the traveling public. Boeing needed to decide whether to ratchet up the development schedule for its potentially lucrative 787 model (The Dreamliner) in order to preempt the new Airbus 350 model that was in development, or create a "stretch" version of the 787 to better compete with the larger Airbus A380 which was scheduled to roll out the next year. Ratcheting up the schedule to get into production sooner might put significant pressure on their suppliers, thereby raising costs, causing shortages and cutting profitability. Developing a stretch 787 would cost more in the short run, but might also blunt Airbus should this market grow quickly.

Airbus needed to decide whether to significantly redesign its A350 model to better compete with the 787 that was already taking an enormous share of the midsize 200-300 seat market pre-order sales. In combination with the fact that the A350 was already two years behind schedule, further delays would more than triple its development price from $4 billion to $14 billion.

Boeing's 787 was the most expensive development program in company history, with an estimated total cost of $32 billion. This represents roughly 10 times the annual net income for the company, and the 787 was just one of many R&D projects. The 787 represented more than just a financial "bet;" it was also a technological bet and a market bet. The airplane was to incorporate technologies never before used in commercial aviation - composite materials for the fuselage, mostly electronics for flight systems, and lithium ion batteries. Because of the long development cycle and the length of years that new models are in service, in the airline business "such strategic moves usually occur only once or twice in a decade."[6]

Boeing was also betting very differently on how the entire commercial aviation market would unfold in decades to come. The Airbus A380 was targeting at very long hauls between huge "hub" markets. But the Dreamliner 787 provided greater flexibility for airlines who wanted to fly long hauls between moderate-sized cities, so that passengers may not need to catch connections. Only time will tell which way the industry goes.

This short story richly illustrates important dimensions of strategy: the long-lasting effects that strategic decisions can have, and how decisions made early on can lead to significant differences between competitors. The Boeing 717 model flew for forty years, and now both Boeing and Airbus are making commitments and staking competitive positions for long into the future through the development of new classes of planes.

Do you think Google, Microsoft, Amazon, or Apple be able to sustain competitive advantage for another 40-50 years?

What Makes Strategic Decisions Special?

The commercial aircraft manufacturing story brings us to the third critical dimension that describes strategy. We want to separate the kinds of decisions and actions that are truly strategic from those that are not. Deciding how to get up in the morning or get to work on time may be important, but those decisions and plans are not strategic, in part because they are not fundamentally dealing with the questions of competitive advantage, sustainability or long-term outcomes. Additionally they are also not strategic because they do not exhibit the critical characteristics that define a strategic decision.[7] Strategic decisions are different from other types of decisions in that they:

1. Are ill-structured and non-routine.

2. Significantly affect the subsequent actions of functions and departments across the entire organization.

3. Involve a significant commitment of resources (broadly defined).

4. Are difficult to reverse both economically and politically.

5. Involve making a clear choice among competing alternatives.

6. Are easily identified with the success or failure of the organization.

Ill-structured and non-routine situations. Though companies are continuously reviewing their strategy, executing it, and monitoring their strategic progress, decisions on major new strategic initiatives are not made on a regular basis. Making a significant decision on strategy is unlike the decision a brand manager at Procter & Gamble might make regarding a new advertising campaign, and unlike the decision a company makes to raise capital by issuing new bonds. Corporations regularly raise capital by issuing bonds. The design and execution of new ad campaigns occurs with some regularity in a packaged goods company and there is a generally prescribed method for managing and implementing these efforts.

This is simply not true for major strategic decisions. Here we are talking about the need to confront unique and changing market conditions, and competitive circumstances for which there is often no historical record of similar types of decisions. Furthermore, beyond generic advice, company executives find that there is little off-the-shelf information readily available. Strategic decision making deals with a level of ambiguity not only about conditions in the present but also about how decisions made today will affect the company years down the road. This is actually what makes the practice of strategy so exciting and interesting: the opportunity for the decision maker to use intuition, creativity, and analysis - a combination of art and science.

Affects subsequent actions. Strategy is also unique in the field of management because effective strategy requires that all of the functional areas of a business (marketing, finance, operations, accounting, sales, etc.) act in ways that consistently support the overall approach to the market. A company's strategy may, for example, involve continuous innovation and new product development. Nevertheless should the finance function not support the investment spending in R&D, or if the production department refuses to allow for adequate test production runs in the factory, or if sales fails to place sufficient emphasis on new products in their customer calls, then the overall approach is likely to fail. Strategy requires internal consistency across all functions in a company. Indeed, a clear statement (mission and/or vision) and understanding about the strategy of the company is one of the most important means of ensuring that all functional areas consistently support one another in the implementation of strategic direction in all of their individual activities.

Significant commitment of resources. Because outstanding accomplishments rarely come from limited efforts or small initiatives, strategic decisions most often involve significant commitments of resources. To create unique competitive differences that are well valued in the marketplace, and to sustain those differences, a company must commit itself to a challenging path. When Amazon started up, it relied upon publishers to warehouse and ship books that its customers were ordering online. As the volume of business increased, however, shipping times and quality control suffered. It became clear to Jeff Bezos (founder and CEO) that publishers did not share his view of what constituted quality customer service. Amazon was positioning itself on customer service, information, and rapid results. Amazon made the decision to build and operate its own regional distribution warehouses, fully stocked with best-selling books. We think of Amazon as a "digital" company, but look at the physical assets carried on its balance sheet! The effort cost the company tens of millions of dollars, and once set in motion could not be pulled back without severe penalties. The effort ensured the quality of service Amazon promised, distanced itself from its competitors, and helped launch the company on an unparalleled growth trajectory.

Difficult to reverse. Suggested by the discussion earlier about long-term sustainability, strategic decisions have a long-lasting impact on the company and the competition in the market. Strategy is not like riding a bicycle, where you know immediately if you have erred because you fall down and scrape your knee. Strategy is more like navigating a high-speed oil supertanker far out at sea: you turn the rudder to change direction, but because of the inertia and the size of the ship, the turn may take many miles to complete. You cannot "turn on a dime." Decisions made today to move forward with strategic investments will not usually manifest themselves in results until many years down the road.

This dimension is actually of significant concern to leaders, who want to know as time goes by whether or not positive progress is being made on strategic initiatives. We will discuss methods for keeping track of strategy progress in Chapter 12.

Making a clear choice. We mentioned earlier that strategy is about deciding what a company will do and what it will not do. It involves making a choice. We will read later on about companies trying to be "all things to all people" by going in multiple directions, and thus winding up "stuck in the middle" (a dangerous place to be). But think about what we have just said above about strategy: affects the entire organization, involves significant commitment of resources, difficult to reverse. These characteristics of strategy and strategic decision-making suggest that companies must not try to go simultaneously down different paths. It's too expensive, it can result in mediocre results in several areas rather than superior results in a distinctive domain, and it can create organizational schizophrenia!

Identified with success or failure. It is for the reasons just described that strategic decisions have the greatest impact on a company's performance. They involve huge commitments of resources over long periods of time. They focus attention on specific opportunities, meaning that other possible opportunities are passed up. These focused commitments are designed to create a unique and sustainable competitive position. Strategy sets the goals of the overall organization as well as establishes how all the functional areas will work both individually and in concert. This is not to say that functional area issues and decisions are unimportant. Quite the contrary, when a problem occurs within a functional area, it is because it can affect strategy for the company – and therefore all the other functions that must be seamlessly integrated – that overall company performance may be put at risk.

What Is the Nature of Strategy in a Multi-business Firm?

A completely unique issue in strategy involves the issue of corporate strategy, that is, the efforts involved in companies that operate multiple business units under the same corporate banner. Corporate-level strategy is fundamentally concerned with acquiring, managing, and divesting various business units in an effort to create a portfolio that achieves economic returns in excess of what the individual business units could produce on their own. This is done primarily through resource sharing and efforts to achieve economies of scale and scope within the organization. Corporate-level strategy is often discussed today in the context of the relatedness of a company's diversification efforts. 3M Corporation (formerly Minnesota Mining & Manufacturing Company) was founded in 1902 by a group of businessmen to exploit abrasive mineral deposits. On the basis of several successful product launches in the 1920s, 3M began to acquire other promising businesses with the help of a set of wealthy investors. Today 3M has over 90,000 employees, sales of nearly $30 billion, and operates companies in five different strategic segments: Consumer; Safety and Graphics; Electronics and Energy; Health Care; and Industrial. 3M management oversees the entire operation from St. Paul, Minnesota, and regularly acquires and divests various components within the different business segments. In their 2015 annual report CEO Inge Thulin highlights how important managing the "corporate portfolio" is in achieving superior results:

"Portfolio management is an ongoing process, and is all about strengthening and focusing our portfolio of businesses. This includes prioritizing the allocation of capital across our portfolio. It also includes combining businesses within 3M, along with acquisitions and divestitures."

Corporate-level strategy will be covered in great detail in Chapter 10.

How Is Strategic Effectiveness Measured?

Because the nature of strategic decisions focuses attention on the performance of the company, companies must employ metrics. These can be qualitative and quantitative measures that allow the firm to measure the effectiveness of its strategy. The customary manner in which the effectiveness of strategy is assessed is by financial performance metrics. Included here are measures such as return on equity (ROE) or one of its constituent components.

Even more important than simple return measures, the assessment of strategic effectiveness usually involves a measure or set of measures that compare how well a company did *relative* to its competitors in the industry. Figure 1.2a shows recent performance, defined by a profitability metric (net income divided by sales revenue) for key competitors in the retail grocery store industry in 2015. The average for the industry during the period was only about 1.4 percent; this "thin margin" results from intense competition among traditional players, the advent of Walmart and Costco, and international companies extending into U.S. markets. Publix and Whole Foods both far exceed the industry average, while Supervalu significantly trails the industry. Publix is an example of a strategically high-performing company partially because it is by definition delivering "above-average profitability" through its business model. An above-average profitability metric means that Publix may be more attractive to financial markets; it most likely has superior cash flows enabling it to reinvest back in its business to further enhance its position and growth.

Figure 1.2 a
Recent Performance in Retail Grocery Store Industry

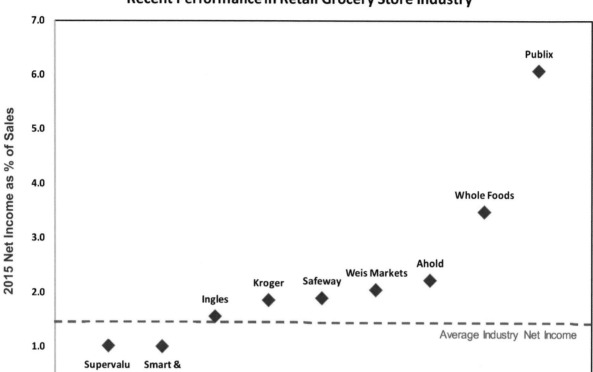

But wait! Recall that strategy is about impact over the long run and about longer-term results. Figure 1.2a shows that Weis Markets performed slightly above average on the profitability metric during 2015. But a longer term measurement of performance provides a more nuanced view. In Figure 1.2b are listed the 3-year average return on assets (ROA) for each of the companies pictured in the above graph. Here we see that Weis Markets exceeds even Publix and Whole Foods in longer term financial performance.

There are several customary types of financial metrics used to gauge effective strategic performance, such as ROA and ROE. A CEO always pays attention to the financial markets' response to the company's performance, since stock prices and debt ratings can significantly impact how and when a company can raise capital. Increasingly, corporate executives are also considering how well their companies create value for a variety of stakeholders. In Chapter 2 we will further explore dimensions of performance, including financial and nonfinancial measures.

The essential goal of strategy is the creation of competitive advantage that can be developed, refined, and sustained such that the company will achieve superior performance over time relative to its competitors. Superior performance refers to outcomes that exceed the average for the industry in which the company competes; those firms

Figure 1.2 b Grocery Stores 3-Year ROA 2013-2015	
Weis Markets	14.5 %
Publix	11.9
Whole Foods	9.8
Kroger	5.6
Ahold	5.4
Supervalu	4.2
Ingles	2.6
Smart & Final	1.5
Safeway	1.0

whose performance is average or below average are less attractive. This kind of relative evaluation allows the firm to compare its most important measures of performance against those of its direct competitors. The strategy approach to performance emphasizes an evaluative system that rewards those who are capable of moving their organization consistently beyond the average expectations in the industry. In Chapter 4 we will further discuss the nature of above-average returns.

HISTORY OF THE FIELD OF STRATEGY

How did the field of strategy get to this point, in which it is defined by the five questions just discussed, and where both value creation and opportunity recognition are absolutely imperative for any company? While there might be some disagreement regarding the roots of the field, the field has an intellectual foundation some 2,500 years ago with Sun Tzu general and military strategist and his writings in *The Art of War*. Thirteen chapters in this succinct text helped codify many of the fundamental concepts of strategy that are still important today. These include:

1. A complete understanding of the nature of the competitive marketplace is the first step in a winning campaign.

2. A deep understanding of the mindset of your competitors and how they might react to various moves enables you to anticipate competitive challenges.

3. The realization that preparation, understanding, and a deep commitment to excellence allows one to preempt competition. An organization that is focused on its business, that is constantly refining and improving its ability to compete with attention to the finer details, and that is on the cutting edge of best practices in its arena may actually prevent others from even attempting to compete. Therefore victory (in its most pure form) is defined as never having to enter battle.

4. An evaluation of the resources and capabilities of the organization will point toward the best ways to compete and win.

Reading Sun Tzu through the lens of business provides many insights about the most basic nature of strategy analysis, formulation, and implementation. An illustration some of the chapters of Sun Tzu's book is included in Figure 1.3.

Figure 1.3
Strategy Excerpts from *The Art of War* (Sun Tzu, 500 B.C.)

Chapter & Title	Quotation and Interesting Strategy Points
1 Estimations	"Warfare is a great matter to a nation; it is the ground of death and of life; it is the way of survival and of destruction, and must be examined." • Calculation and rational thought are keys to success. • Important factors to evaluate include moral influence, leadership, competitive arena, and plans. • Example: In contrast to other commercial banks, BB&T has avoided significant credit risk by rational analysis and objective evaluation of its loan applications.

2 Waging War	"When doing battle, seek a quick victory. A protracted battle will blunt weapons and dampen ardor…If the army is exposed to a prolonged campaign, the nation's resources will not suffice." • Continuous battling depletes resources and makes you vulnerable. • Example: When Microsoft decided to compete in the internet browsing business against Netscape, it offered its Internet Explorer software for free, seeking to drive Netscape out of business quickly.
3 Planning	"To gain a hundred victories in a hundred battles is not the highest excellence; to subjugate the enemy's army without doing battle is the highest of excellence. Therefore, the best warfare strategy is to attack the enemy's plans, next is to attack alliances, next is to attack the army…." • Example: After September 11, 2001, the United States initiated a series of security policies designed to detain suspected terrorists and ferret out terrorist plans before they could be implemented.
6 Vacuity & Substance	"In order to prevent the enemy from coming forth, show them the potential harm. In order to cause the enemy to come of their own volition, extend some apparent profit." • Erect barriers to entry to keep potential competitors away. • Form alliances or joint ventures with competitors to achieve shared goals. • Examples: Pharmaceutical companies seek patent protection on new drugs to prevent competitors from invading their product space. Before they merged, competitors United Airlines and Continental agreed to share schedules and mileage programs to increase passenger volume on each carrier.
7 Military Combat	"Accordingly, if the army does not have baggage and heavy equipment it will be lost; if it does not have provisions it will be lost; if it does not have stores it will be lost." • Failure is guaranteed without the right resources, effectively organized. • Examples: Atari pretty much invented the video game category in the 1970s, but failed because it lacked sophisticated game programmers in the 1980s. A&P supermarkets failed in 2015 because it lacked financial resources needed to scale up to compete with other lower cost food chains.
9 Maneuvering the Army	"If orders are consistently implemented to instruct the people, then the people will submit." • Communication of mission drives coordinated effort. • Example: Disney's mission "to produce unparalleled entertainment experiences" is known and practiced daily by its employees. It so epitomizes excellent customer service that other companies visit Disney to learn how they, too, can improve.

11 Nine Terrains	"When the soldiers and officers have penetrated deeply into [enemy territory], they will cling together. When there is no alternative, they will fight." • Where significant exit barriers exist, competitors will retaliate and fight viciously. • Example: When auto sales flattened out in the 2008-2011 recession, the auto manufacturers offer steep discounting, rebates, and 0% financing. Companies are willing to lose money on a sale to keep from shutting down plants and hurting ROA.
13 Spies	"The means by which enlightened rulers and sagacious generals moved and conquered others, that their achievements surpassed the masses, was advance knowledge." • Importance of prospective information that guides the future. • Example: When Staples opened its first stores in Boston, it collected detailed data on customers and their spending, allowing the company to quickly learn what sort of neighborhoods were most successful for their stores. This enabled them to quickly expand down the eastern seaboard.

Sun Tzu never actually used the term "strategy." The seeds of strategy and strategic management in business were only sown about one hundred years ago, as economies moved out of the industrial revolution and into an era of big business. The development of large industrial giants such as Standard Oil of New Jersey led to antitrust legislation in the United States that aimed to ensure free market competition. New labor legislation was also passed to protect the rights of workers in what were becoming huge factories where the work was distant from the office. As legislation sought to create a level playing field in competitive markets, large companies began to look internally for sources of advantage over competitors. In the early 1900s, Frederick Taylor conducted "science of work" time-and-motion studies that helped identify more efficient production processes and ideas about structure and hierarchy. These studies contributed to more effective structure and organization in progressively larger companies. Mass assembly lines, pioneered by Henry Ford in the 1930s and thus nicknamed "Fordism," contributed to even greater efficiencies and a lowering of costs in manufacturing.

In 1962 a Harvard professor, Alfred Chandler, catalogued the growth and administrative changes which had occurred over the previous fifty years at four giant pillars of industry at the turn of the twentieth century (General Motors, Sears, Standard Oil, and Dupont).[8] As these companies grew, top executives found that they were increasingly removed from day-to-day business activities. The complexity of their businesses and the sheer number of activities made it virtually impossible to manage in the same ways that business owners had in the past. Chandler explained how senior managers discovered new roles for themselves making long-term decisions about the direction of their diverse enterprises. They made investments and modified organizational structures to increase the efficiency and generate higher returns. Chandler called these long-term plans "strategy," the first time the term was used to describe business processes. The term derives from two Greek root words, *strat* and *egos*, meaning "general of the army," or more directly from the combined ancient Greek word *strategos*, meaning "art of the general."

The popular model for strategy in the 1960s and 1970s included the concepts of "policy" and "long-range planning." Policies were simply guidelines within which managers could make decisions. Long-range planning came to be very popular; almost every firm instituted an annual long-range planning exercise. The mainstay of this exercise was the budget process, where programmed activities essentially remained the same, but new updated numbers were plugged in for the next year. Consequently, long-range planning became more of an extrapolation of the past than a real look to the future. This complacent business approach and a belief that the U.S. economy defied all models ran headlong into a strong group of rising global businesses headquartered outside of the United States.

Figure 1.4
Historical U.S. Retail Gasoline Prices

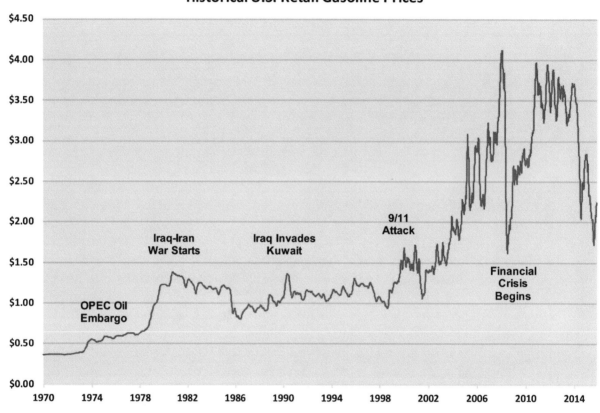

Beginning in the early 1970s American industry suffered a number of significant macro-economic jolts, which forever changed the way businesses plan. The first of these was the 1973 Arab oil embargo, which resulted in gas prices increasing roughly 35 percent overnight, from under 40¢ per gallon to 55¢ per gallon on average nationwide (Figure 1.4). Significant shortages and prices over $1 per gallon in many local areas, and people recall 1-2 hour waiting lines at gas stations because gas was so scarce. It had taken over forty years for gas prices to rise from 21¢ to 38¢ per gallon, but only five more years before prices topped $1 nationwide in 1979. Americans started questioning the wisdom of buying large, gas-guzzling automobiles, opening the door for a host of foreign competitors who were already trying to enter the market with smaller fuel-efficient cars. Honda, Toyota, Datsun (now Nissan), and other international car companies aggressively sought a foothold in the U.S. market. In 1973 foreign companies had a tiny percentage of the U.S. auto market, but within ten years their market share increased to over 35 percent. U.S. auto manufacturers never foresaw this as a possibility, because they had simply been extrapolating past trends into the future. They never really considered a situation where competitive conditions might change so dramatically and so rapidly. Moreover, it took nearly five years to bring a new automobile model to market as U.S. companies had been trying to maximize the "life" of their previous models, so any sort of rapid response to the new competitive threats was virtually impossible. These developments had an enormous cascading impact, as well, in other industries (steel, rubber, parts, and other industries). The intense competition and stumbling in the U.S. automobile industry caused a significant rethinking by American business about how to sustain superior performance in a new global environment.

At the same time, a fundamental shift was occurring in the sources of industrial growth. There was movement toward a more service and technology-based economy that shifted the emphasis away from manufacturing. Consumer tastes increasingly appreciated better quality and superior service. Easy access to information and markets diminished the value of being nearby, and made foreign competition even more viable. An aging U.S. manufacturing infrastructure compromised the ability of many companies to deliver these new values, while foreign competitors could do so more easily with their newer plants built in the aftermath of World War II. From the 1970s until the mid-1980s in industry after industry, American firms lost out competitively to international firms. During this period, more than half of all U.S. industry categories lost market share (Figure 1.5).

Figure 1.5
U.S. Industry Gains & Losses, 1978-1985

Industry type	Share Gains	Share Losses
Raw materials	27	23
Manufacturing	18	28
Consumption	38	46
	83	97

U.S. firms had been like the proverbial frog in the pot of slowly heating water: they had been fairly content in their positions and had not recognized the change going on around them or the need to jump out as the water temperature rose. Traditional planning largely downplayed external competitive forces and most often consisted of doing no more than what had worked in the past.

The field of strategy as we know it today was thus born, when people in industry and professors in business schools realized that newer approaches were required for companies to develop and maintain competitive advantage as a means to deliver superior performance. A number of important books and articles published during the 1970s began to articulate the kinds of ideas we now teach in strategy, ideas that might have helped American companies avoid their declines in the previous decade.[9] In his seminal 1980 book *Competitive Strategy,* Michael Porter described competitive strategy as "positioning a business to maximize the value of the capabilities that distinguish it from its competitors."[10]

The need for strategy is even more important in 2016. Look once more at Figure 1.4 to see what has happened to fuel prices over the last few years since the 2008 financial crisis and ensuing recession. When the crisis began, prices for crude oil and refined petroleum products dropped precipitously. A result of supply and demand, when world financial markets seized up, demand for oil dropped and so did prices. Then things returned to "normal" with gas prices rising back up to nearly $4 per gallon. But since 2015 the price of oil has plummeted, and gas prices followed. Supply and demand again: the slowing China economy has had ripple effects across the globe, decreasing demand for fuel. And the Mideast oil cartels have continued to pump as much oil as possible, creating excess world supply.

These are positive events for companies whose business relies on fuel as a major cost element. Commercial airlines and automobiles are great examples. Airlines are more profitable today than they have been in two decades. In 2015 auto manufacturers set records for new auto sales, especially SUVs and pickups, because buyers don't mind buying "big" since gas costs less than $2.50 per gallon. On the other hand, imagine how difficult strategic planning and execution is for companies when raw materials costs are so volatile. It has taken awhile, but in 2016 the major oil drilling and exploration companies are shutting down many operations, which can't be economically justified at such low market prices. Do you think low-priced oil and gas will last? For how long? What if it rises as quickly in 2017 as it dropped in 2015? The need for sharp, long term strategic thinking is even greater today than ever before!

VISION, ETHICS, LEADERSHIP

We cannot talk about or teach strategy today without simultaneously considering issues of vision, ethics, and leadership. Where the goal of effective strategy is superior competitive performance and superior financial performance, these other dimensions of strategic management are always lurking just beneath the surface. That is to say, these dimensions are not always discussed explicitly when we talk about a particular aspect of strategy, however they are always implicit in the conversation. It's smart to be aware that they are relevant and important as we move along in this book, and as you move along in your careers.

We will actually have a lot more to say about vision shortly - in fact, a whole chapter (Chapter 3). Suffice it to say here, though, that part of the problems encountered by U.S. companies in the 1970s was a lack of vision. Mere extrapolations from the past, combined with a sort of complacent attitude about what changes the future might bring, led to the situation described earlier. The contemporary view of strategy that has since emerged now emphasizes the need to sustain competitive differences over time. A longer-term view is called for to help guide the company and its employees in the right direction. More importantly, calls for today's strategic imperatives of value creation and opportunity recognition demand that companies be forward-looking and anticipate dynamic changes in the business environment while at the same time leveraging what they do best. As we will describe later, articulating vision (and mission) is one effective means for helping to bridge between the present and the future.

Recent headlines have screamed about unethical behavior at companies such as Volkswagon, Enron and Tyco. In 2015 Volkswagon admitted that mid-level engineers installed software in engines over several years so that its cars could pass lab emissions tests. Is it possible they did this on their own, without their superiors knowing? How far up the hierarchy did knowledge about this misleading practice go? The 2008 financial markets crisis was fueled by factors such as unusual mortgage lending activity and baffling financial instruments. These events trigger cries about the ethical behavior of senior executives, and in fact 2016 U.S. Presidential candidate Bernie Sanders made this a centerpiece of his populist campaign. But ethics in strategy covers a far broader range of behaviors than strange accounting techniques or mysterious financial innovations. Externally, managers need to carefully consider decisions such as advertising to children, manufacturing in offshore locations where sweatshops are prevalent, or how "green" a company should be in its business practices. Internally, we need to carefully consider decisions such as how fairly employees are treated and provided opportunities, the kinds of health-care benefits provided, or how privacy and personal data is secured. Many strategic decisions concern initiatives or actions that may be technically legal and highly effective from a competitive point of view, but which may be morally challenged. Throughout this book you will encounter a discussion of strategy where dimensions of ethics surface, and where you will need to balance different factors in the decision situation.

Strategic leadership is crucial at all levels of a company, and will be important to you as you start your career. No doubt you have already encountered in other courses some dimensions of leadership – such as setting direction, establishing goals, making decisions and allocating resources, building culture, engaging in symbolic behavior. Articulating vision and establishing ethical guidelines are also part of the responsibility of strategic managers. However, there is also an interesting contradiction about strategy. Senior management, who we usually think of as in charge of strategy, often knows *less* about what is really working (or falling apart) in their company than do people further down in the organization. The closer you get to dealing with competition, the closer you get to dealing with customers, the closer you get to the actual operations in your company, the more aware you will become of the two strategic imperatives mentioned earlier: value creation and opportunity recognition. Because you will be closer to "the action," you will notice details and nuances that senior management cannot possibly comprehend from 30,000 feet. You will have a strategic responsibility to feed this information up the line when and where you see the company doing exceptionally well or poorly, and when and where you see new opportunities emerge that the company can pursue. You will be on the "firing line," where the balance often plays itself out in real terms between ethical behavior and actions that further increase competitive advantage or financial performance. You can exert strategic leadership, even at your lower level, to help others articulate and further develop these ideas. Today, every employee in an organization has a strategic leadership role to play.

STRATEGIC MANAGEMENT PROCESS

So far we have briefly reviewed the history of strategy in business and why it became so important. We have also described the characteristics and chief concerns of strategic decisions, and how these are very different from other areas of management that you may have studied already. The strategic management process is what the rest of this book is about –a concise and practical guide to analyzing, formulating, implementing, and evaluating strategy. Figure 1.6 provides a blueprint of how the rest of the book is organized to present the topics critical to the strategic process.

What you might notice first about Figure 1.6 is that the next Chapter 2 is on the *right* side of the figure, traditionally indicating the end. You might be asking yourself, why would the authors begin the book at the end? We do so to emphasize the need for keeping our eye on the ball. The "ball" is superior performance, the fundamental goal of strategic management. So to emphasize superior performance as the ultimate goal, we concentrate on it in our very next chapter, before we describe in more specific detail how to achieve it in the subsequent chapters.

After considering performance, we move into the processes of analysis and formulation (Chapters 3 - 7). But as the circular arrow in the center of this block of chapters suggests, there should be a constant cycling back and forth between analysis and formulation. The remaining sections of the book (Chapters 8 - 12) explore topics that contextualize strategy in the process of its implementation. Here we will cover practical methods for how to organize for particular strategic challenges, and how to evaluate whether a strategy will ultimately lead to the desired outcome of superior performance.

Figure 1.6
Strategic Management Model and Outline for This Book

Analysis and Formulation

As indicated by the circular arrow in the middle of the left group of chapters in Figure 1.6, the process of analysis and formulation is not really linear. For instance, even though a high degree of analysis might be required before a company's vision and mission can be solidly established, a company needs to formulate a vision and mission statement to effectively sum up what the company is all about. Therefore, before getting into a discussion of the analysis process (Chapters 4 - 6), mission and vision are covered in Chapter 3. This chapter describes the necessity of establishing a vision that guides the company into the future, a mission statement that enhances day-to-day consistency and coordination of activities in support of the vision, and objectives that represent tangible targets for a company and its employees to work toward.

The analysis chapters yield a more detailed understanding of what works in a particular competitive environment and why, while helping us understand how well our company's activities and resources are suited to the competitive environment. Often, the industry a company competes in or how a company competes is a reflection of an earlier choice that management made about its long-term direction.

Types of analysis. Every attempt to grapple with strategy formulation and implementation relies upon a strong foundation of analysis. The analysis process described will begin with an "external analysis" at the industry level, and then drill down into the company of interest. A detailed analysis of industries and competitors (Chapter 4) builds a solid understanding of the competitive context, how it is evolving, and what competitive dimensions appear to be growing in importance. This analysis also offers insight into the intentions of key competitors. Probing this broader industry and competitive context contributes to a better understanding of how a particular company will be able to effectively compete.

The "internal analysis" of the company encompasses two perspectives. The first is the value chain (Chapter 5), because value creation is a central theme in this book. Value chain analysis takes into account two sets of activities that create value and offer the potential for competitive advantage: 1) activities by people and departments within the walls of the company, and 2) activities transacted between the company and its suppliers and customers. It will be pointed out that companies themselves are merely an organization of a set of activities in a chain of value-adding activity across an industry. We will also learn that products and services produced by a company are simply a manifestation of sets of activities that occur within the company. Therefore, if we are interested in the source of competitive advantage in a market, we need to carefully examine how value is created by a company through what people actually do. We will also examine when it makes strategic sense for a company to outsource important activities instead of performing them in house.

The second internal analysis method is resource-based analysis (Chapter 6). This is an exciting and relatively new area of study for strategy that offers the opportunity to better understand how to develop *sustainable* competitive advantage. While the value-chain perspective in Chapter 5 helps answer the first key question about strategy (Why are firms different?), the resource-based perspective in Chapter 6 helps answer the second question (How are competitive differences sustained?).

One final comment on the analysis chapters: Recall from the earlier discussion that strategic decisions are special for a variety of reasons. The nature of strategy (dealing with ill-structured situations, uncertainty, and making decisions for the long term) will necessarily require decision makers to "make bets." Strategists must make decisions and investments today whose payoff is often far down the road; it's simply the nature of this area of management. When a strategic decision is made, the decision maker is essentially building on a logic that he or she has developed about cause and effect in the marketplace, saying "If we do X now and over time, then Y will occur in the future." The best way to build that logic is through strong, foundational analysis. This enables decisions to be made, based not upon "I hope this will work," but based upon "I have developed a sufficient case to believe that this will work for my company."

Formulation. In Chapter 7, we consider business-level strategic approaches to the marketplace and competition, focusing especially on low-cost and differentiating approaches. Having analyzed the industry and a company's internal resources and value-creating activities, and taking into account its long-term vision, we are now in a position to formulate a precise and actionable approach to building a business, engage competition, and produce superior returns.

The competitive environment is dynamic, and so changes in factors affecting whole industries or new initiatives by competitors may make previously hatched approaches or existing sets of resources less relevant going forward. Similarly, new resources we develop or new initiatives we put into play in our company may shake up an industry and competitors, calling for our own re-analysis of this dimension.

Implementation: Strategy in the Marketplace

Will all of the effort put into analysis and formulation be successful for the company in developing sustainable competitive advantage? The answer you will often hear is "It depends." What does effective strategic performance depend on? It depends on precisely these evolving contexts in the marketplace that confront the company, and this next section explores some of these contexts. Chapter 8 outlines interesting strategy issues that occur in different stages of the life cycle of both companies and industries. The resources, activities, and strategic approach of a young company are likely to be very different from those of an established competitor in the same industry. In fact, there are specific market entry strategy issues faced by new ventures and young companies that existing companies need not worry about. Similarly, there are differences in strategic approaches that depend on the nature of the industry itself. What works in a young, growing industry may not work well at all when that same industry begins to mature. What works in fragmented industries may not be appropriate for consolidated industries. Finally, this chapter tackles what to do when the industry or the company enters a mature stage and additional growth is required. Here we explore ways to redefine the value chain as a way of uncovering new growth opportunities. One especially important area for potential growth may be international expansion, and so here we also look at the unique challenges presented by this type of expansion.

What do you do when your competitors start taking actions in response to your strategic moves? Chapter 9 explores many possibilities of competitive dynamics. For those students who enjoy gaming and sports, there are some very interesting parallels here to your out-of-class activities. Cooperation has recently become of great interest to companies (remember what Sun Tzu said), so here we also examine when it makes sense to cooperate versus compete.

Chapter 10 concerns itself with a different avenue for growth, specifically growth achieved by buying or merging with other companies. This is a chapter on corporate strategy, that is, the strategic management of a company that owns and operates more than one type of business. Mergers and acquisitions (or their "divestitures" counterpart) are often front-page news in the *Wall Street Journal*. It is important to understand what motivates this approach to growth, critical dimensions of the acquisition process, and how to manage a diversified company.

Implementation and Evaluation

The missing piece in so many discussions of strategy is the practical internal implementation of the plan and its ongoing evaluation. A well-developed strategy involves the coordination of a tremendous number of areas within the organization, including its structure and systems. Chapter 11 walks us through different ways to coordinate important value-creating activities, their relationship to the sort of strategic approach adopted by the company, and the various organizational structures that are then appropriate. Ensuring the success of strategy entails setting up internal control procedures and establishing a system to keep track of key performance metrics. Chapter 12 tackles this agenda. The chapter concludes by revisiting comments we have made here in Chapter 1 about the critical importance of strategic leadership and principled decision making.

Iterative Processes

The model in Figure 1.6 makes the strategy process appear to be linear and sequential, where one step logically follows another and where one cannot take a step until others before it have been completed. This isn't really the case in practice, though. For the purposes of studying strategic management, particularly for the first-time student, it is easier to lay the process out as we have done in Figure 1.6. However, note that there are arrows feeding from the Marketplace and Implementation/Evaluation sections back to Analysis and Formulation. This is a visual way of suggesting that there is a "continuous dialogue" that occurs among portions of this process. As we read earlier in this chapter on strategic imperatives, the nature of markets today requires that the strategy process be synthetic and integrative across all the areas pictured in the process diagram. Therefore, the creation of strategy is both intentional and emergent. We conduct analyses, draw conclusions, lay plans, and implement those plans with programs and actions. Yet the nature of markets and competition will change the context in which we did our planning and require us to make modifications as we go along. At the same time, if we are prepared, we will recognize new opportunities that changing markets expose, and we will elect to make modifications in our plans to take advantage of them.

CHAPTER SUMMARY

We began this chapter with a discussion of the real meaning of strategy. The field of strategy is generally defined as addressing five critical questions in business:

1. Why are firms different?

2. How are competitive differences sustained?

3. What is special about strategic decisions?

4. What is the nature of strategy in a multibusiness firm?

5. How is strategic performance measured?

A review of the history of strategy from its earliest foundations with Sun Tzu to its emergence following the 1970s demonstrated that firms needed to think more clearly about how to create and sustain valuable differences versus their competition leading to superior performance. The need for strategy is even greater in the twenty-first century with the advent of technology, globalization, ease of access to financial markets, and other macro-economic trends. As a result of these forces, strategy must increasingly concern itself with two imperatives:

1. *Value creation imperative*

2. *Opportunity recognition imperative*

Sustained superior performance depends upon these capabilities. The structure of this book follows a model for strategic planning. We recognize that strategy planning and implementation requires continuous monitoring of the competitive environment and constant reevaluation and adjustment of plans.

Learning Objectives Review

1. *Identify and discuss the two strategic imperatives facing every company today.*

- **Opportunity recognition**. Identifying and exploiting where the market is heading.

- **Value creation**. Understanding and delivering new values appreciated by both existing and new customers and other stakeholders.

2. *Define the term "Strategy" and describe the five critical questions encompassing what we study in strategy.*

- **Strategy**. The overall concept for how a company organizes itself and all its activities in order to conduct business successfully, out-perform competitors, and deliver superior returns to its shareholders.

- **Questions defining what we study in strategy**.

    1. Why are firms different? Why do some firms perform better than others?

    2. How are competitive differences sustained?

    3. What is special about strategic decisions?

    4. What is the province of strategy in multibusiness firms?

    5. How is strategic effectiveness measured?

3. *Explain the evolution of the field of strategy and why it is important today.*

- **Sun Tzu**. Author of The Art of War, an ancient Chinese book on military strategy.

- **Frederick Taylor**. Father of the "science of work" time and motion studies that helped identify more efficient processes and ideas about structure and hierarchy.

- **Long-range planning**. A traditional approach to planning used before 1980 that often extrapolated into the future what the company had done well in the past.

- **1970s-1980s**. Macro-economic shocks to U.S. industries and technological advances led to foreign competition, share losses in many important industries, and the realization that long-range planning was insufficient.

- **Michael Porter**. Leading proponent of the move from long-range planning to strategy. His two early books on the subject, Competitive Strategy and Competitive Advantage, described competitive strategy as "positioning a business to maximize the value of the capabilities that distinguish it from its competitors."

- **Importance today**. Strategy is the glue that binds different parts of an organization together into a consistent approach to the marketplace. Strategy enables companies to create value and meet the growing desires of customers and other stakeholders. Strategy delivers superior performance to owners of companies. Strategy encourages explicit consideration of ethics in business.

4. *Connect the concept of strategy with leadership and ethics.*

- Every aspect of strategy and the strategic management process depends on effective leadership. Articulating vision and establishing ethical guidelines are part of the responsibility of both leaders. However, senior management often knows less about what is really going on in their company than do people further down in the organization. Employees closer to the action notice details and nuances, see where the company is doing well or poorly, notice new opportunities emerging, and see where ethical behavior and actions impact performance. You can exert strategic leadership, even at your lower level, to help others articulate and further develop these ideas. Today, every employee in an organization has a strategic leadership role to play.

5. *Describe the process for developing and implementing strategy.*

- **Analysis**. Careful "external analysis" of an industry and "internal analysis" of a company's strengths, resources and ways of creating value.

- **Formulation**. Articulating vision, mission, goals, and a type of strategic approach to adopt.

- **Implementation**. Putting strategy into effect by allocating resources, structuring the organization, and motivating employees.

- **Evaluation**. Ensuring strategy-consistent actions across departments, and establishing performance metrics to ensure that progress is being made toward long term goals.

Key Terms

Corporate strategy - The strategy involved in managing multiple business units under the same corporate banner.

Frederick Taylor - Father of the "science of work" time and motion studies that helped identify more efficient production processes and ideas about structure and hierarchy.

Long-range planning - A traditional approach to planning used before 1980 that often simply extrapolated into the future what the company had done well in the past.

Metrics - Qualitative and quantitative measures that allow the firm to measure the effectiveness of its business strategy.

Michael Porter - Leading proponent of the move from long-range planning to strategy. His two early books on the subject, *Competitive Strategy* and *Competitive Advantage*, described competitive strategy as "positioning a business to maximize the value of the capabilities that distinguish it from its competitors.

Opportunity recognition - the critical need in business to identify and exploit where the market is heading.

Strategic decisions - Strategic decisions exhibit five characteristics: 1) are relevant to ill-structured and non-routine situations; 2) significantly affect the subsequent actions of the entire organization; 3) involve a significant commitment of resources; 4) are difficult to reverse both economically and politically; and 5) are easily identified with the success or failure of the organization.

Strategic management - The process through which strategy is developed, executed, and evaluated. There are typically four stages of the strategic management process: analysis, formulation, implementation, and evaluation.

Strategy - The overall concept for how a company organizes itself and all its activities in order to conduct business successfully, outperform competitors and deliver superior returns to its shareholders.

Sun Tzu - Author of *The Art of War*, an ancient Chinese book on military strategy.

Superior performance - As used in the field of strategy, refers to performance outcomes that exceed the average for the industry in which the company competes.

Value chain - Provides a systematic way of examining all the activities a firm performs and how those activities interact with each other to find a basis for competitive advantage.

Value creation - The primary goal of strategy. The value created is widely accounted for by all the stakeholders of the company.

Short Answer Review Questions

1. Imagine that you have arrived back home from your first class in strategy and you receive a call from your father asking you about your class. How would you explain to him what strategy is?

2. How was strategy operationalized during the early part of the 1900s?

3. How has strategy evolved over the past forty years?

4. If you were asked for some advice about how strategy can help a business develop and grow, what are the areas in which you would suggest that strategy could make a difference?

5. Who are Sun Tzu, Michael Porter, and Frederick Taylor?

6. What do you expect to be able to do after you finish this course in strategy?

7. How might your understanding of other areas of your business studies (finance, accounting, marketing, management, and information systems) be affected by your ability to apply the concepts of strategy?

8. Why is being better than average in an industry an important strategy concept?

9. Who uses strategy in a typical company?

10. What elements help distinguish a strategic decision from one that is tactical?

11. What are some measures of an effective strategy?

12. Why is opportunity recognition such an important concept in strategy?

13. What strategic concept encompasses a detailed understanding of the processes within an organization?

14. Describe five types of strategy decisions in which ethical concerns must also be accounted for. Search the Internet for a business article that discusses this type of decision for a real company.

Group Review Exercises

1. Hewlett-Packard is facing some significant strategic dilemmas. The most compelling is for the company to find a means of creating a value for its product. Consumers can personal computers from any one of a number of companies, and they are all pretty much identical to each other. Form a group of three to five people and answer the following questions:

   a. How is HP different from Dell, Toshiba, Lenovo, Acer and many other brands?

   b. How might you create new value in this industry and make it the centerpiece of how the company does business?

   c. How should HP measure its success?

2. Oil prices have significantly affected every business. Business models that were highly profitable when gas prices were lower have been completely upset by higher gas prices. Form a group of three to five people and address the following:

   a. Are some businesses not affected by the price of oil?

   b. How have the airlines tried to cope with the new higher prices of fuel?

   c. What would you suggest as a sustainable strategy for profitability in the trucking industry?

   d. Assuming that there are always new ways for companies to charge more for what they provide, what would you suggest to the owner of an independent trucking company?

3. Blockbuster was significantly challenged by mail rental businesses such as Netflix, by discount retailers such as Walmart that sell DVDs at low prices, and by the advent of kiosks like Redbox. In your group discuss the following:

   a. What was the strategic approach and resources that made Blockbuster successful in the past?

   b. How did this strategy and these resources assist and/or constrain the company's approach to the market?

c. Now discuss the similar challenges faced by Netflix as it faces competition from video streaming sources such as cable TV and phone companies.

References

[1] Two upstarts vie for dominance in satellite radio, Wall Street Journal, March 30, 2005, A1; Steve Finlay, XM Radio ventures beyond audio services, Ward's Dealer Business, July, 2005, 8; Steve Finlay, XM Radio looks beyond audio, Ward's Auto World, June 2005, 18; Noel Bussey, Can satellite radio become a serious medium? Campaign, January 27, 2006, 17; XM Satellite director resigns after expressing cost concerns, Wall Street Journal, February 17, 2006, A3; Wildstrom, Stephan, Copyrights and Wrongs, BusinessWeek, July 3, 2006, 24; Edwards, Cliff, Taking XM Out for a Stroll, BusinessWeek, August 14, 2006, 18; Until recently full of promise, satellite radio runs into static, Wall Street Journal, August 15, 2006, A1; Tom Lowry & Paula Lehman, Grudge match, BusinessWeek, August 21/28, 2006, 86; Record Companies Sue XM Radio for Copyright Infringement, The Computer & Internet Lawyer, September 2006, 38; Sirius XM sends signals of change, Wall Street Journal, September 15, 2008; Sirius unveils raft of options for programs, Wall Street Journal, October 3, 2008; Is Sirius falling to Earth? BusinessWeek, November 3, 2008, 86; Liberty Media unveils plans for Sirius, Wall Street Journal, February 14, 2014, B1; XM Radio (http://www.xmradio.com); Sirius Satellite Radio (http://www.sirius.com); SiriusXM (http://siriusxm.com); Sirius XM's Strong Subscriber Growth Bolsters Outlook, Forbes, May 1, 2015; Number of Sirius XM Holdings' subscribers in the United States from 1st quarter 2011 to 4th quarter 2015, Statista, http://www.statista.com.

[2] R. A. D'Aveni, 1994, Hypercompetition, Free Press: New York.

[3] S. Venkatraman, 2004, Regional transformation through technological entrepreneurship, Journal of Business Venturing, 19 (1): 153 - 167; G. P. West & C. E. Bamford, 2005, Creating a technology-based entrepreneurial economy: A resource-based theory perspective, Journal of Technology Transfer, 30 (4): 433 - 451.

[4] R. P. Rumelt, D. E. Schendel, & D. J. Teece (eds.), 1994, Fundamental Issues in Strategy, Boston: Harvard Business School Press.

[5] M. E. Porter, 1985, Competitive Advantage: Creating and Sustaining Superior Performance, Free Press, 33.

[6] D. Michaels & J. L. Lunsford, Jet makers reach crossroads, Wall Street Journal, May 12, 2006, A4.

[7] Schwenk, C.R. 1988. "The Essence of Strategic Decision Making," Lexington Books, New York, NY.

[8] A. D. Chandler, 1962, Strategy and Structure, Cambridge, MA: MIT Press.

[9] K. R. Andrews, 1971, The Concept of Corporate Strategy. Homewood, IL: Irwin; C. W. Hofer & D. Schendel, 1978, Strategy Formulation: Analytic Concepts, New York: West Publishing; R. E.

Miles & C. C. Snow, 1978, Organizational Strategy, Structure, and Process. New York: McGraw-Hill; H. Mintzberg, 1977, The strategy concept I: Five P's for strategy, California Management Review, Fall: 11 - 24; H. Mintzberg, 1978. Patterns in strategy formation, Management Science, 24 (9): 934 - 948; R. P. Rumelt, 1974, Strategy, Structure, and Economic Performance, Cambridge, MA: Harvard University Press.

[10] M. E. Porter, 1980, Competitive Strategy: Techniques for Analyzing Industries and Competitors, Free Press, 47.

Chapter 2: Strategy and Performance

LEARNING OBJECTIVES:

1. Explain the value of using both financial and nonfinancial performance dimensions to measure strategy effectiveness.

2. Describe the relationship between financial performance and a sustainable competitive advantage.

3. Use financial analysis to examine company strategy.

4. Explain the economic logic of industries and companies.

5. Examine and explain the interaction between strategy formulation and financial analysis.

Turbulence Then Smooth Flying in the Friendly Skies[1]

The first ten years of the new millennium witnessed brutal competition and dynamic changes in the domestic airline industry. According to one airline CEO, it was "tough" and "sloppy" for U.S. airlines and for the traveling public. In the United States, five of the "legacy" airline carriers operated under Chapter 11 bankruptcy (American, Delta, Northwest, United, and US Airways), reflecting an industry that had lost $6 billion and laid off 150,000 workers.

Recessions during 2001-02 and 2009-11 resulted in less demand for air travel. Legacy carriers in the United States felt increased competitive pressure from the expansion of low-cost carriers such as Southwest Airlines, JetBlue, and Frontier. U.S. carriers that relied upon profitable overseas routes were also assaulted by startups Odyssey Airlines and La Compagnie, which plan to steal market share in the lucrative business-class segment to Europe. Fuel costs skyrocketed with the surge in oil prices, challenging all carriers to deal with rising costs. Domestic carriers were burdened with labor costs through pre-existing union agreements. American Airlines tried to avoid bankruptcy by yanking pillows out of planes, cramming more seats into coach class, and experimenting with charging customers for soft drinks. Many airlines instituted fees for checked-bag and pre-assigned seat reservations, in attempts to generate revenue offsetting their costs.

Amidst this backdrop, mergers dominated headlines throughout these years. Fresh off its merger with America West, US Airways came out of bankruptcy and made an unsolicited bid to acquire Delta in an attempt to grow larger and improve operating efficiency. The offer was rejected, but in 2013 the airline merged with American. United Airlines consummated a 2010 deal with Continental, and Northwest was acquired by Delta in 2008. Speaking of its merger proposals, US Airways CEO Doug Parker stated, "The airline industry remains extremely fragmented with substantial levels of excess capacity…. Our industry stands at a crossroads. We can continue down the current path of boom and bust uncertainty, or we can chart a new course."

The traveling public experienced significant headaches while (and maybe because) the airlines were in trouble. Domestic ticket prices had risen roughly 30% in four years, and 41% since the 1990s. New security procedures involving full-body scans and the banning of carry-on liquids created long lines and short tempers at airports. Since new security prompted customers to check more bags, lost baggage plagued many airlines. In 2008 system wide mishandled baggage reports had increased 37% over 2004. Overbooking by airlines resulted in a 14% increase in passenger "bumping" off flights.

But then the airlines started flying in the clear by about 2013. With emergence from the financial crisis passenger traffic picked up. Refraining from adding additional capacity as demand grew, the industry-wide "load factor" grew from 40% in the early 2000s to nearly 85% by 2015.[2] With capacity at record levels the competing air carriers have avoided discounting fares, which is what they used to do to fill seats in planes. Jet fuel costs have declined for two years, and airlines are replacing aging jets with more fuel-efficient equipment.

2015 Selected Domestic Airline Financial Performance					
	American	Delta	JetBlue	Southwest	United
Revenue (millions)	$ 40,990	$ 40,704	$ 6,416	$ 19,820	$ 37,864
Net Income (millions)	$ 7,610	$ 4,526	$ 677	$ 2,181	$ 7,340
Net Income %	18.6 %	11.1 %	10.6 %	11.0 %	19.4 %
Earnings Per Share	$ 11.39	$ 5.68	$ 2.15	$ 3.30	$ 19.52
Stock Price Range 2015	$37.62 – 55.45	$40.00 – 52.26	$14.55 – 27.02	$32.52 – 49.58	$50.78 – 73.72
Stock Price 12/31/15	$ 42.35	$ 50.69	$ 22.65	$ 43.06	$ 57.30
Stock Price 12/31/12	$ 0.80	$ 13.50	$ 5.72	$ 10.23	$ 23.38
4-Year Return on Assets	2.4 %	4.2 %	4.3 %	5.5 %	5.2 %
4-Year Return On Equity	n/a*	n/a*	12.9 %	15.7 %	n/a*

* Experienced losses and/or negative equity during the 4-year period

Financial performance of the U.S. airlines was mixed during the first decade of the 2000s. By 2012 both American and United Continental, two of the largest carriers by revenue, were losing money. Because of prior bankruptcies and recapitalization efforts, balance sheets were in disarray and shareholders were not earning positive returns on equity. Financial markets had beat down stock prices to uncomfortably low levels. A handful of airlines managed to avoid these financial challenges, for example Southwest Airlines was profitable despite its lower load factor.

But by 2016 the financial performance story has changed considerably. In a traditionally commoditized business known for its low margins, net income percentages now range between

10-20%. Stock prices have ballooned in the face of strong customer demand, lower costs, and discipline to avoid fare discounts. There is growing evidence, though, that operational performance has been slightly compromised during the last two years from 2013-15. Increased customer traffic has resulted in longer check-in lines at airports, an increase in mis-handled baggage averaging 21% among the top four carriers, and an increase of 11% in arrival time delays.

2015 Selected Domestic Airline Operating Performance					
	American	Delta	JetBlue	Southwest	United
ASMs (millions)*	117,741	122,449	39,250	136,863	107,607
Load Factor	86.2 %	87.3 %	85.1 %	83.7 %	86.3 %
Cost Per ASM (cents)	14.3	15.0	10.6	11.2	14.9
On-Time Arrival	80 %	86 %	76 %	80 %	78 %
Average Delay (mins.)	60	61	61	52	65
* Available seat miles					

QUESTIONS

1. Since all domestic airlines confront identical industry conditions, why did certain airlines enjoy superior financial performance?

2. How was Southwest able to report the highest 4-year return on assets (ROA) despite having the lowest industry load factor?

FOCUS ON PERFORMANCE

In the first chapter we highlighted the need for strategy in today's competitive and ever-changing world, and we discussed several critical questions that help us understand dimensions that define what strategy is actually about. Throughout that discussion we often used terms or expressions that referred to performance. These included phrases such as "superior performance," "substantial positive return," and "above average profitability." This is because performance is one of the key outcomes of interest for students studying strategy and for managers who are responsible for formulating and implementing a company's strategy. Remember Figure 1.6 in the first chapter, where performance is both the culmination of the strategy model and a starting point for continual refinement. In fact, such importance is placed on performance that we locate this chapter on performance right here near the beginning of this book.

Sound strategy helps to create a position of sustainable competitive advantage in the marketplace, the results of which should be superior performance. Recall that strategic decisions involve *non-routine situations* calling for a *significant commitment of resources and effort* that affect the *entire organization* over the *long run*. When managers are called upon to make such decisions, they must be able to reason that the company's subsequent performance will justify their resource investments and spending commitments. A consistent pattern of decision making that doesn't result in superior performance is often a signal that it is time to replace those making such impactful decisions. So as you study strategy this semester by examining company cases and situations, you should always be considering the performance implications of the strategic moves and actions. By discussing performance early in the study of strategy, we have learned that students can be far more insightful about and discriminating in their company evaluations.

Customary Performance Dimensions

There are three aspects of performance that are important to consider from a strategy point of view (Figure 2.1). First, since strategic decisions and actions involve virtually the entire organization, the types of performance measures we pay the greatest attention to are those that reflect the company's achievement as a whole. A marketing department may be interested in market share gains or advertising effectiveness as key performance outcomes, and a finance department might work toward an optimal capital structure or lowering the company's cost of capital as an outcome. However, at the strategic

> **Figure 2.1**
> **Key Strategy Performance Dimensions**
>
> Summary performance
> Relative to competition
> Over the long run

level we are interested in summary accomplishments of the entire company that roll up and include these functional area effects, as well as the performance in other functional areas. Since strategy requires consistency and coordination across all functions, the key performance measures of interest should be those that reflect the impact of integrated efforts across the entire company.

Second, the kinds of performance measures we will pay the greatest attention to are those that can be compared to other companies. As mentioned in the first chapter, the goal of strategy is to produce *superior* performance, and so strategists are by definition relativists. Reporting that net income per employee increased by 3 percent over last year is interesting; however, realizing that the comparative average in the industry was up only 1 percent makes the result remarkable and indicates a significantly better approach. In Figure 1.2 in the last chapter we saw that, although its 3.5% profitability did not by itself appear astounding, Whole Foods exceeded the retail grocery store industry average by a multiple of over 2 and bested most of its competitors. Relative to competition, the company was doing very well. Therefore, it is especially helpful to consider key performance measures that can be easily compared to other companies.

Finally, since the nature of strategy is about commitment and sustainability, the kind of performance measures we pay the greatest attention to are those that reflect the company's long-term commitment. There is normally a long lead time between strategic investments and the

outcomes of those investments. Imagine, for example, the decision made by Walmart in 2010 to begin to test the use of RFID radio chips on certain types of clothing merchandise flowing through its massive distribution system. This requires a long-term investment in technology and infrastructure by the company in its own stores, as well as parallel commitments by companies that sell to Walmart. The decision also sparked privacy concerns by consumer groups, prompting significant involvement by the company's marketing and public relations departments.[3] Costly to set up initially, its true economic benefit will be years down the road, once the technology is fully implemented across all merchandise. So it may be misleading to evaluate performance over a short time frame, simply because the time between this strategic investment and its strategic impact can be substantial.

A more complete view of strategic performance, therefore, would require assessing whether a company is delivering superior returns consistently over time. Using performance measures that implicitly or explicitly incorporate dimensions of a company's long-term commitments are usually more insightful. For example, a financial measure such as profitability (e.g. net income percentage) reports on current period activity, but implicitly takes into account manufacturing infrastructure that produces efficiency, asset investments that must be depreciated, and the interest burden associated with long-term debt. Return on equity (ROE) evaluates current period profitability with reference to the company's equity basis (which ordinarily does not exhibit short-term variability). It is no coincidence that financial analysts often list ROE under the category of "Management Effectiveness" since it reflects the strategic accomplishments of senior management.

Better than single-year statistics, though, are measures which calculate firm performance over longer periods. Look at the first table in the airline story which began this chapter. Here you will see both 4-year ROA and 4-year ROE – each presenting views of how well the airlines performed at a summary level over a longer period. Note that Southwest exceeded all competitors on both dimensions! As importantly, note that three of the legacy airlines were unable to report ROE, since in some of the 4 years they reported losses or actually had negative stockholder equity accounts due to bankruptcy and recapitalization proceedings.

Emerging Stakeholder Performance Dimensions

Despite the Southwest example and others that emphasize financial measures of performance, effective strategy also demands consideration of other more qualitative dimensions of the strategic performance question. Whole Foods creates more than just economic value for its shareholders. The company has created markets for organic and natural foods that were previously underdeveloped. This effort has served to legitimize producers of these foodstuffs such that even Walmart is now offering organic products in their superstores. In this way the company has helped create value upstream for its suppliers. There is also a social benefit to communities in which Whole Foods stores are located, as consumers in these areas are now provided with shopping choices previously unavailable to them. Since the company sponsors cooking and health seminars as part of its operations, additional noneconomic benefits accrue to communities in which the company locates stores.

One of the more recent moves by companies that benefit both society and the organization is the effort at becoming a "green" organization. Many businesses now design and occupy office buildings which are LEED-certified (Leadership in Energy and Environmental Design). Using natural light, installing natural power generation, reducing the use of water and eliminating waste, such businesses present a more attractive work environment for their employees and communities. Selling products that are made in a sustainable way lead to significant benefits for society and are rapidly being seen as a means of competitive advantage for companies.[4]

These ideas emphasize that strategy is about value creation which can take many forms – economic, cultural, social, and knowledge-based – and which are not just for the benefit of those with formalized economic claims on a company. Businesses are sometimes perceived as being managed using a purely economic transactional view of their relationships, with an exclusive focus on enhancing profitability for shareholders to the exclusion of other goals. This approach has occasionally been associated with what we now consider abuses of the public good, such as the belching smokestacks in heavy industry, the use of child labor for clothing manufacturing in emerging nations, untreated animal farm runoff in the Southeast, or the tearing down of a neighborhood health clinic to make room for a parking garage for corporate executives in the skyscraper next door.

But today a more holistic view of business exists, a view that recognizes that business operates in both a competitive and social context. In this more emergent view, firms consider performance with respect to a broader range of stakeholders. Stakeholders are those individuals or groups who have an interest in or an influence on the business and operations of a company. They generally fall into two categories - internal stakeholders and external stakeholders (Figure 2.2). As awareness of stakeholder issues has become more prevalent over the last decade, a vibrant debate has sprung up as to whether firm performance should be focused purely on financial measures or on a broader selection of measures that account for stakeholder

Figure 2.2
Stakeholders

Internal	External	
Employees	Suppliers	Governments
Managers & Officers	Unions	Communities
Board of Directors	Creditors	Interest Groups
Stockholders	Customers	

interests. This debate implies that profitability and stakeholder performance may be at odds with each other; however, there is growing realization that addressing broader stakeholder goals may also further the financial goals of most companies.[5] For instance, Toyota's groundbreaking efforts on the Prius hybrid automobile not only responded to society's concerns about the impact of automobile exhaust on global warming, but also catapulted the company to the forefront of the industry as gas prices rose and the more efficient car was sought. Microsoft embarked on a drive to enhance information technology education in community colleges across America. This effort provides much-needed resources to schools in a time of constrained state and federal spending, and also responds to the company's long-term need to hire a large number of new advanced-trained IT graduates.

Taking into consideration the interests of a range of stakeholders is consistent with the two strategic imperatives we discussed in the first chapter: the value creation imperative, and the opportunity recognition imperative. Supporting the more enlightened view that business organizations and society are mutually dependent on each other, new trends becoming prevalent in society and industry can represent opportunities for both existing and new businesses. Some new companies actually start up

with social objectives stated explicitly, in addition to ordinary corporate profitability objectives, and by doing so create a valued connection with consumers that goes beyond merely the benefits of the products they sell. Newman's Own started in 1982 with the goal of selling a few bottles of salad dressing and donating whatever profits they might earn to charity. The company attracted considerable consumer attention and has grown dramatically. Over the past three decades it has donated in excess of $450 million to thousands of charities worldwide. Ben & Jerry's similarly attracted a broad following and achieved phenomenal economic performance by combining an economic mission ("sustainable financial growth") with a social mission ("innovative ways to make the world a better place"). Reporting on their efforts in its 2014 annual report, CEO Jostein Solheim writes:

"We are dedicated to a sustainable corporate concept of linked prosperity.... The idea is as simple as it is radical: as the company prospers, all those touched by the company must also prosper, including employees, suppliers, customers, and communities.... it benefits people through some of our more well-known examples: our livable wage policy; ongoing support for family dairy farms, supporting small-holder producers by purchasing Fair-trade-certified ingredients and values-led sourcing partnerships.... Or you could think of linked prosperity as benefitting the planet we share by supporting sustainable forms of agriculture.

"We are finding practical ways to implement business decisions that manifest our best aspirations.... We came to the understanding that we need to deeply focus Ben & Jerry's on two overarching priorities: Climate Justice and Social Equity. The two intersect in profound ways. The work that we do as an agriculturally-based business, sourcing ingredients from the global north and south, selling ice cream around the world, compels us to stand on the two platforms of Climate Justice and Social Equity and deliver some significant results. That sets the table for 2015-2020 and, quite frankly, well beyond."[6]

The integration of corporate financial performance and corporate social performance goes beyond simply attracting like-minded customers. Increasingly, companies are finding ways to make a difference in socially important issues as they go about the day-to-day activities that have

to do with their core business. In Walmart's South African division, Massmart helps to preserve small-scale farming by sourcing raw materials for its produce sections from small family farmers, while Sysco's reliance on small family farms also ensures the provisioning of fresh, locally grown produce for their foodservice and restaurant supply operations. Marriott provides job training for chronically unemployed workers, which helps the communities in which Marriott does business and also aids the company in its recruitment of entry-level workers.[7] Known for its industrial climate and security technologies, Ingersoll Rand leveraged its capabilities and collaborated with local firms to develop a sustainable new business in affordable refrigeration addressing a vast need among poor families in India who are living at the "bottom of the pyramid."

Corporate social performance has now become proactive, stretching beyond the customary activities of companies. In 2016 legislation was passed in North Carolina which had the effect of limiting gay and transgender rights. Alcoa, Dow Chemical, and Northrop Grumman have all waded into the public debate, condemning these measures and lobbying elected officials for change. This reflects a new reality that corporate activism may be expected; in fact, 78% of Americans support corporate political engagement on social issues. Although this sort of corporate activity can have a beneficial effect in communities and with their stakeholders, it also presents challenges for leaders. Expending corporate resources on issues unrelated to the core business may not be wise, and taking positions on social issues – while consistent with espoused corporate values – may also be controversial.

Reflecting these newer orientations of many for-profit companies, over the last few years the concept of the triple bottom line has emerged. Companies that embrace the triple bottom line concept measure their performance in economic, social and ecological (or environmental) terms. They develop internal processes and measures to ensure that they are making progress on each of these performance dimensions over the long run (see Chapter 12 for monitoring progress on key strategic performance dimensions). Often these companies also provide significant disclosure – on their websites and in their annual reports – about the progress they are making. Marks and Spencer, for example, is a leading UK-based retailer of fashion clothing, home products, and food. In 2007 they launched "Plan A," involving 180 environmental and social commitments to achieve by 2015. They update their progress on this strategic initiative regularly on their website (http://plana.marksandspencer.com/) and in their annual report, and have recently extended their goals to 2020.

> **Triple Bottom Line**
>
> Economic performance
> Social performance
> Ecological performance

Finally, the increasing application of strategic management principles in the nonprofit sector and in government has also heightened attention to nonfinancial measures of performance. Since by definition these organizations do not produce profits and do not have shareholders, we must deal with important questions about how to measure their performance. In both these instances the key to measuring performance is to focus on the values appreciated by the organization's various stakeholders. Profits in ordinary businesses are an outcome measure reflecting successful value creation that results in a greater number of new customers and/or greater purchasing by existing customers. Similarly, measurement for nonprofits and governments should begin with how well stakeholders are being served. Some nonprofits have very focused missions, in which case the summary performance measures that report how well the entire organization has functioned are relatively easy to describe and measure. Feeding America, the largest national charitable food donation network, collects and distributes food to people in need at community kitchens, food pantries, homeless shelters, Kids Cafe, senior centers, soup kitchens, and youth programs. Their performance is measured by tonnage of distribution, and by the proportion of cash donations received which are devoted to programs rather than to administration (the "charitable commitment rating"). Figure 2.3 illustrates performance measures for valued receiver stakeholders for this relatively focused nonprofit organization.[8] In contrast, any government entity is likely to have a far more complex network of stakeholders –individual citizens, interest groups, businesses, arts and entertainment organizations, schools, municipal employees, etc. –so that gauging performance would likely require an array of measures.

Figure 2.3
Feeding America, 2015 Performance

✓ Distributed 3.7 billion pounds of food nationwide
✓ 68% of distributed food was classified as "foods to encourage"
✓ Served 1.2 billion meals, a 14% increase over 2014
✓ 47% increase in targeted meals for seniors
✓ Raised $110 million in donations, with 98.6% charitable commitment rating (% of funds going to programs)
✓ Expanded public awareness of Feeding America to 45%

FINANCIAL PERFORMANCE AND COMPETITIVE ADVANTAGE

Having made the case that strategy should be assessed by a balance of both customary financial and emerging nonfinancial measures, we turn back now to more carefully examine aspects of financial performance and their relationship with strategy. Once again we begin with the premise that effective strategy is connected with *superior* financial performance –that is, something *more* than what the average competitor achieves. When people invest in a company and become shareholders, their expectation is that the return they will earn through their investment is at least equal to the kind of return they could earn on average by investing elsewhere in the marketplace at the same level of risk. Otherwise, why would they invest in this company? Normal profit may be viewed as the minimum return earned by a company that is necessary to attract and secure the owners' inputs. Long ago, however, economist Alfred Marshall distinguished economic profit from normal profit.[9] Economic profit represents the *residual income* above and beyond normal profit that accrues to owners, deriving from the prowess of management in planning, supervision, and control (i.e. from effective strategic management). Residual income associated with economic profit occurs when a company's return on equity (ROE) is greater than its cost of equity capital.[10] This is precisely the logic behind the focus of CEOs (and strategy students) on ROE as one of the key strategy performance indicators. If a company produces higher ROE than the average in the marketplace, without incurring any additional risk, then the company is earning economic profit –or as we usually refer to it in strategy, above-average profitability.

	Profitability	Asset Productivity	Financial Leverage	ROE
	$\frac{\text{Net Income}}{\text{Sales}}$	$\frac{\text{Sales}}{\text{Assets}}$	$\frac{\text{Assets}}{\text{Shareholder Equity}}$	$\frac{\text{Net Income}}{\text{Shareholder Equity}}$
JetBlue	10.6 %	0.74	2.70	21.1 %
Southwest	11.0 %	0.93	2.90	29.6 %

Figure 2.4
DuPont Analysis: Decomposing 2015 Return On Equity (ROE)

In turn, we must now ask, in practical terms, how can strategy impact a company's return on equity? To partially answer this question, we can break ROE down into its component parts. This is called a "DuPont Analysis" because it originated in the 1920s with that company. Figure 2.4 decomposes ROE into its three different ratios: profitability, asset productivity, and financial leverage. When these three ratios are calculated and then multiplied together, the resulting product is the return on equity percentage for the company. The three ratios provide the insight that there are different ways in which superior returns can be created, either through a focus on one area or through some combination of areas within the company. As your grandmother probably said, "there are several ways to skin a cat." Illustrating this, the figure provides a breakdown of ROE in 2015 for the two discount airlines profiled in the opening story for this chapter. Here we see why JetBlue's 21.1% ROE was lower than that of Southwest: the combination of lower asset productivity and lower financial leverage constitute the sources of the difference in performance.

The decomposition of ROE into its component ratios can be taken further to provide greater ammunition for the strategist. In Figure 2.4 we observe that Southwest's Profitability is slightly higher than JetBlue's, despite having a higher cost per available seat mile in 2015 (see earlier table). So Southwest must be doing something else much better than JetBlue to generate better profitability. There are many financial ratios that can be used to develop an even more refined view of the sources of advantage within each of the three components. Figure 2.5 lists many such subcomponent ratios that are helpful in assessing company performance, identifying advantages that can be leveraged, and calling out areas that might require management attention. Remembering that our performance evaluation should be relative to our competitors' performance, we may see that one company's profitability is lower than that of its competitors. Closer examination may reveal that the sources of that inferior position can be traced back to its higher cost of goods sold, higher selling general and administrative costs (SG&A), or some other non-operating characteristics of the business. These areas might then receive greater focus by management to improve profitability and overall return on equity. The Appendix to this chapter provides a review of financial ratios that may be helpful in analyzing companies and their strategic performance. Use these ratios when you examine cases and companies in your strategy course.

Figure 2.5
Financial Ratios Providing Strategic Insight

Return on Equity		
Profitability	**Asset Productivity**	**Financial Leverage**
Cost of goods sold / sales	Current asset turnover	Current ratio
Gross profit / sales	Working capital turnover	Quick ratio
SG&A / sales	Accounts receivable	Cash ratio
Operating income / sales	turnover	Operating cash ratio
Non-operating gains & losses	Inventory turnover	Liabilities / equity
/ sales	Accounts payable turnover	Debt / equity
EBIT / sales	Days' receivables	Debt / capital
Taxes / sales	Days' inventory	Interest coverage ratio
	PP&E turnover	

Strategy performance is gauged "over the long term," however, as we have said earlier in this chapter. So we need to be very careful about looking at just one year's performance. Figure 2.4 derives ROE for the two airlines for just 2015. However, viewing a longer time period provides a better measure of the sustainability of superior performance. For the ten years leading up through 2012 – a brutal period that included both expansion and contraction in the U.S. economy – Southwest's ROE was 6.2 percent while JetBlue's was only 3.5 percent. This is because Southwest managed to stay profitable during the post-September 11 decline in airline traffic and following the 2008 recession. JetBlue was unprofitable during three years of this period. An excellent question to ask here is, why was Southwest able to sustain its performance while JetBlue and other airlines were not? To understand Southwest's strategy and the sources of its superior performance, we will have to dig deeper into the company using ideas coming up in the next few chapters.

So far the measure return on equity has been highlighted as being particularly important, because of its direct relationship to the strategy goal of superior performance. However, there are other market-based measures of performance that are also used by CEOs, analysts, and strategy students to quantitatively assess how well companies are performing. While there are a variety of other such measures, four seem to be used most frequently: sales revenue growth, returns to common stock, some measure of a company's market value such as market capitalization, and return on invested capital (ROIC).[11]

Revenue growth is generally of great interest to the senior executives of most companies. The ability to grow a company's revenue demonstrates that the company continues to develop relationships with existing and new customers, is able to expand into new geographic territories, and is staying relevant to the marketplace. Unfortunately, revenue growth often occurs at the expense of growth in profitability, since the factors that generally drive up sales (e.g., more advertising, investment in new product development, building a more effective sales force) often add expenses that diminish the bottom line. So there is a certain yin and yang quality to sales growth and ROE (which depends on the profitability ratio). Senior managers who can increase both sales *and* profitability simultaneously are highly regarded, since in practice this does not happen very often (only 9 out of 1,077 companies in a recent McKinsey survey achieved this feat).[12]

Common stock returns and market capitalization are the other two measures of firm performance that are commonly mentioned. Common stock returns take into account both the dividends paid by a company to its shareholders as well as increases in the price of the shares. Abnormally high returns, relative to common stock returns for competing companies, are desirable and indicative of high-performing companies. A well-known and popular business book, *Good to Great*, used abnormally high returns as the starting point for examining the strategic moves of those special companies. The eleven companies (out of 1,435 analyzed) that formed the basis of the book were identified by examining this type of performance metric over long periods of time.[13]

Market capitalization, defined as the market value of outstanding shares of stock, also depends on stock price and characterizes the total value of the company. While both these measures provide perspective on the performance of a company, they also mirror investors' anticipation of future performance and assume that all available information is reflected in the stock price. Investors partially base their evaluations of companies on traditional metrics such as ROE and revenue growth rates. Yet we have recently witnessed times when an "irrational exuberance" (an unaccountable and unsupported opinion that things will keep getting better and better) among investors drives stock prices so high that they bear absolutely no relationship to a company's fundamental economics (e.g., the "dot bomb" era). Since a purely market-based evaluation of a company's performance might be misleading, it is always important to evaluate companies using several measures.

Lately there has been interest in return on invested capital (ROIC) as an alternative to, or enhancement of, ROE. This is a metric which measures how efficient a company is in earning cash flow from its strategic investments of invested equity capital and debt. Says General Motors CFO Chuck Stevens: "ROIC provides the clearest picture of how we are managing our capital and our business. It's really starting to become part of the DNA of our decisions." Since higher levels of ROIC are correlated with superior performance versus rival companies, increasingly executive long-term bonuses are being tied to this measure.

INSIGHTS FROM DETAILED FINANCIAL ANALYSIS

Although companies often make public statements about their strategies and discuss broad strategic initiatives in shareholder meetings or analysts' conference calls, they generally do not "publish" great detail about their strategies. This is because they don't really want to reveal their deepest, most critical thinking to competitors. Strategy should be articulated to and understood by important external constituents, but not so much revealed that it can be easily imitated. So then how can we determine what a company's strategy really is, what is really at the core?

Financial analysis of companies and competitors is a tool that should be used in parallel to the forthcoming strategy frameworks you will read about in this textbook. This is because, as companies implement their strategies, their implementation results in patterns of investments, asset allocations, and sets of interrelated activities that ultimately manifest themselves in financial results. The key to utilizing strategic financial analysis is that the patterns revealed by the numbers demonstrate what companies are really doing and how they are actually operating in the marketplace, regardless of what they say they are doing. In combination with the strategy frameworks we will be developing in later chapters, we can then induce what their intended and actual strategies really are. Another way of thinking about this is that a company may state what

its overall strategic approach will be, but the numbers show what they are actually doing. It should come as no great surprise to anyone that Walmart pursues a low-cost strategy; we hear about it all the time, from them in their ads as well as from others. But you can really understand how the company makes this an effective strategic approach by carefully examining its financial statements. Here is where we can see what they are actually doing.

Current Financial Statements

Financial statements paint a picture about how companies are operating. A quick example can illustrate this quite easily. Figure 2.6 (a) provides recent income statement and balance sheet information for three types of well-known national retail chains – a supermarket, a drug store, and a department store. Without telling you their names (the three chains are labeled A, B, and C), we can examine the financial detail to determine which is which. The financials show us that each type of retailer operates very differently, and will reveal dimensions of their strategies to us.

At the outset we can make a couple of obvious comments and draw preliminary inferences. Chain A produces more than 1/2 the net income of Chain B on only about 1/4 the sales revenue, while using an asset base that is roughly 2/3 that of Chain B. At the same time, Chain C is producing 250% of the net income of Chain B on a revenue base that is only 40% higher. So it appears as if Chain B is conducting business in a low-margin industry, is experiencing significant operational issues that cost more, or is facing strong competition that polices its pricing. Apparently size or scale is less important for the industry in which Chain A competes, since it is more profitable on a much lower revenue base. All three companies carry considerable inventories and have significant investment in physical infrastructure (property, plant, and equipment) that is financed by varying combinations of long-term debt and equity. Chain C, however, has a far higher level of receivables than the other two chains, even in light of its high annual sales revenue. Of course, this means it relies much more on credit, versus cash, transactions.

Figure 2.6 (a)
Financial Data For Three Retail Chains (millions)

	Chain A	Chain B	Chain C
Income Statement			
Revenues	$ 27,079	$ 109,830	$ 153,290
Cost of goods sold	16,496	85,496	126,762
Gross profit	10,583	24,334	26,528
Selling, general & admin (SG&A)	7,195	18,669	14,982
Depreciation & amortization	1,061	2,089	2,092
Other expense / income	286	10	-7
Operating income	2,041	3,566	9,461
Interest expense	363	482	838
Taxes	608	1,045	3,386
Net income	**1,070**	**2,039**	**5,237**

	Chain A	Chain B	Chain C
Balance Sheet			
Assets			
Cash & short term investments	$ 1,109	$ 1,200	$ 2,547
Receivables	558	1,734	11,888
Inventories	5,506	6,168	14,001
Property, plant, equipment (net)	7,616	19,619	9,855
Other assets	5,787	5,176	55,366
Total Assets	**20,576**	**33,897**	**93,657**
Liabilities & Shareholder Equity			
Accounts payable	$ 3,333	$ 5,728	$ 7,490
Other current liabilities	2,395	7,243	15,679
Long term debt	6,995	9,769	26,267
Other liabilities	3,600	4,359	7,025
Equity & retained earnings	4,253	6,798	37,196
Total Liabilities & Equity	**20,576**	**33,897**	**93,657**

It is often difficult to get a clear picture when comparing companies of different sizes. So a more useful view can be developed by converting the financial statements to common-sized statements. This is done for income statements by setting revenue for each company equal to 100 percent, and for balance sheets by setting each side of the balance sheet to 100 percent. Figure 2.6 (b) shows the common-sized statements for the three retail chains.

It can now be observed that Chain C has the highest cost of goods sold as a percentage of sales, but makes up for this slightly through its lower SG&A expense. Its receivables represent fully 13% of its assets, significantly higher than the other two retailers, and its "other assets" represent a whopping 59% of the total. Its property, plant and equipment is smaller in percentage terms than A or B. This sounds like a chain which operates in smaller buildings with less distribution infrastructure or could be leasing store locations, sells expensive merchandise, and whose customers take time to pay for their purchases. Chain B has the largest portion of its assets in property, and produces a 1.9% razor thin bottom line with little margin for error (literally). This sounds like a business that is primarily distribution-focused selling volumes of low margin goods. Compare sales, general and administrative (GS&A) expenses across the three chains. A spends significantly more than both B and C. This seems to be a retailer that is dealing with administrative complexity and must advertise regularly to bring customers through the doors.

Figure 2.6 (b)
Common Sized Data For Three Retail Chains (%)

	Chain A	Chain B	Chain C
Income Statement			
Revenues	100.0 %	100.0 %	100.0 %
Cost of goods sold	60.9	77.8	82.7
Gross profit	39.1	22.2	17.3
Selling, general & admin (SG&A)	26.6	17.0	9.8
Depreciation & amortization	3.9	1.9	1.4
Other expense / income	1.1	0.0	0.0
Operating income	7.5	3.2	6.2
Interest expense	1.3	0.4	0.5
Taxes	2.2	1.0	2.2
Net income	**4.0**	**1.9**	**3.4**

	Chain A	Chain B	Chain C
Balance Sheet			
Assets			
Cash & short term investments	5	4	3
Receivables	3	5	13
Inventories	27	18	15
Property, plant & equipment	37	58	11
Other assets	28	16	59
Total Assets	**100 %**	**100 %**	**100 %**
Liabilities & Shareholder Equity			
Accounts payable	16	17	8
Other current liabilities	12	21	17
Long term debt	34	29	28
Other liabilities	18	13	8
Equity & retained earnings	21	20	40
Total Liabilities & Equity	**100 %**	**100 %**	**100 %**

	Chain A	Chain B	Chain C
Selected Financial Ratios			
Current assets / current liabilities	1.34	0.76	1.31
Inventory turnover (x per year)	3.00	13.86	9.05
Receivables collection (days)	7.52	5.76	28.31
Total debt / total assets	0.79	0.80	0.80
Net income / sales (Profitability)	4.0 %	1.9 %	3.4 %
Sales / assets (Asset productivity)	1.32	3.24	1.64
Assets / equity (Financial leverage)	4.84	4.99	2.52
Net income / equity (ROE)	25.2 %	30.0 %	14.1 %

Selected financial ratios provide further insight into who is who. Chain B turns its inventory over almost 14 times each year. What kind of merchandise would we hope and expect to be turning more frequently – clothing, drugs and sundries, or food? There are also very different receivables collection periods for the three companies. Chains A and B average collection periods are under 8 days; these are almost a pure cash or immediate transaction business. On the other hand, Chain C's collection period is 28 days, suggesting that it extends credit to many of its customers.

We can start drawing conclusions about these observed differences: Chain C with smaller stores and expensive inventory that turns slowly, versus Chain B with large investment in property and low value inventory that turns over rapidly. The sum of these differences, in fact, describes the kinds of different operating characteristics that we should expect to see across three types of retail chains:

Chain A - Department store chain (Macy's)
- large stores with basic display furnishings
- carries a vast array of moderately priced merchandise
- requirement for variety in styles and sizes produces low inventory turnover
- must advertise in order to compete with other retailers and online shopping
- some use of store credit card increases receivables collection versus pure cash and third party bank credit cards

Chain B - Supermarket chain (Kroger)
- large stores with sophisticated furnishings (freezers, coolers, bakery) and heavy investment in warehousing and transportation logistics
- lower priced, everyday merchandise that sells through quickly
- largely a cash, debit card, or bank credit card business
- competition with other chains ensures low prices and thin margins

Chain C - Drug chain (CVS Caremark)
- smaller stores than supermarkets or department stores, leased in strip shopping centers
- higher priced merchandise because of carrying costs of expensive medications
- reimbursement from insurance companies for medications sold takes a long time
- high asset value in "other" assets due to capitalizing intangibles from acquisitions and the value of long term medication supply contracts

Interestingly, although the supermarket develops half the net income percentage of the drug chain and less than half the net income percentage of the department store chain, its ROE is the greatest of these three companies. This is because B also exhibits superior asset productivity (3.24) as well as superior financial leverage (4.99), so that in combination its ROE is competitive with other retailers.

Trend Analysis

In the preceding example we have examined three companies at a point in time, using the financial data from one year's performance. The differences we observe illustrate different approaches to the marketplace. It can also be helpful to evaluate the financial statements of a company over a series of years. Figure 2.7 provides five years of historical financial data, from 1997 through 2001, for a company you probably know quite well – Amazon. These five years are when Amazon really took off. The financial trends in evidence here provide insight into what the company was actually doing strategically as it grew from a very small online retailer into a much larger, dominating internet powerhouse.

Figure 2.7
Selected Financial Data For Amazon.com (millions)

	2001	2000	1999	1998	1997
Income Statement					
Revenues	3,122	2,762	1,640	610	148
Cost of goods sold	2,323	2,106	1,349	476	119
Gross profit	799	656	291	134	29
Selling, general & admin (GS&A)					
Fulfillment & marketing	512	594	413	133	40
Technology	241	269	160	46	13
All other	457	657	323	64	8
Operating income (loss)	(412)	(864)	(606)	(109)	(33)
Interest expense (income)	139	131	85	27	0
Net income	(567)	(1,411)	(720)	(125)	(31)

We could spend considerable time picking apart these statements, as you should when you conduct your own strategic analysis of a company. But let's highlight a couple key areas that go to the heart of this company's successful growth trajectory. First we observe that the company's gross profit increased from 19.5% in 1997 to 25.6% by 2001. This might mean that the company had been able to raise its prices to consumers during this time, or that it was receiving more favorable prices from its suppliers. We know that the retail book business is fairly competitive and that Amazon was seeking to drive more buyer volume to its website, so it is not likely it was raising its prices. Instead, the much greater volume of business they were doing by 2001 ($3 billion in sales versus $148 million only five years earlier) suggests they struck agreements with suppliers (likely facilitated by a higher volume of business).

How did the company manage to grow so quickly? The statements tell us they were making massive investments in fulfillment and marketing, technology, and administrative support. These investments helped make their website especially attractive and easy to use (for example, their "One-Click" checkout innovation), helped drive consumers to their website, and made sure there was sufficient staff and infrastructure to support the added business. In 1999 and 2000 the company's intangibles increased considerably, indicating it was purchasing other companies and/or booking significant technological innovations onto its balance sheet.

	2001	2000	1999	1998	1997
Balance Sheet					
Assets					
Cash & marketable securities	997	1,100	706	373	125
Inventories	144	175	221	30	9
Fixed assets	272	366	318	30	9
Goodwill & intangibles	80	255	730	179	0
Other assets	145	238	496	37	5
Total Assets	**1,638**	**2,135**	**2,472**	**648**	**149**
Liabilities & Shareholder Equity					
Accounts payable	445	485	463	113	33
Other liabilities	476	490	276	49	11
Long term debt	2,156	2,127	1,466	348	76
Equity & paid-in capital	1,467	1,342	1,199	302	65
Other equity	(45)	(16)	(51)	(1)	(2)
Retained earnings	(2,861)	(2,293)	(882)	(162)	(34)
Total Liabilities & Equity	**1,638**	**2,135**	**2,472**	**648**	**149**

A closer look at the balance sheet data reveals startling increases during this period of time in a number of categories. As the company's business volume grew, it began to build its own inventory and distribution warehouses to make sure that ordering customers received their books quickly. So we see that fixed assets skyrocketed in one year from $30 million to over $300 million. How could the company afford to make such large investments in warehousing, marketing, and technology? It continued to lose money throughout this period, as illustrated by its net loss of hundreds of millions of dollars each year! Its growth was financed by both long-term debt and the sale of additional shares of stock (paid in capital); both categories combined to provide the company $2.8 billion in cash between 1998 and 2000.

At the time this was going on many people wondered why anyone would invest in shares of a company that was losing so much money every year, a company that had not produced positive ROE at any time in its history and wasn't likely to for the foreseeable future? Hindsight is wonderful, but in 1998-99 no one knew what the future held! The company's success – and the investor's return – would depend critically on the market and the company's strategy in that market. These are areas we will be tackling in the next few chapters. Stay tuned!

The preceding examples have illustrated two key points about how strategy and financial performance mirror each other:

1. Strategy is implemented by taking actions and operating in the marketplace in certain ways, which result in certain financial performance characteristics we can see in the financial statements; and

2. Financial performance characteristics reveal the way in which a company is operating in the market, which follows from the company's strategic direction and decisions.

Analyzing a company's operations and financial performance provides evidence about its strategy (the coordinating pattern of decisions and investments affecting the entire company over a long time period). It also provides insight into whether the company is actually pursuing the strategy that it claims to be. Strategy is not just words and intentions; it is about action and the commitment of resources. A stated strategy that is not backed by sufficient investment and supportive actions is not a strategy at all.

ECONOMIC LOGIC AND OPERATING CHARACTERISTICS

If you step back from a detailed analysis of financial statements, you can often discover that there is a core economic logic that helps in understanding a successful company's strategic thinking and operational execution. Economic logic is sort of a "recipe" by which the successful company seeks to generate a return that is greater than what competitors earn and greater than its cost of capital.[14] The economic logic for warehouse club retailing, such as Sam's Club stores, can be described as being "pile it high, mark it down, and move vast quantities." Successful retailers whose strategies embrace this logic are likely to develop healthy ROE by increasing the asset productivity component as a consequence of sales throughput. In contrast Saks Fifth Avenue's approach might be characterized as "merchandise beautifully, pamper the clientele, and charge premium prices." Such operations are relatively less interested in asset productivity and more interested in profitability as a route to superior ROE. Although Sam's and Saks Fifth Avenue compete in different industries, in some industries sufficient strategic variety exists that we might witness very different economic logics being used by different competitors. In grocery retailing, Wegman's and Whole Foods have a very different economic logic in mind (premium quality, wide variety of selection, higher prices) when compared to Food Lion (commonly needed household foods priced to sell).

In other industries conditions may exist where a core economic logic drives all competitors to a great extent. For example, commercial banks have historically earned profits by focusing on "net interest margin," the difference between interest rates they pay to borrow capital and the interest rates they charge to lend that capital out. Online discount stock brokers such as e*Trade and online auctions such as eBay earn extremely small fees on each of their transactions, and therefore seek to drive up their sheer volume of transactions. This is a low-margin, high-volume economic logic. In several technology-based industries (e.g., inkjet printers, gaming, computer

operating systems), the logic for competing often involves establishing a broad "installed base" of users while earning little in the process of doing so. Having established the base, returns are then earned through future transactions that installed base users must engage in (e.g., replacement ink cartridges, buying additional games for the game platform). None of these overarching economic logics dictate exactly what strategy any individual competitor in an industry must follow or how they are to operate. Yet once we understand the economic logics that tend to operate in an industry, we have a better chance of accurately diagnosing the strategy of a particular company in which we are interested.

Along with the core economic logic that helps to frame a company's approach in an industry, strategy analysis should also pay close attention to important operating characteristics that describe how well the company addresses the economic logic at play. In the commercial airline industry, which was profiled at the beginning of this chapter, the economic logic reflects an industry that has become commoditized. This is where the combination of low costs and high passenger volume might be the key to success. What drives profitability for every carrier are low costs per available seat mile flown, in combination with passenger load factors (although that model is in the process of changing with their new efforts to charge for everything that used to be included with a ticket). These two operating characteristics are closely watched by the financial news media, because they are so critical to airline profitability, and thus they command great attention from senior managers in charge of strategy. Referring back to the tables in the opening story of the chapter, Southwest Airlines has a lower load factor than the other airlines listed, yet it also has the lowest cost per available seat mile of any of its major competitors. Though the low-cost-high-volume economic logic applies to every carrier in the industry, it does not dictate a particular strategic approach. In this case Southwest achieves its low-cost position through a combination of exceptionally strong human resource practices that create a coherent workforce, fast gate turnarounds at airports, use of identical aircraft to save on maintenance costs, crew training, crew availability and downtime, routes that take passengers to less expensive airports near major cities, and other unique investments the company has made. In Chapters 5 through 7 we will learn more about designing unique and sustainable strategic approaches, such as those developed by Southwest.

Every industry has combinations of operating characteristics that provide insight on how well competitors are faring. Important operating characteristics in retailing include, among others, sales per square foot of retail space and same-store sales increases (for stores open at least one year). Wholesaling and distribution companies are interested in metrics such as warehouse turns and percent of complete orders shipped/received on time. The cable TV industry pays close attention to net subscriber additions, churn (the tendency of subscribers to drop out quickly), average revenue per subscriber, cash costs per subscriber, and average minutes of use per subscriber. Your analysis of companies and industries will be aided by researching important operating characteristics that are consistent with the economic logics you have identified. This might include standard measures of performance as well as measures that are unique to the strategy they are pursuing.

STRATEGY PLANNING

The important connection we have made in this chapter between strategy and performance is a two-way street. By that we mean that the student of strategy should strive to develop comfort in going back and forth between a strategy and its financial outcomes. Financial statements can be revealing about strategy, while a type of strategy should result in certain patterns in financial statements (Figure 2.8).

Figure 2.8
Relationship Between Strategy and Financial Statements

Most of what we have just covered illustrates how the analysis of financial statements can reveal dimensions of important strategic behavior. This is because, as we mentioned earlier in this chapter, strategy really involves a pattern of asset allocations and inter-related activities that ultimately manifest themselves in financial results. It is nice to have a statement of the company's strategy that the financial media and analyst communities can consume. However, a company's strategy is given real force when the company *acts* - when it organizes itself to support its pronouncements, when it pursues a segment of a particular industry that matches its investments, and when it commits resources to specific projects and initiatives. The allocation of resources and the activities that people in the company engage in are often below the radar of competitors and the financial community in specific terms, but ultimately reveal themselves in financial statements. So understanding a company's strategy through financial statement analysis is sort of like what Yogi Berra once said: "You can observe a lot by watching."

At the same time, we want to emphasize that excellence in strategy *formulation* also requires excellence in financial analysis. When you are the architect of a new strategy for your company, it means that the company will need to act in new ways in organizing itself and allocating human, physical, and financial resources. Every strong strategic plan projects out what these new activities and resource allocations will look like financially. In addition, every strong strategic plan ensures that desired outcome of "above-average profitability" or "superior performance" will be the financial outcome realized. Remember, though, as we mentioned in Chapter 1 and also illustrated by the Amazon.com example, that the financial outcome of superior performance will often involve long time horizons.

CHAPTER SUMMARY

Performance (both quantitative and qualitative) is the key outcome of interest for those studying strategy and managing strategy. Three dimensions of performance are important: 1) summary measures that reflect the impact of integrated efforts across the entire company, 2) measures that can be compared to competitors, and 3) measures that account for longer periods of time. Return on equity (ROE) is the most common performance measure used by executives. ROE can be broken down into three component ratios in the DuPont Analysis that provide insight on company profitability, asset productivity, and financial leverage. Each of these components may be further broken down into additional financial ratios to provide more specific information about sources of strengths and weaknesses.

Other financial dimensions are also used frequently to assess performance resulting from strategy (stockholder returns, market capitalization, sales revenue growth, ROIC). Nonfinancial performance dimensions account for two other important considerations: 1) the realizations that companies may create social, cultural, and knowledge value in addition to economic value; and 2) the emerging view that there are a variety of stakeholders (internal and external) who have interests in a company. Whereas debates have existed in the past as to whether companies should be single-mindedly focused on providing returns to shareholders, the emerging view suggests that attention to stakeholders can create profitable new growth opportunities for companies and simultaneously strengthen their existing franchises.

Insight can be gained about company strategy through three methods: 1) detailed financial statement analysis, often using common-sized statements to compare competitors; 2) identifying the economic logic(s) that may operate within an industry as a means of framing how companies operate; and 3) identifying and evaluating important operational characteristics that portray how well companies appear to be addressing economic logics. Together, these techniques can provide a better understanding of the nature of a company's strategy.

Learning Objectives Review

1. *Explain the value of using both financial and nonfinancial performance dimensions to measure strategy effectiveness.*

- **Stockholders**. For-profit companies are expected to produce positive financial returns for investors who buy their stock. A company's stock will be more attractive to investors if it produces above-average returns, without requiring investors to accept greater risk. This is consistent with the goal of strategy. Certain financial measures of performance (ROE, sales growth, common stock returns, market capitalization) are indicative of strategic performance when considered over a longer time horizon.

- **Stakeholders**. Many corporations today create value for other stakeholders, and thus embrace the idea of triple bottom line performance measurement. Non-financial measures of performance (e.g. "green" environmental benefits, supplier relationships, employee satisfaction, company culture) can lead to a stronger business and enhanced opportunity to accomplish strategic goals.

- **Non-profits and governments**. Strategy is equally important in the management and administration of non-profits and governments that have important long term goals. Non-financial measures that relate to each organization's value-creation model are important to us to evaluate progress.

2. *Describe the relationship between financial performance and a sustainable competitive advantage.*

- **Above average profitability**. The goal of strategy is superior competitive performance. This should translate to above-average profitability and other superior measures of financial performance.

- **Long run performance**. Strategy involves directions and investments that produce superior competitive position and superior performance over the long run. Corporations are challenged to maintain competitive performance in the short run, while developing superior performance in the long run. A company may produce slightly more or less financial return in any given year, however its long run financial performance relative to competitors is of greater interest.

3. *Use financial analysis to examine company strategy.*

- **Return on equity (ROE)**. This is the primary measure used to assess strategic management effectiveness.

- **Composition of ROE**. ROE is composed of three ratios: profitability, asset productivity, financial leverage. Companies may achieve superior ROE by excelling in any one ratio, or by some combination of ratios. Each ratio may be further decomposed into contributing dimensions that reveal sources of performance differences versus competitors.

- **Current financial statement analysis**. A strategy involves a pattern of investments, asset allocations, and sets of activities in pursuit of a specific direction. These are manifested in financial statements, examination of which can reveal what companies are actually doing in the conduct of their business. It is helpful to develop "common sized" financial statements to compare competitors of different sizes.

- **Trended financial statement analysis**. Evaluating a company's financial statements over time is like watching a movie of its strategy in actions (i.e. its pattern of investments, asset allocations, and sets of activities). It can reveal areas of activity where the company is moving very quickly, and can help determine whether its strategic objectives are being accomplished.

4. *Explain the economic logic of industries and companies.*

- **Economic logic**. This is a general description, or a "recipe," for how a successful company seeks to earn superior economic returns in its industry. You can identify the recipe by stepping back from the specific detailed activities that a company engages in, to describe in broad terms what it is trying to do. Example in retailing: "pile it high, mark it down, move vast quantities. There can often exist more than one workable economic logic in an industry.

- **Operating characteristics**. Usually there exist key operational metrics that companies must pay attention to, given the economic logic they employ. These metrics tend to reveal which companies will do well financially, and which will struggle. Example in airline industry: cost per available seat mile.

5. *Examine and explain the interaction between strategy formulation and financial analysis.*

- A formulated strategy indicates long term direction for a company and calls for a pattern of investments, asset allocations, and sets of activities. Strategists must project out the financial implications of these investments, allocations, and activities, and develop proforma financial statements that will be the result.

Key Terms

Common-sized statements - A method of financial analysis that facilitates comparisons between different size companies. For income statements set revenue for each company equal to 100 percent, and for balance sheets set each side of the balance sheet to 100 percent.

Common stock returns - Takes into account both the dividends paid by a company to its shareholders as well as increases in the price of shares.

Economic logic - A "recipe" by which the successful company seeks to generate a return that is greater than what competitors earn and greater than its cost of capital. A broad description of the way the company will operate in its industry.

Economic profit - The residual income above and beyond normal profit that accrues to owners, deriving from the prowess of management n planning, supervision, and control.

Market capitalization - The market value of outstanding shares of stock. Stock price multiplied by all outstanding shares.

Normal profit - The minimum return earned by a company that is necessary to attract and secure the owners' inputs. Generally defined as the cost of equity capital multiplied by the amount of shareholder equity.

Stakeholders - Individuals or groups who have an interest in or an influence on the business and operations of a company. They fall into two categories - internal stakeholders and external stakeholders.

Triple bottom line - Measuring performance in economic, social and ecological (or environmental) terms.

Short Answer Review Questions

1. What three dimensions of performance are most critical?

2. What is the most common performance measure used by executive management? Why? What components make this particular measure so useful?

3. What are non-financial performance measures?

4. What three methods of performance analysis provide the greatest insight into company strategy?

5. Explain the performance considerations necessary when we involve stakeholder's desired outcomes.

6. How do financial ratios provide insight into a company's true strategy?

7. Why is revenue growth such a critical performance measure?

8. How would you determine what strategic approach a company is actually pursuing?

Group Review Exercises

1. Examine the last five years of annual financial statements from a public company that you think you already know fairly well from your own personal experiences (for example, Starbucks or Apple).

- Identify patterns in the income statements and balance sheets, and discuss their possible meanings.

- Use the financial ratios in Appendix A to compare the company to its closest competitor.

- What differences do you now observe about the company's strategic approach to the market, as compared to observations from your personal experiences or ideas you hear about the company in the news media?

- Do you believe this company is achieving superior performance? Why or why not?

2. Choose a nonprofit organization that you are interested in. Examine its publications and documents to determine how it measures its performance.

3. Nobel Prize winner, Milton Friedman, claimed many years ago that the only business of business is to earn a profit for its shareholders. In 2008 successful businessman Bill Gates, founder of Microsoft, advocated corporations to practice "creative capitalism" where they use their capabilities to "do good" while not sacrificing "doing well" for shareholders. The public outcry for greater corporate social responsibility is great. In your group discuss whether you believe corporations should focus only on economic performance for shareholders, or should they also address broader social and community concerns in their day-to-day activities and goals.

4. In 2008 Exxon Mobil (XOM) came under intense public scrutiny because it had reported $11 billion in net income in each of its preceding quarterly statements, at the same time that gas prices were rising to over $4 per gallon for the American public. Some political candidates were recommending a tax on excess oil company profits. According to Thomson Financial, XOM's net income represented 11.3% of revenues, its corporate tax rate was 48% (paid $30 billion during 2007 fiscal year), and its return on equity was 9.36%. Discuss whether you think it would be prudent for government to place additional financial regulation on oil companies.

5. Many of the financial ratios appearing in Figure 2.6 (b) exhibit a wide range across the three companies. But ROE stays within a fairly narrow range. Why do you suppose this would be the case? Why wouldn't we see greater variability in ROE? Discuss this with other members of your class. We will explore the answer to this question in the next chapter on Industry and Competitive Analysis.

References

[1] Several sources were used for this blue. S. McCartney, 2007, A report card on the nation's airlines, Wall Street Journal, February 6: D1; M. Trottman, 2006, Airline CEO's novel strategy: No bankruptcy, Wall Street Journal, April 17: B1; K. Wingfield, 2007, A dogfight in business class, Wall Street Journal, January 25; International Airline Transport Association; U.S. Department of Transportation; Thomson One Banker. Financials reflect 12-month performance through 2006.

[2] Load factor is calculated by dividing the number of revenue passenger miles flown by the number of available seat miles.

[3] M. Bustillo, 2010, Walmart radio tags to track clothing, Wall Street Journal, July 23: B1.

[4] E. L. Plambeck, 2007, The greening of Walmart's supply chain, Supply Chain Management Review, July 1, 2007.

[5] M. E. Porter & M. R. Kramer, 2011, Creating shared value, Harvard Business Review, 90 (1): 62-77.

[6] http://www.benjerry.com/about-us/sear-reports/2014-sear-report.

[7] Porter & Kramer, op. cit.

[8] Feeding America annual report, 2015.

[9] A. Marshall, 1890, Principles of Economics, London: Macmillan Press.

[10] Using the capital asset pricing model, the cost of equity capital for a company depends on the company's sensitivity to market risk (which is captured by the company's ß). When we discuss economic profit, we refer to the ability of a company to earn above-average returns without

requiring shareholders to assume enhanced risk (higher ß). In this case the company earning economic profit produces an ROE that is greater than the expected return using the capital asset pricing model.

[11] B. S. Chakravarthy, 1986, Measuring strategic performance, Strategic Management Journal, 7: 437 - 458; G. G. Dess & R. B. Robinson Jr., 1984, Measuring organizational performance in the absence of objective measures: The case of the privately held firm and conglomerate business unit, Strategic Management Journal, 5: 265 - 273; M. Lubatkin & R. E. Shrieves, 1986, Towards a reconciliation of market performance measures to strategic management research, Academy of Management Review, 11 (3): 497 – 512; D. Benoit, 2016, Finance's hot new metric: ROIC, Wall Street Journal, May 3, C1.

[12] J. Devan, M. B. Klusas, & T. W. Ruefli, 2007, The elusive goal of corporate outperformance, The McKinsey Quarterly, May.

[13] J. Collins, 2001, Good to Great, New York: HarperCollins Publishers.

[14] D. C. Hambrick & J. W. Fredrickson, 2001, Are you sure you have a strategy? Academy of Management Executive, 15 (4): 48 - 59.

APPENDIX

Financial Ratios Useful in Strategy Analysis

PROFITABILITY

Measure	How to calculate it	What it means
Return on equity (ROE)	Profitability x Asset productivity x Financial leverage	Profitability of shareholder investment
Profitability	Net income / Sales	Profitability per dollar of sale
Asset productivity	Sales / Assets	Sales generated per dollar of assets
Financial leverage	Assets / Shareholder equity	Assets in place per dollar is equity investment
Return on assets (ROA)	Net income / Assets	Profitability of assets employed by the company
Return on invested capital (ROIC)	EBIT x (1 − tax rate) / [(Debt + Equity) - (Cash + Equivalents)]	How much new cash is generated from capital investments
Gross profit margin	Gross profit / Sales	Gross profit % per dollar of sales
Operating profit margin	Operating profit / Sales	Profitability of ongoing operations of the company

LIQUIDITY – SHORT TERM

Measure	How to calculate it	What it means
Current ratio	Current assets / Current liabilities	Ability to meet current obligations
Quick ratio	(Current assets − inventories) / Current liabilities	Ability to meet current obligations without having to sell inventory
Cash ratio	Cash / Current liabilities	Ability to meet current obligations relying only on existing cash
Inventory to working capital	Inventory / (Current assets − Current liabilities)	How much working capital is tied up in inventory

LIQUIDITY – LONG TERM

Measure	How to calculate it	What it means
Total debt ratio	(Assets – Shareholder equity) / Assets	Reveals percentage of balance sheet tied up in debt
Debt-to-assets ratio	Total debt / Assets	Reveals percentage of assets financed by debt
Debt-to-equity ratio	Total debt / Shareholder equity	Ratio of borrowed funds to funds provided by shareholders
Long-term debt to equity	Long-term debt / Shareholder equity	Ratio of long-term borrowings to equity contributions
Times interest earned (coverage ratio)	EBIT / Interest	Ability to meet interest payments
Cash coverage ratio	(EBIT + Depreciation) / Interest	Ability to meet interest payments using operating cash

ACTIVITY RATIOS

Measure	How to calculate it	What it means
Inventory turnover	Cost of Goods Sold / Inventory	Number of times a firm sells its inventory each year
Asset productivity	Sales / Assets	Sales generated per dollar of assets
Fixed asset turnover	Sales / Fixed assets	Sales generated per dollar of fixed assets
Capital intensity	Assets / Sales	Dollar investment in assets needed to generate each dollar in sales (the inverse of Asset Productivity ratio)
Accounts receivable turnover	Annual credit sales / Accounts receivable	Number of times each year a company collects on credit sales
Receivables collection period (days)	Accounts receivable / Average daily sales	How long it takes for the company to collect payment for sales

SHAREHOLDER RETURNS

Measure	How to calculate it	What it means
Dividend yield	Dividend per share / Current market price per share	Return to common stockholders through dividends
Dividend payout ratio	Dividend per share / Net income per share	Approximation of profits returned to investors versus those kept to reinvest in the business
Price-to-earnings ratio PE	Current market price per share / Earnings per share	How much investors are willing to pay per dollar of current earnings
Market capitalization	Current market price per share× Total shares outstanding	Total value of all the company's stock at current stock market prices

Chapter 3: Strategic Direction: Vision, Mission, Principles

LEARNING OBJECTIVES

1. Examine how vision and mission statements can be used to provide effective direction for a firm.

2. Describe the process of developing a vision statement.

3. Explain the steps involved in developing an effective mission statement.

4. Name five techniques for communicating vision and mission.

5. Explain how principles and values can lead to superior performance.

Alphabet Soup?[1]

"Google and Walmart are the business world's version of yin and yang." Now a division of Alphabet, Google is a high growth, extremely high margin company. 61,000 employees produce annual sales of $75 billion, or $1.23 million per worker. Operating cash flow exceeds $425,000 per worker per year. The typical Google worker possesses a very high IQ, and about half of their employees hold advanced degrees in science or engineering, most from elite universities.

Since Alphabet was created as the holding company in 2015, its mission may be changing. Google's original mission was "to organize the world's information and make it universally accessible and useful." But Alphabet is engaging in enterprises far afield from this mantra: glucose-sensing contact lenses, driverless car technology, biotech on aging, think tank on global challenges, and more. With the reorganization Google can refocus on its original mission. What is the glue that binds together all the other Alphabet companies?

Laser Focused

Walmart ✴
Save money. Live better.

In many ways, Walmart appears to be the opposite of Google. It is the world's largest company by sales – $482 billion – but its net income of $15 billion is typical of low margin retail. Walmart has the world's largest private workforce of 2.3 million employees who generate $209,565 in sales apiece. Operating cash flow per Walmart worker is very small, only $13,000, only about 3% of what Google employees achieve.

Walmart is laser focused. Its everyday mission is "Saving people money so they can live better," and to do so they relentlessly drive down their costs and the prices we pay in their stores. One economist estimates Walmart saves shoppers $450 per year on groceries. Walmart's vision is to leverage this focus into the future: "To be the best retailer in the hearts and minds of consumers and employees." Each year they strive toward the achievement of this "stretch" goal.

Google and Walmart have become huge successes, each in their own very different ways. But the two have the following in common:

- Each company has a simple mission. These companies know who they are. As they diversify into new lines of business, they still know who they are.
- The brand and the mission statement of each are aligned. Picture Google and Walmart in your head. There's no confusion about what these companies do. Neither is there confusion for their employees.
- Each company's offerings are simple to understand and use. Shopping at Walmart does not take a heroic intellectual effort. But neither does using Google, even though the search engine behind the curtain is the product of a prodigious intellectual feat.

Principles, What Principles?

In 2008 Volkswagen announced its "Strategy 2018" plan: "…make Volkswagen the most successful, fascinating and sustainable automaker in the world….Our particular focus is on the environmentally friendly orientation and profitability of our vehicle projects…." In 2013 the company reiterated its principles to "offer attractive, safe and environmentally sound vehicles." In 2015 it came to light that it had been installing software in engines so they passed laboratory emissions tests but belched out dangerous nitrogen oxides when on the road. They had been doing this for years in 11 million vehicles sold. Although CEO Martin Winterkorn said "I am endlessly sorry that we have betrayed that trust," in 2016 it was discovered that he knew about the cheating scandal more than a year before it was admitted. Principles and values run deep in companies, and those at the top can set clear examples for acceptable behavior to those down the line.

STRATEGIC DIRECTION

We will learn in the chapters to come that every organization must possess a set of resources and capabilities (Chapter 6) that will allow it to achieve superior and sustainable returns. We will emphasize that one way of doing this is through the value chain of the organization (Chapter 5), which involves tight coordination and internal consistency of activities across the company. The coherence that results from coordinating all the activities is critical. It is also imperative that we have a deep understanding of the competitive environment, our company's position in that environment, and how we may profit from that position. But at the same time we face these complicated challenges, we must consider whether *where* we compete and *how* we intend to compete are consistent with the *direction* we choose to take for our company, and whether everyone in the company is pulling in unison in that direction.

Getting all or even most of the individuals in a corporation to move in the same direction is infinitely more difficult than "herding cats." Without a true understanding of a company's guiding purpose, people – like cats – will tend to wander wherever each thinks it is best to go. A mission statement helps because it is a brief statement that summarizes how and where the firm will compete in the present. A vision statement also provides guidance because it presents a more compelling, overarching image of the organization in the future that motivates employees to focus their actions toward a common point.

Students and managers often get mission and vision confused. Mission statements have a significantly more bounded nature than broader, longer-term vision statements. Think about it this way. Imagine you are James Bond and Eve Moneypenny working for the MI6 intelligence agency. You are sent on a mission to recover the stolen NOC list ("non-official cover) of undercover agents around the globe. This mission is actually part of a grander long-term vision to reduce and ultimately destroy Spectre and its influence. Mission has to do with what we do in the immediate moment, and how we go about doing it based on our current strengths and capabilities. "Tempus fugit."

Statements of principles (or values) are also important in today's environment. Because companies are large with employees dispersed around the world, espoused principles guide the sort of behavior that is acceptable and unacceptable in pursuing the mission. As the above Volkswagen example illustrates, a principles vacuum at the top – or a principles policy that is only words with no substance – can lead to inappropriate behavior way down inside the organization. Statements espousing principles are also important in recruiting, since young people today are especially interested in matching personal goals and ethics with those of prospective employers.

The combination of a vision statement, mission statement, and statement of values or principles provides fundamental guidance by laying out the unique purpose of the organization and its defining approach.[2] Defining the mission and vision for a business are two of the most difficult, yet equally most critical, elements in any company's long-term success. In fact, some have referred to the creation of vision and mission statements as a "wicked problem" because the problem is ill-formulated, the process can involve many people with conflicting values, and the result has ramifications for the whole business system.[3] What constitutes a good mission and vision statement? How can these statements be developed? What impact will an effective set of statements have on the overall strategy and performance of the business?

Business, by definition, is a place of coordinated action that cannot be effectively accomplished by the individual. However, studies have consistently demonstrated that significant differences of opinion exist among senior-level executives about both strategic goals and the means to accomplish them.[4] Mere consent to others' goals, or worse, disagreement about goals and the means by which to achieve them, will have a cascading negative effect on employee behavior across the company. Employees left without a clear corporate direction will intuitively and explicitly try to guess what their bosses really want them to do. A sobering question for senior management is: "Does the company have any confidence that what employees are doing on a day-to-day basis is consistent with senior management's overarching goals for the organization?"

Evidence from industry suggests that the resounding answer to this question in many cases is *NO!* In fact, only about half of the Fortune 500 companies have developed and published comprehensive mission statements. Of those companies, some have added loads of superfluous elements to their mission statements, hoping to satisfy as many stakeholders as possible without upsetting others, with the result that they fail to provide clear guidance. Roughly 5 percent of the Fortune 500 has neither a mission nor a vision statement, but they do have written values or principles. Most surprising, after years of admonitions about the value of mission statements, fully 25 percent of the world's largest companies have no written statement at all that would serve to guide their organizations.[5]

Providing Direction and Purpose

Before we proceed to the details of developing effective mission and vision statements, let's consider a larger question first: Why does it even matter whether a company has a defined mission or vision statement? The majority of employees at any company come to work every day with the intention of working hard, doing something of real value for their company, and finding a personal and professional sense of accomplishment. What motivates employees to do their work? It is unrealistic to believe that a paycheck is their primary motivation. The question is, what *is* the glue that binds employees' collective actions on a daily basis into a consistent and unified effort for the company? This is the purpose of mission and vision statements.

Why is any company in business? To some this may sound like a foolish question, but as we pointed out in Chapter 1, companies most certainly are *not* in business just to make money. As appealing as it may be to believe this, customers will never purchase a product or service just because the company needs to make money. Imagine the company's mission statement that would accompany such a goal:

Company X Mission

Because our fiduciary responsibility is to maximize shareholder value, we strive to make the most money possible within the legal constraints of the countries within which we do business.

Without a doubt, all employees would understand their task each day. The employees would simply explain to customers, suppliers, and fellow employees that since the organization must make as much money as possible, this is why they are: 1) charging more for the same value or providing less for the same price, 2) requiring pay, benefit, or work condition concessions, 3) demanding reduced prices for raw materials, etc. It is not the employees' fault; they are simply pursuing the mission. Furthermore, this mission statement would be so generic as to be applicable to virtually every company in the world, because any type of technically legal business activity would be acceptable.

Similarly, a company is not in business to meet its "fiduciary responsibility to maximize shareholder value," since once again this provides no direction for the company's employees and therefore provides no unifying reason for its existence. Profitability and shareholder value are the *results* of a strategically focused organization, not its reason for being. Customers purchase a product or service because of the value they receive in exchange for the money and time invested. The reason that companies are in business is to provide a product or service that creates value for customers, who in exchange are willing to profitably compensate them for their efforts.

An organization exists to create and deliver value in ways that an individual cannot accomplish alone in free-market transactions. We call a company an "organization" because everything it does involves the organization of the efforts of more than one individual. The most pressing issue that develops as the company grows is one of coordination and consistency of effort toward a common purpose. As was pointed out many years ago by Henry Mintzberg in his definitive book *The Structuring of Organizations*, the issue of coordination is the continual struggle to get more and more employees' efforts focused on the mission of the organization.[6] All employees have a series of routines and tactics they use to handle situations on a day-to-day basis. These routines and tactics should be guided by the set of objectives that reflect each employee's job description and upon which each employee is compensated. In turn, their objectives are arrived at as a subset of the strategic plans of the organization, and those plans are a direct result of the mission that company wishes to accomplish. Vision initiates the whole process by laying out the compelling, overarching focal image guiding everyone in the organization in a certain direction. A mission statement then provides guidance on what the company does in the present. Therefore, vision and mission statements help to answer two basic questions for every employee in an organization:

1. What am I expected to be doing today? Answer: Mission statement, which characterizes how the company competes in today's market.

2. Why are my co-workers and I expected to act this way? Answer: Vision statement, because this is what we want the company to become.

Figure 3.1 illustrates the relationship between vision, mission, and activities. Everything an organization and its employees do should have an under-girding foundation of values and principles.

Figure 3.1
Strategy Planning Hierarchy

VISION AND VISION STATEMENTS

Whereas the mission defines specifically what the organization does in the present, the vision is the desired future state of the organization. What is the organization's purpose and why should everyone who works for the organization care? The vision of the organization (sometimes referred to as the statement of purpose) helps define the long-term future for the company, which management guru Peter Drucker described as "what should our business be."[7] Figure 3.2 lists the elements that characterize effective vision statements.

The benefits of having a shared vision can be remarkable. Employees can not only execute on a daily basis

Figure 3.2
Effective Vision Statement Elements

Incorporates foresight
Provides event horizon
Connects with current capabilities
Incorporates enduring values
Is short
Is memorable

more easily if there is a collective understanding of where they are headed, but they can also better imagine how they will be rewarded through the accomplishment of the vision. When people are inspired and see how their individual efforts can work toward a grand future, their collective efforts can make a powerful difference. On January 11, 1987, the Denver Broncos football team fell 7 points behind the Cleveland Browns late in the fourth quarter of the AFC Championship game. Gaining possession of the ball on their own 2-yard line with 98 yards to go to tie the game, quarterback John Elway announced in the offensive huddle that the Broncos "now had them right where they wanted them." During "The Drive"[8] the team marched up the field and tied the game ultimately leading to an overtime win. Members of the offensive line commented that the vision of superiority that Elway implanted had inspired and enabled them to rise to the challenge.

Figure 3.3
Henry V's Speech at Agincourt, 1415

"That he which hath no stomach to this fight,
Let him depart; his passport shall be made
And crowns for convoy put into his purse:
We would not die in that man's company
That fears his fellowship to die with us.
This day is called the feast of Crispian:
He that outlives this day, and comes safe home,
Will stand a tip-toe when the day is named,
And rouse him at the name of Crispian.
He that shall live this day, and see old age,
Will yearly on the vigil feast his neighbours,
And say 'To-morrow is Saint Crispian:'
Then will he strip his sleeve and show his scars.
And say 'These wounds I had on Crispin's day.'
Old men forget: yet all shall be forgot,
But he'll remember with advantages
What feats he did that day: then shall our names

Familiar in his mouth as household words
Harry the king, Bedford and Exeter,
Warwick and Talbot, Salisbury and Gloucester,
Be in their flowing cups freshly remember'd.
This story shall the good man teach his son;
And Crispin Crispian shall ne'er go by,
From this day to the ending of the world,
But we in it shall be remember'd;
We few, we happy few, we band of brothers;
For he today that sheds his blood with me
Shall be my brother; be he ne'er so vile,
This day shall gentle his condition:
And gentlemen in England now a-bed
Shall think themselves accursed they were not here,
And hold their manhoods cheap whiles any speaks
That fought with us upon Saint Crispin's day."

A more compelling example of how vision motivates occurred on October 15, 1415, when King Henry V of England confronted the French army in Agincourt, France. With only 5-6,000 soldiers against an estimated 20,000 French soldiers, the odds were against the English. Henry delivered his visionary "band of brothers" message to his troops, later immortalized by Shakespeare (Figure 3.3), and his troops went on to defeat the French in what is regarded as the most lopsided military victory in history.[9] Henry's vision inspired his troops to imagine themselves years later as old men, when others would still recount their heroism in victory at Agincourt. It worked! 600 years later, we are still recounting this story!

Designing a vision is an exercise that balances foresight with a deep understanding of the company's present resources. On the one hand, senior management wishes to establish long-term direction that will require the company to grow significantly beyond its present position and capabilities. On the other hand, the vision cannot afford to imagine a future that is simply unattainable, given current capabilities and position.

Through this process the vision should establish an event horizon that guides current practices within the company. There should be a specific and discernible endpoint in mind – for example, the goal line, living to old age, etc. – that is at the horizon but is not further than the eye can see. So, the vision statement encourages the organization to significantly stretch its strategic capabilities, in order to achieve a valuable and secure position in an unfolding future. The event horizon presents a motivational, attainable goal that is true to the vision statement. The former CEO of Rubbermaid articulated the vision for the company as being able to go into any supermarket and walk down an "aisle of Rubbermaid." Can you imagine an entire aisle of Rubbermaid products in a store!? It sounds a bit funny to us, but to employees it crystallized in their minds what they wanted the company to become, and it led to significant and effective innovation and new product introductions over the next few years.

**Figure 3.4
Horizon for Vision**

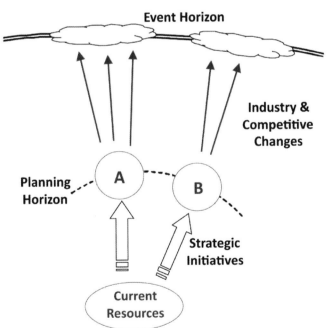

Typically the time horizon for a vision statement will be something close to a decade. This makes sense when we think about the fulfillment time required for ongoing strategic initiatives, which can often take three to five years to pan out (recall the character of strategic decisions discussed in Chapter 1). This means that the event horizon is beyond the more immediate boundary that marks the longer-term outcomes of current strategic initiatives and in all likelihood beyond what can be accomplished with just existing capabilities. Setting an event horizon thus requires management to consider carefully not only how external forces will shape competitive markets, but also how current capabilities may be enhanced or supplemented to develop a portfolio of possibilities. Figure 3.4 captures the sense of this discussion. Here a company builds on two of its resource positions as it engages in strategic initiatives that are estimated to have A and B as outcomes. The horizon for the company's vision, however, extends well beyond outcomes A and B, to fuzzy sets of possibilities that might build further on A or B and the resource positions that led to them.

Examples of successful visioning such as this can further illustrate the nature of longer-term horizons. President John F. Kennedy propelled NASA in the 1960s with his very clear and well-articulated vision of putting a man on the moon and returning him safely to earth within the decade. In his speech to Congress on May 21, 1961, he resolutely laid out his stretch goals for the United States while recognizing its current technological capabilities, and asked us to imagine how proud we would all feel in such an accomplishment (Figure 3.5). Management author Jim Collins referred to this type of statement as a "*BHAG*," that is, a Big, Hairy, Audacious Goal.[10]

Figure 3.5
John F. Kennedy's 1961 Speech

"Finally, if we are to win the battle that is now going on around the world between freedom and tyranny, the dramatic achievements in space which occurred in recent weeks should have made clear to us all…the impact of this adventure on the minds of men everywhere, who are attempting to make a determination of which road they should take…. Now it is time to take longer strides – time for a great new American enterprise – time for this nation to take a clearly leading role in space achievement, which in many ways may hold the key to our future on earth. I believe we possess all the resources and talents necessary…. I believe that this nation should commit itself to achieving the goal, before this decade is out, of landing a man on the moon and returning him safely to the earth…. But in a very real sense, it will not be one man going to the moon – if we make this judgment affirmatively, it will be an entire nation. For all of us must work to put him there."

A more recent example of vision is the case of Amazon.com, which started up as a new business named Cadabra.com in 1994. As an Internet startup in the dawn of the Internet age, the original vision espoused by founder Jeff Bezos was to be the "biggest bookstore" – quite a stretch for a small technology company that relied on book distributors for its merchandise. After the company's business took off in the late 1990s, Bezos established an updated vision as "earth's most customer-centric company … a place where people can come to find and discover anything they might want to buy online."[11] Since then, Amazon has been reinvesting in technology to deliver superior online selling performance, as well as establishing relationships with providers of a tremendous variety of merchandise.

As suggested earlier, vision statements should be memorable and inspiring to everyone throughout the organization. Though politicians and Shakespeare are accustomed to using "words, words, words"[12] in their inspirational passages, vision statements for organizations should be short. Whirlpool Corporation has a simple, but compelling vision: "Every home… Everywhere… with Pride, Passion, and Performance." The vision sets forth an event horizon for the business that can easily be used as a guidepost for current activities and tactics. Other useful examples are presented in Figure 3.6.

Figure 3.6
Effective Vision Statements

Company	Vision
Microsoft	To enable people and businesses throughout the world to realize their full potential.
Chevron	To be the global energy company most admired for its people, partnership and performance.
Johnson Controls	A more comfortable, safe and sustainable world.
Avon Products	To be the Company that best understands and satisfies the product, service and self-fulfillment needs of women -- globally.
Progressive Insurance	To reduce the human trauma and economic costs associated with automobile accidents.
Cornerstone Health Care	To be the model for physician -led health care in America.

Developing the Vision

Developing a vision for the organization is a process that can be full of ambiguity. There is no one way to develop an effective vision statement, although there are clearly methods that seem to assist in the process. Gaining buy-in from the entire organization is crucial in the initial development process, however. This is not to say that everyone in the company has a great sense of what the vision should be, but it is to suggest that everyone should have input on the values that are reflected in the long-term direction. As Jim Collins suggests, leaders at the top cannot "set" or "install" organizational values; values can only be discovered.[13] This can be approached through a solicitation to the whole organization for direct input, yet in large companies with many employees this process may result in a deluge of communication that becomes difficult to sift through for meaningful content.

Instead, another more effective method used to bring together core values as well as an understanding of present capabilities is to compose a small team of five to seven people who embody the deeply held values of employees. If employees are asked to nominate members of the team, often the result is a group of individuals that employees look up to because they stand as exemplars for the company's important values and knowledge. Together with top management, the group should consider several critical questions to generate a compelling vision:

1. What do we hold to be "true" and meaningful in our business, factors that should never change as we go forward?

2. What does it mean to work in this organization? After ten more years what would I want to look back upon and be proud of for having worked in this organization?

3. At the core, what are we particularly good at doing? What is our core competence, and what extraordinary resources do we possess?

4. What are the compelling changes and opportunities in the competitive environment that we should be taking advantage of?

5. Where should our company be in ten years?

These questions spur the development of a vision statement that can be used by every individual in the course of his or her daily interactions. The actual writing of the statement is an iterative process, attempting to capture the richness of a company in a statement that is short, memorable, and inspiring.

Lena Pope Home Inc., Part 1

The Lena Pope Home was established in the 1930s in Fort Worth, Texas, as a place for all foster children to feel welcome. Lena H. Pope developed a place where high expectations were set. They wish to equip their youth with an education, job skills, and in some cases, rehabilitation. However, they also want a place that teaches integrity, personal responsibility, fairness, and good citizenship.

Today their efforts have expanded to include both children and their families. Each year they serve more than 20,000 families in over 3800 community organizations. They operate a foster care agency, a counseling operation, and an extensive school program for kids no longer welcome at the public schools, and teach courses in family preservation as well as assist in adoptions.

A few years ago, the organization had grown to a point where it was financially independent and the leading provider of services to children and their families in the Dallas-Fort Worth Metro-complex. The Board of Directors was faced with the imminent retirement of their outstanding, long-term Director. The Board also recognized that the agency had grown to employ hundreds of people in many different areas. In order to ensure a smooth transition and to get the whole organization on a path moving forward, they embarked upon an effort to reset the organization for the coming decade.

They wanted a new mission statement that encompassed who they were now, and they wanted a singular vision statement to use as guidance for the employees and the community.

Their web page site is: http://www.lenapope.org.

QUESTIONS

1. Given what you've read about the organization, how do you view their overarching aim?

2. How would you go about developing a new vision and mission statement for the organization?

3. Given what you're read about the organization, try to write a vision statement of the Lena Pope Home, Inc.

MISSION STATEMENTS

The firm's mission helps the corporation by targeting its current efforts in specific arenas and on specific opportunities. No business can or should attempt to serve up all things to all people. Instead, the business needs to focus on those areas where it possesses extraordinary resources and creates value in ways that competitors cannot. Research over the past thirty years has shown that corporate performance improves as firms focus their resources and capabilities on a narrower, not broader, set of activities.[14] The firm's mission helps the business achieve focus because it specifies what the company does best. In a wonderfully related manner, a well-developed mission statement also helps the business *stay away from* areas that opportunistically sound promising, but which actually take the business away from its principal focus. Take note of the fact that as a business diversifies into other areas of competition, it loses focus on its core area of business. If that occurs, history suggests that there are always singularly focused companies in any market that are ready to capitalize on the fragmentation of effort that can result.

Developing a Mission Statement

The mission statement is the vehicle that captures the immediate purpose of the company and its unique way of fulfilling that purpose. The process of developing an effective mission statement requires that the top management team simultaneously align five key criteria (Figure 3.7). These criteria can be further described as follows:

1. Short. Does it fit on a coffee mug?

2. Simple. It has to be something that can be easily learned and understood.

3. Company-Specific. A mission should tell everyone exactly what the company does and by definition it will tell them what the company does not do.

4. Actionable. It has to be able to guide every individual each and every day.

5. Measurable. The company should be able to develop a metric for every part of the statement.

Figure 3.7
Elements OF Effective Mission Statements

Short
Simple
Company specific
Actionable
Measurable

These five criteria are not sequential, but an overall design that companies should try to achieve. Let's look at each of these criteria in more detail.

Keep It Short

We recognize that there are two schools of thought in creating mission statements: keeping them short and succinct, or using them to summarize many desirable elements of what a company is all about. We prefer keeping them short, since such statements are more easily remembered and therefore more easily relied upon for day-to-day actions and decisions.

Some of the most often mentioned historical guides have suggested a long list of items that must be included in order to create a comprehensive mission statement. This advice holds that a mission statement must include many or all of the following elements:[15]

1. Customers
2. Products/Services
3. Geographic Markets
4. Technology
5. Concern for Survival/Growth
6. Philosophy
7. Public Image
8. Employees
9. Distinctive Competence

As you may imagine, the effect of this approach is to create a list so inclusive that the statement will no doubt be acceptable to every stakeholder inside or outside of the company. As a result, some company mission statements have become multi-sentence or even multi-paragraph tomes that are geared to avoid conflict rather than guide employees. These become mission statements that cannot be easily recalled – unless an individual has a photographic memory – and therefore cannot be acted upon. An all-encompassing mission statement that cannot be easily recalled and used by employees is simply an exercise in frustration, expense, and occasionally outright derision by employees.

Does it fit on a coffee mug? This may be the single most important element of a well-designed mission statement. It is not an essay that describes everything that a company has done or might do, such that the organization can cover every single avenue of potential profit. An effective mission statement is best described as a short, direct statement that precisely encapsulates what approach the organization takes as it seeks to accomplish its purpose.

One of the truly outstanding companies in the United States is Caterpillar. Unfortunately, this manufacturer of enormous earthmoving equipment used to have a mission statement that fails every tenet of effective mission statement development. Consider the following:

Caterpillar (older). *Caterpillar will be the leader in providing the best value in machines, engines and support services for customers dedicated to building the world's infrastructure and developing and transporting its resources. We provide the best value to customers. Caterpillar people will increase shareholder value by aggressively pursuing growth and profit opportunities that leverage our engineering, manufacturing, distribution, information management and financial services expertise. We grow profitably. Caterpillar will provide its worldwide workforce with an environment that stimulates diversity, innovation, teamwork, continuous learning and improvement and rewards individual performance. We develop and reward people. Caterpillar is dedicated to improving the quality of life while sustaining the quality of our earth. We encourage social responsibility.*

This statement certainly encompasses every aspect of potential influence for the business. It has the look and feel of a checklist with a series of ideas that, while not objectionable, are not going to be remembered by people in the organization. An effective mission statement does not

86

explain in detail how the mission will be done. However, it does state the purpose of the company and the basic approach the company will use to accomplish that purpose. An effective modification of the Caterpillar mission might look something like this:

Caterpillar (newer). *Our mission is to enable economic growth through infrastructure and energy development, and to provide solutions that support communities and protect the planet.*

It simply states the mission of the organization. It is easily recalled, and leaves the detailed means of attainment up to the experts within the organization.

Another unclear example that an excellent company formerly used is as follows:

Halliburton Company (older). *The world needs energy resources and commercial and industrial facilities to fulfill the need of its communities in a safe and environmentally sound manner. Halliburton Company is dedicated to leading the way in meeting this need through demonstrated excellence in providing a broad spectrum of services and products for finding and developing energy resources; designing, constructing, operating and maintaining facilities; and protecting the environment. We will afford our employees opportunities to contribute to our Company's success. Through their skills and abilities, we will continuously improve the quality of services and products we supply our customers. We will provide a fair return for our shareholders and good opportunities for our business partners and suppliers, and be good citizens of our communities.*

Reading carefully, we can see that this statement contains a smorgasbord of ideas. While everyone within the organization would be hard pressed to find something they would disagree with, neither would most employees be able to remember or execute against this lengthy statement. What might be the alternative to this lengthy statement? The company recently retooled its mission statement to the following:

Halliburton Company (newer). *To create sustainable value by delivering outstanding products, services and Digital Asset solutions that help our customers succeed by:*

> *Maximizing production and recovery;*
> *Realizing reserves from difficult environments;*
> *Improving operational efficiency.*

Keep It Simple

A well-designed mission statement has to be something that everyone in the organization can learn and understand. A mission statement that does not incorporate shared language and meaning for all employees has little value to the organization. Learning and understanding require that the statement be relatively simple. The senior management team needs to ensure that the words and concepts employed in the statement are straightforward and have a clear meaning to all who hear or read them. If you saw the movie *Pirates of the Caribbean*, you may recall the entertaining language at play when Captain Barbossa replies tongue-in-cheek to his upper class captive, "I'm disinclined to acquiesce to your request," pauses for moment, and turns back to his captive and says, "Means NO!"

Consider the following corporate mission statement from a very focused and successful company, which certainly meets the first criteria of keeping it short but fails on the dimension of simplicity:

Waste Management. *To maximize shareholder value, while adhering to the laws of the jurisdictions within which it operates and observing the highest of ethical standards.*

Try to imagine the army of trash truck drivers being told to use this mission statement in the course of their daily pickups. The terms "adhering," "jurisdictions," and "ethical standards" are all fine concepts and yet are of little practical value in advising on day-to-day activities to most employees. Why is Waste Management in business? Why would a customer want to use them? What are their resource-based advantages? Where do they attain extraordinary returns in their value chain? Don't all corporations (or should we say, *shouldn't* all corporations) adhere to the laws? As an employee, what exactly is useful to take from this? What are the alternatives? Would any corporation seriously suggest that it will *minimize* shareholder value? We're being a tad facetious here to make an important point. It is not to suggest that Waste Management isn't a fine organization; it is simply to suggest that the true mission of the organization is not what is stated in the mission statement, and this lack of focus does not help the organization move consistently toward a goal in a unified fashion. The use of terms that have no meaning to the employees, suppliers, customers, or the investing community provides inadequate direction, opening up the possibility to both an unfocused future and a group of employees who will "interpret" the mission of the organization in different and possibly creative ways.

The ability to learn and understand a mission statement requires that it be written in such a manner that virtually everyone can obtain significant meaning from it and know how to apply it. Take a look at the following short, simple, and effective mission statement:

Parker Hannifin. *We manufacture highly engineered components and systems that facilitate motion and the controlled flow of liquids and gasses for a wide variety of global markets to increase our customers' productivity and profitability..*

Keep It Company-Specific
There are occasions where a short and simple mission can also miss the mark of being company-specific:

J.P. Morgan Chase. *To create exceptional value for our clients, employees and investors by delivering our deep, broad and integrated capabilities.*

We hesitate to guess what the result of this statement would be if it were used to make daily decisions. These ideas are so vague that few could possibly understand what the company does or how employees are to conduct themselves for the company to achieve its goals. This mission is not company-specific. Without the name we attached to it, this could be a statement about virtually any company.

Mission statements that stay at too general a level are like the mass mailings that show up in your mailbox from aspiring political candidates. They seek to curry favor with the entire population. Everything seems so agreeable; who could disagree? Just as the mailings provide no precise definition of the candidates or even what political parties they actually belong to, these types of statements provide virtually no clear definition of the company in question. A mission statement that is not clear and specific to the company invites continual questions as to purpose and direction.

One of our favorite companies (primarily because of its focus and quality leadership) nonetheless has a mission statement that would actually prevent employees and others from learning or understanding what the company seeks to achieve. GM Financial, along with its

AmeriCredit division, is one of the leading companies in subprime (individuals with less than stellar credit records) automobile lending. Yet their mission statement reads:

GM Financial. *To create value for our stakeholders by constantly improving our services, investing in innovative solutions and information-based strategies, and promoting a culture of teamwork, excellence and integrity.*

Upon a first reading one would be inclined to believe that they had read the mission statement of a software company or a Web-based business. You could easily take this mission statement and apply it to virtually any organization, anywhere in the world, and while it would be equally useless, it would nonetheless be perfectly applicable.

Other well-known and respected companies also suffer from this type of ineffective mission statement writing. Take a look at some of the following mission statements:

Merck. *The mission of Merck is to provide society with superior products and services by developing innovations and solutions that improve the quality of life and satisfy customer needs, and to provide employees with meaningful work and advancement opportunities, and investors with a superior rate of return.*

Albertson's (older). *Guided by relentless focus on our five imperatives, we will constantly strive to implement the critical initiatives required to achieve our vision. In doing this, we will deliver operational excellence in every corner of the Company and meet or exceed our commitments to the many constituencies we serve. All of our long-term strategies and short-term actions will be molded by a set of core values that are shared by each and every associate.*

If all you had in front of you were these mission statements, how might you know what these companies actually do? Can you tell that Merck develops and manufactures pharmaceuticals, and that Albertson's is a supermarket? How might these statements help anyone in their organizations to make decisions? These statements are certainly not disagreeable, but in fact could be interchangeably attached to virtually any company anywhere in the world. There appears to be nothing outside of their "opportunity space." It is not unusual to read comments from corporate executives that state that one of their goals is not to close any doors on any opportunity. This is an unrealistic view of strategy and is counter to the weight of more than thirty years' worth of studies and consulting practice showing that strategic focus is one of the most important factors in company success.

Interestingly, Albertson's was acquired a few years ago by an investor group that combined it with other supermarkets around the U.S. In the process they retooled the mission statement, which today reads as a much more focused business:

Albertson's (newer). *We want to run really great stores and provide great customer service.*

One of the primary goals of an effective mission statement is, therefore, its ability to allow (often empower) employees at all levels to use their directed judgment in the execution of their daily responsibilities. Employees are constantly faced with decisions that may have both an individual as well as a cumulative strategic impact. An effective mission statement tells everyone exactly what to "DO" and therefore, by omission, what "NOT TO DO." The focus within the mission statement must go beyond a laundry list of areas covered in the business; instead it should be narrowly defined as "an organization's unique and enduring purpose...."[16] Consider the following mission statement:

Autoliv. *To create, manufacture & sell state-of-the-art automotive safety systems.*

Every employee, customer, and supplier knows exactly what Autoliv does and does not do. If an employee is approached by a vendor with an interesting new product that might improve the sound quality within an automobile, the employee knows instantly that this product is outside the stated purview of the company. Management has made the decision to focus their time, energy, and resources upon the creation, manufacture, and sale of state-of-the-art automotive safety systems. This focus prevents the company from wasting valuable time and resources pursuing areas outside of its core competence.

Keep It Actionable

One of the measures of a high-quality mission statement is its ability to guide every individual in the company each and every day. Virtually every employee is faced with a large number of decisions in their daily jobs. Therefore, an effective mission statement needs to be actionable for every employee. An effective mission is one grounded in specificity, creating a bounded business model that allows every company to be the best at some aspect of their business. The mission statement must highlight and focus the energy of all the employees upon the direction that the top management team believes is best for the business.

The Parker Hannifin mission from earlier in this chapter achieves just that. It takes extraordinary care to develop a statement that can guide the entire organization and at the same time be effectively utilized by every employee of the company, regardless of their level in the organization. Imagine the customer service employee who every day deals with customers calling in with concerns and complaints. If the mission statement of the organization is a long, multi-paragraph affair that essentially says "we do it all," or if it is like so many statements and simply extols the employees to "maximize shareholder value," then how is the customer service employee to act? As we said previously, what is most likely to happen is that they will simply do their best, given some mix between their own common sense and the combination of advice and admonishments of their immediate superior. An effective statement is one that helps the employees make active decisions in the moment without always having to refer every decision up the chain of command. A mission statement that comes fairly close to simultaneously achieving all of the components that we have thus far discussed is the one for Southwest Airlines.

Southwest Airlines. *The mission of Southwest Airlines is dedication to the highest quality of customer service delivered with a sense of warmth, friendliness, individual pride, and company spirit.*

Reading this mission statement, some of you may argue that it could be applied generically to just about any organization. Although Southwest is clearly an airline company, they view their business as one of customer service. Virtually every aspect of the activities performed by employees on a day-to-day basis are focused on providing exceptional service to the company's customers.

Keep It Measurable

The final element of an effective mission statement is a bit more complex and time consuming than the previous four. The mission statement is only as valuable as it is practical. While all corporations have a set of metrics to evaluate the organization as a whole, the metrics developed from an effective mission statement focus the company's efforts upon its unifying approach to gaining competitive advantages.

Many mission statements exhibit one of three types of performance dimensions: 1) "feel-good" goals, 2) specific financial goals, or 3) general financial or vague market goals. Feel-good goals, such as "provide employees with meaningful work and advancement opportunities," tend to be ineffective. This is because they focus on qualitative dimensions that cannot be easily measured on a regular basis. If they cannot be measured, they are of little help in providing direction for the company. In contrast, highly specified financial goals appear to lock management and employees into specific targets, potentially compromising strategic actions that are better suited for sustained performance over long periods. Financial performance goals are ethically neutral and therefore may lead to a distortion in the activities of employees by possibly encouraging short-termism. Employees may have compelling reasons to achieve financial targets regardless of the strategic impact on the company. This is not unlike the challenges faced by public companies in managing toward short-term earnings targets. General financial goals or vague market goals are also not very helpful in connecting mission statements to performance. This is because it is difficult to connect specific actions and practices that fulfill a mission to such fuzzy goals.

Studies strongly suggest that alignment between a well-written mission statement and the firm's performance evaluation system helps to magnify the impact on performance of the mission statement.[17] Metrics of this sort generally fall into two categories, those that are quantitative and those that are qualitative. A good rule of thumb is to develop several metrics with approximately some being quantitative and some being qualitative. Since we emphasize the importance of action at the individual level that is facilitated by an effective mission statement, some of the quantitative metrics should presumably be tied to the firm's personnel performance evaluation system. For example, since innovation is central to the mission of 3M Corporation, each employee is encouraged and expected to devote a percentage of his or her workweek to investigating new business ideas. The actual time percentage spent by each employee in this area can be captured on an individual basis, and then aggregated to a departmental, divisional, or corporate level.

A great check on the quality of a mission statement is to note whether metrics can be designed to measure each and every part of the mission. Consider the following mission statement:

New York Times. *Enhance society by creating, collecting and distributing high quality news, information and entertainment.*

This well-designed mission statement allows for the development of metrics (performance measures) that will provide an effective measure of their success at achieving their mission. *The New York Times* aims to do three things (create, collect, and distribute) across three areas (high-quality news, high-quality information, and high-quality entertainment) in order to accomplish one goal (enhance society). All of these can then be translated into a mix of qualitative and quantitative metrics given the top management's interpretation about what constitutes high quality. Examples might be:

1. Number of high-quality news articles written by *NY Times* staff writers divided by the total number of news articles appearing in the *NY Times*. This could be measured daily.

2. Perception of the quality of articles in *NY Times*.

3. Number of *NY Times* articles that are picked up by other news sources.

The metrics designed for the *NY Times* will be unique to that organization and truly measure how it is succeeding in its mission.

Take a look at the following mission statement from an office products manufacturer:

Steelcase. *Our mission is to provide the world's best office environment products, services, systems, and intelligence ... designed to help people in offices work more effectively.*

Steelcase does one thing ("provide," which can be defined as producing, outsourcing, or simply purchasing for resale) across four areas of expertise (products, services, systems, and intelligence) aimed at one arena (office environments) with one goal (helping people work more effectively). The specificity of the items appearing in the statement not only focuses employees on sets of activities, but also provides substantial opportunity for the development of metrics.

Well-Designed Mission Statements

Combining all of these qualities into an effective mission statement is both an art and a science. Figure 3.8 shows several examples of well written mission statements.

No mission statement is ever perfect, and everyone in the organization will have their own ideas of how the five concepts presented might best be articulated. However, the effort made to design a quality mission statement has a high potential payoff for the business that undertakes its creation.

Figure 3.8
Examples of Mission Statements

Company	Vision
H&R Block	To help our clients achieve their financial objectives by serving as their tax and financial partner.
Host Marriot	To be the premier hospitality real estate company.
Collins & Aikman	To be recognized as a leading-edge automotive systems supplier and an innovator of world-class NVH (noise, vibration, harshness) and acoustic technologies.
MGM Mirage	To design and operate an unmatched collection of resort-casinos and provide unsurpassed service and amenities to our guests.
AMGEN	To be the world leader in the developing and delivering of important, cost-effective therapeutics based on advances in cellular and molecular biology.

Lena Pope Home, Inc., Part 2

The Lena Pope Home management and employees met in a multiday session to evaluate their key value drivers and talk about who they were and who they wanted to be in the future. The organization determined that the following four areas constituted their potential competitive advantage:

- ✓ Exceptional Value
- ✓ Reputation For Excellence
- ✓ Complete Continuum of Care
- ✓ When No One Could, LPH Did

With this decided, the group designed the following Mission Statement:
Lena Pope Home is committed to help create a future of hope, happiness, and success for children and families.

QUESTIONS

1. How well does their new mission statement meet the five criteria established for effective Mission Statements?

2. What would you change in their mission statement and why?

3. How would you suggest they use this mission statement?

COMMUNICATING THE VISION AND MISSION

The strategy department of Thyssenkrupp, a German industrial company with 155,000 employees, conducted an electronic survey in 2015 to learn how well the company's mission and vision statements were understood by the workforce. The results were underwhelming: roughly 50% of the company's employees had no clue what was the mission of the company!

The computer manufacturer Dell wanted to retool its code of principles a few years ago. The goal of the company's Chief Ethics and Compliance Officer was to get employees to be "believers" rather than mere "obeyers," and felt achieving such a goal would require employee engagement. Dell created a game challenging employees to work through an ethics scenario. Within the first few days after the game's introduction, over 5,000 Dell employees participated. A subsequent voluntary survey about the game generated over 30,000 employee responses.[18]

The best statements are of little value if they are not communicated to all employees. Following the tenets of good practice, this communication should be in as many forms as are available. Employees learn in different ways and it is crucial that they learn and incorporate the vision and mission into their everyday processes at work. An organization's culture and means of interacting are not consistent throughout a company and therefore, the means of communicating must be tailored.[19] Furthermore, organizations have their own sub-unit communication systems that generally vary by area. The key is to increase the coherence across the organization. It is the responsibility of senior management to ensure that the vision and mission are both known and used by their employees. This can be done in a number of ways:

1. Creating Narratives - One of the newer means of embedding the vision and mission in an organization is the use of one of the oldest communication techniques known to humankind – storytelling. Telling stories that point to the understanding and use of the vision and mission is an extremely effective method of relaying important, actionable concepts. A story allows the listener or reader to visualize the situation and the result. Individuals have a much higher recall level with good stories than they do with bulleted items, lists, or verbal presentations.[19] When Sony was developing the first music CD in 1982, at a time when cassette tapes and

albums dominated, they took a prototype CD to Stevie Wonder at his Los Angeles home. He was enamored with the sound quality and excited about its possibilities for sound reproduction. This story was repeated throughout Sony, inspiring further commitment to the new direction. In an earlier case, Sony founder Akio Morita said "I'll leave Sony if we don't do the Walkman," a story that was repeatedly told throughout the company, which mobilized the entire organization to become the first mover in the portable listening device field.[20]

2. Role Models - Management has a profound ability to affect the actions of their employees by serving as a role model in the embodiment of the vision and mission. Strong, consistent actions by top management demonstrating to all employees that the vision and mission are the measures by which they evaluate their actions provides direct and compelling evidence of its importance to all employees. Recently the Chinese president Xi Jinping has forgone luxury class accommodations as he travels. Lower-level Chinese government officials are now following his lead, saving the government tens of millions of RMB as the country's economic growth slows down.

3. Specific Short-Term Objectives - Translating the loftier and more general direction provided by the vision and mission into specific, short-term objectives clarifies the actions expected of individual employees and provides a quick reinforcement that employees are headed in the right direction. Simplicity and focus are crucial. General Mills (Big G cereals, Betty Crocker desserts) says its mission is "building leading brands that our consumers trust around the world." This provides guidance for employees to focus on great tasting products made with superior quality, and acting in ways that enhance the company's image. We will discuss other techniques available to guide employee actions in Chapters 11 and 12.

4. Personalizing the Vision and Mission - Employees are encouraged to develop their own vision and mission that are consistent with the ones developed by the organization. The ability to personalize the vision and mission for themselves not only has the effect of internalizing what is needed, it also acts as an effective check to ensure that senior management has developed a set of statements that resonate with the organization's employees. Whole Foods includes the following in its mission statement: "to satisfy and delight our customers – and to support Team Member happiness and excellence." The company seeks employees who share a similar vision and mission, believing this consonance is a source of strategic superiority.

5. Create Objects that Display the Vision and Mission - Placing the vision and mission on a coffee mug and distributing one to every employee has been used as a communication device to set the stage for constant reinforcement of the company's approach to business. Printing the vision and mission on posters, banners, and/or plaques that can be prominently displayed helps reinforce their importance to the future of the organization. When he was CEO and Chairman of Pepsico, Steve Reinemund carried in his wallet a card that listed the mission statement and values of the company. Every employee was provided the same card.

Here's a story to remember. Medtronic is a leading medical device company that specializes in cardiac and spinal products. Its mission statement reads: "To contribute to human welfare by application of biomedical engineering in the research, design, manufacture, and sale of instruments or appliances that alleviate pain, restore health, and extend life." To this end, one of the founders of the company had a medallion cast with the image of a patient rising from the operating table. Every new employee, when he or she is hired, is presented a medallion by a member of the senior management team at a ceremony. Employees are encouraged to keep the medallion at their desk to remind them of the goal of the organization.[21] The organization celebrates its ability to accomplish this mission with events throughout the year and honors employees who exemplify their approach to this business. It is part of what separates them in a very competitive field.

"We believe our first responsibility is to use technology to enhance the gift of life; to develop therapy-driven products that alleviate pain and promote biological healing and restore function."

PRINCIPLES AND VALUES

We have spent most of this chapter discussing the importance of vision and mission statements for achieving coherence across the company and guiding employee behavior. But if you now refer back to Figure 3.1, you will remember that vision, mission, objectives, and the activities of any company rest on a foundation of principles and values. In the aftermath of corporate scandals such as Volkswagen, Enron, Tyco, and the BP Gulf oil spill during the first decade of the 2000s, and of the 2008 financial crisis, it has become increasingly fashionable for major corporations to publicize a set of principles or values that they purport to live by.

If you evaluate values espoused by companies on the Fortune 500, you would often see listed ideas such as social responsibility, diversity, honesty, trust, and more. In fact, three words – integrity, respect, and innovation – occur most frequently in the principles and values statements of these companies. These sound great, don't they? But here's the problem. First, they all sound the same, offering no clarity regarding what is unique and special about a particular organization. If all companies sport "integrity," then how is calling this out supposed to indicate how this company is different and better? More importantly, what company would ever assert that "integrity" is *not* one of its principles?

So the more fundamental question is whether or not corporations actually use and apply such principles in the day-to-day conduct of their business. Such lofty ideas only become meaningful if senior management communicates their importance regularly, serves as a role model for their importance, and aligns performance incentives with them.

Some corporations develop statements of values and principles because it is in vogue. It is "expected" of them and provides a defense if and when they encounter trouble rooted in unethical behavior. Some corporations develop these statements because senior management believes this approach will hopefully keep the company out of trouble while possibly also enhancing performance. But some corporations do this because senior management actually believes such principles are vital for corporate success and personal employee happiness.

The challenge in developing statements of values and principles is that, while they are espoused by the corporation, the values extolled must be internalized by employees to be effective.

It's one thing to say we have integrity; it's quite another for every employee to act regularly with integrity. Part of the problem here is definition: if you ask ten employees what integrity means, you will get a variety of different responses. So in developing statements of principles and values, management must take two essential steps. First, each principle or value must be defined and explained so that every employee has the same understanding of what it is and how it can contribute to the company's mission. Second, management must regularly and continuously reinforce the espoused principles so that they become living, breathing dimensions of how work is performed in the company.

We briefly mentioned BB&T in Chapter 1 as one such corporation which embraced principled decision making. BB&T publishes a booklet for all its employees titled "The BB&T Philosophy," in which ten critical values are listed:

1. Reality (fact-based) - the foundation for quality decision making.

2. Reason - thinking through the facts logically to objectively make the best decisions.

3. Independent thinking - each employee is responsible.

4. Productivity - creativity, productivity, and turning thoughts into action improve economic well-being.

5. Honesty - say what we mean, mean what we say.

6. Integrity - always acting consistent with our principles.

7. Justice (fairness) - individuals are evaluated and rewarded based upon contributions toward the mission.

8. Pride - performing work in a manner to be justly proud.

9. Self-esteem - self-motivation leads to goals accomplishment.

10. Teamwork - respect for fellow employees while acting in a mutually supportive manner.

In addition to publishing the principles internally on a regular basis, including them in annual reports and listing them on the company's website, former CEO John Allison spent years visiting offices and far-flung branches of the bank to meet employees and reiterate these ideas. The application of these ideas to the bank's business during the 2000s prompted loan officers to refrain from extensive sub-prime and Alt-A mortgage lending that crippled other large national bank competitors. During the 2008 financial markets crisis and ensuing years, BB&T outperformed many of its competitors and continued to grow its deposits base.

CHAPTER SUMMARY

This chapter has focused on: 1) Understanding the importance of effective vision, mission, and principles for an organization; 2) Developing the criteria for evaluating and writing the statements; and 3) Understanding the process of developing them. Truly great companies have developed a vision and mission that provides direction and accountability for their businesses.[22] As in much of strategy, the process, evaluation, and use of both a vision and a mission statement is a combination of both art and science. The ability to apply the science and practice the art provides a strong foundation for your business career. Increasingly, companies are also beginning to develop statements of values and principles. Like mission statements, the effectiveness of statements of principles depends on their communication throughout the company and on substantive support from senior leadership.

Effective vision statements incorporate six elements: 1) Incorporate foresight; 2) Provide an event horizon; 3) Connect with current capabilities of the organization; 4) Incorporate enduring core values; 5) Be short; and 6) Be memorable.

Effective mission statements incorporate five criteria in their design. They can be evaluated by their simultaneous accomplishment of the following characteristics: 1) Be short; 2) Be simple; 3) Be company-specific; 4) Be actionable; and 5) Be measurable.

Statements of principles become effective when management finds ways to personalize expressed values with every employee, and when management behavior serves as an exemplar of principled conduct.

Learning Objectives Review

1. *Examine how vision and mission statements can be used to provide effective direction for a firm.*

- **Provides direction and purpose**. Establishing a vision for a company provides every employee (and suppliers and customers) with a view to the long term direction the company wishes to take.

- **Defines immediate approach**. Establishing a mission statement provides fundamental guidance for how employees should act in the present toward more immediate goals. The mission statement helps distill an overall strategic approach in the market into a more actionable guideline for day-to-day behavior.

- **Complements strategy**. Strategy plans are often developed and usually endorsed by senior management, far removed from employees at lower levels. Vision and mission statements help overcome the coordination problem that exists in large, complex organizations.

2. *Describe the process of developing a vision statement.*

- **Assemble a small team**. The team of five to seven employees should represent key employee groups and understand deeply held values of the company.

- **Consider important questions**. What are we particularly good at doing now? What are the compelling changes and opportunities in the competitive environment that will leverage these capabilities, or require us to develop new ones? What is meaningful in our business that should never change? Where should we be in ten years? What should we look back on and be proud of after ten years?

- **Establish an event horizon**. Where will we be if we establish stretch goals for our strategy?

3. *Explain the steps involved in developing an effective mission statement.*

- **Short**. This makes it memorable.

- **Simple**. This makes it easily learned and understood.
- **Company-Specific**. This makes it relevant.
- **Actionable**. This provides day-to-day guidance.
- **Measurable**. This provides feedback on how consistent employee actions are with strategy and direction.

4. *Name five techniques for communicating vision and mission.*

- **Creating Narratives**. Telling stories makes it memorable.
- **Acting as Role Models**. "Walking the walk" demonstrates the ideas in action.
- **Establishing Specific Short-Term Objectives**. Clarifies actions expected of employees.
- **Personalizing**. Encourages employees to internalize company values.
- **Creating Objects that Display**. Keeps the message visible.

5. *Explain how principles and values can lead to superior performance.*

- **Establishes trust**. Employees, suppliers, and customers will trust the company and its actions. Helps to communicate the pursuit of business *as* a moral undertaking.
- **Provides ethical boundaries of action**. Helps employees understand moral obligations and ethical basis of decision-making.
- **Leads to positive outcomes, and avoids unhealthy outcomes**. Positive outcomes gained through ethical practices are personally rewarding for employees and perceived as positive by markets.
- **Establishes distinctive platform compared with many competitors**.

Key Terms

Mission statement - A brief statement that summarizes how and where the firm will compete in the present.

Vision statement - More compelling and overarching than the mission statement, an image of the organization in the future that motivates employees to focus their actions toward a common point.

Short Answer Review Questions

1. How is a vision statement used in organizations?
2. What criteria should be kept in mind for writing an effective vision statement?
3. Why is it important to keep a mission statement short?
4. How are vision and mission statements best communicated to employees in an organization?

5. What is a BHAG?

6. How would you evaluate a mission statement?

7. How can you make a mission statement actionable?

8. How would you suggest a company create narratives for its vision and mission statements?

9. How does a company's sustainable competitive advantage guide its vision and mission?

10. Describe how a mission statement can encourage ethical behavior in a company.

Group Review Exercises

1. Using the information presented in this chapter, create a vision statement for your business school.

   a. How well did the process work?

   b. Who else would you include if you were to do this again?

   c. What might you do differently if you were to try this again?

   d. How accurately does your vision statement present the school and its future?

2. Have your team agree on five large, publically traded companies. Using the Internet, try to locate the vision and/or mission statement for each.

   a. How many were you able to find?

   b. Evaluate each vision/mission on how well it meets the criteria laid out in the chapter.

   c. Do you have any excellent statements? Any horrible ones? Which are they and why did you evaluate them as such?

   d. In what part of their websites did you locate the statements? Why do you suppose the statements are there? Do they mention if they communicate the statements to employees?

3. Look at the following list of mission statements. Match them to the company listed at the end. Company # 1 - One team, one plan, one goal. People working together as a lean, global enterprise for automotive leadership, as measured by: customer, employee, dealer, investor, supplier, union/council, and community satisfaction.

Company # 2 - Use our pioneering spirit to responsibly deliver energy to the world.

Company # 3 - To be the most creative, innovative and efficient company in high-quality interactive entertainment experiences across a range of genres.

Company # 4 - To be a leader in the distribution and merchandising of food, health, personal care, and related consumable products and services.

Company # 5 - To be one of the world's leading producers and providers of entertainment and information. Using our portfolio of brands to differentiate our content, services and consumer products, we seek to develop the most creative, innovative and profitable entertainment experiences and related products in the world.

Company # 6 - To continually provide our members with quality goods and services at the lowest possible prices.

Company # 7 - We seek to be Earth's most customer-centric company for four primary customer sets: consumers, sellers, enterprises, and content creators.

Company # 8 - We will become the world's most valued company to patients, customers, colleagues, investors, business partners, and the communities where we work and live.

Possible Answers	
Amazon.com	Pfizer
Conoco Phillips	Safeway
Costco	Sam's Club
ExxonMobil	Take Two Interactive
Ford	Toyota
GlaxoSmithKline	Walt Disney
Kroger	Wells Fargo

References

[1] R. Karlgaard, 2005, YingYang, Big Bang. Forbes, March 14, 175 (5): 33; The Economist, Measuring the Walmart effect, February 25: 80; W. Boston & S. Sloat, 2015, Volkswagon emissions scandal relates to 11 million cars, Wall Street Journal, September 22: A1; C. Bryant & R. Milne, 2015, Boardroom politics at heart of VW scandal, Financial Times, October 4: 1; P. Knapp, 2015, Alphabet might appease shareholders but has it lost its vision? The Guardian, August 14: 1.

[2] J. A. Pearce & F. David, 1987, Corporate mission statements: The bottom line, Academy of Management Executive, 1 (2): 109 - 116.

[3] J. E. Conklin & W. Weil, 1997. Wicked Problems: Naming the Pain in Organizations. Washington, DC: Group Decision Support Systems Inc.

[4] For perspectives on top management team disagreement see Bourgeois, 1980, Performance and consensus, Strategic Management Journal, 1: 227 - 248, or Eisenhardt, Kahwajy, & Bourgeois, 1997, How management teams can have a good fight, Harvard Business Review, 75 (4): 77 - 85.

[5] Many of the largest corporations in the world are highly diversified in unrelated businesses. It may be that these corporations refrain from offering a corporate mission statement because such statements should be focused. Evidence suggests, however, that many operating divisions of such diversified corporations still do not have mission statements.

6 H. Mintzberg, 1978, The Structuring of Organizations, Prentice Hall.

7 P. Drucker, 1974, Management: Tasks, Responsibilities, Practices, New York: Harper & Row.

8 www.profootballhof.com/history/decades/1980s/the_drive.jsp.

9 J. Barker, 2006, Agincourt: Henry V and the Battle That Made England. New York: Little, Brown.

10 J. Collins, 2001. Good to Great. New York: HarperBusiness.

11 Amazon.com investor relations (http://phx.corporate-ir.net/phoenix.zhtml?c=97664&p=irol-faq).

12 W. Shakespeare, Hamlet, act 2, scene 2.

13 J. Collins, 1996, Aligning actions and values, Leader to Leader, 1: 19 - 24.

14 L. E. Palich, L. B. Cardinal, & C. C. Miller, 2000, Curvilinearity in the diversification-performance linkage: An examination of over three decades of research, Strategic Management Journal, 21: 155 - 174.

15 F. R. David & F. R. David, 2003. It's time to redraft your mission statement, Journal of Business Strategy, 24 (1): 11 - 14; R. D. Ireland & M. A. Hitt, 1992, Mission statements: Importance, challenge, and recommendations for development, Business Horizons, 35 (3): 34 - 42; J. A. Pearce & F. R. David, 1987, Corporate mission statements: The bottom line, Academy of Management Executive, 1 (2): 109 - 116.

16 C. K. Bart & M. C. Baetz, 1998, The relationship between mission statements and firm performance: An exploratory study, Journal of Management Studies, 35 (6): 823 - 854.

17 Ibid.

18 B. DiPietro, 2014, Turning employees into ethics believers, Risk and Compliance Journal, September 26, http://on.wsj.com/1sxyzic.

19 R. Goffee & B. Jones, 1996, What holds the modern company together? Harvard Business Review, November - December 1996: 133 - 148.

20 G. Shaw, R. Brown, & P. Bromily, 1998, Strategic stories: How 3M is rewriting business planning, Harvard Business Review, May/June 1998 (Reprint # 98310).

21 S. A. Buckler & K. A. Zien, 1996, The spirituality of innovation: Learning from stories, Journal of Product Innovation Management, 13 (5): 391 - 405.

22 Medtronic Corporate Mission.

[23] J. C. Collins & J. I. Porras, 1991, Organization vision and visionary organizations, California Management Review, Fall: 30 - 52.

[24] 1 = Ford, 2 = Conoco Phillips, 3 = Take Two Interactive, 4 = Kroger, 5 = Walt Disney, 6 = Costco, 7 = Amazon.com, 8 = Pfizer.

Section B: Strategy Analysis Fundamentals

In the first three chapters of this book we laid a foundation for understanding strategic management. The first chapter outlined the nature of strategy as the direction for the firm that is reflected in an ongoing stream of decisions impacting all areas of the company. Through its strategy the firm seeks to achieve a level of performance that is superior to competing firms in the short term, and offers the potential to sustain performance differences over time. We also discussed the two fundamental imperatives that impact every strategic management process today. Rapidly-evolving markets and aggressive competitors make it exceedingly difficult to sustain superior levels of performance. So the imperatives of "value creation" and "opportunity recognition" become absolutely critical. This context makes developing and executing strategy complex, challenging, exciting, and fun!

Chapters 2 and 3 provided a set of "bookends" for the strategic management process. In the beginning management needs to develop a vision for the direction the company is heading, a mission that describes how it is going to get there, and principles that help guide decisions and behavior. The result that strategy seeks is superior performance, and we discussed ways in which the performance of companies can be evaluated.

Given this, you are probably still asking yourself "What is strategy, really? What the book has done so far is provide an outline, but it hasn't really described it in detail." Let's get specific. The next four chapters of the book take up the challenge of how to develop strategy and sustainable competitive advantage. There are two basic steps in the design and development of a strategy: 1) examine the industry and competitors in order to develop a deep understanding of the market and how your firm must operate within it in order to be successful; 2) examine your own company in order to develop a list of activities and capabilities that potentially provide competitive advantage.

EXTERNAL ANALYSIS OF INDUSTRY

This model originates from a branch of Economics called Industrial Organizational Economics, and focuses on the economic structure of an industry. Attractive industries are those where the conditions are favorable for a company to earn above-average returns. An industry's attractiveness as a place to do business is largely determined by industry characteristics outside the company. These characteristics suggest "key success factors" that any strategic approach should address, and in turn the strategic approach requires the company to assemble or develop certain kinds of capabilities and resources. According to this approach, effective execution of the strategy using these capabilities and resources would then lead to superior performance.

Here's a quick example of this approach. Before mp3 music and players were available, the only way musicians could grow beyond playing in local clubs to make it big was to get a contract with an established music label. The music label companies would then provide studio time to record, schedule the artist on tours, and provide marketing and promotional support. The "barriers to entry" to this industry were significant. Then along came digital. First, compressed files and file-sharing platforms like Napster, then Apple's iTunes, made distribution of music much easier. Then social media platforms like Facebook, and then music sharing services like Spotify, made it inexpensive for musicians to gain visibility. Successful companies in the music industry have now completely re-engineered their strategy approaches and capabilities, in light of the new industry context.

The Industry Analysis methodology is covered in Chapter 4, along with several means of analyzing specific competitors.

INTERNAL ANALYSIS OF COMPANY

The second approach begins with a detailed internal examination of the company. This model begins with: 1) a detailed analysis of the entire business via a value chain analysis; 2) an examination of the company's current resources and capabilities; and 3) a determination of which resources and value-adding activities are truly extraordinary, providing a foundation for sustainable competitive advantage. The result of this analysis will suggest a type of strategic approach that leverages the resources and activities, which in turn suggests the kinds of industries or businesses to compete in (those that will leverage the company's existing skills). Successfully implementing this approach in new circumstances will lead to superior returns for the company.

Another quick example to illustrate. GoPro, the manufacturer of action cameras often used in extreme-action videography and part of the connected sport movement, started up in 2002. Founder Nick Woodman was first mover into an untapped market, and his company developed moderate quality wearable video capture technology. Its activities and capabilities centered around unique designs and making inroads into action sports to generate sales. But as the industry grew and competitors entered the market, GoPro's activities and capabilities became increasingly irrelevant. Competitors had higher quality technology that was cheaper, and were out-maneuvering the company in ways to sell technology through retail distribution and online. The competitive dynamic of the industry had shifted, but GoPro failed to keep up. By early

104

2016 the company's revenue was down 49% versus a year earlier, it lost $108 million in the first quarter, and its market value had declined 80%.

Chapter 5 covers the Value Chain and its associated analysis techniques, while Chapter 6 explores Resources and the associated application of a resource-based analysis.

FORMULATING A STRATEGIC APPROACH

In practice most companies do external industry analysis and internal company analysis simultaneously, and on a continuous basis. They must! Industries are dynamic, and so ongoing attention to emerging competitors is critical. But companies are also not static. They get better and better at some things they have done for awhile, and this sort of improvement can present new opportunity in the market. But along the way they may also discover new things they can become particularly adept at. Good strategy blends all these perspectives together.

Chapter 7 puts the three chapters together in a discussion of Business-Level Strategies as ways to approach the marketplace. Specific strategic approaches must respond to the requirements dictated by industry conditions, but must also build on sets of activities or resources and capabilities that enable a company to create and deliver value in a superior fashion to competition. At the same time, managers must have a sense of trajectory that accounts for anticipated dynamic changes in the industry and competition, but that also builds and follows a vision for the company.

Chapter 4: Industry and Competitive Analysis

LEARNING OBJECTIVES

1. Explain how the phrase "competitive advantage" is connected to company strategy and performance.

2. Describe how an industry definition can affect conclusions drawn from an industry analysis.

3. Explain the impact that forces other than competition can have on company strategy and performance.

4. Employ strategy mapping techniques to identify strategic groups in an industry.

5. Explain how an industry is shaped by driving forces.

6. Explain how dynamic changes in industries and competitive positions will impact a company's strategy.

Afraid of Concentration in Office Supplies Industry

In 1996 Staples and Office Depot announced their plans to merge together their two chains of office supply stores. Office Depot had 571 North American outlets and Staples had 553 superstores in 100 U.S. markets, so their combined operations would exceed 1,100 stores and generate over $10 billion in revenue.

The potential merger between two intense competitors raised immediate suspicions of dominating market power. Many feared that the nearest competitor – Office Max with 425 stores and $3.3 billion in revenue – would be left "in the dustbin." Suppliers, competitors, and customers filed comments of concern with the Federal Trade Commission (FTC).

In response Thomas Sternburg, founder and CEO of Staples, said that office products are sold in a fragmented $185 billion market in which the merged firm would have a meager 6 percent market share. Furthermore, with larger operations the new company would achieve efficiencies, eliminate redundancies, and develop greater buying power with their suppliers. In combination these would lead to price reductions and bigger savings for both business and individual customers. Staples and Office Depot placed ads in major newspapers around the United States assuring the public that the proposed merger would be beneficial.

The FTC disagreed with Sternburg, and announced that it would seek an injunction against the merger. FTC research determined that there were higher retail prices for office supplies in markets where there was high industry concentration of office supply stores. It entertained a much narrower definition of the market. Staples and Office Depot claimed that they were in competition not only with traditional office supply stores, but also with other large outlets such as Walmart and Best Buy who also sold office machines, paper, pens and pencils. The FTC took a different view of the market, as "one-stop-shop" office supply stores. In this narrower market definition, the merged company would have a 70 percent market share. Under pressure from the FTC, the merger never went through.

Fast forward 17-20 years. In 2013 Office Depot and Office Max announced they would be merging in a $1.2 billion stock deal. The merged company would have a combined market share of nearly 42 percent, compared to Staples' 35 percent share. This time the FTC was fairly silent, and the deal was finalized in 2013.

But then in 2015 Staples and Office Depot once again announced their intention to merge into a combined entity with a 75% market share, $39 billion sales and over 4000 stores. Over the previous years the retail office supplies industry had peaked, then declined, and each retail chain had experienced rough going. Following its merger with Office Max, Office Depot revenue declined 10%. Between 2013-15 Staples' revenue dropped 9% and net income declined 39%. In 2015 Amazon launched Amazon Business to cater to corporate customers. Staples and Office Depot again maintained that competition in the industry was vibrant. The FTC again disagreed, and filed suit to stop the merger. FTC research showed that customers were damaged in concentrated markets because office supplies were priced higher. In April 2016 a federal judge upheld the FTC's case, and the two companies gave up (again) on their plans.

Tough Industry for Startup Championship Foods

Traditionally the food manufacturing industry has experienced a very high level of entrepreneurial activity. This is because the barriers to entry have been fairly low. Nearly everyone's grandma has passed down a special food recipe, so coming up with a unique and tasty food product idea has never been a problem. In addition, everyone has access to a "manufacturing plant" to try out new concoctions. It's called your kitchen at home with a sink, refrigerator, stove, and ingredients easily accessible.

Championship Foods started off exactly this way, with a recipe for prepared chili that had won the Texas State Championship and other national chili cook-offs. The company intended to sell its chili in supermarkets, shelved next to Hormel and other canned products. Championship Chili was made with fresh ingredients and high-quality beef, and it was packed in glass jars to exude homemade quality. Who would buy gross canned chili when Championship was available?

The company encountered market forces that made it exceedingly difficult to earn profits. While food ingredients are readily available from a variety of suppliers, glass and manufacturing capacity are not. Glass manufacturing is heavily concentrated, while glass users are not. Glass suppliers charged exorbitant prices for their products sold in smaller quantities, and Championship had no recourse. Manufacturing chili that contained beef required USDA inspected plants, and these plants tended to be huge in size compared to small startup companies. As a small startup, the company had no opportunity to negotiate for better prices or terms from its suppliers.

On the other end of the spectrum, the company's supermarket buyers were fairly concentrated. Championship started business in a city where only three supermarket chains controlled roughly 85 percent of the market. Supermarket buyers entertained many possible new products to place in their stores, and asked all manufacturers to pay "slotting allowances" to gain initial shelf space as well as special advertising and display programs. This concentration of buyers, with no mass market alternatives, makes it unprofitable for small manufacturers.

The food industry is characterized by intense rivalry. Look at the ads on TV every day, and notice the volume of coupons that appear in local newspapers on Wednesdays and Sundays. To create consumer awareness, trial, and repeat purchases, Championship had to play the game where rules were set by the likes of Kraft, Procter & Gamble, and other large food manufacturers. Hormel and other incumbent chili brands engaged in competitive retaliation when Championship's products first appeared on store shelves.

THE NATURE OF MARKETS AND OPPORTUNITY FOR COMPETITIVE ADVANTAGE

We continue our discussion of strategic management with a chapter on the external analysis of markets. Why do we begin here? First, every company exists in a market of some sort, and as the chapter's opening stories illustrate there are varying market forces exerting influences on companies. These forces pressure every company to behave in certain ways in order to be successful, and to not behave in other ways. Second, when we think about achieving "competitive advantage," which is the goal of strategic management, we are acknowledging that there are many companies that may be competitively close to our business. Sets of competitors, in fact, help to define markets. Abraham Lincoln once said, "If we can know where we are and something about how we got there, we might see where we are trending - and if the outcomes which lie naturally in our course are unacceptable, to make timely change."[1] Understanding the market in which a company competes will be helpful in guiding the company in its strategic direction and choices.

But let's first step back in time a bit earlier than Lincoln, to the eighteenth century and economist Adam Smith. You will probably recall from one of your first economics courses that in 1776 he published *Wealth of Nations*. To Adam Smith what created the successful functioning of an economy was the pursuit by each individual of self-interest:

> "... and by directing industry in such a manner as its produce may be of greatest value, he intends only his own gain and he is in this, as in many other cases, lead by an invisible hand to promote an end which was no part of his intention. By pursuing his own interest he frequently promotes that of society more effectually...."[2]

Here and elsewhere in his book we find Smith arguing that there is an efficiency in markets that is guided by the aggregated pursuits of individuals. Resources are efficiently allocated, and the demands and needs of the marketplace are met.

If it is true that markets can efficiently allocate resources and meet demand through the actions of individuals, then why do business organizations even exist? Why shouldn't commerce simply be conducted by transacting individuals? The answer, of course, is that businesses can do a number of things that individuals cannot. They can achieve administrative efficiency and more easily organize the specialization of labor. They can gain access to capital unavailable to individuals and therefore have the ability to construct large facilities and achieve **economies of scale** and scope that individuals cannot achieve by themselves. In today's world business firms can also shield managers and employees from some of the legal liabilities of the business itself as well as from the risks taken on by the firm's investors. So the existence of business organizations opens up a much wider range of possible transactions and approaches in a market.

In Chapter 1 we pointed out that strategy concerns itself with five basic questions, two of which are particularly relevant here: 1) why are firms in an industry different – that is, why are some firms more successful than others; and 2) how and why are those differences between successful and unsuccessful firms sustained over time? The slight deviation we have taken here into Adam Smith and the nature of markets provides us with a very important starting point for exploring these questions. Adam Smith and two centuries of economists have focused on the efficiency of markets in allocating resources and meeting demands, with perfect competition as an elegant concept that illuminates this efficiency. In contrast, the ability of firms to create sustainable differences versus other firms is only possible because of the *failure* of perfectly competitive markets.

Let's explain this carefully. Recall from your economics courses the characteristics that describe perfectly competitive markets: all firms are identical, produce exactly the same products, and no firm earns any profits at all. This is because in this type of market every firm enjoys perfect information about what is going on in the industry, there are no costs associated with making adjustments in how or what a firm produces, and there are no costs for new firms to enter the industry. If Billy Bob's Barbeque somehow figures out how to make a better sauce and starts generating more business as a result, in a perfectly competitive market all the other barbecue joints would see this change instantaneously and just as instantaneously imitate it exactly. Why wouldn't they? Why would they allow Billy Bob to generate more business and more profit, if they can produce exactly the same award-winning sauce? As soon as one firm has figured out how to make more money, in a perfectly competitive market all the other firms will immediately imitate that recipe for success. In addition, because there are no costs to enter the industry, if Fred and Heather on the outside observe that the barbecue sauce companies are making money while they are not, then they will enter the industry to participate in the profit-making. This process will continue until all the profits have been competed away. As the economists say, the market equilibrates at the point where once again all firms are virtually identical and no firm is making any profit.[3]

Perfect competition is on one end of a continuum of types of markets. Commodities markets are an example of a market that closely resembles perfect competition. The other end of the continuum is the exact opposite of perfect competition. Instead of lots of firms, which are all identical and none of which is earning a profit, on the other end there is just one firm and it earns all the profits. This is called a monopoly (Figure 4.1). Here one company owns all of the business in an industry. Without the policing effect of an efficient market populated by competitors, the monopoly firm can usually charge what it wants for its products or services. Because it is the only game in town, it can likely extract economic concessions from its suppliers that lower its costs and raise its profits even further. Because government regulators believe the public interest is usually not well-served by monopolies, it seeks to prevent them from being created or rein them in when they naturally occur. Microsoft has historically enjoyed a huge installed base of users of its operating system on personal computers, making it difficult for other software companies to be successful in this market. Although it now experiences more competition than before, it has been targeted by both the U.S. government and the European Union for its monopolistic position and the aggressive business practices it engages in with the market power it exerts.

Monopoly companies are sometimes protected from new firms entering the industry and from substitute products or services taking away their customers. Local gas and electricity utility companies and cable TV providers are examples of monopolies that have been historically protected through government regulation that keeps competitors at bay.

Competitive advantage is therefore possible when there is a *failure* of perfectly competitive markets. In a perfectly competitive market, no firm has or can gain a competitive advantage and no firm earns profits. In a monopoly market, one firm exerts market power and one firm earns all of the profits. If we think about the goal of strategy as being the creation of sustainable differences between companies that result in higher profits, then we see that the possibility for competitive advantage and higher profits are more likely when our company exists in a market that is at a point on the continuum further away from perfect competition and closer to the monopoly position.

At the beginning of this chapter we profiled the possible merger between Staples and Office Depot in the office supplies industry. The Federal Trade Commission has now twice prevented the merger from going through, because the combined company would have been too far to the right in Figure 4.1 and would have possessed too much market power. The FTC came into existence in the early years of the twentieth century in order to regulate and prevent precisely this type of powerful business combination. To do so they often examine the structure of industries and how industry structure can increase or reduce competition. In the 1970s Harvard Business School professor Michael Porter proposed that instead of using principles of industry structure analysis to prevent monopolies from developing, the very same principles could be productively used by companies to guide them in the development of strategies that will create and sustain positions of advantage.[4] Companies want to be careful about not getting too close to the endpoint of the market continuum and creating a monopoly. Google has been so successful in dominating the "search" industry that it is now under the microscope by both domestic and foreign regulators. However, the great insight of the industry analysis view is that a firm can generate competitive advantage and earn above-average profits if it uses tactics to move the market away from perfect competition.

How do companies do this? In Chapters 5 through 7 we will explore how companies can develop specific types of activities and resources to create value uniquely. The strategic approaches that depend on these activities and resources will often involve consciously creating "barriers to entry" to prevent new companies from entering the industry, as well as "barriers to mobility" that make it difficult for other companies already in the industry to imitate what the company is doing. By creating these kinds of barriers, the company makes the industry less perfectly competitive. Sustainable competitive advantage is then possible when companies figure out how to take advantage of this type of imperfect market.[5]

So what had changed by 2013-15 that made it possible now for Office Depot and Office Max to consummate a merger while Staples was denied its move? This is a complicated question which this chapter will help shed light on. Step back for a second and think about where your parents went shopping for electronics and office supplies when you were a kid, and where you might first look for these items today. Retailing has changed dramatically in a number of industries, in large part thanks to Amazon.com. It is likely that the regulatory examiners at the FTC are just as likely themselves to be shopping via the internet as to visit an office supplies retail store. So the sort of industry fragmentation that CEO Sternburg argued for many years ago is now recognized as more prevalent in the retail landscape. On the other hand, allowing the latest merger proposal to go through would have resulted in an uncomfortable – and possibly damaging – level of industry concentration. The lesson here is that industries may change over time, but a chief concern remains the competitiveness of industries as a function of their structure.

STRUCTURE – CONDUCT – PERFORMANCE

The structural analysis of an industry will allow us to develop clear insight about characteristics of the industry that are helpful to a company in developing and executing its strategic approach. Through industry analysis we can 1) determine how attractive an industry is, and 2) identify key success factors that provide guidance on how to earn above-average profits.

Potential for Above-Average Profits

Industry analysis is a means by which we examine whether the nature of competitive forces makes an industry attractive or unattractive. In industries that are less perfectly competitive, the potential is greater for a company to earn superior returns. At this point one might ask, "Why is this important, since my company is already in an industry? Whatever that industry is, we just have to deal with it." The answer is that companies often make strategic choices to participate in an industry, or not. Today most large companies operate in several industries, and companies are often engaged in acquisitions that may diversify their operations further into new industries (we will discuss this in depth in Chapter 10). Not every industry is equally profitable; see Figure 4.2 for example.[6] The prepackaged software industry earned the highest return on invested capital over this 10-year period. Microsoft, a competitor in this industry, has amassed huge sums of cash as a consequence of its very profitable operations, and has used that cash to acquire other companies. While Microsoft might be interested in participating in the delivery of entertainment to the home, the profitability of the cable TV industry is well below the national average. Therefore, its route to get into home entertainment delivery would in all likelihood not involve starting up or acquiring a company in the cable TV industry. When your grandfather took you fishing, he may have told you that "it's best to fish where the fish are," and that's why he bushwhacked his way into that remote stream or pond. In this case it is generally better to participate in industries where there is a stronger likelihood of earning profits rather than in industries where the average profitability is already depressed.

Figure 4.2
Selected Industries Return on Invested Capital, 1998-2008

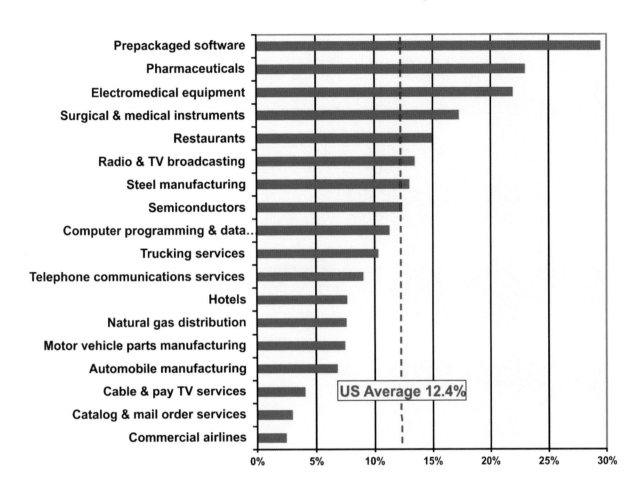

Key Success Factors

If your company is going to participate in an industry, industry analysis can provide guidance on how it should be done. The structure of every industry imposes constraints on and defines options for firms competing in it. For example, an agricultural business operating in the wheat market could not charge higher prices than the current market rate for wheat, because wheat is bought and sold as a commodity with a virtually identical product readily available from many competitors. A company manufacturing PCs and laptops cannot afford to forgo innovation and product line upgrades, because its suppliers push new technology and its customers demand continual progress. In any industry there will always be a small number of key factors that characterize how to navigate the challenges that the industry presents. These key success factors (KSFs) are "rules of thumb" for operating that reflect the structural conditions of the industry. The KSFs identify the aspects of business that each

Strategy Acronym: KSF

The "rules" of an industry

K   Key
S   Success
F   Factors

112

company must pay attention to - and make strategic investments in - if it is to be successful in the industry.

Think about an industry in the same way you might think about a game such as *Fallout 4*, the video game released by Bethesda Game Studios in 2015 for the Playstation 4 and Xbox One platforms.[7] By mid-2016 it has already become the best-selling video game worldwide. The game operates a certain way, and there are actions that players must follow in order to earn experience points and level up their character, the Sole Survivor. The Sole Survivor can roam anywhere on the map and can freely craft settlements and be joined by companions; these may be entertaining, but pursuing these can increase the player's risk and distract the player from accomplishing the primary mission of finding Shaun who was kidnapped by the Institute. Completing different challenges and contracts, and using different types of weapons will earn more experience points and move the player to deeper levels. Similarly, focusing on the key success factors in an industry also increases the odds of success for the company.

We now see that the potential to earn superior returns in an industry partially results from the structure of the industry. We also see that the structure of an industry will suggest that there are certain fundamental rules, which are referred to as key success factors. These ideas help explain what is commonly known as the Structure-Conduct-Performance (SCP) paradigm in strategic management. SCP was historically used to describe the performance of entire industries, but has now become one of the foundations in strategic management for improving company performance.[8] The SCP perspective tells us that the structure of an industry helps determine rules for competing, forcing companies to conduct their business according to the rules. The company's conduct refers to its strategic approach and the types of strategic investments it makes (like manufacturing infrastructure or field sales force development) that support its approach. If the conduct of the company aligns with the KSFs suggested by the current structure of the industry, and presuming the company is effective in its actions, then the company's performance should be enhanced.

Strategy Acronym: SCP
Connecting industry analysis and firm performance
S   Structure
C   Conduct
P   Performance

DEFINING AN INDUSTRY

Before we move on to analyzing an industry, we need to be clear what we mean by an "industry." An industry can generally be defined as a group of productive, profit-making, or value-creating enterprises[9] that draw upon related suppliers of various sorts, develop different kinds of customers, and compete with each other. Economists like to further narrow this definition by focusing on two types of possible substitutions: 1) substitutions for the consumption of a company's output, and 2) substitutions in supply/inputs to the company's production process.[10] A firm is included as a competitor in an industry if its products or services present alternatives for other companies' products or services in the eyes of customers. If a price rise in another company's product would cause someone to buy your company's product instead, then the other company is considered a competitor (Figure 4.3). This is usually how we think about competition. However, competitors may also exist on the supply side of what a company does. Imagine a high-tech firm located in Silicon Valley, for example, that is seeking to expand its business and needs to hire well-trained programmers. Although the software that the company intends to produce is different from that offered by Apple, Oracle, and other software developers, the company must still compete with these companies for the trained programmers that will ensure its success. So a firm is also included as a competitor in an industry if it uses similar raw materials or employs similar production methods as other companies, even if the final products produced are not entirely similar for consumers. In this case, since the company already competes with other companies for production inputs, it might then easily compete for customer business by producing similar products if the lure of potential profits is great enough.

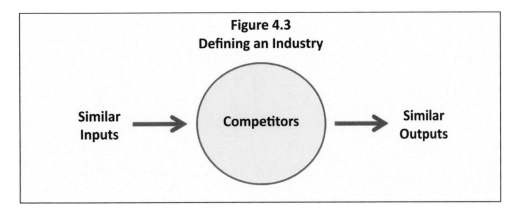

It is important to recognize that industries can be defined differently, depending on who's doing the talking. We saw earlier in this chapter that Staples and Office Depot sought to describe the office supplies market as encompassing competitors as diverse as Best Buy (who largely sells audio and video equipment) and Walmart (who largely sells general merchandise and food). On the other hand, the FTC defined the industry very narrowly, including only "one-stop-shop" office supply stores like Office Max and the local mom-and-pop shops that traditionally sold these goods. The narrowest industry definitions ordinarily involve the group of competitors who produce similar outputs *and* utilize similar inputs.

Sometimes industry definitions can be very confusing. For example, what industry classification do cell phones exist in? Until the mid-1990s it seemed very clear that cell phone manufacturers and cell phone service providers competed in the telephone industry, that is, in local and long distance calling. But consider the nature of cell phone capabilities just a few years later, serving multiple functions competing with products and services in multiple industries (Figure 4.4).[11] If a company is in the cell phone business today (equipment or service), it is not entirely clear how it might draw the boundaries around its industry. Here's another example: consider the "home entertainment" industry. Not long ago this industry included manufacturers of various kinds of equipment such as stereos, TVs, VCRs, and DVD players. But within the last few years technology has now enabled a host of new types of firms to go after the consumer home entertainment dollar. These include new equipment manufacturers as well as content providers: video game manufacturers, Internet-based gaming sites, video on demand from cable, downloadable music and video from Apple, Internet sites, and even your cell phone service provider. How to define the boundaries of an industry can be complicated, and can affect the kinds of conclusions drawn from an industry analysis.

Figure 4.4
Industries May Be Hard to Define

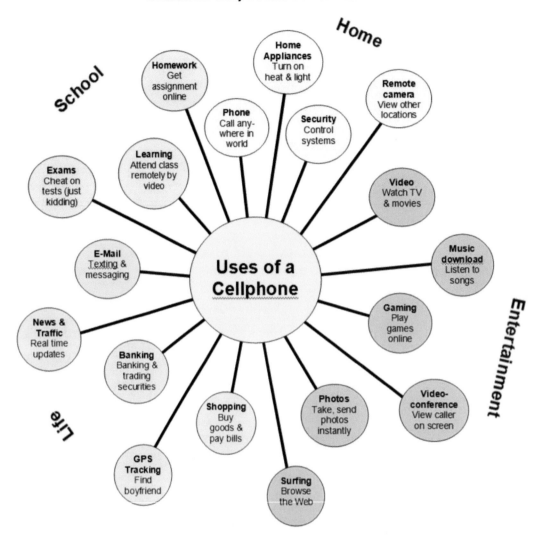

As we shall see later on, an industry definition is very important to come to grips with. Broadly defined industries will usually require companies to engage in a variety of value-creating activities (Chapter 5) that depend upon developing broad and deep resource positions (Chapter 6) in order to be successful. Broadly defined industries usually encounter international competition or require international development, which of course place additional demands on companies. Narrowly defined industries, in contrast, allow companies to focus their efforts and resource investments more carefully. So the definition of the industry has real implications for the boundaries of the firm, the kinds of capabilities it has to develop, and the competitors it will encounter.

Basic information on virtually any industry can be obtained from the Internet, library, or data search engines. This data gathering should start with locating the NAICS code (North American Industry Classification System) for the industry. An NAICS code (formerly known as a SIC or Standard Industrial Classification Code) is generated by the U.S. government in an effort to gather, track, and publish data on specific industries.[12] The code can vary from two to seven digits; the more digits, the more specific the industry classification. Figure 4.5 illustrates the

NAICS classifications in which the office supplies industry (code 45321) is found, where Office Depot and Staples compete.

```
                          Figure 4.5
               NAICS Codes for Office Supplies Industry

        Code        Classification

        45          Retail trade
        453            Miscellaneous store retailers
        4532              Office supplies, stationery, gift stores
        45321                Office supplies & stationery stores
        45322                Gift, novelty & souvenir stores
```

While there are many ways to obtain this code, there are two relatively simple means available. The first is to consult the list of NAICS codes available from the U.S. government (either at a library or on the Internet).[13] The second is to locate either your company or a public company that might be a direct competitor to your business and simply use their NAICS code to look up overall industry data on the industry (via *Dun & Bradstreet, Lexis/Nexis*, etc.).

At an aggregated national level the data gathered on a firm's industry has some value; however, it is the rare business that draws customers equally from all parts of the United States. Most of the data available will be on a national basis, but provides little understanding of the local, regional, or territory-specific competitive environment. The national industry may be doing very poorly while in a local area there may be few competitors or the industry is doing very well. Effective analysis requires a definition of the industry that is broad enough to be inclusive of all potential competitors, but not so broad as to negate effective evaluation. Ferreting out important details like this is one part of the art of strategic management.

STEEPG – THE GENERAL ENVIRONMENT

It is important to recognize that every industry is surrounded by a rich array of outside forces in the general environment that have the ability to impact the growth of the industry and the nature of competition. These driving forces are conditions and trends in the general environment that no one company can change, but that every company in the industry must incorporate into its planning. Driving forces can have a variety of significant effects on an industry and the competition within it:

- Increase or decrease demand
- Increase or decrease supply or supply alternatives
- Create opportunity to provide greater value to customers
- Create higher costs for suppliers or buyers
- Create higher costs for rivals
- Lower barriers to entry and elevate the threat of new entrants
- Create a wider pool of potential substitutes

These possible effects need to be figured into your analysis of the industry, because they suggest ways in which the nature of the industry may change over time.

Consider driving forces as equivalent to trying to drive on a really steep grade in a car or a four-wheel drive vehicle. No matter where you're trying to go, the grade is so steep that it will affect your direction and your speed, and if it is steep enough you may not get where you're trying to go. Therefore an easy way to remember these forces is by using the acronym STEEPG, which is the combination of the first letters of each of the driving forces: social, technological, economic, environmental, political/legal, and global. Figure 4.6 provides a comprehensive list that categorizes types of driving forces in the general environment, with key dimensions for each category. While a comprehensive study of the various dimensions of these forces could take up an entire book by itself, we will highlight a few of these more carefully below to provide a sense of how powerful they may be.

Strategy Acronym: STEEPG
Driving Forces

S	Social
T	Technological
E	Economic
E	Environmental
P	Political
G	Global

Figure 4.6
STEEPG: Driving Forces in the External Environment

Social

Demographic
- population size & trends
- age structure
- geographic distribution
- ethnic composition & segment growth
- income distribution

Psychographic & cultural
- lifestyle
- entertainment
- convenience
- women in workforce
- work/home balance

Technology
- discoveries in basic science
- governmental support for R&D
- broader availability of new technologies

Environmental
- increasing pressure for sustainable approaches
- increasing attention to externalities of pollution
- greater scrutiny about accessing natural resources

Economic
- inflation & interest rates
- general economic conditions—growth vs. recession
- capital market availability
- unemployment rates
- exchange rates for currency translations

Political / Legal
- antitrust laws & philosophy of enforcement
- tax laws
- legislation on corporate governance and financial regulation
- SEC regulations
- labor issues—minimum wage, health insurance, pension coverage
- patent laws & changes
- social expectations that can lead to political and legal initiatives

Global
- political events
- consolidating institutions—OPEC, European Economic Community
- emerging markets—consumption, supply, finance
- cultural sensitivities—moderating vs. escalating
- terrorism and security issues

Social driving forces are of two varieties: 1) demographic, and 2) psychographic, or cultural. Basic demographic structure and changes can have a dramatic impact on the nature of competition within industries. The clearest example of this impact is illustrated by your parents'

117

generation, the often-discussed "baby boomers," which refers to U.S. citizens born in the years 1946-1964 (Figure 4.7). During this time U.S. birth rates spiked, creating a large new demographic segment defined by age. As this segment has aged through the decades, it has dramatically affected demand in an array of industries, including soft drinks, education, real estate, vacation homes, automobiles, investments, and now retirement planning. But it is the *combination* of basic demographics and the "psychographic," or

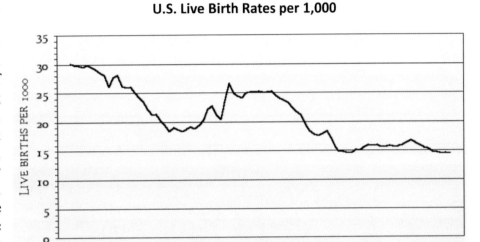

Figure 4.7
U.S. Live Birth Rates per 1,000

cultural, factors that have affected industry growth, decline, and competition. For example, the first minivan was introduced by Chrysler in the 1980s, just as baby boomers were entering the lifestyle years of having their own families with young children. In contrast to other automobile manufacturers, Chrysler sensed the opportunity for a new kind of passenger vehicle by doing psychographic customer research rather than traditional demographic studies, in order to identify lifestyle needs of potential buyers.[14] During the same time period Sony and BMW made great headway in U.S. markets because this generation began to value "high status" possessions such as Walkman portable tape players and engineered imported cars.

Other major cultural factors are worth mentioning. 59 percent of women in America are in the workforce in 2016. Where this has resulted in a family with two working adults, it has had an economic effect in the form of higher disposable income per family and has led to the dramatic changes in industries as diverse as daycare and luxury vacations. On the other hand 34% of all U.S. children (and 72% of African-American children) live in single-parent homes,[15] which considerably impacts available income and time for a range of economic activities.

In the example mentioned earlier about the home entertainment industry, technology advances in microchip design, fiber optics, file compression algorithms, and many other developments have enabled new companies to begin competing with the traditional equipment manufacturers. These types of technological developments most often originate in other firms outside the industry or are discoveries made in science and research laboratories. Yet the new developments will diffuse throughout the economy and be used productively within many different industries. This can change the nature of competition.

Environmental factors are increasingly seen as driving forces in many industries today. It might seem that these effects would be most pronounced in basic manufacturing and in the kinds of suppliers that manufacturers rely upon for raw materials. So we read about pollution control equipment requirements on smokestacks and in runoff from factories that use large amounts of water. However, environmental concerns are expressed in ways that affect us in our daily lives, as well. For example, Hewlett Packard and other companies that provide laser and inkjet toner cartridges now include recycling instructions and mail-back envelopes in every package they sell.

Hotels which have embraced water-saving practices (low pressure shower heads, re-usable towels) are in greater demand. The Environmental Protection Agency recently issued a report clearing the way for lawn mowers, watercraft, and other users of small gas-powered engines below 50 horsepower to meet tougher emissions standards.[16] Engineering these more stringent standards into small engines will raise the cost of manufacturing these products and we will likely see higher prices in stores. On the plus side, of course, our back yards and lakes will have much cleaner air as a result!

Political and legal forces can come and go, but their presence is always felt. During the 1990s there was relatively less attention on antitrust issues than has been the case at other times in recent history. On the other hand, a high level of mergers and acquisitions by U.S. firms during the same decade led to the issuance of new Financial Accounting and Standards Boards (FASB) regulations in 2001 that governed how the combining of two businesses must be treated by the accounting profession. FASB eliminated "pooling of interests" as an acceptable method of accounting for business combinations, which allowed companies to add together the book values of their net assets without indicating which entity was the "purchaser" and which was the "purchased." When this method was used, investors often had difficulty telling who was buying whom or determining how to evaluate the transactions. Instead, FASB favored the "purchase method" of accounting for mergers. With the purchase method, one company is identified as the buyer and records the assets of the company being acquired on its books at the price it actually paid. This led to greater transparency for investors. Other more comprehensive, frame-breaking pieces of legislation to directly affecting business practices are the Sarbanes-Oxley Act (SOX) in 2002 and Dodd-Frank in 2010 after the financial markets crisis. The SOX legislative initiative responded to violations of financial reporting and imposed stiff new demands on companies and their auditors to ensure that published financial statements are accurate. Dodd-Frank added reams of additional regulation on financial services companies.

In addition to explicit political and legal forces, we add a final dimension to this category that has been increasingly important for companies to pay attention to: social expectations that could become political and legal initiatives. SOX is an example of a social concern about business that was institutionalized into a body of law, largely because companies were often perceived as acting in ways detrimental to their shareholders. There is a whole class of social issues that falls into this gray area, such as environmental concerns, offshoring jobs to countries with lower wage rates, or privacy and data protection issues. A survey by *McKinsey Quarterly* found an overwhelming majority of their readers felt that corporations needed to take on a wider role in dealing with these issues, something that goes beyond simply producing returns for their investors.[17] The implied social contract that businesses have today with the communities and societies within which they exist has become a standard that is embraced by the public and will most likely result in greater regulation that affects how industries function.

FIVE-FORCES ANALYSIS

An analysis of the industry is possible once the industry has been defined and we gain a better understanding of the forces in the general environment that can affect it. There are a number of techniques available to perform this type of analysis, with five forces and competitive mapping being the most popular.

The Harvard Business School professor we mentioned earlier, Michael Porter, developed the five-forces model in the 1970s to examine the five main structural elements in any industry;

Figure 4.8 provides a summary of these forces. This model expands the way we think about competition. To the untrained eye, one might view only direct competitors and their competitive success as the primary dimension affecting the economic performance of a company. However, the five-forces model explicitly acknowledges the roles that new entrants, substitutes, buyers, and suppliers also play in this equation, in addition to rivalry. In the process of considering the five forces, every effort should be made to evaluate the extent to which each force influences how the industry is either more or less profitable for the entire set of competitors. This is because when each of these five forces is strong, it will tend to reduce the profitability in the industry. Five-forces analysis is also used to understand how one industry compares to another regarding the opportunity to earn above-average profits.

Figure 4.8
Five Forces of Industry Structure

← Potential Competitors →

Threat of New Entrants
➢ Capital requirements
➢ Economies of scale
➢ Absolute cost advantages
➢ Access to inputs
➢ Access to distribution channels
➢ Need for product differentiation
➢ Switching costs
➢ Expected retaliation
➢ Government regulation

Threat of Substitutes
➢ Relative price/performance of substitutes
➢ Switching costs of buyers
➢ Buyer propensity to substitute

Rivalry
➢ Industry growth rate
➢ Fixed costs as % of total costs
➢ Overcapacity in industry
➢ Low product differentiation
➢ Low switching costs
➢ Informational complexity
➢ Numerous or equally balanced competition
➢ High strategic stakes
➢ Exit barriers

Bargaining Power of Suppliers
➢ Supplier concentration (vs. rivals' concentration)
➢ Importance of volume to supplier
➢ Switching costs of suppliers
➢ Differentiation of inputs required
➢ Presence of substitute inputs
➢ Cost of input relative to total costs
➢ Threat of forward integration

Bargaining Power of Buyers
➢ Buyer concentration (vs. rivals' concentration)
➢ Buyer volume
➢ Switching costs of buyers
➢ Buyer information
➢ Threat of backward integration
➢ Availability of substitutes

← Industry Chain of Activity →

Threat of New Entrants

Industries that tend to be profitable (see Figure 4.2) are attractive to companies outside the industry because they see the possibility of entering the industry and participating in the profit-making. New entrants may take the form of either startup companies going into business for the first time, or existing companies that decide to grow by acquiring their way in to the industry.

120

Existing companies are the most challenging new competitors when they enter an industry since they may already possess a set of capabilities and financial resources that allow them to enter in a big way. Regardless of whether they are a start-up or an existing company, new entrants will tend to do two things that can hurt the profitability of incumbent firms: expand capacity and steal their customers. New firms often expand industry capacity as they seek to sell goods and services to the same customers. Expanded capacity has the tendency to lead to downward pricing pressure on industry competitors for several reasons: 1) each company wants to ensure that its existing capacity continues to be fully utilized; 2) companies feel the overwhelming need to grow sales regardless of industry dynamics; 3) companies may mistakenly believe that market share is of primary importance; and 4) greater availability generally leads buyers to compare products and look for bargains. Competition for the same customers will lead to higher levels of marketing, sales, and promotional expenses by all competitors as the requirements for differentiation continually increase (i.e., the "why should I buy from you?" question). So unless new entrants to an industry can significantly expand overall industry revenue, the profit pool that is available in any given year will be spread across a greater number of competitors, on average reducing the potential profits available to any one company. Therefore, the combination of a greater number of competitors, lower prices, and increased expenses diminish the potential for the existing firms in the industry to generate revenue and profits.

Figure 4.9
Threat of New Entrants

➤ Capital requirements
➤ Economies of scale
➤ Absolute cost advantages
➤ Access to inputs
➤ Access to distribution channels
➤ Need for product differentiation
➤ Switching costs
➤ Expected retaliation
➤ Government regulation

This threat of new entrants is considerably reduced if substantive barriers to entry can be erected. Existing competitors attempt to reduce the threat of new entrants by building entry barriers to raise the costs to start business in the industry. Higher entry costs then prompt potential entrants to question whether they can afford to enter the industry, or make sufficient profits once they have entered. On the flip side, current competitors must weigh the cost of erecting barriers with the potential downside of additional competitors. There are several varieties of barriers to entry that affect the threat of new entrants (Figure 4.9), and we discuss each of these next.

Capital requirements. Starting up a new business in an industry generally involves a significant commitment of capital. For example, in a manufacturing industry a new entrant would need to invest in a manufacturing facility, production assembly line, tools and dies, as well as build inventories of raw materials and finished goods. Depending on the industry, this can involve a huge outlay. The restaurant industry experiences a very high level of new entrants, and yet establishing even one restaurant location can be costly. A typical stand-alone Krispy Kreme outlet, which makes only doughnuts and coffee, might cost $1.5 million or more to build. If a company wanted to compete against Best Buy in the home electronics retailing industry, the inventory alone to set up and stock a comparable-sized store would cost millions of dollars. In our experience, students often believe that it would be fairly easy to set up an Internet business by developing a Web site fairly quickly. However, the kinds of Web-based businesses that promise the potential for sustainable advantage will usually involve making an initial investment upwards of $500,000 to develop a sophisticated Web site, back-end database, and the programming that smoothly integrates the two.

Economies of scale. In some industries the ability to compete will depend on whether a company can produce its product or service at a cost that is low enough to offer low competitive prices. Low costs are sometimes achieved because companies produce on a large scale where the benefits of volume translate directly to unit cost reductions. Economies of scale characterize many industries, including automobiles, packaged consumer products, and computer manufacturing. They are often achieved as a direct result of huge investments in physical infrastructure, which raises the initial capital requirements (e.g., barrier to entry) mentioned above.

Absolute cost advantages. New entrants may be deterred from entering an industry if the incumbent firms in the industry enjoy a cost advantage that comes from having been in the industry for a while. The usual type of absolute cost advantage derives from what is known as the experience curve, in which cost reductions per unit produced are based upon cumulative production over time (in contrast to economies of scale, in which unit cost reductions are associated with volume during a fixed time interval). With greater experience the company learns about subtle and not-so-subtle new procedures that can contribute to cost reductions. Figure 4.10 diagrams the classic experience curve relationship. It is important to note that the entry barrier of experience holds only if the learning that comes through experience cannot be easily appropriated by new entrants through hiring away a competitor's employees, purchasing machinery or equipment that incorporates the refined production practices, or somehow copying what the competitor is doing. A second type of absolute cost advantage occurs when an existing competitor has developed a unique and proprietary design for a product or manufacturing process that may be obvious to others, but which is protected through patents. In this case a new entrant would have to invent a new way to produce a particular product, and often this will involve significantly greater expense.

Figure 4.10
Experience Curve

Unit Cost

Cumulative Production Over Time

Access to inputs. Barriers to entry exist when raw materials or important inputs are not available to potential new entrants. A group wishing to start a new hamburger restaurant needs a good-quality, high-traffic location. However, the best street corner locations in your community might already be occupied by other businesses (or by McDonald's itself!). Once these prime corner locations are occupied, then there are simply no more available. Moving from the mundane to the sublime, the De Beers Company has nearly exclusive access to South African diamond mines, making it exceedingly difficult for any other potential competitor to gain access to the raw materials. In 2016 a "global scramble" began to secure supplies of lithium, the demand for which is skyrocketing among automobile manufacturers and battery producers. CITIC, a Chinese state-controlled company, made overtures to acquire part of SQM which is the largest lithium producer in Chile.

Access to distribution channels. Companies that desire to enter an industry may discover that they are unable to gain access to customers. If a new company wanted to introduce a cola or lemon-flavored soda into the soft drink industry, for example, it would need to find a bottler to mix its concentrate with water and CO_2, bottle it, and distribute it. However, the major bottlers and canners are contractually locked into long-term deals with existing soft drink competitors and are therefore prevented from bottling competing cola or lemon soda products. In other cases, access to distribution may be difficult because prospective customers simply place limits on the number of companies with whom they do business. In the food business, supermarkets have limited shelf space and are only interested in carrying proven products that will sell quickly. Therefore, supermarkets charge exorbitant fees to manufacturers who seek to sell new products. In the financial industry, companies often provide a limited set of mutual fund alternatives to employees for investing through their retirement programs, so other financial firms seeking to offer new mutual funds may be excluded from consideration.

Switching costs. Customer resistance to new entrants may also arise due to the costs to switch to the new competitor's product or service (both real and perceived). The costs involved in changing buying habits include the real costs of time, price, new buying patterns, inventory turnover, and customer service. Perceived costs are important, too – including reputation, history, market image, and comfort. Many folks who began using personal computers in the early 1980s have been forced to learn a continuing series of newer word processing, spreadsheet, and systems packages throughout the years. Switching from Edline to WordStar to VolksWriter Deluxe to WordPerfect to Microsoft Word was a painful, slow process that appeared necessary to be able to enjoy the benefits of writing on computers. Today it is difficult to convince those same people to switch to using Google docs or other online shared programs, as both the real and perceived costs to switch from Word would appear enormous.

Real switching costs can take many forms. For instance, those individuals who live near and fly out of Atlanta generally fly on Delta, and by doing so accumulate mileage under Delta's SkyMiles program. This program encourages customers to remain loyal to the airline, and creates real switching costs for those customers when they consider flying on another airline. A Platinum traveler on Delta has priority boarding, a high chance for upgrading to first class on many flights, and a reduced membership fee for the Delta Room Club. Each of these items has a real, tangible value that would have to be overcome by a competitor for a traveler to switch to another airline.

Consider the switching costs related to changing soft drinks. There are virtually no real switching costs involved. Actual consumers do not have to learn how to open the can or bottle in a new way, swallowing is unchanged, the purchase price is virtually identical, and availability is not an issue. For the retailer who stocks soft drinks, the same size cans and bottles require no new handling in their warehouses or stores, and promotional displays are built the same way as before. However, there are enormous *perceived* switching costs involved in convincing a Coke drinker to move to Pepsi or vice versa. Take a look at a typical advertisement by these two rivals. The ads focus exclusively on perceptions, not on their quality ingredients, extraordinarily clean environments, or on their Rocky Mountain spring water! Similarly, for most retailers the strength of long-term supply relationships with Coca-Cola and Pepsi may make it difficult to switch out to Uncle Jethro's Wicked Cola or some other new concoction. Or if you have your entire music library on iTunes, imagine your angst in being forced to convert it over to the android platform after you have dropped and cracked your iPhone.

Need for product differentiation. In most industries, existing competitors have carefully crafted a brand image and reputation that helps generate a continuing customer base. One of the key elements of strategy is the positioning of the business in a space that differentiates it in the mind of customers relative to the businesses' competitors. Similarly, in established industries new entrants most often find they must effectively differentiate each of their products or services. Often this will involve major marketing and sales expenditures on advertising, promotion, sales force development, and penetration in order to create a unique positioning in the minds of customers.[18]

Government regulation. "Big Brother" - in the form of federal, state, and local government - can have an enormous effect on the propensity for new firms to enter an industry. In order to enter the food manufacturing industry, every new entrant must at a minimum be in compliance with FDA rules or may be required to have all of the new firm's products, packaging, and processes approved in advance and regularly inspected by USDA. Starting a restaurant requires that the new business meet all state and local health regulations, submit to regular inspections, and post those results in the public view. All of this takes significant time and expense, which is only indirectly related to the reason that customers patronize the business. Every industry has its own unique set of regulations, required licenses, and personnel to ensure compliance. If the costs of starting a new business are onerous, then the rate of new entrants will be dramatically reduced. Despite the enormous operational advantages to the use of nuclear power, new power stations in the United States have been at a virtual standstill since the late 1970s. The primary reason has been government regulation. Those wishing to build, operate, attain fuel rods, and then dispose of those same fuel rods face an almost Herculean set of regulations and regulators. The impact of the government regulation has been crushing to the growth of this and other industries in the United States.

When new start-up companies are possible new entrants, regulation by various countries' governments can be a significant constraining force. Whereas in the United States it takes an average of about five days to complete five procedures to start up a new company and costs only 1.5 percent of average personal income, government regulations in some other countries are onerous and can significantly impede foreign new-venture competition. For example, in Greece new companies must complete fifteen separate steps that take thirty-eight days on average, at a cost of nearly 25 percent of average personal income.

Expected retaliation. New entrants in any established industry should not expect existing competitors to sit idly by and watch another company suddenly show up and start competing for their customers. Retaliation by existing competitors is increased when the following conditions exist: 1) there is a history of such retaliation in the industry; 2) the existing competitors have deep pockets and plenty of resources to devote to more intense competition; 3) the existing competitors have already sunk significant costs in building infrastructure or establishing a market position, and a loss of business would create financial pressures; and 4) the industry is not growing quickly, meaning that any business for a new entrant must come from an existing competitor. In April 2006, low-cost carrier JetBlue Airlines announced that they would begin daily nonstop service from Charlotte to New York City's LaGuardia Airport. Tickets went on sale for the equivalent of half the current market price of the major airlines flying out of Charlotte. Within two weeks all of the major airlines announced dramatic fare reductions to NYC in a bid to retain their customers. When Tiger Woods broke into the professional golf circuit and started winning tournaments by out-driving other pros off the tee and showing pinpoint short-club accuracy, what did the other pros do? They increased their physical training regimens and began spending longer hours in practice. His entry changed the game.

Threat of Substitutes

Substitutes are products or services that perform the same function or meet the same need as the products or services in the industry under study, but which are produced using different raw materials and inputs. The classic example that economists use is coffee, tea, milk, and sodas; the competitors to Starbucks or Folgers would be other brands of coffee, whereas Lipton tea and Coca-Cola would be viewed as substitutes. The availability of substitutes can have two impacts on industry competition and profitability. First, they establish a price ceiling for products and services in the industry; exceeding the ceiling would prompt customers to take flight to the substitute products that are available. Second, substitutes can prompt the competitors in an industry to ramp up their marketing and promotional efforts to stem the outflow of customers. Together these put pressure on competitors in the industry to keep prices low enough, enhance the performance of their products, and to spend more to attract and retain customers - all of which can depress sales and profits. Today bottled water and sports drinks, as substitutes, have significantly impacted the traditional soft-drink industry, which in 2005 experienced its first volume decline in U.S. sales in twenty years.[19]

Three factors determine how strong the threat of substitutes will be for an industry. These include: 1) the relative price/performance of the substitute products; 2) the switching costs for the buyer to obtain and use the substitute; and 3) buyers' propensity to try substitute products or services. Substitution tends to increase when the substitute's price is equal to or lower than prices of incumbents and the value to the buyer is equal to or greater. In this case the value to buyers can sometimes be satisfied more economically by turning

Figure 4.11
Threat of Substitutes

Factors Increasing Substitution | **Examples**

Better relative price and Performance combination	Making airline reservations online, compared to using a travel agency.
	Downloading mp3 music to your iPod, compared to buying CDs in stores.
Low switching costs	Soft drink companies used corn syrup as a sweetener instead of sugar, because it required no changes in operations.
	Consumers buy electricity for their homes from wind farms, by merely signing a form with their power company.

to companies outside the industry. If the switching costs for buyers to move to substitutes are also fairly low, then even greater pressure may be exerted on the competitors' ability to generate sales, as buyers then have even less reason to remain loyal. Think about the growth of tablets versus laptops computers recently. Although tablet users sacrifice some performance (e.g. ease of printing), the overall combination of price and performance has made these extremely attractive substitutes.

Finally, although many buyers and consumers maintain loyalty to companies and brands, today there appears to be a greater psychological willingness to experiment and try alternatives. Often this willingness to experiment with substitutes springs from characteristics of the relationship between companies and their customers, going far beyond mere product or service characteristics. Figure 4.11 offers additional examples of increasing substitution.

Whereas the threat of new entrants will usually depend on the attractiveness of the industry, an increase in the threat of substitutes depends on the dynamics of *other* industries. Competitors should watch for warning signals that pressure from substitutes may be increasing. For example, in the early 1990s the soft-drink aisle in most supermarkets contained beverages on one side and snacks and chips on the other side. By the late 1990s the aisle had become the "beverage" aisle, with soft drinks on one side and bottled waters on the other. It was obvious that consumers were flocking to bottled waters, and beginning to drink them instead of soft drinks. The major soft-drink companies all made the move to add bottled water to their product offerings. Warning signs that companies in substitute product industries might be getting more aggressive include production capacity increases, significant accumulations of cash, merger and acquisition activity, as well as significant technological changes. The addition of production capacity signals that substitute producers might want to get more aggressive in pricing and marketing in order to fully utilize available capacity. In addition when profits are growing, such companies might consider investing additional marketing dollars to broaden their customer base.

Bargaining Power of Buyers

Buyers affect the profitability of the industry's competitors with their purchase choices. The profitability levels in any industry are determined by the bargaining power that buyers have in purchasing goods and services offered. Buyers may affect profitability by demanding that competitors spend money to deliver other valued dimensions such as enhanced product quality, extended payment terms, promotional support, and other services. Buyers will often pit competitors against one another in order to negotiate the best terms possible. The ability of buyers to extract various economic concessions depends on the variety of factors shown in Figure 4.12.

Figure 4.12
Bargaining Power of Buyers

➢ Buyer concentration (vs. rivals' concentration)
➢ Buyer volume
➢ Switching costs of buyers
➢ Buyer information
➢ Threat of backward integration
➢ Availability of substitutes

Buyer concentration. It is important to remember that an industry analysis is an examination of the *structure* of the entire industry. This reminder is very important when we talk about the bargaining power of buyers that may result from buyer concentration. Here we are not discussing the bargaining power that any one buyer (such as Walmart) may have with its suppliers; instead we are referring to the structure of buyers as an entire group. A high level of buyer concentration means that there are just a few major buyers in an industry, and each one on average commands a significant share of the market. Under these circumstances competitors have few meaningful alternative places to sell their products. Furthermore, the loss of any one buyer to a competitor would create a dramatic shift in the industry: the company would lose significant sales and market share, which would be entirely taken up by a direct competitor. These conditions make it likely that buyers would be able to exert significant pressure on the companies in this industry to either reduce prices or provide additional services, or both.

Figure 4.13
Calculating Industry Concentration

Concentration Ratio

The concentration ratio uses the formula:

$$CR_m = s_1 + s_2 + s_3 + \ldots \ldots + s_m$$

where m is the number of firms to be examined, and s_j is the market share of the jth firm.

Evaluation of CR_4:

< 40	very competitive industry
40-70	moderately concentrated
> 70	highly concentrated

Herfindahl-Hirschman Index (HHI)

The HHI uses the formula:

$$HHI = s_1^2 + s_2^2 + s_3^2 + \ldots \ldots + s_n^2$$

where n is the number of firms in the industry, and s_j is the market share of the jth firm.

Evaluation of HHI:

< 1000	very competitive industry
1001-1800	moderately concentrated
> 1800	highly concentrated

Increases in HHI by more than 100-200 raise serious anti-trust concerns in markets where HHI is greater than 1800.

Buyer concentration can be measured in one of a couple ways. A relatively easily calculated measure of concentration is simply referred to as the concentration ratio, which is the percentage of market share in the industry owned by the largest buyer firms. The U.S. government often looks closely at the concentration ratio of the largest four firms, known as CR4. If this measure is less than 40 percent, then it suggests the industry is very competitive, with no buyer owning a very large market position. Concentration ratios are the "quick and dirty" method for determining concentration, but the measure is incomplete because it captures only the largest firms in the industry. In its place, the Herfindahl-Hirschman Index (HHI) is often used, because it provides a more complete portrayal of industry concentration. The HHI uses the market shares of all the firms in an industry to calculate a measure that can range from 0 to 10,000 (see Figure 4.13

for how to calculate the concentration ratio and HHI). The FTC uses HHI as a guideline for evaluating mergers. An HHI between 1,000 and 1,800 signals moderate concentration, while an HHI exceeding 1,800 reflects an industry that is highly concentrated. In the opening story of this chapter, the merger of Staples and Office Depot would have produced an HHI greater than 5,000, while in the second story the HHI for the supermarket buyers in the city where Championship Chili started up was greater than 2,600. In these two cases, companies selling to these highly concentrated groups would be subject to intense bargaining power of buyers.

The impact of concentration is best evaluated on a relative basis. When buyers as a group are significantly more concentrated than are firms in the industry you are studying, then concentration can surely impact the attractiveness of the industry. So when the HHI for supermarkets is 2600 but the HHI for manufacturers might be only 750, the buyers as a group can make demands and cause the food manufacturing industry to be less profitable, and therefore less attractive. But if the relative concentration is balanced – for example, where both buyers and producers have HHI levels of 2100 – even though categorized as "highly concentrated" the bargaining power between the two groups is balanced.

Buyer volume. Similar to buyer concentration, if buyers purchase a high percentage of goods and services produced by companies in the industry, it means that the producing companies cannot afford to lose that business. Under these circumstances buyers have the potential to demand additional services, changes, and/or price concessions. 63% of appliance manufacturer sales are to retailers, and among retailers only five chains account for roughly 75% of this volume. Not only is appliance retailing concentrated, but they also account for a critically large share of the manufacturers' business.

Switching costs of buyers. In a similar manner to the earlier discussion about switching costs under the "Threat of New Entrants" section, as switching costs (both real and perceived) go down, the relative power of the buyers is increased. With lower switching costs there is less to keep buyers loyal to incumbent producers. Switching costs tend to decline as the standardization of an industry's products or services increases. For this reason producers in many industries seek novel improvements in their offerings.

A cautionary note is in order here. Remember that this is a discussion about *industry* structure. So when we discuss a dimension like switching costs, keep in mind we are not referring to the ability of just one customer to switch. We are referring to the ability of a significant block of customers to switch. This then becomes a structural condition of the producer-buyer relationship which enables a critical mass of buyers to seek more from the producers. This puts pressure on rival producers to lower their prices, develop new doohickeys that will satisfy customers, provide them with extra services to complement the existing business, etc. All of these efforts cost the rival producers, and thus lower the profits they are able to make.

Buyer information. The advance of technology has dramatically increased the power of buyers. Whereas most buyers were previously limited in their knowledge of competitive pricing, product availability, and comparisons of the features of competitive products, the advent of technology has created an empowered buyer. Until the mid-1980s, for example, food manufacturers used to conduct their own research on product sales and market shares in supermarkets using third-party research firms like A. C. Nielsen, and would then present their findings to supermarket category buyers. With the advent of UPC scanning technology and personal computers, supermarket buyers now capture data instantaneously about sales in their stores, and have more information than do manufacturers. The rollout of RFID (radio frequency identification) technology allows even greater information about sales, inventory levels, product locations, and more. Information asymmetry refers to a situation where either buyers or sellers have more complete information. If buyers are in this position, their bargaining power can increase.

Threat of backward integration. Buyers may decide to simply produce the product or service that was previously being purchased from someone in the industry. Frustration with the current companies in the industry, an excess amount of buyer cash, the desire to control the whole process, ego, and a host of other factors may encourage certain buyers to integrate a business backward by developing or acquiring capacity in the industry. This is particularly true if buying organizations observe that the competitive rivals in an industry are earning attractive levels of profits and returns. This is one reason why many supermarket chains now produce and stock their own "private label" food products.

Bargaining Power of Suppliers

Similar to buyers, suppliers have the ability to exert their own power upon the competitors in an industry. This power manifests itself in price pressures, availability issues, services provided, and speed of technological advancement. Figure 4.14 presents a list of factors that can impact supplier power.

Supplier concentration. The same methods of concentration analysis are performed for supplier concentration analysis as they are for the buyer analysis. As the number of suppliers becomes more concentrated in a few businesses, the more they will be able to control the interactions between the producers and themselves. Intel and AMD, for example, have manufactured a majority of the computer chips used as the "brain" in personal computers for the past three decades. This power has allowed them to set the pricing, availability, and features available to the many manufacturers of personal computers. Several businesses have attempted to enter this business with the strong backing of the personal computer manufacturers; however their success has been limited.

Figure 4.14
Bargaining Power of Suppliers

➢Supplier concentration (vs. rivals' concentration)
➢Importance of volume to supplier
➢Switching costs of suppliers
➢Differentiation of inputs required
➢Presence of substitute inputs
➢Cost of input relative to total costs
➢Threat of forward integration

Importance of volume to supplier. As the volume of material that businesses buy from the suppliers increases, the importance of the suppliers to the businesses increases. A common theme in the business press is one of reducing the number of suppliers and forging long-term relationships with a few suppliers. While this does provide an element of control to the process, those selected suppliers are also in an increasingly powerful role relative to the company they supply.

Presence of substitute inputs. Businesses work very hard to develop their products with particular inputs going into the final product. In cases of supply disruption, raw material shortages, or supplier efforts to raise prices, the presence of effective substitutes will dampen the impact of that supplier's power. For example, though the perfect input for fueling your car as it is currently manufactured is a petroleum oil derivative, corn-based ethanol can be a powerful substitute when government subsidies make it price competitive with gasoline.

Cost of input relative to total costs. The power of suppliers is increased as the cost of the input increases relative to the total cost of the product or service produced. If the suppliers' input represents 25 percent of the value of the total product produced, then suppliers will have significantly more leverage when compared to an industry where the suppliers' part is worth only 1 percent of the final value of the product. This is especially true if substitutes for the input are not available.

Switching costs of suppliers. Once again, the cost to switch suppliers (both real and perceived) is a factor in the power of the supplier. The more companies in an industry tie their operations to certain types of supplies or highly specified inputs, the more power such suppliers have with these companies. In today's market, many companies are tying their operations very closely with select suppliers in order to get guaranteed just-in-time deliveries, advanced access to new technology, more favorable pricing, guaranteed prices, and first options on raw materials. Supplier management is a two-edged sword since the higher degree to which producers lock themselves in to suppliers, the greater leverage such suppliers will then have to exact economic concessions from the producers.

Threat of forward integration. Just as buyers have the ability to integrate backward to replace their suppliers, suppliers have the ability to integrate forward and become a competitor to the businesses that they may still supply. Honda has produced engines for many small pieces of power equipment. In addition, they now sell their own line of lawn maintenance equipment and portable generators. Similarly, Home Depot acquired one of the major plumbing supply operations in the United States. This supply business is one of the main sources from which plumbers have historically purchased items for their own business. In addition, Home Depot now offers plumbing services to its customers, thus moving into the business of the plumbers.

Intensity of Rivalry

The intensity of competition among rivals varies from industry to industry. Although we often read that many organizations believe they are in a chaotic, intense, cost-conscious, highly competitive industry, the fact remains that not all industries experience the same level of intensity. Each industry or industry subset should be evaluated with a set of criteria (Figure 4.15) that may then be used to understand the intensity of competition. Recall that it is important to first define the

Figure 4.15
Intensity of Rivalry

➤ Industry growth rate
➤ Fixed costs as % of total costs
➤ Overcapacity in industry
➤ Low product differentiation
➤ Low switching costs
➤ Informational complexity
➤ Numerous or equally balanced competition
➤ High strategic stakes
➤ Exit barriers

industry and the rivals in it; the most important rivals are those companies who are in direct competition with a company for its customers and for the same types of supplies or inputs to production. This may or may not be the entire industry as defined by the government or the popular press.

Industry growth rate. Every industry has a rate of growth that ranges from negative to explosively positive. While one might believe that either of the extremes would lead to more intense rivalry amongst competitors, the simple fact is that slowing or negative industry growth rates lead to destructive patterns of corporate behavior and dramatically increase the rivalry. Consider the U.S. automobile industry during periods of average-to-poor growth in sales. If one of the auto manufacturers wants to increase sales revenue over its previous year, in a flat or declining industry the only way to do this is to take business away from one of its competitors. In contrast, "a rising tide lifts all boats." When an industry is enjoying fast growth in revenue dollars and units shipped, then an individual company may also increase sales without necessarily having to take it from a competitor. In growth markets all companies may grow and prosper, but in a stagnant or declining market companies will become extremely aggressive in either trying to grow their business or prevent declines.

Industry capacity. The sheer capacity of the industry has a significant effect upon industry rivalry. Throughout the 1980s, many firms spent billions laying fiber optic cable in a bid to take advantage of the cutting-edge needs of an expanding Internet. Within several years the bubble burst as cable supply far outstripped demand. By 2001, utilization rates ran around 40 percent and prices dropped almost 80 percent as cable operators tried competitively low rates in order to generate enough business to pay back the investment they made in laying the fiber optics.[20] The same dynamic is true in the auto industry. Here excess plant capacity as well as fixed union contracts represent huge financial burdens. So U.S. manufacturers have repeatedly turned to intensely competitive "employee pricing" and "dealer rebate" schemes in order to generate sales and keep the plants producing and the paid union workers making cars.

Industries with too little capacity to meet the buying desires of customers will find that there is less intense rivalry relative to an industry where there is dramatic overcapacity. Where industry demand exceeds industry capacity, rivals do not need to turn to intensely competitive tactics. If we were to examine the narrow industry subsegment of electric cars, for example, we would find that consumer demand far exceeds industry supply. So in 2006 while Ford was discounting F-150 pickups trucks and General Motors was discounting Impala four-door sedans, Toyota did not discount the Prius, which sold close to MSRP (manufacturer's suggested retail price).[21] Now that Ford, GM, and others have increased manufacturing capacity to produce hybrid vehicles, the intensity of rivalry has increased in this segment.

Numerous or equally balanced rivals. Another means for evaluating the relative intensity in the industry is to examine the source of sales in the industry. A widely fragmented market with lots of competitors leads to practices that are detrimental to the success of any one company. Dry cleaners appear on many corners of populated areas in the United States. Price changes and competitive moves to differentiate oneself in this industry are quickly copied by all the other companies in the immediate area. Similarly, rivalry can become intense even in fairly concentrated industries with only a few major players, such as the personal computer manufacturing industry. Here price changes and moves to differentiate one's self are also quickly copied by competitors in an effort to maintain market share. The key point here is that relative equality among competitors - whether in a fragmented or concentrated industry environment - tends to make those competitors fight against each other to a greater extent as each seeks to develop a superior position.

Product or service differentiation. The degree of separation between the offerings of different companies has a significant impact upon the intensity of rivalry. In industries where the competitors have been able to establish a significant level of differentiation among their products, the intensity of rivalry is sharply reduced. Charlotte, North Carolina, is like so many other communities across the United States in that it has several member-only country clubs within the area. While each offers its members golf, tennis, and restaurant privileges, each has effectively carved out its own unique clientele and specialty offerings within this regional industry. There is a healthy competition among the various clubs, but the level of rivalry is quite low. In contrast, the New York City health and fitness club industry competes intensely for working professional memberships. These clubs all provide Stairmasters, elliptical equipment, free weights, Nautilus, aerobics, Pilates classes, juice bars, and socializing areas. Like dry cleaning stores, health clubs in the city are often just around the corner. Because of the similarities, therefore, each company competes very hard to acquire and retain members.

Switching costs. Similar in fashion to each of the other four competitive threats, switching costs have an impact on the intensity of rivalry. When products or services are nearly identical and switching costs to buyers are low, competitors fight fiercely to keep their existing customers and attract new customers. This leads to rivals expending significant resources in marketing, promotions, price concessions, innovation, and other costly initiatives that reduce their profitability.

Exit barriers. High costs to exit a business cause competitors to perform in ways that are often counterproductive to both company and industry performance. Exit barriers can exist in the form of fixed manufacturing plants, long-term contracts, costly infrastructure, ownership of basic inputs, governmental limitations, or specialized and unique assets, sometimes complicated by declining markets in which there are simply no buyers. Rather than write off millions of dollars of manufacturing assets, companies will often continue to operate plants at less than capacity and lose money.

However, exit barriers can also be perceived, and perceived barriers can be just as compelling. These include a long history in the industry, prior decisions or statements by senior management that would look questionable in the face of exit, nostalgia, a desire to protect a community and the employees, as well as a stubborn desire to prove that the business is still viable. The combination of real and perceived exit barriers causes competitors to fight very hard to maintain their business. Eastern Airlines fought a losing battle in a post-regulated world in the 1980s. The major airlines have extremely high fixed costs and a strong need to fill seats on each plane that takes off. As new, low-cost carriers entered the market and other established airlines were able to negotiate cost-effective contracts with their workers, Eastern suffered with a pre-deregulation high cost structure, a debilitating inability to work with their labor unions, and a series of highly publicized crashes. Despite all this, the airline continued to fly unprofitably until 1991 before it was finally forced to cease operations. High exit barriers impacted the business decisions and were a significant influencing factor in the industry.

EXTENDING INDUSTRY ANALYSIS

Conclusions on Industry

Having gone carefully through the five forces, and having considered driving forces from the external environment, it is now possible to draw together some conclusions from those observations and to put those conclusions to practical use. Recall that there are two types of conclusions that should be drawn from this analysis: 1) the attractiveness of the industry, and 2) the identification of key success factors.

Industry attractiveness. Each of the five forces will exert influence on an industry that either enhances or detracts from the potential for any individual company to earn above-average profits. Summarizing the effect of all of the five forces at one time provides a clearer picture of the industry. The "Five-Forces Analysis Checklist" in Figure 4.16 provides a convenient means to create this summary. Every factor within each of the five forces should be evaluated with an indication as to whether the effect of the factor is strong or weak on that force in the industry being evaluated. Having profiled each of the factors, this checklist provides a summary for making an informed judgment about how each of the five forces affects potential profitability in the industry. Developing judgments about the impact of each of the five forces allows for drawing conclusions about the attractiveness of the industry as a whole. The industry appears attractive when the five forces work in a way that helps to insulate the profit-making potential of the business. It looks much less attractive when the five forces in combination indicate that potential profits for the rivals in the industry are being siphoned off to suppliers, buyers, new entrants, and substitutes, or possibly because the

Figure 4.16 Five Forces Analysis Checklist		
	Strong	Weak
Threat of new entrants is low when		
Capital requirements	★	
Economies of scale	★	
Absolute cost advantages	★	
Access to inputs		★
Access to distribution		★
Need for differentiation	★	
Switching costs for buyers	★	
Government regulation	★	
Expected retaliation	★	
Threat of substitutes is low when		
Relative price/performance		★
Switching costs of buyers	★	
Buyer bargaining power is low when		
Buyer concentration		★
Buyer volume		★
Switching costs of buyers	★	
Buyer information		★
Availability of substitutes		★
Threat of backward integration		★
Supplier bargaining power is low when		
Supplier concentration		★
Importance of volume to supplier		★
Presence of substitute inputs		★
Differentiation of inputs required		★
Cost of input relative to total costs		★
Switching costs of suppliers	★	
Threat of forward integration		★
Intensity of rivalry is low when		
Industry growth rate	★	
Overcapacity in industry		★
Fixed costs as % of total costs		★
Product differentiation	★	
Informational complexity	★	
Switching costs of buyers	★	
Numerous or equally balanced competitors		★
Strategic stakes		★
Exit barriers		★

intense rivalry among competitors causes all of the companies in the industry to spend at higher levels and commit additional resources in order to compete (Figure 4.17).

Figure 4.17 Potential to earn superior returns in industry		
Five Forces	**Good Potential**	**Poor Potential**
Threat of new entrants	Low	High
Threat of substitutes	Low	High
Bargaining power of buyers	Low	High
Bargaining power of suppliers	Low	High
Intensity of rivalry	Low	High

Key success factors. We mentioned earlier in this chapter that key success factors (KSFs) are like the "rules" of the industry; they indicate the kinds of activities that every company needs to focus on in order to succeed. Unlike external driving forces, which affect an entire industry and which no company can impact, the KSF-related activities are critical dimensions that companies can affect through their strategic investments. The extent to which companies pay attention to KSFs and succeed in addressing them will distinguish the winners from the losers in an industry.

Every industry will have its own unique set of KSFs, and in each industry there are likely to be no more than four to six such factors. While there are a vast number of competitive factors within any industry, KSFs are those that are the most critical to success. Because the KSFs are a "short list," it is important to understand that not every company in an industry will be forced to compete in exactly the same way in order to succeed. In fact, one of the most challenging and interesting aspects of strategic management is that strategic variety not only exists within most industries, but also that there is equifinality – the idea that there are many means to achieve success. That is, despite the fact that there are only a limited number of KSFs, companies compete quite successfully for industry profits in many different ways. KSFs provide guidance for being strategically competitive, but do not dictate specific actions that companies must take. In ancient history it used to be said that "all roads lead to Rome." Here in the twenty-first century, the roads are the KSFs: they guide companies to the destination of superior performance. Companies vary in the roads they may take, the chariots and horses they use, the training of the charioteers, and the speed or deliberation in their journeys.

Having conducted a five-forces analysis, identifying KSFs becomes a more straightforward exercise. There are two key questions to answer in this identification process (Figure 4.18):

1. *How is value created for customers in this industry?* In the five-forces analysis we considered the conditions under which customer bargaining power is increased, with the result being that customer power may actually diminish the profitability of competitors in the industry. Though the power of customers in the industry can negatively impact industry profitability, it is important to remember that customers are the fundamental source of revenue and profit for companies. Customers in any industry will prize certain product or service features and

characteristics over others. They will also value a certain type of relationship with a company that provides them with products or services. Carefully defining the values that are most appreciated by customers will lead a company to take actions to deliver those critical values. Earlier, for example, we mentioned that consumers increasingly demand that cutting-edge technology be incorporated into the PCs and laptops they use. To deliver on this value, PC and laptop manufacturers must engage in continuous innovation. In the fast food business consumers value convenience, which has led companies like McDonald's and Burger King to develop expertise in real estate site selection for the new restaurants in order to ensure that each new restaurant is centrally located and easily accessible to their customers.

Figure 4.18
Identifying Key Success Factors

2. *How must we compete against rivals to succeed? What are the critical dimensions of rivalry that enable a company to successfully compete in delivering values to customers?* This question should be addressed as a multifaceted problem to be solved with the best combination of approaches. What is it that the company will have to do in order to compete effectively and survive in the industry? The other way to phrase the question is "what are the factors that will cause the company to fail if we do not attend to them?" Five-forces analysis goes a long way toward addressing these questions. The threat of new entrants often prompts existing competitors to either create or increase economic barriers to entry or to establish stronger brand reputations that will differentiate their products. This might lead existing competitors to build larger manufacturing facilities or to increase the amount they spend on advertising and image development. The pressure on costs from suppliers as well as on prices from buyers, and potential substitutes, generally causes companies to seek ways to develop a low cost structure so that they can offer more competitive pricing.

Answering these questions completely often requires a process of thinking through the reasons that lie beneath the surface dimensions that might be initially identified. We have already noted that in the PC industry customers value the opportunity to shop for cutting-edge technology, which in turn means that PC manufacturers must focus on innovation as a fundamental KSF. However, the customer desire for innovation is balanced by the desire to have technology that is also manufactured around a commonly accepted standard. Standardized product offerings allow customers to comparison shop more easily among competing models, instill confidence that the technology will work well, and ensure the customer that the product can be repaired easily if something goes wrong. There are two implications derived from the parallel need for innovation and standardization in the PC industry. First, companies must find ways to produce standardized models inexpensively, because their competitors will be producing to the same standards, and price competition will likely be fierce. This suggests that cost management is an important KSF in this industry. Second, companies must seek to move their models incorporating new technology standards into the marketplace quickly, suggesting that speed to market is also a KSF.

Changes in key success factors. By answering the two questions posed earlier, we should be able to identify a short list of KSFs for any industry. Before moving on, however, we want to re-emphasize that industries change over time. Therefore the important KSFs might also change. This is especially true as an industry matures and its growth rate of new customers or revenues begins to flatten out, or as the presence of viable substitutes becomes increasingly important. The U.S. automobile industry has seen a continuous evolution of KSFs over the last seventy-five years, moving from purely low cost and basic functionality, to style and design, to quality and performance, and now to economic performance. General Motors and its unionized workforce remained so mired in a model of business dating back to the 1960s and 1970s that the company failed to recognize a fundamental shift in the kinds of KSFs that were emerging in the 1980s and 1990s. Poor anticipation of major shifts that generate new sets of KSFs led many of the U.S. automakers into "critical condition" during the mid-2000s. General Motors was forced into cutting jobs and costs, was forced into a government-mandated bailout, and then went through bankruptcy.[22] Therefore, the ability to identify changing and emerging KSFs helps a company to better anticipate possible threats to its existing business.

By the same token, a company can identify new opportunities through its efforts to better anticipate the changes in KSFs that its industry will be experiencing. Recall that in Chapter 1 we discussed "opportunity recognition" as one of two key strategic imperatives. By answering slightly reworded questions in Figure 4.18, a company can potentially develop insight about new opportunities before its competitors do. The questions now become "what kinds of value should be created for customers in the future?" and "how will we need to compete against rivals to succeed?" Companies that develop regular activities and routines to constantly ask and answer these questions can do a better job of scoping out significant opportunities and threats. We will have much more to say about threats, opportunities, and activities in the next chapter.

Competitive KSF Analysis

Identifying key success factors that are currently important in the industry is an important step that allows for the evaluation of each primary competitor along each KSF dimension. This is best completed by looking at how well each primary competitor addresses the KSFs that distinguish between success and failure in the industry. A comparison of competitors on each KSF dimension highlights the relative positions of strength in the marketplace. This is important on many levels, not the least of which is that companies need to be careful about making strategic moves that attack a competitor's position of strength. You will recall from Chapter 1, where we paraphrased lessons from the ancient writings of Sun Tzu, that this was one of the lessons he taught. Attacking the strength of a competitor is an attempt to win based upon the competitor's strengths and experience rather than based upon the unique capabilities of the company doing the attacking. Comparative analysis also reveals relative positions of weakness in the marketplace and thus reveals possible areas of exploitation through strategic moves. This sort of comparative analysis was central to Sun Tzu's beliefs about how to succeed.

The goal of a competitive KSF analysis is to produce a table that resembles that in Figure 4.19. Here the KSFs we have just identified are listed across the top, and the chief competitors in the industry are listed down the side. This type of analysis requires us to evaluate the strength or competency of each firm on each of the KSFs. In evaluating each firm it is important not to "guesstimate" or simply "eyeball" how well or how poorly the competitor does on a particular dimension. This analysis should be based on hard facts and data, not simply upon opinions and subjective evaluations. Since the KSFs are the critical dimensions that distinguish success from failure in the industry, basing strategic decisions on factual evidence will be

Figure 4.19
Competitive KSF analysis table

	Key Success Factors			
	KSF #1	KSF #2	KSF #3	KSF #4
Firm A				
Firm B				
Firm C				
Firm D				

particularly helpful. In contrast, basing important strategic decisions on estimates and opinions may lead a company to under or over-estimate a particular competitor.

Here is an illustration. We have referred to the PC manufacturing industry several times in providing examples for aspects of industry analysis. We have suggested that innovation is a KSF in this industry. The question, then, is how innovative are competitors in this industry? We need to measure innovation somehow, and there are several ways we might consider:

- Dollars of R&D spending each year

- R&D spending as a percentage of revenue

- Number of new models introduced each year

- Degree of improvement in performance characteristics of new models

Dollars spent on research and development (R&D) each year is an industry standard means of assessing the level of commitment that companies are putting into discovery and innovation. However, there is a wide variation in size, with some companies (e.g., Apple) being significantly larger than other companies competing in this industry, and therefore simply having more dollars available to spend on discovery. In fact, during 2015 Apple spent $8.1 billion on R&D, while HP spent only $3.5 billion. It looks like Apple is outspending HP by a ratio of over 2-to-1. Another way of evaluating innovation, therefore, is to "common-size" R&D spending by looking at it as a percentage of sales revenue. A different picture emerges: during 2015 Apple spent 3.5 percent of sales on R&D, and HP spent 3.4 percent – so the relative difference is not as great. It is likely that the R&D spending for each company is spread across multiple product lines – computers, iPhones, iPads and Apple Watch for Apple; HP is focused on computers, printers, and servers. However, we are particularly concerned with how innovation impacts the PC industry. So perhaps a more salient metric to evaluate – and one that would be more relevant for customers like Best Buy or for competitors – is how many new PC models each firm introduces in a given period of time. While R&D information is generally available on the Internet by accessing an annual report, data on models introduced are not. These are data that require careful investigation to obtain, such as interviewing purchasing managers at Best Buy or finding and reviewing historical price lists of the companies. However, in the PC industry Dell and HP are significantly larger than Apple or Asus. One might expect that larger companies with broader lines would tend to introduce a larger number of new models during any given period. Therefore, a fourth possible measure for innovation is one of relative degree, that is, how much have new models improved in computing performance over existing models? Here one might examine specific operating characteristics of new PCs such as increases in speed, capacity, or size relative to power.

This brief discussion illustrates that selecting the best metrics to evaluate companies on KSF dimensions involves choosing among a range of options. While there is no one best set of metrics, each tends to lead the company to a slightly different conclusion. The best choices will usually be the type of measurement techniques that best align the needs and desires of the core customers with the resources and capabilities of the company.

Strategy Maps and Strategic Groups

We can take the analysis of competition one step further by using KSFs to provide greater insight on strategic positions within an industry. "Mapping" the position of competitors in an industry allows for the identification of important strategic groups. A strategic group is a collection of companies that tend to behave in relatively the same way strategically because they are making investments on the same subsets of KSFs. They therefore occupy positions in an industry that are close enough to each other that they become primary competitors with each other. A competitive KSF analysis (Figure 4.19) can help identify companies that are very similar to each other on key competitive dimensions. However, a strategy map is a visual tool that takes this one step further by revealing competitors' relative positions and competitive advantages. A strategy map is created by using a pair of the identified KSFs as axes in a graph, and then plotting the companies on the graph according to their measures for each of the KSFs.

Constructing strategy maps. Let's use the PC manufacturing industry once again to illustrate the creation of strategic maps and the identification of strategic groups. There are several steps in the process:

1. Identify the KSFs in the industry and, as objectively as possible, measure each competitor on these dimensions. Earlier, for instance, we identified that two of the KSFs in the industry are innovation and low-cost manufacturing. Choose two of the KSFs and plot the competitors in the industry in a graph using these dimensions as the axes (Figure 4.20). By convention we put the "desirable" condition for each KSF toward the outer end of each axis. So in this case "Low" for Unit Cost (one objective measurement of the Low Cost KSF) is toward the right end of the horizontal axis, and "high" for Innovation is toward the top of the vertical axis. This makes the upper-right portion of each graph the most desirable part of the graph to be, in this case low unit cost and highly innovative. Note that no company currently occupies that position in "strategic space." It can be seen that Dell has pushed the frontier of low-cost production with an average level of innovation, while Apple is significantly higher on the innovation dimension but less advanced in unit cost manufacturing.

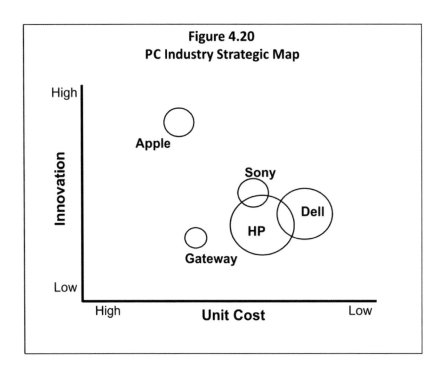

Figure 4.20
PC Industry Strategic Map

2. At the point where competitors are located on the graph, draw circles for each competitor. The size of the circle should represent the relative size of the competitor, in either market share of the industry or annual revenue. In Figure 4.20, for instance, PC manufacturers are represented by circles whose size approximates market share for each company; thus HP is slightly larger than Dell and four to five times the size of Apple.

3. Assess the presence of strategic groups. In this example, Sony, Dell, and HP make up a strategic group because they are extremely close to each other on these two critical strategic dimensions in the industry. Dell and Sony should be most concerned about the way in which HP will be competing in the marketplace, because HP tends to create value for customers in much the same way and represents a greater threat to take business away from them. So HP is the competitor that threatens them the most. Dell would be much less concerned about Apple, who appears to compete more on the dimension of innovation and less on the cost/price dimension.

4. Use other combinations of KSFs to draw additional maps. With four KSFs identified in an industry, there will be six possible graphs to draw using combinations of any two KSFs. Other graph combinations can also be revealing about industry competition. In the PC industry a graph showing Unit Cost versus Speed to Market might also portray a strategic group made up of Sony, Dell, and HP. This finding should elevate the attention paid by any one of those competitors to the other two, because it reinforces the relationship seen in Figure 4.20.

5. Make sure that KSFs provide unique information. Sometimes industry KSFs turn out to be highly correlated with each other. Figure 4.21 is a strategic map of the fast food industry in which Food Quality and Low Costs were previously identified as KSFs. The alignment of all the companies along the downward sloping diagonal indicates that there is a high degree of correlation between food quality and unit costs: the lower the unit costs, the lower the food

139

quality. Therefore the addition of Food Quality to the list of industry KSFs does not impart any new information that is not already captured by the Low Cost KSF. If Food Quality similarly aligns with other KSFs identified in the industry analysis, then it should be removed from the list of KSFs, because it does not distinguish between success and failure any better than the other KSFs do.

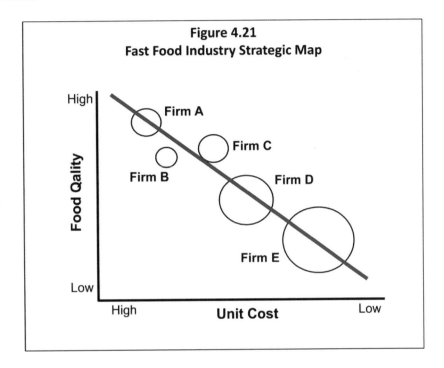

Identifying strategic trajectories. Another advantage of strategy maps is that they can be used to illustrate the trajectories of strategy development that have occurred in an industry. A single strategy map is similar to a photo: it is a static view that is a representation of the industry at a defined point in time. A series of strategy maps developed over time would be like a movie, showing the dynamic character of the industry over a period of time. This type of dynamic view would help illuminate the historical trajectories that competitors have taken throughout this period of time.

Building further on the PC industry strategy map developed earlier, Figure 4.22 now provides a dynamic view of the changes in strategic position over time for two key competitors in the industry. Apple has always been an innovative company since its founding in the 1970s. A few years ago Dell was superior to Apple on the Unit Cost KSF, but was inferior to Apple on the Innovation KSF. Over time Dell has worked diligently to continue lowering its unit cost structure, and its trajectory from the past to its present-day position illustrates its accomplishments. At the same time, it has only marginally improved its Innovation position since it relies heavily upon Intel, Microsoft, and other suppliers of subassemblies for its basic PC models. In contrast, Apple has continued to push an innovation agenda, evidenced by its introduction of the iMac with Retina display, Mac Book and Mac mini, OS X, and more. Apple has also recognized the need to become more price competitive, which has caused it to make substantial improvements in its unit cost dimension. The solid arrows in Figure 4.22 illustrate the trajectories each company has followed over the last few years.

Figure 4.22
Strategic Map Trajectories Over Time

These historical trajectories are manifestations of the strategic approach each company has taken in the marketplace in order to improve its competitive position. To pursue these trajectories each company has made strategic investments in certain resources and activities that allow it to make significant progress. In Chapter 6 we will discuss in some detail the nature of these types of resource investments and how they can lead to competitive advantage. The point that should be emphasized here is that such investments are major commitments by a company and, like most strategic decisions, are not easily reversed. They are "sticky," meaning that once you build a capability for innovation, that capability will stick with you for a long period of time.

Past strategic intentions are indicators of future strategic direction. Because the strategic investments made by each company are indicative of strategic intention and are sticky, it is reasonable to expect that each company will continue to move in a similar direction. In Figure 4.22 the dotted-line arrows suggest the direction that each company will move in the near future, assuming each will continue to build on past strategic investments. Anticipating the direction in which one of your competitors will move can be extremely helpful. To achieve further reductions in unit cost, for instance, Dell can expect that Apple will be evaluating a range of strategic options that will help fulfill this intention. Since PC manufacturing costs have been well-connected with economies of scale, one option that Apple may consider would be a way to make their PCs more attractive to a wider audience. It should come as no surprise, then, that in early 2006 Apple developed its own software enabling users to run Windows and Windows-based software on its Apple computers, has expanded Apple Stores to more than 460 nationwide by 2016, and now sells its machines through Best Buy and other popular retailers.[23] This instantly makes the Apple computing platform a viable and highly-available option for tens of millions of computer users who would experience significant switching costs to give up the Windows environment in order to use an Apple.

Identifying strategic opportunities. The strategy map can also be a useful tool for identifying new opportunities for strategic distinction. In Figure 4.20 Sony appears to be

141

competing directly with both HP and Dell, two larger companies in the PC business. Direct competition seldom has positive results for smaller companies, simply because the smaller company has fewer resources at its disposal to fight the good fight (another lesson from Sun Tzu). This is one of the reasons why competitors frequently score goals in lacrosse or ice hockey when a player on a team has to sit out in the penalty box. Additional resources generally lead to higher performance. So what options are available for Sony to compete, while at the same time trying to remove itself from a battle of attrition? The map in Figure 4.20 suggests that opportunity for Sony lies in the space in the upper-right corner. The anticipated trajectories Dell and HP appear to be taking are primarily to the right, as they pursue an agenda of unit cost reductions. Therefore, Sony might consider making new strategic investments in innovation capabilities, which would create strategic separation from Dell and HP and allow them to move into a currently unoccupied part of the "strategic space."

Effect of industry definitions. Earlier in this chapter we discussed the difficulty that can arise in defining the precise boundaries of an industry. Similarly, industry boundary definitions can make a difference in how strategy maps are interpreted. Let's assume that we are conducting an industry analysis of the pizza industry, and that two of the KSFs that have been identified are Quality and Convenience. Figure 4.23 portrays a hypothetical strategy map of the industry. Pizza Hut, Domino's, and Papa John's dominate the industry and constitute a strategic

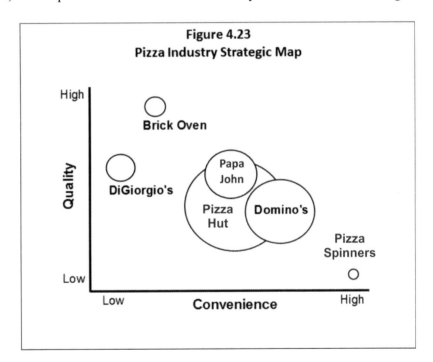

group of companies that court the consumer in much the same way. Brick Oven is a sit-down restaurant producing high quality pizzas, while Pizza Spinners is the local late-night place that students call only if everything else is closed. We also plug in DiGiorgio's Pizza, which is purchased in supermarket frozen food sections, simply to acknowledge that this brand is also a competitor of delivery and restaurant pizzas.

A broader industry definition can lead to a very different view of the main competitive strategic group. In fact, consumers often choose pizza instead of some other type of fast food, and vice versa. So if the industry analysis is broadened to account for the wider variety and values that consumers seek when they make choices, a different strategy map emerges. Figure 4.24 illustrates the strategy map when the industry definition is broadened to "fast food." In this instance we observe that McDonald's and Burger King have been added to the map, and they appear to compete for the consumer in precisely the same manner as do the delivery pizza restaurants. Consequently, Domino's must worry about not only the competitive efforts of Papa John's in producing moderate quality pizzas and delivering them in a timely fashion. They must also worry about McDonald's efforts to deliver the same values to consumers – convenience and moderate quality – available through their drive-up windows. Presumably the broader definition of the industry would also have implications for relative strengths on other KSFs, such as Price/Value.

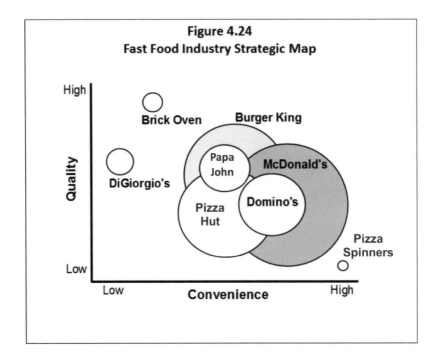

Figure 4.24
Fast Food Industry Strategic Map

CHAPTER SUMMARY

Industry analysis is a tool that provides objective evaluation of where an industry stands on a continuum that ranges from a perfectly competitive market to one that is a monopoly. In perfectly competitive markets (which are rare), it is difficult for any company to earn superior profits. Imperfect markets are characterized by the potential to sustain differences between companies, which can lead to superior profits. The examination of five structural forces of an industry provides insight on the extent to which there is potential for companies to earn profits. These forces include the threat of new entrants, threat of substitutes, bargaining power of buyers, bargaining power of suppliers, and the intensity of rivalry among competitors. The stronger each of these forces is, the lower the potential for the target company to earn superior returns.

Through industry analysis, inferences may be drawn about the critical strategic dimensions of competition that distinguish between successful and unsuccessful companies. These are referred to as key success factors (KSFs). KSFs can be used to evaluate the relative strengths and weaknesses of competitors in the industry as well as to construct visual strategy maps, which may reveal groups of companies that compete in very similar ways.

Industry analysis involves the following steps:

1. Define the industry of interest. Narrow industry definitions involve companies whose inputs are very similar, whose geographic markets are similar, and whose customers are very similar.

2. Examine the general environment for driving forces that will affect the industry and every company in it. These forces include social, technological, economic, environmental, political/legal, and global forces.

3. Examine the five forces in the industry to understand how the structure of the industry affects the potential to earn profits. Each force is evaluated through a series of characteristics that will indicate whether profits for competitors are insulated or may be drawn off.

4. Complete the five-forces analysis checklist. Draw conclusions about the attractiveness of the industry for earning profits.

5. Identify key success factors by answering two pivotal questions: 1) how is value created for customers; and 2) how must we compete in order to succeed?

6. Determine the appropriate way to measure companies in the industry on each of the KSFs.

7. Complete the competitive KSF analysis table, in order to easily compare companies on the KSF dimensions.

8. Draw strategy maps using paired combinations of KSFs. Identify strategic groups of closely competing companies. Identify historical trajectories of competitors, as well as anticipated direction of future development.

9. Change the industry definition used, and re-examine KSFs and strategy maps for new insights on the nature of competition.

10. Anticipate how KSFs in the industry might change in the future, based upon your earlier driving forces analysis.

Learning Objectives Review

1. Explain how the phrase "competitive advantage" is connected to company strategy and performance.

- Competitive advantage can be achieved in an industry that is not perfectly competitive, where there are differences among companies. In this environment some companies can earn higher profits than others. Strategy is about the sets of decisions and investments that result in a position of "above average profits."

2. Describe how an industry definition can affect conclusions drawn from an industry analysis.

- Different industry definitions will result in different sets of competitors, and in different key success factors.

- Broadly-defined industries usually require companies to engage in a wider variety of value-creating activities that depend on developing broad and deep resource positions. Broadly-defined industries usually encounter international competition or require international development.

- Narrowly-defined industries allow companies to focus their resource investments and efforts more carefully.

3. *Explain the impact that forces other than competition can have on company strategy and performance.*

- There are four forces internal to an industry, in addition to competition, than affect company strategy and performance: threat of new entrants, substitutes, bargaining power of suppliers, bargaining power of buyers. When any one of these four other forces is strong, it prompts incumbent competitors to spend more to develop new products or meet escalating demands, or to lower prices to remain more competitive. Each such effort reduces the profitability of incumbents.

- Customers are stolen away by new entrants and by substitute products and services, resulting in lower revenue to incumbent competitors.

- External driving forces can have either beneficial effects on an industry (e.g. increasing target population) or detrimental effects (e.g. more government regulation; technology that obsoletes products).

4. *Employ strategy mapping techniques to identify strategic groups in an industry.*

- Identify key success factors in the industry. Plot the location of competitors on a graph using objective measures for two of the KSFs.

- Draw a circle for each competitor at its plot location, where the size of the circle represents the size of the company.

- Repeat these steps using other pairs of KSFs. Identify groups of competitors that are close to each other on the sets of graphs.

5. *Explain how an industry is shaped by driving forces.*

- External driving forces can have either beneficial effects on an industry (e.g. increasing target population) or detrimental effects (e.g. more government regulation; technology that obsoletes products).

6. *Explain how dynamic changes in industries and competitive positions will impact a company's strategy.*

- Driving forces can produce changes in industries over time. This may lead to newly emerging key success factors that companies will need to invest in. External driving forces can also lead to the emergence of new industries whose products and services increasingly serve as substitutes to existing products and services.

- Understanding changes in the positions of competitors can lead companies to pay more attention to some competitors and less attention to others.

Key Terms

Concentration ratio - The percentage of market share in the industry owned by the largest firms.

Dodd-Frank - The legislative initiative enacted in 2010, following the 2008-09 economic crisis, that imposes significant new regulations on financial institutions.

Driving forces - Forces outside the control of the company, but which the company must pay attention to.

Economies of scale - Low unit costs that result from producing on a large scale.

Equifinality - There are multiple paths to achieve success.

Experience curve - Reductions in cost per unit that are achieved through the learning that occurs in cumulative production over time (in contrast to economies of scale, in which unit cost reductions are associated with volume during a fixed time interval).

Five-forces model - A model originally identified by Michael Porter as a means to examine the aspects of an industry's competitive environment. The model consists of the threat of new entrants, substitutes, suppliers, buyers, and rivalry.

Incumbent firms - Established firms in the industry.

Industry analysis - Method through which the examination of competitive determines whether an industry is attractive or unattractive, i.e. whether there is an opportunity for a company to earn above average profits.

Key success factors (KSF) - Rules of thumb for doing business in an industry that reflect the structural conditions of the industry.

Monopoly - An industry where a single firm virtually constitutes the entire industry and earns all the profits.

NAICS (North American Industry Classification System) - A U. S. government coding method to gather, track, and publish data on industries. See
(http://www.census.gov/epcd/www/naics.html).

Perfect competition - A marketplace in which there is perfect information, zero transactions costs and costless entry, so that all firms become virtually identical and no firm earns any profit.

Profit pool - Generally, the amount of profit available in the industry in a particular period of time.

Sarbanes-Oxley Act (SOX) - The legislative initiative enacted in 2002 that imposes stiff new demands on companies and their auditors to ensure that published financial statements are accurate.

Social contract - Implied relationship between businesses and the communities in which they operate.

Strategic group - A group of companies competing in the same manner.

Strategy map - A two-dimensional map showing the positions of competitors using a quantitatively defined set of criteria.

Substitutes - Products or services that perform the same function or meet the same need as the products or services in the industry under study, but which are produced using different raw materials and inputs.

Short Answer Review Questions

1. What did Adam Smith have to say about efficient markets?

2. How do key success factors (KSF) inform us about a particular market?

3. What elements help us define an industry?

4. How are NAICS codes utilized in industry analysis?

5. What criticisms do you have of the five-forces model? What does it not explain that you believe is important in competitive strategy?

6. How can we use the five-forces model to examine industries?

7. What factors help limit the entry of new competitors into an industry?

8. What are the types of absolute cost advantage, and how do they impact the five forces?

9. What are perceived switching costs?

10. Provide examples of real switching costs.

11. How do substitutes affect an industry's attractiveness? What are appropriate responses by competitors when possible substitutes emerge?

12. What are the three factors that determine how strong the threat of substitutes will be for an industry?

13. How would you explain buyer concentration?

14. In what ways do suppliers impact the attractiveness of an industry?

15. Name the elements that affect the attractiveness of an industry and explain their impact.

16. The general environment impacts industries and companies. Explain how the Internet has affected competitive rivalry and the attractiveness of the airline industry.

Group Exercises

1. Classifying a company is the first step in analyzing an industry. Take two businesses that are close to the university and use the NAICS classification system to classify them. Try to get the code as specific as possible.

a. How difficult was it to get the classification code to five digits?

b. What other businesses fall under the same classification code?

c. What insights does this classification provide you in your analysis of a particular company?

2. Take one of the businesses that you used in Exercise #1 and develop a five-forces analysis for the industry in which it competes.

a. What conclusions can you reach about the competitiveness of the industry?

b. What areas of the industry concern you most?

c. What aspects of the industry appear to provide the best opportunities for those already in the industry?

d. What conclusions have you reached about the general competitiveness of this industry?

3. Take the same business for which you developed a five-forces map in Exercise #2 and create a strategic map for the industry in which it competes.

a. What conclusions can you reach about the industry's KSFs?

b. What recommendations would you provide a company that wished to enter this industry?

References

[1] Basler, R. P. (ed.). 1953. Collected works of Abraham Lincoln. Piscataway, NJ: Rutgers University Press.

[2] Smith, A. 1977. An inquiry into the nature and causes of the wealth of nations. New York: Dutton.

[3] Technically, the economists would say that the market equilibrates when the firm's marginal revenue equals its marginal cost. Since every firm is identical, this means that no firm is earning a profit. At this point there would be no inducement for firms to change what they are doing or for other firms to enter the industry.

[4] Porter, M. E. 1980. Competitive strategy. New York: Free Press.

[5] Goodman, R. A., and M. W. Lawless. 1994. Technology and strategy: Conceptual models and diagnostics. New York: Oxford University Press.

[6] Chart derived from data in Porter, M. E., 2008, The Five Competitive Forces That Shape Strategy, Harvard Business Review (January), and author's additional calculations.

[7] See https://bethesda.net/.

[8] Saloner, G., A. Shepard, and J. Podolny. 2001. Strategic management. New York: John Wiley.

[9] We distinguish between profit-making and value-creating enterprises for the moment. Value-creating enterprises might include for-profit companies that produce economic value, but a broader view will include nonprofits as well because they create social value. Nonprofits also exist in industries, and compete with other firms for resources and customers.

[10] Scherer, F. M., and D. Ross. 1990. Industrial market structure and economic performance (3rd ed.). Boston: Houghton Mifflin.

[11] Lewis, P. 2004. Broadband wonderland. Fortune. September 20: 191 - 198.

[12] See http://www.census.gov/epcd/www/naics.html.

[13] See http://www.census.gov/eos/www/naics.

[14] West, G. P., III, and J. O. DeCastro. 2001. The Achilles heel of firm strategy: Resource weaknesses and distinctive inadequacies. Journal of Management Studies 38(3): 417 - 442.

[15] Pew Research Center. http://www.pewresearch.org.

[16] EPA. 2006. Cleaner small engines are safe. March 17. http://yosemite.epa.gov/opa/admpress.nsf/a8f952395381d3968525701c005e65b5/db1ecd1d6a79 3d5185257134006945e0!OpenDocument.

[17] Bonini, S. M., L. T. Mendonca, and J. M. Oppenheim. 2006. When social issues become strategic. McKinsey Quarterly (2): 20 - 32.

[18] Ries, A., and J. Trout. 2000. Positioning: The battle for your mind (3rd ed.). New York: McGraw Hill.

[19] Terhune, C. 2006. Coke attempts to paint it 'black.' Wall Street Journal. April 1: A2.

[20] Kalla, S. 2001. Fiber glut: It's real. Network Fusion News. September 10.

[21] See http://www.edmunds.com.
[22] Loomis, C. J. 2006. The tragedy of General Motors. Fortune. February 20: 59 - 75.

[23] Mossberg, W. S. 2006. Boot camp turns your Mac into a reliable Windows PC. Wall Street Journal. April 6: B1.

Chapter 5: Value Chain Analysis

LEARNING OBJECTIVES

1. Explain the differences between internal analysis and external analysis.

2. Explain the benefits and drawbacks of using SWOT analysis.

3. Describe how value is created through a firm's internal sets of activities (value chain).

4. Assess how the value chain perspective provides insight on sources of competitive advantage.

5. Perform a value chain analysis.

Xbox One Market Introduction

Competition in the $13 billion video game industry is intense. In 2005 Microsoft introduced the Xbox 360, pre-empting Sony's PS3 the following year. The earlier introduction of the Xbox was part of Microsoft's strategy in the video game market. The more machines they can sell, the more game makers will be encouraged to design their games for the Xbox game console. When more games and better games (like *Call of Duty Black Ops III* and *Star Wars: Battlefront*) are designed for a particular machine, more customers will be inclined to buy that machine. It becomes a self-reinforcing cycle. Sony was not to be pre-empted again. In 2013 it introduced the PS4 only 8 days before Microsoft's Xbox One hit the market in the U.S., and by mid-2016 has outsold the Xbox One by 86%.

Designing the Xbox One, and then producing several million consoles in a short period of time, called for the development of a unique and well-integrated value chain for Microsoft. Its design team learned from costly decisions made on the first Xbox model in 2001 and the Xbox 360. Figure 5.1 illustrates the many areas of the value chain that needed to be coordinated. They collaborated with AMD on the design of the core chip, which contains 5 billion transistors and is manufactured by a Taiwan company. The Microsoft team internally developed the Windows 10 and Microsoft cloud computing interfaces, and redeveloped the popular Kinect sensor as an optional add-on. Then the team had to think through what other components were necessary to fulfill the company's vision for this cutting-edge product, create specifications, and identify suppliers. Each Xbox console has 1,700 components produced by 250 suppliers worldwide. The components were shipped to assembly factories in China that are operated by contract manufacturers Foxconn and Flextronics. The shortage of any one component at either of the factories brings production of the Xbox to a screeching halt. Each factory pushed out tens of thousands of consoles each day, in order to meet the company's sales objectives.

Once produced, the machines were shipped to Hong Kong and then packed into containers for transoceanic shipping bound for three international ports. The Xbox Ones bound for the United States entered through Long Beach, California, and were then routed through a central distribution facility in Memphis. At that point they were loaded onto freight trains and semi-trucks, which delivered the products to large retailers.

The Xbox One introduction was a volatile event at the year-end holiday season, for both Microsoft and the industry. To ensure an uninterrupted supply the company had to forecast anticipated demand. Despite their advance planning they sold out in some stores, forcing the company to revise production and shipping plans on the fly. Sony and Nintendo both amped up their holiday advertising and promotions in order to remain competitive.

Figure 5.1
Xbox One Value Chain

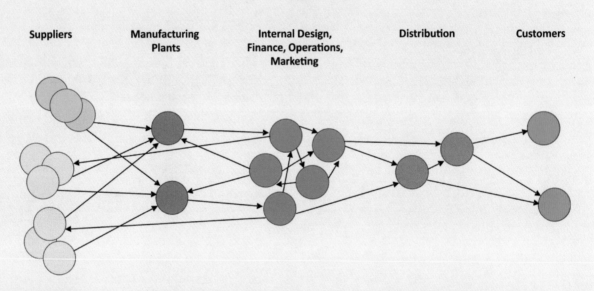

QUESTIONS

1. What is it about the Xbox One console that provides competitive advantage for Microsoft?

2. What activities does Microsoft's perform particularly well, and how do they affect the company's venture into the gaming industry?

3. What is it that Microsoft does that competitors cannot imitate very easily?

Value Creation in the Travel Agency Industry

Less than twenty years ago, the travel agency industry was a vibrant, fast-growing industry. The large "baby boom" generation was aging into peak traveling years, and their growing disposable income allowed them to travel more often than their parents did. Travel agencies reaped the advantage of these trends, since airlines sold tickets only over the phone, and complicated trip planning services were not available elsewhere.

The advent of technology and the internet changed how value is created in this industry. Whereas previously the travel agency was the primary intermediary between the airlines and customers, now both airlines and online travel agencies (such as Expedia and Priceline) can reach customers both effectively and efficiently. Figure 5.2 illustrates the new value chain in the industry. For incremental costs far lower than what travel agencies used to charge in commissions, airlines and online travel sites can book and deliver airline tickets much faster.

By 2000 e-tickets already accounted for over 60 percent of all airline ticket volume, and online travel sales had risen from $400 million to over $15 billion. Since travel agencies had previously booked 67 percent of domestic airline travel and 80 percent of international airline travel, these new developments had dire implications for the industry. Between 1997 and 2002 the number of U.S. travel agencies declined from over 29,000 to under 22,000, and employment in the industry dropped from 183,000 to 147,000. By 2016 only 84,000 people worked for these agencies.

Figure 5.2
Travel Agency Value Chain

But a funny thing happened on the way to this new marketplace. Although the airline companies had expected to reap significantly greater profits from using the internet to directly connect purchasers to their own websites, intermediary companies that handle computerized reservations for the airlines create and capture the greatest value in this process. These companies work in between travel agencies and the airlines, charging an airline a $12 fee for handling a round trip reservation and passing on only a small portion to travel agencies. In 2012 these middlemen organizations (Sabre, Amadeus, Galileo, etc.) earned $7 billion in fees, while the airline industry only earned $3 billion in net profits.[1]

QUESTIONS

1. If your family owned and operated a travel agency business, what initiatives would you recommend that they undertake in order to survive and grow?

2. How is value created by online services compared to the airlines' own ticketing operations?

3. What are airlines best at doing? Should the airlines even engage in ticket distribution?

INTERNAL ANALYSIS VERSUS EXTERNAL ANALYSIS

In the last chapter we had a chance to explore the impact of industry structure on the strategies of firms and their ability to earn profits. Out of the analysis of the five industry forces, we are able to draw conclusions about key success factors and driving forces. These factors and forces partially determine how firms must act if they are to succeed. Key success factors can also be used to plot the locations of competitors on a strategic map, determine if there are groups of companies that seek to compete in similar ways, provide insight on the trajectories that companies are following strategically, and identify both potential threats and opportunities.

Figure 5.3
Pharmaceutical Company Return on Assets, Average of 2003-2007

Despite the insight gained about competitors and firm strategy through industry analysis, understanding strategy requires us to go to a much deeper level. As you may recall from Chapter 4, different industries exhibit very different levels of profitability. Industry analysis helps us understand why some industries tend to be more profitable than others. However, this is only part of the picture. The pharmaceutical industry enjoyed one of the highest average levels of returns between 1988 and 2008. However, we see in Figure 5.3 that there is tremendous variation in the performance of companies within this one industry. Usana (which manufactures drug-related products) earned stellar returns, GlaxoSmithKline and J&J earned strong returns, while Boston Scientific and Schering earned far below the average for the industry. Figure 5.4 demonstrates that variations in performance also hold true in a super-competitive industry characterized by low returns, such as the passenger airline industry.

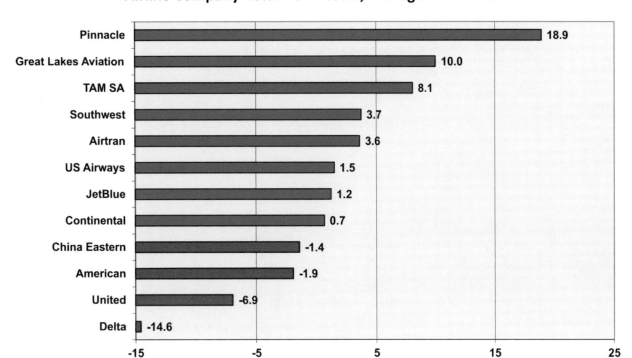

Figure 5.4
Airline Company Return on Assets, Average of 2003-2007

Sophisticated strategy research has demonstrated that industry structure and conditions can explain only a small portion of the variance in the performance of firms within an industry.[2] In fact, only about 20 percent of the differences in performance among firms within an industry can be explained using the tools of industry analysis. While that insight is critical and important as a starting point for strategy analysis and planning efforts, it is simply not enough! As strategic managers we need to develop more than 1-in-5 odds of understanding the marketplace. Much more of the performance differences between companies in an industry can be understood by looking *inside* the companies to examine what they do, what they fail to do, and how they operate. Through "internal analysis" of companies it is possible to gain much greater insight into the sources of competitive advantage that enable them to occupy leading (or lagging) positions in an industry, and to better understand what strategic paths they will follow based on their activities and resource investments. This can be accomplished by delving deeply into companies in order to better answer the key questions we posed in Chapter 1: why do some firms perform better than others, and why are those differences sustainable over a long period of time? It's to the internal analysis of firms that we now turn our attention.

There are three basic methods for conducting an internal analysis that will provide insight into a company's strategic potential: resource-based analysis, SWOT analysis, and value chain analysis. Resource-based analysis is a very popular topic among many strategy professors and professionals, and it deserves separate focus as a technique. The next chapter of this book (Chapter 6) takes up resource-based analysis, primarily because it builds upon ideas in this chapter about the value chain.

The focus of this chapter is on SWOT and value chain. There is a big distinction between these two internal analysis methods. SWOT provides a snapshot of what a company *is*, while the value chain provides perspective on what a company *does*. When asked what music you are listening to today, you share information that is both momentary and dependent upon your mood that day. That music choice describes you at a point in time, just as a SWOT approach attempts to summarize the perception of a company's situation at the moment. When we look at your playlist we can see how many times you listen to a particular song and get a pretty good perspective on the type of music you listen to the most over time. It is the patterns of behavior over time, which lead to your present state and suggest a future path of development, that the Value Chain idea seeks to capture. So you might think about the differences between the methods like the differences between a photograph and a movie: SWOT is a static view of a company at a point in time, and value chain is a dynamic view over time. Each has its uses and benefits, but each also has inherent drawbacks.

SWOT

There is hardly a firm of any size or age that is not familiar with the concept of SWOT, and it is important for you to be familiar with it as well. SWOT consists of four categories: strengths, weaknesses, opportunities, and threats. SWOT analysis has been taught in business schools for nearly forty years. Almost without exception, every large corporation will go through an annual or biannual strategic planning process. SWOT analysis is on the front end of that process in nearly every case. Like fireworks on the 4th of July, it is a familiar – and therefore comfortable – process to anyone involved in strategic planning. As testimony to its ubiquitous nature, a simple Google search for the term "SWOT" turns up almost 18 million hits! Wow!

Strategy Acronym: SWOT	
S	Strengths
W	Weaknesses
O	Opportunities
T	Threats

SWOT is usually conducted by a team. Several individuals representing various functions in a company will convene to discuss and agree upon the strengths and weaknesses inherent in their company, and to identify the opportunities and threats that the company faces. The initial conversations are designed to identify these characteristics and can happen at different levels of management. Sometimes senior management will participate, while in other circumstances a middle management team will do the initial work and then present their ideas to senior management for approval. The result of a SWOT analysis is usually a list of factors that the team agrees on as being most important for management to consider as a very early first step in the formulation and adjustment of their strategic plans.

Strengths and weaknesses are ordinarily thought of as characteristics of the company, while opportunities or threats are ordinarily construed as either elements of the competitive environment or outside factors, such as the driving forces discussed in the last chapter. In fact, the output of the KSF analysis and strategic mapping exercises done in an industry and competitive analysis (Chapter 4) can be an important input into the process of identifying areas of potential threat (e.g., encroaching competitors on a particular KSF or in a strategic group) and opportunity (e.g., uncontested space in a strategy map). Figure 5.5 shows a typical SWOT analysis, in this case for a manufacturing company that is creating a website to sell directly to its end users.

Figure 5.5
Manufacturing Company SWOT Analysis

Strengths	Opportunities
• Product quality and reliability. • Superior product performance. • Flexible manufacturing capacity. • Staff with end-user experience & perspective. • Possess lists of heavy-user customers. • Strong innovation capability for new products. • Achieved superior industry certifications. • Good information systems support. • Experienced management team.	• New products desired by customers. • Few competitors in international markets. • Suppliers are generally unhappy with manufacturers. • New Capabilities enabled by advances in technology.
Weaknesses	**Threats**
• Customer service unproven. • Products do not cover full range. • Small size relative to competition. • No direct marketing experience. • Limited distribution capacity for all markets. • Sales force thin. • Limited access to outside financing. • Poor long term planning; greatest attention on short term needs	• Pending legislation on safety and standards. • Unclear if recent market growth reflects fad or long term trend. • Possible cannibalizing core business. • Retention of management and staff. • Vulnerable to reactive attack by major competitors.

SWOT Benefits

Easy to understand and use. One of several benefits that arise to companies that use SWOT analysis is that it is a fairly simplistic method of internal analysis that nearly everyone can understand with little formal training. For this reason it is easy for management to involve a broad cross-section of departments and employees in the process. Although companies ordinarily do not extend SWOT involvement to the lowest levels of a company's hierarchy – such as production line workers, salespeople, and customer service reps – the simplicity of the method does at least offer this potential. This may actually be a missed opportunity for many companies because these employees on the "firing line" are often the first to observe how well or how poorly certain company initiatives are faring, or how customers might react. Therefore they tend to have early, first-hand knowledge about potential strengths and weaknesses.

Alignment. Matching up items that are identified in a SWOT analysis can be helpful in determining whether a company is prepared for and properly aligned to deal with looming threats and opportunities. Here the management team compares each of the elements with the other three to make judgments of the following kinds:

- Will our strengths play into emerging opportunities?
- Are there emerging threats that might marginalize our existing strengths?
- Do our weaknesses seriously compromise the company, even though it has strengths?
- Can our strengths overcome looming threats?

As an illustration, let's take a brief look at 3M. 3M is widely recognized as being an innovative company, a success story they have created because they have institutionalized innovation throughout their business practices. Reflecting its "primary and defining strategy of organic growth through innovation,"[3] the company has a stated goal that it seeks to develop 40 percent of its sales from new products introduced within the last four years. In fact, they encourage all employees to take 15 percent of their time – nearly one full day each work week – to experiment with new ideas. So innovation has become a virtue for the company, but it has implications for the nature of opportunities they are realistically able to pursue. In 2015 the company achieved over $30 billion in worldwide revenue. So achieving the 40 percent new business goal sets a target of $12 billion in revenue per year over the next four years from products that do not exist today. This is larger than the annual revenue of more than half the companies in the S&P 500! With this goal in mind, 3M can pursue only large business opportunities. Smaller opportunities (like the original Post-It

Notes product line) are likely to be passed over, because the company would need to start up dozens and dozens of such smaller businesses in order to reach their revenue goals. This example illustrates that matching strength to opportunity can reveal appropriate development direction.

Suggests overall direction. Occasionally management teams will use the matching process to develop overall guidance for the direction of the company. This is accomplished through the use of a TOWS matrix (which is a great strategy acronym, but in this case does not stand for anything except SWOT spelled backwards!). Figure 5.6 shows a TOWS matrix that provides general guidance for what direction a company might take. When new opportunities present themselves, for example, the company may decide to expend efforts to overcome existing weaknesses instead of leveraging its current strengths. If threats are looming, the company may focus greater attention on defensive actions to protect the downside from some combination of threat and apparent weakness. In the 3M example above, we saw that its large size prevented 3M from pursuing smaller new business opportunities. One possible way to overcome a weakness associated with large size would be to spin off a new product development group into a separate operation that is unconstrained by size, such as Hewlett-Packard did in the 1980s with its inkjet printer division. Freed from corporate policies and constraints, that division became very successful with new technology and by 2015, it accounted for over 20% of HP's $103 billion annual revenue.

Figure 5.6
TOWS Matrix

	Opportunities	Threats
Strengths	Use strengths to take advantage of opportunities	Use strengths to avoid threats
Weaknesses	Take advantage of opportunities by overcoming weaknesses	Defensive measures to minimize weaknesses and avoid threats

Competitive analysis. With SWOT, the management team may also begin to make comparisons between its company and competitors. This would involve a process similar to the Key Success Factor competitive comparisons discussed in the previous chapter. Having identified a list of strengths and weaknesses, the team would need to decide how to accurately measure each of its own and competitors' SWOT items using accessible data and information. In this way an objective assessment would reveal the relative strengths and weaknesses of the company versus its competition. Comparisons such as these might lead to decisions to further invest in strength-building initiatives, or to find ways to minimize areas of weakness that competitors might take advantage of.

Strong starting point. Perhaps the greatest value gained by identifying the SWOT components is that the process provides a really good starting point for in-depth discussion and analysis of company strategy and competitive position. Preparing a SWOT list is a first step to focus attention on critical components. Then management needs to engage in a deeper conversation about the nature of its business and its competitive environment.

Potential SWOT Drawbacks

Results in a laundry list. One of the key dangers in a SWOT analysis is that the list of items identified across the four categories becomes very large. This can often occur because the items on the list are usually based upon the opinions of the team members, without supporting data or critical analysis. Since teams are ordinarily composed of managers from different functions in the company, each functional area would like to see its own critical issues included in the list. Other team members may not have sufficient expertise to judge whether function-specific issues outside their areas of expertise are important enough. So inclusion tends to occur more than exclusion. The result is that a SWOT list can include an immense number of items. For instance a SWOT analysis done for the City of Burnet, Texas, produced 83 items in the four categories,[4] while an Iowa State University SWOT analysis contains 43 items.[5] Figure 5.5 shows a more typical list of items generated by a manufacturing company that is considering starting up its own website for sales directly to competitors. When the list becomes even this long, it becomes very difficult to use in practice. Try to imagine the challenge for 6-7 key team managers from different departments in a company trying to substantively address up to 25 important issues each year as part of the planning process, while at the same time taking care of their ongoing daily departmental management responsibilities.[6] With long lists it is hard to know where to focus.

Over simplification. The items that are listed in SWOT often tend to sound fairly general, lacking the kind of specificity that creates meaning. Where "new product development capability" is listed as a strength, for instance, the generality of the item tends to disguise whether this is really a successful business practice, and if so what is behind it. Is the company strong in this dimension because they are excellent at sourcing new ideas, excellent at translating ideas from concept to actual product, able to move through the process very quickly, or adept in their marketing and sales methods for introducing new products to the market? A manufacturing company in North Carolina listed "new product development capability" as one of their strengths even though sales from products introduced in the past four years accounted for less than 1% of sales. General descriptions often hide more than they reveal. In addition, the guidance provided by the use of the TOWS matrix also tends to be fairly general, not focusing on specific products, services, or operations. Finally, the method provides little guidance on the appropriate balance of effort that should be devoted to different cells in the TOWS matrix.

Definitions may vary. In many cases it is not clear to management whether a particular item represents a strength or a weakness, or perhaps both. 3M's size clearly presents a strength for the company in that size confers market power, better access to financial markets, and other advantages. However size also represents a weakness since the company is unable to pursue the smaller business opportunities that once made it successful, and is not particularly agile in responding to sudden competitive moves. If size is both a strength and a weakness simultaneously, the management implications may be difficult to determine. In the case of Apple, their CEO Steve Jobs masterminded the company's revival in the 1990s-2000s. His imagination, focus on design, and demanding management style represented a significant strength for the company. Later on he underwent treatment for pancreatic cancer at a time when there was no executive succession plan in place, and he passed away in 2011. Timothy Cook became CEO. Five years later, the marketplace is still not ready to acknowledge that Apple continues to retain the creative and imaginative ingenuity that Jobs brought to the company. Strength or weakness, or possibly both? Hard to tell.

Are they relevant? Simply because a company has a particular strength does not mean it can effectively compete in its industry. If a company's strengths or weaknesses have relevance for the key success factors in the industry, then attention devoted to them can be important. However business history is rife with examples of companies which developed amazing strengths that were incredibly irrelevant for their industries. Sharper Image, which finally went bankrupt in 2008, originally thrived on its knack and pizzazz in sourcing and presenting high-tech personal gadgets such as ion air purifiers, jogging watches, and nose hair trimmers (!). Unfortunately, the kind of creative force that was the foundation of the business became irrelevant to consumers and retailing in the 2000s.

Static view. The most discouraging part of SWOT is that the list developed during each planning cycle only provides a picture of the company at a fixed point in time. Remember that we said SWOT is like a snapshot. From one planning cycle to the next it is not uncommon to find new strengths appear and previously held strengths disappear. A company conducts its strategic planning biannually, and in successive plans has identified the strengths pictured in Figure 5.7. Items A, B, and F remain strengths consistently over this period, but C has morphed into something slightly different as C*. Meanwhile new strengths E and G have appeared and D has for some reason dropped off the list. As time goes by and companies encounter changing market conditions

**Figure 5.7
Strengths in Successive SWOT Analyses**

Year 1	Year 3
A ——————→ A
B ——————→ B
C —————→ C*
D ———————•
—————→ E
F ——————→ F
—————→ G

with evolving competition, it is not unusual to witness these kinds of changes in perceived strengths taking place. In the process of creating the list there is little attention devoted to

159

understanding why or how a company came to possess a certain strength or develop a certain weakness to begin with. Without developing an understanding of cause-and-effect, management is not provided with guidance on what kinds of steps to take going forward.

A dynamic view of a company's strategic potential is more appropriate and more useful. As strategic managers we are interested in understanding not only that strengths and weaknesses may exist, but also what it is that creates strengths and prevents weaknesses from developing, which in turn will allow us to develop competitive advantage. Do you recall the quotation from Abraham Lincoln in Chapter 1? If we understand how actions and activities undertaken in the past result in our current strategic position, then we can make better judgments about the effects that our current actions and activities will have going forward. This is the vital distinction between SWOT and the value chain perspective, to which we turn below.

The Greenbrier Resort, Part 1

The Greenbrier resort has stood in the mountains of West Virginia for more than a hundred years. Founded as a haven for those seeking the healing powers of the nearby White Sulphur Springs, the resort really came into being as more than a hotel when the C&O Railroad purchased the property in 1910. Today the enormous property has more than 700 rooms, 10 lobbies and a complete conference center. The resort boasts three championship golf courses, tennis courts, a spa, and more than 6,500 acres of land. The Greenbrier has been awarded the AAA Five Diamond status since the inception of the award and is one of only three properties to have earned this distinction for 33 consecutive years.

During good times, the resort has prospered as a destination resort for the rich and famous as well as families looking for an elegant vacation getaway. Among the more interesting features of the resort is the vast underground bunkers built to house the President and Congress in the event of a national emergency.

While not easy to travel to, one of the real appeals to the resort is its relative proximity to major cities in the eastern United States.

QUESTIONS

1. What are the Strengths and Weaknesses of the resort?

2. What are the Opportunities and Threats for the resort?

3. How would you suggest they take advantage of their Strengths and minimize their Weaknesses?

4. How would you suggest they take advantage of their Opportunities and minimize their Threats?

VALUE CHAIN

Much like SWOT, the concept of the value chain was first explored in strategic management roughly thirty years ago, when management scholars started thinking about the sets of activities that are combined by a company to form a successful "business system." The value chain provides "a systematic way of examining all the activities a firm performs and how they interact ..." in order to find a basis for competitive advantage.[7] In the first chapter of this textbook, we stressed that value creation is one of the core concepts at the heart of effective strategic management. As a method of internal analysis, exploring the value chain requires us to go significantly deeper into a company than does the SWOT approach. The basic rationale of the value chain is that some types of activities are observed when a company competes one way, while other sets of activities are observed when another company competes in a different way. Therefore through the value chain we move below summary ideas about a company's strong or weak points; instead, we examine the nature of activities performed in or by the company, and we estimate how such activities are able to uniquely create value in the industry vis-à-vis competitors.

Industry and Company Value Chains

The value chain concept recognizes that a company is one of many entities that participate in an entire chain of value-adding activity within any given industry (see Figure 5.8).

Figure 5.8
Chain of Industry Value-Adding Activities

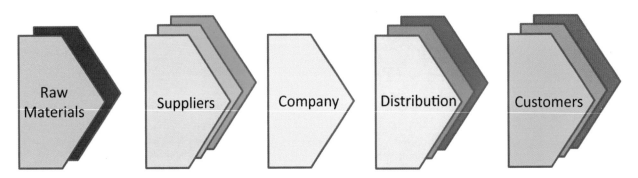

When you open up a can of soda at home, it is because a complex array of integrated activities has taken place across an industry or industries that provide you this enjoyment. The chain of activities starts with basic raw materials and extends all the way to the finished product in your hand. Consider just the can itself: from mining bauxite ore, to the smelter, to mixing aluminum with manganese and magnesium, to extruding and roll casting aluminum sheets, to cutting and forming cans, to filling them with soda on a high-speed production line (that in itself is a complicated process involving multiple parts of an industry), to packed 24-can cases loaded onto pallets and shipped in semi-trucks, and then finally distributed to your supermarket. The Xbox 360 story at the beginning of this chapter also illustrates some of the sophisticated array of activities across an industry value chain that manifests a new game console in your dorm room or apartment. The travel agency story demonstrates that an identical product or service may be provided through one of several different sets of industry-wide activities. In this case an electronic

161

airline ticket and other travel reservations can be sourced directly from an airline carrier, purchased through an online intermediary such as Expedia or Priceline, or procured through a travel agency where the traveler can meet in person with a travel consultant to discuss personal plans and preferences. Each method involves a different set of activities, but each results in a similar outcome for the traveler.

In addition to value chain activities across a single industry or multiple industries, there are value chain activities within each company competing in the industry. Although we may tend to think about competing companies in terms of the products or services that we see them providing, the value chain concept instead focuses on the different sets of activities that ultimately lead to the production of their products or services. This is the great insight about strategy that the value chain perspective provides: a company is nothing more than a set of organized activities, and that products or services are simply the outcomes of the activities that have led to their creation. When we refer to a company as an organization, occasionally we might be referring to an organization of people, such as through departmental structure and hierarchy. However, at a very foundational level a company is structured so that employees *act* in certain ways. It is their *activities* that describe how a company actually conducts its business and produces products or services.

It is relatively easy to observe examples of how different activity sets define the differences between competitors and their approaches in an industry. In the photo finishing business Kodak was known for its focus on producing high-quality paper that was used by camera shops to print pictures. With the advent of digital photography, Canon – previously known for its strengths in plain paper copiers and printers – entered the camera market and encouraged end users to print pictures on Canon printers. In response Kodak developed the Easy-Share camera-printer docking combination, and rapidly expanded its photo kiosks in drug stores and other retail locations nationwide. In book retailing the activity sets that distinguish Amazon.com from "bricks and mortar" based Barnes & Noble are quite dramatic. Figure 5.9 provides other examples that illustrate how competitors' strategic approaches are characterized by different activity sets.[8]

Figure 5.9
Company Value Chains Differ

Industry	Company & value chain activity	Company & value chain activity
Book retailing	Barnes & Noble bricks 'n mortar stores	Amazon online retailing
Business education	Harvard real professors in physical classrooms	University of Phoenix directed self-education diplomas by mail
Personal computers	Dell, HP modular design mass customization JIT manufacturing	Apple proprietary design limited model selection
Movie rental	Redbox neighborhood kiosks	Netflix access by mail & streaming
Steel	Arcelor-Mittal blast furnaces large volume from iron ore	Nucor electric arc furnaces mini-mills using scrap
Food retailing	Whole Foods exceptional quality organics & naturals	Food Lion average quality wide selection

Primary and Support Activities

Looking carefully within any company, we can differentiate between two kinds of important value-adding activities. When we mention "Toyota," most people will think of Celicas, Prius's, 4Runners and other cars and trucks; when we say "Starbucks," it calls to mind something like a "vente latte double shot no whip skim extra hot" (yikes!). When we used Priceline as an example earlier, we tend to think of the inexpensive ticket we were able to get on their website. That is, most people naturally tend to associate companies with their products and types of services. Along the bottom of the company value chain diagram in Figure 5.10 are "primary activities." These are the activities engaged in to tangibly produce the products and services that come to mind when a company's name is mentioned. If we walked into a Pepsi facility, we would expect to see these activities on the bottom of the figure taking place: ingredients and packaging materials coming in the back warehouse door, the high-speed lines queuing and filling cans, preparing the finished goods for shipping, and so on. We also regularly observe the Pepsi trucks delivering product to local stores, and we see their ads on TV with their most current "hip" pitch person.

Figure 5.10
Company Value Chain

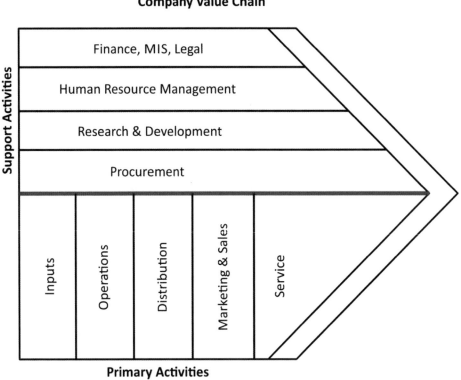

In contrast, in the top half of Figure 5.10 are what have been called "support activities." These include much of the white collar work done in companies such as finance, information systems, human resources, legal work, research and development, and purchasing efforts. When we consider any type of company and its products or services, we generally do not think too much about the people performing these so-called support functions despite the fact that those jobs are usually more coveted by new college graduates. When we step into the Pepsi plant, we are struck with the furious production activity going on before our eyes, not with what the person in the cubicle upstairs or in the corner office is working on.

163

Which type of activities – primary or support – do you think are more important from the standpoint of strategic management? One perspective on this comes from a study on employment in the United States conducted a few years ago, examining the importance of both manufacturing and service jobs in America. Whereas manufacturing jobs involve handling physical objects, service jobs involve "anything … that could not be dropped on your foot."[9] Service activities include such areas as finance, HR, purchasing, research, design, engineering, administration, and legal, even in traditional manufacturing companies. Figure 5.11 reproduces the results of this study.[10] In a dramatic shift from earlier in the twentieth century, by the beginning of the next century the manufacturing activities constituted less than 20 percent of U.S. employment while service activities represented more than 75 percent. Service activities, which include primarily all the activities in the top half of the company value chain in

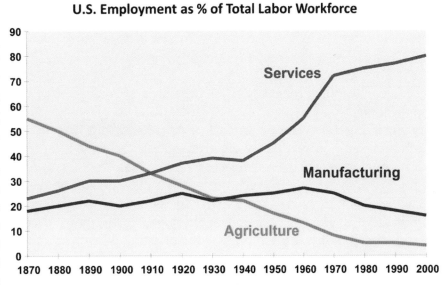

Figure 5.11
U.S. Employment as % of Total Labor Workforce

Figure 5.10, are where employment is concentrated. Here, and in the coordination that must occur between support activities and primary activities, is where significant strategic value is truly added.[11]

Value Chain Benefits

Illustrates derivation of strengths and weaknesses. We pointed out earlier that the list of strengths and weaknesses is likely to change over time, but that SWOT does not substantively explore the reasons behind such changes. The value chain perspective can answer these questions because it is the activities that a company undertakes that lead to positions of superiority (strength) or contribute to positions of weakness. Examining the activities therefore focuses attention on the causes of internal strengths and weaknesses. For example, "we are particularly strong in new products because of how well our marketing research and R&D staff works together to move new ideas rapidly into development and production."

Dynamic. One of the most important differences from SWOT is that the value chain approach focuses more on what a company does, not what a company is. Consistent with the idea of a business system, the activities that take place within companies are often organized and systemized ways of conducting affairs. When companies are successful, like a well-oiled machine they seek to reproduce and fine-tune on an ongoing basis the actions they took that made them successful. For these reasons the actions that lead to success tend to persist over periods of time. If companies are not successful, then they try to change the ways they conduct business in order to find more effective methods. When weaknesses that have developed remain stubbornly persistent, it is likely that a company's actions are perpetuating them. So a focus on the activities,

164

which reflect patterns of behavior over a period of time, has a dynamic quality to it that the static SWOT approach invariably misses.

More predictable path of development. When the analysis focuses on how patterns of activities result in performance, it becomes much easier to predict - at least in the near term – what future developments will take place for a company. If it is true that examining activities helps develop a cause-and-effect understanding of successes and failures, then that same logic can be used productively to look ahead. Since managing strategically involves setting goals and objectives for the future, an understanding of the effects of actions and behaviors can guide goal setting. This understanding can also reveal gaps that exist between goals that have been set and the predicted results of activities the company currently engages in.

Spotlights internal synchronization and consistency of effort. One of the hallmarks of strategic decisions discussed in Chapter 1 is that they significantly affect all parts of the organization. Coordination across departments and functional areas (marketing, finance, operations, etc.) is integral to effective strategic management. While many activities highlighted in a value chain analysis will occur within these functional areas, the value chain explicitly recognizes the need to coordinate with other departments, so that the company accomplishes the required level of cross-department integration and consistency of effort in its approach to competitive markets. Therefore identifying and managing the coordinating activities become extremely important. This important dimension will be further discussed in the next section.

Provides more actionable information for managing strategy. With attention on the day-to-day activities as the means to understand how competitive strengths are developed, it should come as no surprise that value chain analysis can be very useful as a tool of management. Since the analysis has drilled down to the level of actions that departments and people take, decisions to enhance strengths or correct weaknesses can focus on specific activities. By breaking down a conceptual strength (such as "new product development capability") into specific sets of activities that lead to this competitive advantage, management has more actionable information that can guide investments made to enhance the process.

Potential Value Chain Drawbacks

Depends on information systems to provide useful data. It is nice to be able to break down a company's overall strengths into sets of activities that in combination or in sequence produce a positive outcome. Yet the risk remains that these contributing activities are described in only general terms, and this does not go far enough to understand the company's approach relative to competition. Remember from Chapters 1 and 2 that the goal of strategic management is to be different from and better than competitors. The provision and use of objective information is required to draw informed conclusions. One NASCAR team worked diligently to reduce the pit time for its driver, which makes a significant contribution to overall race standings. Yet by collecting metrics to evaluate their improvements relative to their competition, they discovered that competing teams had also reduced their pit times. Moreover, the team that thought it had achieved competitive superiority on this dimension employed a greater number of pit crew workers to accomplish the reduced time, and so the cost/benefit comparison with its competitor looked even worse. A company may conclude, for instance, that its new product development capability is strong because it moves through the R&D process quickly (from idea to finished product).

However, more data is needed to have confidence that this conclusion is warranted. Is the development time, in fact, faster than what competitors have been able to engineer? Is the development time compressed because the company overspends on staff and resources in this area, relative to competition? Even though competitive information may not always be easily available, the company must use data to develop metrics that provide hard evidence supporting preliminary conclusions. Activity-based costing, which students are exposed to in management accounting classes, can be helpful in developing internal cost and performance metrics.

More focus internally, less focus on market. One of the positive features of SWOT is that it explicitly recognizes market threats and opportunities as components of its analysis. With value chain analysis there could be a tendency to simply focus inwardly on activities and behaviors of the company, and not account for the nature of the marketplace. It is not uncommon to find that companies perform sets of activities in certain ways "because they have always done it this way," or because these activities have contributed to past successes and have therefore been reinforced over time. In the 1990s, the pigments manufacturing division of Ciba-Geigy had significantly reduced their costs per ton produced while maintaining product quality. Yet they later discovered that they were losing market share because competition had moved to more adeptly respond to escalating customer requirements by producing higher quality at even lower costs, leaving Ciba-Geigy behind.[12] Value is defined in the marketplace, and the market is constantly shifting based on technological advances, changing customer preferences, and dynamic competition. When companies consider the activities they engage in as part of the "value chain," attention must remain focused on how the marketplace continues to shape the meaning of value.

VALUE CHAIN AND COMPETITIVE ADVANTAGE

Value Creation

What is value, and how is it created? This simple question is really at the very heart of effective strategic management. Value creation occurs when some other party appreciates something that we do for him or her and is willing to execute a profitable transaction with us as a result. Value is thus defined in the marketplace through transactions between willing buyers and willing sellers; it is not defined by either party in isolation from the other. In his California kitchen, Wally Amos created a special recipe for chocolate chip cookies that people loved and which he developed into the Famous Amos brand that has flourished for over 30 years. In contrast, Fortune 44 was a Colorado company that developed sensational tasting fortune cookies, only to discover that few people appreciated a great-tasting fortune cookie enough to buy them. The company went out of business very quickly.

There are several basic ways in which value can be created. The most obvious way to create value appreciated by others is to provide greater benefits to them for the same price they have been accustomed to paying previously. Panel (a) in Figure 5.12 illustrates that Company Y has created value in this fashion, compared to Company X. For example, in 2005, for no extra annual fee The Wall Street Journal added a "weekend edition" delivered on Saturdays to its regular subscribers.

Another means to create value involves just the opposite of these examples, by providing exactly the same benefits as always but at a price that has been reduced below what is normally paid. In panel (b) of Figure 5.12 Company Q has somehow figured out how to deliver to its customers precisely the same benefits they have always received, but at a lower price than Company P still charges (presumably reflecting that Q has discovered ways to effect cost savings). At the dawn of the "browser wars" in the 1990s, Microsoft gave away Internet Explorer for free while Netscape continued to charge customers for its software.

Panel (c) of the figure combines elements of both these basic methods for creating value. In this case Company T has raised its prices over what is normally paid, but it delivers significantly greater benefits than does Company S; here the value created by T is the difference between m and n in the figure. For corporate customers Dell started preloading not only software but also inventory "tag" information on both its PCs and the customer's inventory database, charging $100 more for this service but also creating up to $200 savings in inventory tracking expenses per PC for the corporate customer. Apple's iPhones also fall into this category. They are certainly more expensive than other smartphones. Yet clearly the Apple product is the smartphone of choice because its design and capabilities deliver significantly greater benefits to customers (both real and perceived) that more than offset its higher price.

There is a fourth method of value creation that is not illustrated in the figure. It is also possible to create value by broadening access to benefits to a wider audience, without sacrificing the benefits delivered to existing customers. For many years Coors beer was not distributed east of the Mississippi River – a decision made by the company for both operational and marketing reasons. This created a sort of mystique about the brand on the east coast. In 1981 national distribution was initiated, spreading the highly desirable western brand to those in the east who had never before tried it. eBay and Craigslist become more valuable to existing customers when their networks of users expands, since this provides everyone a more efficient auction environment, through a greater selection of merchandise and a larger group of potential buyers. Often the value created by broadening access involves building a new type of customer base or reaching out to new geographic markets, such as was the case with the Coors expansion.

However, value can also be viewed as a social good, unrelated to products and services provided by companies. Facebook provides a social network for ever larger numbers of people, whose access only enhances the usefulness of the network. Several states have, over the years, managed to reduce unemployment and its associated governmental cost by connecting unemployment compensation applicants with a local jobs database. Value is created for taxpayers because government spending can then be redirected to other vital needs, and value is created for unemployed workers who get connected with potential employers. General Electric initiated a new program labeled "Ecoimagination Vision." As explained by CEO Jeffrey Immelt, "We will establish partnerships with our customers to tackle the most pressing environmental challenges and double our research spending to develop the products and services they want. And we will use these technologies to improve our own energy efficiency and environmental performance. Increasingly, for your business, 'green' is green."[13] In this last statement the profit motive is plainly evident. Yet the benefits of environmentally conscious methods of manufacturing turbines, compressors, locomotives, and other industrial equipment will be enjoyed by the population at large and especially the communities in which GE locates factories.

Although ordinarily value creation is discussed in the context of what companies are able to do for their customers downstream in the industry, it is also appropriate to consider value creation possibilities upstream for suppliers. A company can create value for suppliers in several ways, and then capture that value to enhance its strategic position relative to its competitors. For example, research and development may identify a new manufacturing process that reduces costs previously borne by suppliers in providing highly specified raw material inputs. Another alternative may be that a company will outsource a particular function to a supplier that takes advantage of the supplier's own unique capabilities. Toshiba, for example, used United Parcel Service for pickups and redeliveries in its laptop warranty repair service. Finding that its laptop customers valued "speed" when needing repairs, Toshiba turned to UPS – where speed is a valued organizational process – to outsource the actual laptop repair operation. Laptop customers were pleased because repair time was reduced, and value was created for supplier UPS by delivering new business to them.[14] A new venture often confronts suppliers who are hesitant to do business with an unproven, risky enterprise. However the promise of providing access to entirely new end users is a significant value because it can accelerate supplier growth. On a larger scale Whole Foods has provided precisely this type of broader market access to organic foods manufacturers, whose increased volume and greater efficiencies have now resulted in cost savings for Whole Foods.

Value Capture and Competitive Advantage

For a company to gain competitive advantage it must be able to capture the value that is created. Assume that Company Y in Figure 5.12 has, in fact, figured out a way to provide greater benefits than Company X or the rest of its competitors without charging a higher price. Building on the logic of perfect competition explored in Chapter 4, we might expect that the other competitors will observe what Y is doing and then imitate it. In this way any kind of advantage gained from providing greater benefits will be competed away over some period of time. How, then, is value captured? To capture value a company must perform a set of activities that is superior to the way in which its competition acts. In addition, the company's set of activities must be idiosyncratic, meaning that they must be unique. To perform a set of activities in a unique fashion also means that competitors will not be able to imitate that set of activities, or cannot imitate them very easily or very inexpensively. Therefore, value capture occurs when a company creates value by acting in ways that its competitors cannot or will not act.

What portions of a company's value chain activities are difficult or impossible for a competitor to imitate? Once again, turn to the company value chain diagram in Figure 5.10. In most cases the primary activities associated with the actual production of a manufactured item or a service can be reproduced because they are more observable to outsiders. Although the Coca-Cola secret recipe has been the subject of much speculation and news over the years, any food technologist could easily identify its chemical makeup with commonly available analysis equipment. Knowing the formulation, an exact imitation of the product could be reproduced. With sufficient financial backing, a scale-efficient canning line could also be installed that replicates the manufacturing process for the finished product. Indeed, Sam's Choice Cola was released to the market in 1991 and although sold only in the Walmart chain, has done exceedingly well as a private label brand.[15] Similarly, competitors in the coffee business can closely imitate the physical characteristics of a typical Starbucks shop, the roast of its coffee, and its other beverage selections. These characteristics are more tangible, and can be reverse-engineered and reproduced fairly easily.

Value chain activities that are far less obvious to outsiders and competitors, and therefore far more difficult to imitate, are the support activities. These are unobservable, so that competitors can only surmise how research and development operates, what kinds of human resource practices are employed, the nature of internal financial controls that provide for sound management, or the policies and procedures used by a purchasing department to ensure higher quality inputs and/or lower costs. If a company hires exceptional employees to staff these support domains, and if the company develops particularly effective ways of operating within each of these domains, then it increasingly insulates the company from competitive imitation.

Taking this line of reasoning one step further, the greatest source of value capture resides in the coordination and linkages that exist between and across elements of a company's value chain. Consistent with the nature of strategy, to the extent that a company can tightly organize, coordinate, and orchestrate all of its value-creating activities into a unified, consistent approach to the marketplace, the more it ensures that its value chain is idiosyncratic and not subject to imitation. The intangible, unobservable nature of this sort of coordination – often embedded in routines and tacitly-understood ways of acting – means it is impossible for competitors to copy it. This is really a critical point, and we urge you to thoughtfully re-read the last two paragraphs!

Here are two illustrations. Hackensack University Hospital reduced the time it takes to treat heart attack patients by 30 percent and has a mortality rate for heart attacks 2 percent below the national average. It has achieved these results because of an intense effort to review and establish new cross-functional procedures and coordination.[16] In the $89 billion electronic manufacturing services industry, 77 percent of manufacturing is done outside the United States in order to take advantage of low-wage countries. However Plexus, a Neenah, Wisconsin, company, generates 69 percent of its revenue from components manufactured in the United States. The company uniquely specializes in low-volume production of a high mixture of items. To do so requires tremendous coordination across its internal and external value chains in order to achieve both flexibility to change quickly and inexpensively as well as maintain some control over costs.[17]

Even if a competitor were to hire away a top executive and his or her staff (which has occasionally happened in various industries), the effectiveness of that individual or staff will be impaired in their new organization because the nature of their relationships with other departments will be different. The aspects that work toward coordination and consistency of approach throughout any organization - factors such as culture, communication systems, personal relationships established among employees, long-held cross-organizational routines - are impossible for competitors to observe and extremely difficult for competitors to duplicate. We will talk more about these types of intangibles as critical "resources" in the next chapter.

Value Creation and Capture Through Opportunity Recognition

Implicit in the notion of value creation and capture is that a company is able to identify an opportunity to provide greater benefits for customers or suppliers, or discover ways to reduce costs and prices. There are a great many ways in which new ideas and opportunities are brought to the surface in organizations.[18] Competitive advantage, however, arises to the extent that some company in an industry is more successful in this process than others, and to the extent that its methods for doing so cannot easily be imitated.

The sets of activities through which companies may excel in opportunity recognition include the following: 1) through internal coordination within the company value chain, 2) through external relations downstream with customers and upstream with suppliers, and 3) through other external relations and "boundary-spanning" activities that enhance the company's ability to anticipate emerging trends and industry/competitive dynamics.

The first approach - relying on internal activities and processes - is the traditional approach. Many companies have extremely vibrant and well-funded internal research and development efforts underway. Occasionally, centralized R&D efforts have been broken up into physically separated "skunk works" units in order to shed some corporate policy guidance and loosen up development teams. A trend through the 1990s was to increase the level of cross-departmental coordination on new developments, such as through cross-functional teams involving R&D, marketing, operations, and purchasing to simultaneously provide input rather than sequentially examine new ideas. These methods parallel value capture methods that focus on the linkages across internal company value chain activities.

Working upstream with suppliers and downstream with customers has proved successful for some companies. An investment in activities that regularly feeds back customer preferences and feeds forward supplier ideas can stimulate further internal development activity. Paralleling value-capture methods that work across the industry value chain, investments in these activities can work to combine customer needs identification, supplier research, and the company's own knowledge. Procter & Gamble's CEO A. G. Lafely instituted a "connect and develop" program that produces over 35 percent of the company's innovations and billions of revenue dollars. Through this program they develop new ideas that arise from bringing together information from seventy "technology entrepreneurs" who identify emerging consumer needs with the 50,000 R&D workers employed by fifteen major suppliers.[19]

Former Procter & Gamble CEO A. G. Lafley

The third approach involves boundary-spanning outside the industry. In this fashion companies identify emerging competitive, technological, environmental, economic, and social trends (e.g. STEEPG) that are expected to have a significant impact on their business or industry. Ideas that spring from such broad, prospective activities may often result in small internal efforts to prototype new products or services that could respond to the emergent industry environment. Early prototyping activities enhance the potential for a company to better anticipate and successfully take advantage of significant changes. The types of activities associated with these efforts are often the most challenging to undertake in any organization, because they are intentionally focused on identifying opportunities that do not exist in the present and products or services for whom a customer base has not yet developed.[20] Yet as described in Chapter 1, the nature of industries and markets today suggests that these prospecting capabilities are of growing importance. The ability to create and capture value depends to an increasing extent on the activities that companies structure to develop prescience about their industries and to use such prescient knowledge productively.

The Greenbrier Resort, Part 2

In 2009, the Greenbrier resort reported a sharp drop in hotel stays as the recession wore on. The resort reported a loss of over $35 million in the previous year and announced that they were laying off 650 workers and trying to renegotiate their union contract. The fundamental value model of the business needs to be completely reevaluated. Much as the airlines redid their value model under the stress of the last few years, the hotel needs to reconsider its entire value chain.

QUESTIONS

1. Referring to Figure 5.12 and the ensuing discussion, how has the Greenbrier historically created value?

2. How are the Greenbrier's activities different from another hotel, different from another resort? Which of these value chain activities are unobservable by competitors or cannot be easily imitated?

3. How would you advise Greenbrier's management to modify its value-creating activities in order to respond to the 2009 recession?

CONDUCTING A VALUE CHAIN ANALYSIS

There are five significant results of a value chain analysis. First, the company creates a better understanding of the complete set of value-creating activities it engages in - sort of a roadmap of all the steps it takes to manifest a product or service for its customers. Second, it helps clarify how the activities in different functional areas of the company (marketing, purchasing, production, customer service, etc.) are either working in synch in support of a common strategic approach or may be working at odds with each other. Third, a strong analysis will identify how much of a contribution is made by some of those intangible service activities performed in the company (the top half of the value chain diagram in Figure 5.10), and how important is the intangible coordination activities among departments. Fourth, this type of analysis can shed light on how and where in the company the creation and capture of value can be enhanced and/or where costs can be lowered without sacrificing value. Finally - and again reflecting the strategic imperatives mentioned in Chapter 1 - value chain analysis can provide actionable information on the extent to which the company engages in activities that are specifically designed to help recognize and move on new opportunities emerging in the competitive environment. If we think about a company as an organization of activities designed to create and capture value, then this type of analysis focuses our attention on what the company actually does that makes a difference in achieving superior performance.

There are three primary steps in a value chain analysis:[21]

1. Identify the value chain activities.

2. Evaluate their value-creating properties and cost characteristics.

3. Identify improvements that allow the company to capture greater value.

Step 1: Identify Value Chain Activities

The first step is to identify key value-creating activities throughout the organization. Every functional area of the company should be part of this process since, as we have argued earlier, value is created through activities and there are important activities performed in all departments throughout the organization. Therefore a value chain analysis is one means for understanding how higher-level strategic goals and direction are translating to day-to-day behavior in each functional area.

We are not suggesting that we identify and analyze every single activity performed by every single employee! Looking at the millions of such activities goes way too far. There are some guidelines that help us focus on particular kinds or particular categories of activities. The important activities to pay attention to are those that exhibit any of the following characteristics:

-   They represent a significant percentage of operating cost;

-   What enables the activity to be performed or what it costs to perform the activity is different from what's involved in other activities in the company;

-   The activities are performed by competitors in different ways (competitive analysis on key success factors, strengths and weaknesses is critical); or

-   The activities appear to have great potential to create strategic differences from competition.

Occasionally, these guidelines may focus our attention on a discrete department or function within a company, such as purchasing or marketing, because it is a big operation or because the company is generally known to be particularly good at performing these functions. More often than not, however, simply considering an aggregation of activities at a summary functional level will be inadequate for the outcomes we seek in this type of analysis. There is too much going on within an entire department or function; we need to drill down further. Just as we described earlier how "new product excellence" can be the result of a whole series of different kinds of activities, departmental or functional excellence in all likelihood comes from subsets of activities within its sphere.

Figure 5.13
Activities Associated With Advertising

Let's say, for example, that we believe our company's reputation for excellence in its marketing actually springs from the effectiveness of its advertising. We receive feedback that our advertisements are superior, that they generate high levels of readership, and that consumers cut out our coupons and use them at a higher rate than industry averages would suggest. Value chain analysis would then prompt us to break down the activities associated with advertising, in order to identify more precisely what we do and how we do it so well. Figure 5.13 provides a view of the chain of value-adding activities in this one area within the marketing function. Now we are able to focus in more carefully on what contributes to great advertising, which in turn contributes to great marketing and our ability to out-compete other companies.

Step 2: Evaluate Activities' Value Characteristics and Costs

In the earlier discussion of potential drawbacks to the value chain we mentioned that information systems are required to provide useful data. This is especially true when we seek to understand the cost- and value-creating characteristics of various activities. The typical company does not readily capture specific enough cost information, for example, on the activities in the advertising function outline in Figure 5.13. Yet this type of detail can be especially revealing.

Figure 5.14 shows how helpful it can be to identify important categories of activities as suggested in Step One, and to capture essential cost information about those categories. The information is from a manufacturing company whose key strategic position in the marketplace depends on custom manufacturing of unusually complicated electronics components and a very tight relationship between its sales force in the field and the customers. Before the company ever begins a custom production run of an item, there is a sort of a dance it engages in between the customer, sourcing possible suppliers, and buying the parts needed for the customer's special order, receiving the various parts, and testing and preparing them for use in production. The astute student will recognize that sales and purchasing are both functions that exist in the top half of value chain diagram (you can't "drop them on your foot"), while receiving and testing is on the lower half in the primary activities sector. So this is a company that has to coordinate well across value chain sectors in order to do well in its market.

Figure 5.14
Manufacturing Firm Value Chain Analysis

Traditional accounting		Value chain analysis		
Salaries	$177,400	Sales	Field sales purchase orders	$72,300
Benefits	56,325		Purchase order processing	24,500
Supplies	36,600		Expediting delayed orders	13,500
Fixed costs	11,275			
		Purchasing	Sourcing suppliers	68,000
	$281,600		Issuing supplier orders	36,000
			Tracking supplier order status	7,500
		Receiving	Receiving & handling	8,300
			Resolving supplier quality	24,300
			Reissuing supplier orders	10,700
			Preparation for production	16,500
				$281,600

The left side of Figure 5.14 shows the traditional accounting treatment for the personnel and minor supplies and overhead expenses that are involved in these efforts. These costs would usually get rolled up into a corporate income statement, but they do not tell us anything at all about the essential activities performed by the company. However, company management thought carefully about the categories of activities that were important in their business, and then used an activity-based costing system to produce the figures on the right side. The "Sales" category is really a combination of field sales and internal sales office activities (which themselves are a subset of the Marketing and Sales department). "Purchasing" is a subset of activities within the Procurement department that relate specifically to these types of custom orders, and "Receiving" is also a subset of activities within the entire warehousing function. None of these categories of activities would appear on any regular financial statement. Yet the combinations and categorizations reveal not only where the greatest costs lie but also where there may be opportunities to enhance value capture.

Each activity performed by a company presumably creates value and involves costs, and hopefully many activities will have value-capturing characteristics (meaning that they are unique and cannot be imitated very easily). To better understand how each activity creates value and what determines its cost, we can evaluate it by considering two different kinds of drivers: executional drivers and structural drivers (Figure 5.15). Executional drivers come from the execution of the business activities – involving people, systems, routines, culture, and coordination – and usually have a fairly important learning dimension to them (i.e., get better over time). Structural drivers are derived from the strategic choices made

Figure 5.15
Value Chain Activity Drivers

Executional Drivers
- Work force involvement
- Total quality management
- Plant layout
- Capacity utilization
- Routines & coordination
- Culture

Structural Drivers
- Scale & scope
- Experience curve
- Complexity of products & services
- Technology utilization
- Capital intensity

about the underlying economic logic and structure of the business - such as the scale and scope of its operations, the complexity of its products or services, and its use of technology. Executional and structural drivers can be sources of either value enhancement or cost reduction, and sometimes both simultaneously. In Chapter 7 when we more carefully describe business level strategies, which depend on the value chain ideas we're covering here, we will spend considerably more time discussing the nuances of these types of drivers.

Step 3: Identify Improvements That Allow the Company to Capture Greater Value

The categorization and cost itemization of value chain activities in the previous step ordinarily make this final step much easier, and sometimes almost obvious. For example, in the company profiled in Figure 5.14, management learned that $24.3 million was spent annually in checking the quality of received parts from suppliers, and nearly $11 million on efforts to reorder from suppliers whose received material did not meet specification. Management realized that by investing a bit more in the effort to source quality suppliers to begin with, the company would save costs later on, orders could go into production sooner, and customers would be shipped final product more quickly. Management also realized that an investment in more sophisticated enterprise management software would lead to reduced costs in order processing and tracking, and again lead to smoother flow of orders to manufacturing.

There are five basic questions to ask during this step of value chain analysis. These reflect the ways in which value can be created, shown earlier in Figure 5.12 and its discussion:

1. Can we increase benefits in this activity (or subset of activity), holding costs constant?

2. Can we hold benefits constant while reducing costs?

3. Could we reduce assets required for this activity, while holding both benefits and costs constant?

4. Would a further investment in assets improve the company's ability to either create benefits or improve costs?

5. Can we expand the scale or scope of our activities to a broader audience without sacrificing benefits or costs to our current sets of stakeholders?

It may be that, through identifying sequences of value creating activities, we also realize that outsourcing is a possibility for some activities – that is, they could be handled effectively by other companies. We need to be careful about the decisions used to determine whether even minor sets of activities are outsourced to others, since they could have important strategic consequences. We will return to the topic of outsourcing in Chapter 7, when we describe more carefully the types of strategies companies can follow and the key value chain activities choices they make for each.

CHAPTER SUMMARY

Internal analysis can improve our understanding of why there are performance differences between companies in an industry. By examining carefully what a company does, what it fails to do, and how it operates, one can better identify the sources of strengths (and weaknesses) that enable it to occupy a leading (or lagging) position in an industry. SWOT tends to provide a perceptual snapshot of a company at a point in time. Value chain analysis is a more dynamic view because it exposes causes and effects, draws our attention to the critical concepts of value creation and value capture, and provides important insights on sources of competitive advantage by focusing on unique activities that cannot be imitated by competitors.

The value chain concentrates on activities conducted within a company. Primary activities are those we can easily observe, and are usually associated with the more tangible aspects of products and services that a company produces. Support activities involve the efforts of company employees and management behind the scenes, including functions such as human resources, research and development, finance and accounting, procurement, and administration. Coordinating activities are those that seek to ensure strategic consistency across the company by tightly linking activities across different functional areas of the value chain and making sure they are mutually reinforcing. The uniqueness that provides a foundation for competitive advantage often resides in support activities, and especially in how well coordination occurs across the vale chain.

Companies may prosper by creating value for customers, for suppliers, and for broad stakeholder groups such as communities. Value can also be created through company processes that more effectively detect emerging opportunities and take advantage of them before competitors. Sustained superior returns resulting from these efforts depend on the uniqueness of a company's value-creating activities.

Value chain analysis is a three-step process that helps management identify and understand the subsets of critically important activities in a company. By identifying and categorizing important sets of activities, and by understanding their value creation and cost characteristics, managers are in a better position to explore how to create and capture greater value and/or how to reduce costs and prices without sacrificing benefits.

Chapter 6 will further explore internal analysis by discussing the relationship of resources to sustainable competitive advantage. One of the principal characteristics of strategic resources is that they create value. We will return to value chain analysis in Chapter 7 on Business Level Strategies, which can be better understood as coordinated sets of value-adding activities.

Learning Objectives Review

1. *Explain the differences between internal analysis and external analysis.*

- External analysis examines industry structure and driving forces, in order to assess the attractiveness of an industry and identify key success factors that every company must attend to. External analysis can explain roughly 20% of the variation of performance of firms.

- Internal analysis can be conducted using SWOT analysis or value chain analysis. SWOT tends to present a static snapshot, while value chain tends to present a dynamic view. Internal analysis is intended to identify what a company is particularly adept at doing as well as possible points of weakness. Strengths and weaknesses usually arise because of activities and routines that companies engage in. Value chain analysis helps dig deeper to identify these activities and routines.

2. *Explain the benefits and drawbacks of using SWOT analysis.*

- Benefits: 1) easy to understand and use; 2) helpful in seeing how strengths and weaknesses align with opportunities and threats; 3) provides simple overall direction; 4) enables competitive comparisons using objective data; 5) provides a strong starting point for further in-depth strategic planning.

- Weaknesses: 1) often results in a long list of items, too many to effectively manage; 2) can over-simplify complex business processes; 3) possible confusion between strengths and weaknesses, and these can change over time; 4) may prompt companies to build on strengths that are less relevant to changing markets; 5) provides a static view without insight into the sources of strengths and weaknesses.

3. *Describe how value is created through a firm's internal sets of activities (value chain).*

- There are four ways to create value: 1) provide greater benefits for the same price; 2) provide the same benefits for a lower price; 3) provide greater benefits at an incremental price smaller than the gain in benefits; 4) broadening access to benefits to a broader audience without sacrificing current customers.

- Value can be created for both customers downstream and suppliers upstream.

- Value is created through primary and support activities that companies engage in, and through the extent to which all these activities are internally consistent and well-coordinated.

4. *Assess how the value chain perspective provides insight on sources of competitive advantage.*

- Competitive advantage arises when competitors are unable to easily imitate a successful company. Such barriers to entry and barriers to mobility are often created through actions that a company engages in which its competitors cannot observe. In the value chain the support activities and the efforts to coordinate activities across the company are usually unobservable.

5. *Perform a value chain analysis.*

- There are three steps in conducting a value chain analysis: 1) identify value chain activities; 2) evaluate the value characteristics and costs of these activities; 3) identify activities that allow the company to capture greater value, and those where further improvements are desirable and possible.

Key Terms

Activity-based costing - A managerial accounting method used to assign all direct and indirect costs to a particular activity.

Executional drivers - Performance and cost dimensions of activities that are derived from the execution of the business activities - involving people, systems, routines, culture, and coordination - and usually have a fairly important learning dimension to them.

Idiosyncratic - Unique to the company and which cannot be reproduced by a competitor or imitated very easily.

Outsourcing - Activities that are part of producing a company's products or services which are provided by other companies on a contractual basis.

Structural drivers - Performance and cost dimensions of activities that are derived from the strategic choices made about the underlying economic logic and structure of the business - such as the scale and scope of its operations, the complexity of its products or services, and its use of technology.

SWOT analysis - A form of analysis, resulting in a listing of a company's strengths, weaknesses, opportunities, and threats. It is a static view of the company at a particular point in time.

TOWS matrix - A matrix that compares a company's strengths and weaknesses against its opportunities and threats, providing general direction.

Value capture - When a company creates value by acting in ways that its competitors cannot or will not act.

Value chain - A concept emphasizing that a company is an organization of interrelated activities designed to create value for stakeholders, and that the derivation of superior performance is better understood by focusing on what a company actually does.

Value chain analysis - A method that identifies value-creating activities in a company, categorizes them into important subsets, develops information to understand how the activities create value and what their costs are, and pinpoints opportunities for enhanced value creation and cost reduction. It is a dynamic view of a company's activities.

Value creation - When some other party appreciates something that is done for them and is willing to execute a profitable transaction as a result.

Short Answer Review Questions

1. What does SWOT stand for?

2. How can SWOT be effectively used in organizations?

3. What are some positive characteristics of SWOT?

4. What are some negative characteristics of SWOT?

5. What elements constitute a value chain?

6. What are the big differences between the primary and secondary activities?

7. Where is the best place to look for value in an organization? Why?

8. What can you reasonably expect to result from a value chain analysis?

9. How is a value chain analysis conducted?

10. How do you use a TOWS matrix?

11. What are some of the executional drivers?

12. What are some of the structural drivers?

13. How is opportunity recognition enhanced with the use of value chain analysis?

Group Exercises

1. Draw a value chain for a manufacturing company, such as Dell Computer. Be sure to include industry value chain relationships as well as internal value chain activities. Highlight activities that you believe help insulate Dell from competitive threats.

2. Draw a value chain for an Internet-based company such as Google. Who are the suppliers? Who are the customers? What activities do you imagine Google has engaged in to become the world's premier search engine, and what must they do to sustain this position?

3. Draw a value chain for your business school. Are students to be considered as part of the supply network or part of the customer network? What value chain activities does your business school engage in to develop competitive advantage?

References

[1] "The Ineluctable Middlemen," 2012, *The Economist*, August 25, pp. 49-51.

[2] Rumelt, Richard R. 1991. "How much does industry matter?" *Strategic Management Journal*, 12: 167 - 185.

[3] 3M Annual Report, 2005.

[4] Angelou Economics SWOT Report.

[5] www.iastate.edu/~strategicplan/2010/process/docs/swot.shtml.

[6] For perspective on the capacity to manage in complex environments, see: Miller, George A. 1994. The magical number seven, plus or minus two: Some limits in our capacity for processing information. Psychological Review (101)2: 343 - 352.

[7] Porter, Michael E. 1980. Competitive strategy. New York: Free Press.

[8] Porter, Michael E. 1985. Competitive advantage. New York: Free Press.

[9] Quinn, J. B. 1988. Technology in services: Past myths and future challenges. In B. R. Guile and J. B. Quinn (eds.), Technology in services: Policies for growth, trade, and employment. Washington, D.C.: National Academies Press.

[10] Quinn, J. B. 1992. Intelligent enterprise. New York: Free Press.

[11] There is considerable evidence that significant strategic value is added by support activities and the coordination that occurs between primary and support activities. For example, the Gartner Group recently reported that worldwide spending in 2006 on information technology was estimated to include $682 billion for technology services, but only $485 billion for manufactured hardware and software (which both include significant support activity components). In the strategy press over the last few years there has been significant attention paid to "knowledge" management and other intangible resources that underlie the manifestation of services and products by successful companies. See Blackler, F. 1993. Knowledge and the theory of organizations: Organizations as activity systems and the reframing of management. Journal of Management Studies 30(6): 863 - 883; Grant, R. 1996. Toward a knowledge based theory of the firm. Strategic Management Journal 17: 109 - 122; Winter, S. G. 1987. Knowledge and competence as strategic assets. In D. J. Teece (ed.), The competitive challenge, 159 - 184. New York: Harper & Row. Quinn argues that the "manufacturing-services interface is now the key to most manufacturing organizations." See Quinn, J. B. 1992. Intelligent enterprise. New York: Free Press.

[12] Pascale, R. 1997. Nothing fails like success. Princeton, NJ: Films for the Humanities and Sciences.

[13] www.ecomagination.com/.

[14] Friedman, Thomas. 2005. The world is flat. New York: Farrar, Straus and Giroux.

[15] Discount Store News. 1993. Sam's Choice climbs beverage brand list - Walmart's Sam's American Choice beverage brand. October 4.

[16] Szabo, L. 2006. Hallmark of quality care: Efficiency. USA Today, October 20: 3B.

[17] Bulkeley, W. 2005. Plexus strategy: Smaller runs of more things. Wall Street Journal. October 8: A1.

[18] Baron, R. 2006. Opportunity recognition as pattern recognition: How entrepreneurs "connect the dots" to identify new business opportunities. Academy of Management Perspectives 20(1): 104 - 119.

[19] Huston, L., and N. Sakkab. 2006. Connect and develop. Harvard Business Review, March: 58 - 66.

[20] For a fuller discussion of this challenge, see Christensen, C. 1997. The innovator's dilemma. Boston: Harvard Business School Press.

[21] This section draws on material from Shank, J. K., and V. Govindarajan. 1993. Strategic cost management. New York: Free Press; See also Hammer, M., and J. Champy, 1993, Reengineering

the Corporation, HarperBusiness: New York. See also Grant, R. M., 2005, Contemporary strategy analysis (5th edition). Malden, MA: Blackwell.

Chapter 6: Resource-Based Competitive Advantage

LEARNING OBJECTIVES

1. Demonstrate how to compare the types of company resources, and show which can generate competitive advantage.

2. Explain the difference between resources and capabilities.

3. List the categories of resources that companies may draw upon to develop competitive advantage.

4. Outline a practical model for analyzing which resources and capabilities will work to deliver competitive advantage.

Popping the Cork[1]

Nomacorc Mission: "Our mission is to become the leading innovator and preferred strategic partner to the wine industry, in a joint effort to integrate closure design and wine preservation to ensure consistent consumer enjoyment, just as the winemaker intended."

For over 300 years, since French Benedictine monk Dom Perignon first adapted it to close wine bottles, the wine industry has relied on cork to seal its products. And then along came Nomacorc LLC. Within the last twenty years since its founding in Zebulon, North Carolina, Nomacorc's synthetic corks made from extruded plastics are what seals 15% of full-sized bottles of wine sold worldwide. Today 45% of all red wine in the U.S. is closed with Nomacorc.

Over-production of natural cork in the 1980s led to the prevalence in cork of the naturally occurring chemical TCA, which "tainted" up to 15% of fine wine and rendered it undrinkable. This opened the door for synthetic closures, which have grown to represent fully 30% of the entire wine closure market.

With previous experience in plastic extrusion, Nomacorc entered this industry in 1999. But the company took plastic closures to another level. Focusing on reverence for the tradition of winemaking, the company recognized early on that simple extruded closures do not provide the oxygen transfer properties that had made cork so central to fine wine. Nomacorc invented and

182

patented a process for co-extruding two types of plastics into a single closure – a firm inner core to hold shape, and a spongy exterior creating better fit. They have partnered with wine research institutes and hired PhDs to study "oxygen management" issues related to types of plastic, extrusion methods, and even bottle neck design.

In 2010 the company introduced its Select Series closures to precisely control oxygen ingress into wine. Their research collaborations have explored more than just closures, but a full spectrum of the winemaking processes and their relationship with oxygen. With this knowledge in hand they are now designing co-extruded closures specifically for certain wineries and their varietals. The company owns eleven patents related to closures for containers and process predicting the oxidability of a wine or grape must. In 2014 the *Wine Enthusiast's* number 1 pick for the year (out of 17,500 reviewed) was Abbott Claim Vineyard Pinot Noir, sealed with a Nomacorc closure.

By 2016 Nomacorc has expanded operations to Europe, South America and China. It serves over 5,000 wineries in 40 countries, and will have sold 20 billion wine bottle closures since its inception.

QUESTIONS

1. What are the activities this company performs that create value? Are these unique? Could other companies imitate them easily? Why or why not?

2. Do the company's activities and accomplishments fulfill its mission statement?

In the previous two chapters we explored the industry analysis technique for examining the external competitive environment, and value chain analysis for understanding the means by which a business can create a valuable position in its industry. In this chapter we will extend both of these approaches by outlining a practical framework for understanding how the business can develop a *sustainable* competitive advantage. Now we drill down deeper into the nature of value creation in order to understand the reasons for how and why a particular strategy has the ability to be successful over time. Here we focus on resources that provide the foundation for the firm to succeed in the market. We will see that the careful identification and analysis of a *narrow* set of resources provides a business with the *broadest* possible opportunity to succeed in the marketplace and to sustain that success over time.

THE CHARACTERISTICS OF RESOURCES

Strategic resources of an organization are the foundation of the development of its sustainable competitive advantage. The "resource-based" approach was originally suggested almost fifty years ago, and has been carefully and more fully developed over the last twenty-five years by a number of strategic management scholars.[2] This approach contains a fairly well-developed theoretical framework, but it has often been difficult for people in business to implement the ideas in practice. So this chapter will clearly lay out principles behind the approach, but most importantly will provide a method for how to use it in practice.

Ordinary and Extraordinary Resources

At the outset we need to make a distinction between resources as contemplated by this approach and the way we might normally consider assets possessed by a firm. Whereas assets are typically thought of as those items listed or accounted for in the firm's balance sheet, the resource-based approach contends that not all such "accounting" assets are strategically important to the firm. As an example, the office desks and chairs of any business are indeed assets of the firm accounted for in its financial statements; however, these physical office furnishings do not represent a foundation upon which the firm can develop and sustain a competitive advantage. Having the finest, most ergonomically correct Italian leather chairs and handcrafted desks may feel good, but few customers would buy from the company or pay more for its products because its back-office operation has those accessories.

In contrast, the resource-based approach concentrates on resources of the business that have the potential to be strategically important. There are two types of resources that have the potential to be strategically important: tangible resources and intangible resources. Tangible resources are physical assets such as equipment, buildings, land, furniture, money, and raw materials. Tangible assets are relatively easy to identify, and are usually easy (although sometimes quite expensive) to acquire in the marketplace. While this list often includes items that may have no strategic value, in some instances physical assets do indeed provide the business with a strategic foundation. For instance, it may be possible that those ergonomic Italian leather chairs are found to improve employee morale and job satisfaction to such a high level that it directly leads to enhanced customer service and firm performance (this might be quite a stretch). More often, though, highly-unique raw materials, special manufacturing equipment or facilities, and other customized operational assets[3] are the kinds of tangible resources with strategic importance. Championship Chili (mentioned in Chapter 4) was produced using highly-specialized food manufacturing equipment that other chili companies did not have and could not easily acquire. For the corner gas station in your neighborhood at home, its property is of strategic value because no other competitor can now occupy the location providing convenience for traffic coming from multiple directions.

Intangible resources are those assets that are not physical in nature but are often more critical to the success of the business. Intangible assets include such things as relationships with key suppliers and other businesses, the culture of the organization, processes or routines within the organization, patents and trademarks, as well as the knowledge and skills of the management team or other key employees. The skills and experience of founders, for instance, is often cited as a key intangible asset in the development of new ventures.[4]

Ways to Describe Resources	
Physical Nature	Strategic Value
Tangible Intangible	Ordinary Extraordinary

To this distinction between tangible and intangible resources, we also need to distinguish between ordinary resources and extraordinary resources. Some resources are necessary simply for the business to operate legitimately in an industry, while others may be truly unique to the business and can help set it apart from its competitors. Many (if not most) of the resources possessed by a firm are ordinary resources, those that the firm must possess just to be a credible contender in the industry. If you operate a sit-down restaurant, then you must have refrigerators, food preparation equipment, food preparers, serving staff, utensils, plates, napkins, condiments, a cash register, a credit card transmitter, telephones, a building to operate within, computers, some office furniture, lighting, a payroll system, a business license, and so on. These constitute the minimum resources (both tangible and intangible) that have to be in place for the business to operate as a restaurant.

Similarly, many of the capabilities of the business, such as serving safe food to customers that meets the cleanliness standards of the industry, may be done very well. However, these resources provide no distinctive competitive advantage to the firm. The expectation of customers is that every restaurant possesses this capability. Thus, while necessary to compete in this industry, this set of resources is not sufficient to be a source of sustainable competitive advantage. Every restaurant must possess the same characteristics. Other than curiosity, customers are provided with no compelling reason to spend their money at this restaurant.

We don't mean to suggest that ordinary resources and capabilities are not important. Quite the contrary! They must be developed and they must be developed well, at least as well as the standard in the industry. A restaurant that barely clears its health inspection and receives a low grade may indeed operate. However, since the general expectation of most customers is that restaurants should have an "A" rating from the health department, a restaurant receiving something less is likely to negatively impact its performance. Investment in the ordinary resources required in a particular industry is a *necessary* condition to operate, although they alone are not *sufficient* to develop a competitive advantage.

To create a sustainable competitive advantage with the associated opportunity to earn substantial returns, some of the resources that the business possesses must be extraordinary resources. These are resources that either individually or in combination with each other:

1. Provide the business with the opportunity to produce extraordinary economic returns (i.e. they create value versus competitors);

2. Are unique in the industry;

3. Allow the business exclusive access – to either suppliers or customers – for some period of time;

4. Cannot be easily matched by another business in the short run; and

5. Cannot be easily transferred to or appropriated by another business.

There must be a reason why customers would consider taking their business to a different company. For most people it is far more convenient to continue in their established patterns of behavior than it is to change those patterns. Customers are often not willing to switch unless there is a compelling reason to do so. A company's extraordinary resources can create exceptional value and become the source of that motivation to change.

Why would a customer choose one restaurant over another? Will the restaurant have a unique atmosphere, type of cuisine, level of service, or entertainment when compared to other restaurants? Will its cost structure allow for prices to be set significantly lower than those of the competitors, while still providing comparable value on other dimensions that customers appreciate? Will access to the business location be more convenient? If it is only going to do the same thing that other companies do, why would anyone switch to the business? The strategic focus of every company, therefore, is to identify and develop extraordinary resources that enable the firm to offer an improvement in value which cannot be easily copied by competitors. Extraordinary resources are at the foundation of value creation and value capture, and offer the opportunity to achieve financial gains in excess of ordinary returns produced in a particular industry. Figure 6.1 presents characteristics that help distinguish between ordinary and extraordinary resources.

Figure 6.1
Differences Between Ordinary and Extraordinary Resources

	Tangible Hard assets; on balance sheet	**Intangible** Soft assets; not on balance sheet
Ordinary (Necessary to compete, but not sufficient for advantage)	• Easily viewed • Easily purchased	• Easily recognized • Well known routines • Able to learn easily
Extraordinary (Provides basis for competitive advantage)	• Difficult to acquire • Uncommon in industry • Possible immobile	• Difficult to identify • Difficult to evaluate • May require time to learn • May require experience to understand

The descriptions of extraordinary resources in Figure 6.1 prompt us to recall the discussions in Chapter 4 about imperfect markets and barriers to entry or imitation. Whether tangible or intangible, extraordinary resources are not readily available in competitive markets. Any industry in which firms have been able to develop and utilize extraordinary resources is one that will tend away from the perfectly competitive markets endpoint (Figure 4.1), because barriers to entry or barriers to imitation prevent others from operating similarly. Extraordinary resources also tend to take time to develop, and build further on value chain ideas from Chapter 5. As we shall see in the discussion below, the often-intangible nature of these resources emphasizes the importance of routines that enhance coordination across the value chain.

Five Key Dimensions of Extraordinary Resources

How can one determine if resources are ordinary in nature, or if they are extraordinary and provide a foundation for sustainable competitive advantage? While various strategy textbooks and articles provide somewhat different approaches, in general five elements help answer this critical question. This is the VRIST framework. You might remember it more easily by thinking about the Latin word *verist*, meaning "truth," because any resource that exhibits all five characteristics is truly extraordinary. Truly extraordinary resources present a foundation for the business's strategy.

Strategy Acronym: VRIST **Extraordinary Resource Dimensions**		
V	**Valuable**	It is Valuable
R	**Rare**	It is Rare
I	**Imitation**	It is difficult to Imitate
S	**Substitution**	It cannot be Substituted for
T	**Tradable**	It cannot be Traded for

Is it valuable? Only those resources that have the ability to create value for the company might qualify as extraordinary. In assessing value creation, the truly extraordinary resource must help the company in at least one of several possible ways (Figure 6.2). These mirror the discussion we had in Chapter 5 about the value chain: 1) lower its cost structure relative to competitors for a particular product or service; 2) provide enhanced product or service benefits to customers while maintaining parity on costs and prices; 3) provide the ability to charge more for its products/services and more than offset any related cost increases; or 4) enhance the company's ability to reach target customers more effectively or attract additional customers more efficiently than competitors.

Figure 6.2
Ways to Create Value

Accomplish this	While providing this
Lower costs	Parity on product/service features
Add benefits	Parity on costs and prices
Increase revenue	Revenue increases more than cost increases
New customers	Undiminished value to existing customers

Johnson Controls (JCI) operates in the auto parts industry against literally hundreds of competitors. A major challenge in this industry is keeping track of thousands of auto parts while keeping costs low to remain price-competitive. In 2016 JCI was reaping the benefits of an earlier investment it made in RFID tags and tracking procedures for its reusable shipping boxes and parts storage racks. While maintaining its same level of service and pricing, it has lowered its costs.

Buc-ee's is a small convenience store chain in Texas with 37 shops that was looking for a way to create greater value than its competitors. They decided to create the "World's Cleanest Bathrooms." They invested heavily in the design and maintenance system for their bathrooms, and then slightly raised the prices on many items in the store. Customers stop in because the clean bathrooms are "worth the wait" while driving, and they are inclined to pick up convenience items rather than loading the kids back in the car and heading to another store where they might save a few pennies on each purchase. Now customers go long distances before stopping for a rest break, just so they can enjoy Buc-ee's. The company's approach has resulted in a Facebook account with tens of thousands of followers, more than a half million YouTube views of in-store videos shot by customers, and its website has been visited over 4 million times since 2012. Who shoots videos of convenience stores? Customers adore Buc-ee's! Their sales volume and profits shot up during the following years, returning the investment for the upgrades and providing a continuing value proposition for the company that cannot be easily imitated by competitors.

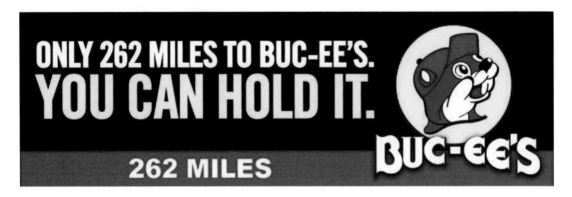

Is it rare? Each potentially extraordinary resource must be evaluated for its uniqueness relative to the competitors in the industry. Krispy Kreme Doughnuts went public in April 2000 with a business model based on a number of rare tangible and intangible resources including its brand name, its heritage in the southeastern United States, a unique recipe, and doughnut making system that utilized proprietary company-designed machinery. These resources were unique in the industry and provided a potential competitive advantage to the company. Prior to the advent of high speed internet and video streaming possibilities, Blockbuster's retail store coverage (5800 U.S. stores at its peak) provided rare access to complete movie libraries for most neighborhoods in America.

One of the reasons McDonald's restaurants are so popular is the general customer perception that they have cleaner food preparation operations and eating areas than other fast food operations. Cleaning standards have, in fact, been incorporated into their franchise manual so that every McDonald's restaurant follows virtually identical procedures. Yet these standards are not actually rare, evidenced by the incorporation of similar procedures at Burger King, Wendy's, and other national fast food restaurants. But a resource that is *perceived* as rare can be just as powerful as a real resource that is rare. The cachet of a brand name is a perception by consumers, and yet may provide a significant resource-based advantage for the firm that simultaneously meets all five of the VRIST criteria.

Is the resource truly unique or rare for the company's industry? The question of rarity should be answered using research and objective data, although occasionally qualitative judgments may be necessary. If the management team finds that the resource or capability does not qualify as rare within the industry then it cannot be categorized as extraordinary.

Starbucks, Part 1

Starbucks is one of the great business success stories of our time. Taking a Seattle-based roasting and coffee bean operation as its base, Howard Schultz had a vision of opening Italian-style coffee houses around the world where people could enjoy great coffee in an atmosphere that would welcome them from the time they walked into the door. Seeking investor money for a business that was going to sell coffee at prices that had never been seen, using Italian names for sizes that no one understood, and encouraging people to hang out in the store: all seemed to be a recipe for disaster, and he was turned down by 95 percent of the investors he approached.

As if that weren't enough, he dramatically changed the model upon which employees would be treated. The company provided all employees (even part-timers) with health insurance coverage, paid living wages, and provided matching contributions for their retirement accounts. The baristas behind the counter were expected to know customers, know coffee, provide great service, and love their store.

QUESTIONS

1. Did these characteristics make the Starbucks model work? Why?

2. Why didn't other companies just imitate their model?

3. What other products or services could Starbucks get into that can further leverage their existing resources?

Is it difficult to imitate? If you have determined that a particular resource is valuable and rare, then the next step is to determine whether some other company might be able to easily imitate it. If it can be imitated, how perfectly can it be copied? One obvious means to prevent imitation is to obtain intellectual property protection for the resource, such as through a patent or trademark. Trademarks protect names and graphic designs associated with a company from being copied. Patents may be granted to unique, nonobvious products and business processes. These make it illegal for a competitor to "reverse engineer" a product and then turn around and produce exactly the same thing in exactly the same way. Qualcomm patented computer chips providing CDMA (code division multiple access) technology for digital cell phones, which became one of the two worldwide industry standards. No other company has been able to infringe on their rights, and every cell phone equipment provider that utilizes CDMA must pay Qualcomm a royalty.

More often than not, however, resources that cannot be imitated involve unobservable routines or processes within a company; they are "behind the scenes" from the physical product produced or service provided. Boeing re-engineered its aircraft design system in the 1990s, so that all its future commercial aircraft would be designed entirely using electronic methods with no paper blueprint drawings ever produced. This was an enormous undertaking because each of their airplanes incorporates 3 million parts and critical aerodynamic features with extremely small tolerances. In turn, this digital conversion made electronic sourcing with thousands of worldwide suppliers much easier. Competitors Airbus and Embraer, unable to observe this process, also began to move in this direction but have had to invent the process for themselves, taking years to do so.

Consider the organ transplant "industry." In 2016 there were over 4,000 Americans actively waiting for heart transplants, but there are only about 2000 transplants done annually in 150 heart transplant facilities nationwide. Why don't more hospitals and their cardiac surgery units get into this field? The answer is that "imitation" of successful practice here is incredibly difficult. These facilities must be pre-approved by hospital boards of directors as well as federal and state health care regulatory agencies, stocked with incredibly expensive diagnostic equipment and specially developed clean areas in a hospital, and staffed by transplant-trained doctors and medical staff, whose surgical techniques and skills cannot be imitated and cannot be easily learned.

Can it be substituted for? Every resource that a company determines to be potentially valuable, rare, and not subject to quick or easy imitation should be evaluated for close substitutes. Here substitution means other ways that competitors can provide comparable value-creating benefits. So a substitute is something that meets the same basic need being satisfied by a company's resource. As with the question of rarity, it is often the case that tangible resources can be easily substituted. Retail or corporate location, machinery, equipment, and raw materials are all usually substitutable. Amazon developed and patented its "One-Click" method for customers to use in buying books and merchandise; however, other online retailers have developed similar systems that allow customer information to be retained and called up easily at the time of purchase.

So substitution most often applies to intangible resources, like internal routines and coordinating efforts across the value chain. General Electric's Superabrasives Division competes with DeBeers in industrial diamonds and cutting tools. Some years ago GE discovered that DeBeers had invented a new process that yielded higher quantities of industrial diamonds, thus lowering their costs and allowing them to price more aggressively in the marketplace. There was no practical substitute for this process that GE could put into place. This is different from the airplane manufacturing example just above, since in that case a "paper and pen" process would still have allowed Airbus to design aircraft and compete with Boeing. But in the GE case they were

189

being priced out of the market, losing business hand over fist. Their only hope was to imitate what DeBeers had already accomplished; developing this was an expensive undertaking and took a long time, giving DeBeers a significant timing advantage in the market.

Occasionally, it is possible to substitute for intangible resources. The "brand management" system of marketing was developed by Procter & Gamble in the 1960s, but other consumer packaged-goods companies (e.g., General Mills, Kraft) developed their own "product management" systems that work equally well in the marketing of consumer products.

From this discussion it should become clear that the questions of imitation and substitution begin to focus our attention on the *durability* of advantage that any developed resource might confer. We will return to the question of durability in the following section.

Can it be traded for? Once again, for those resources that are simultaneously valuable, rare, not subject to imitation, and not easily substitutable, the business must consider tradeability (or transferability) of the resource. How mobile is it? Can it be purchased somehow by another company, and if so will there be a loss in the short- or long-term value-creating benefit of that resource? Is the resource most valuable in a particular geographic location? A potentially extraordinary resource increases value to your company if it is also difficult to transfer.

In the early 1980s John Sculley was president of PepsiCo, after having been promoted up through the organization. He was well known for his marketing acumen; in fact he oversaw the initiation of the Pepsi Challenge, which enabled Pepsi to begin gaining market share from Coca-Cola in U.S. supermarkets. In 1984 Sculley was hired away from Pepsi to become chairman of Apple Computer, while founder Steve Jobs' responsibilities were stripped away. The Apple board believed that Sculley could bring the same kind of marketing success for their company that he had engineered in the soft drink business. However, his tenure at Apple was marked by suboptimal product development plans, failed market launches (e.g., the Newton PDA), and increasing division and dissension within the company. It appeared that the success at Pepsi had been a combination of Sculley and the team of individuals involved, the culture of the company, the cooperation they fostered, and the unique procedures and knowledge base of all the other employees at that company. The Apple board had deemed that this resource could be imported into their growing company, when in reality it was a nontransferable combination of people, culture, and systems. Steve Jobs ultimately returned to run Apple, and navigated the company to its next successful run of strong performance. For the same reasons that Sculley was successful at Pepsi but not at Apple, Jobs was successful at Apple.

Figure 6.3 summarizes these concepts and provides further examples of each of the five VRIST dimensions. Whenever you discuss sources of competitive advantage and the potential for a sustainable position vis à vis competition, you should always use the VRIST framework as an evaluative tool.

Figure 6.3
Extraordinary Resource Criteria

Criteria	Key Question	Illustrations
Valuable	Does the resource lead to a product or service that creates value?	Your company has a staff of highly traveled and experienced agents who custom design premium vacation travel. Customers regularly pay three times the cost of doing it themselves to have your company create the whole package and deliver a total vacation. Paul Newman created a non-profit organization, The Hole-in-the-Wall Gang, providing terminally ill children a no-cost camp experience. Mr. Newman's reputation enabled the non-profit to attract a high level of philanthropic giving to support its mission. Firm XYZ developed a targeted method to reach consumers very active in outdoor activities. Their consumers provide feedback information about camping equipment that XYZ shares with its suppliers to assist suppliers in future new product development.
Rare	How unique is the resource?	After years of research and investment, your organization has developed a new diagnostic process for detecting with 99% accuracy that your computer's hard drive is about to fail.
Imitation	Is it difficult or costly to imitate?	Your programmers have just implemented a new web site that is innovative because it relies on a novel, non-obvious method allowing users to access a public database. Although competitors will be able to view your approach immediately through the website, you have patent protection possibilities that would prevent anyone from replicating your method for a specified period of time.
Substitution	How easily can competitors develop a strategically equivalent resource?	Your firm has an in-house staff of process engineers that enable you to take designs to production in a very efficient manner. However, there are process engineering consulting companies that can be hired by competitors to accomplish essentially the same task. Ride the Rockies Inc. worked out an exclusive agreement with the National Park Service allowing them to run downhill bike tours in Rocky Mount National Park.
Tradeable	How mobile is the resource?	A restaurant whose business depends on drive-through traffic manages to snag the last remaining corner location along the busiest commercial route in town.

Connecting Extraordinary Resources to Sustainable Advantage

The five criteria shown in Figure 6.3, used to determine whether or not resources are extraordinary, also help describe why extraordinary resources are the foundation of a competitive advantage that is *sustainable*. It was earlier pointed out that there may be no unique strategic positions discernible simply as a result of conducting an industry analysis, because the information that feeds into such analyses is commonly available to all companies. A firm's competitive

191

advantage thus depends on the development or possession of an idiosyncratic resource or set of resources that cannot be easily developed or acquired by other firms.

Three of the criteria discussed above – rare, non-tradable, non-substitutable – characterize a resource that is *unique* to the business and that cannot be appropriated by potential competitors. These characteristics confer the possibility to develop an immediate competitive advantage because no competitor has the resource nor can they buy it or substitute for it.

We understand, however, that – while no advantage lasts forever – all businesses wish for their advantage to last as long as possible. Practice suggests that there are two ways to examine and predict the *durability* of advantage. First, there can be an anticipated time lag between the development of a particular competitive advantage and the point where a competitor will be able to closely match that advantage. This lag creates a window where the business can earn extraordinary returns. Second, a competitor may be required make huge investments and devote great amounts of management attention in order to achieve the same result. If so, the competitor may not be able to earn an adequate return on its investment or may believe that too much attention would be diverted away from its existing business. Keeping competitors at bay increases the potential for durability and the ability to earn extraordinary returns in comparison to the industry.

Because the question of durability is so central to sustainable competitive advantage, it is important to know about the three primary sources of durability:[5]

1. *Historical conditions*. The ability to develop unique resources can depend on historical conditions – the time and place in which businesses locate, begin, or grow. For example, real estate entrepreneurs Richard Peery and John Arrillaga began buying California farmland in the early 1960s, subsequently converting it into industrial use and office space. Their original plot of farmland is at the corner of Maude and Mathilda Avenues in downtown Sunnyvale, the very center of what became Silicon Valley. Peery-Arrillaga Properties is one of the largest commercial real estate firms in North America, and the two founders are regularly listed among the world's wealthiest individuals.[6] By virtue of the time period in which they were acquiring the land and their specific location, Peery and Arrillaga were able to control vast land resources, locking up the "supply" of land and preventing other would-be real estate developers from becoming involved.

2. *Causal ambiguity*. Causal ambiguity exists when the link between a business's resources and its competitive advantage is poorly understood. If the linkage is poorly understood, then potential competitors are likely to have a difficult time trying to imitate the "recipe" for success. We might think about causal ambiguity as what occurs when we try to instruct people in how to ride a bicycle when they have never done so before. We can describe the mechanics of peddling and steering but there is a tacit component that is impossible to describe,[7] such as the relationship between speed and turning or understanding how to ride safely on a gravel surface. Experience is necessary to understand how superior performance is achieved, but what is learned from the experience cannot be completely written down or easily communicated to others. For example, General Electric is widely-recognized for its ability to produce exceptional business leaders who go on to run other large corporations. It is more than the GE experience or their system of rotating managers between businesses. What creates this capability cannot be completely explained and competitors have a very difficult time trying to reproduce it.

   You should recognize that there is a sort of paradox about this notion of causal ambiguity.[8] Just as it makes it difficult for a competitor to understand the foundation of your

192

company's strong competitive position, it may also be difficult for your management team to identify why your company is doing so well. Resource positions are not always obvious, even to those who benefit from them. In fact, one of the challenges of growth and development is the accurate internal identification of the kinds of resources that your company can build upon effectively. We will return to the challenge of identifying resources in a few minutes.

3. *Social complexity.* Here the business's resources may result from social complexity, a phenomenon that cannot be systematically managed or influenced. For example, Apple's iPad resulted from a socially complex design/product development process. Highly trained engineers worked closely with designers in a culture that values the unique and exceptional. Other companies may be able to hire away the engineers for their technical or design skills, but the integrated combination of the team, culture, and environment cannot be easily reproduced elsewhere. Social complexity may also extend upstream or downstream to relationships that companies develop with their suppliers or customers, where the business relationship regarding product or service transactions is further cemented by other personal and social relations.

The astute student will recognize that strategic resources are seldom available in the external industry environment. If they are there, then other companies may also acquire them, thereby eliminating the important VRIST dimension of rarity. So rare resources are usually those developed internally.

You will also see that the criteria for assessing whether a resource is "valuable" ties back directly to the discussion in Chapter 5 about the value chain. Resources are *valuable* if they enable the company to implement an approach that achieves superior performance. If the company is unable to utilize a particular resource to earn above-average returns, then while it may be potentially interesting, that resource cannot be classified as extraordinary and does not represent a foundation for competitive advantage. It is not uncommon to have a particular resource meet all four of the other criteria previously mentioned, and yet still be unable to create value by reducing costs relative to competitors, delivering added benefits for the exact same price, increasing revenues, or obtaining more customers. If a firm performs an activity that is rare,

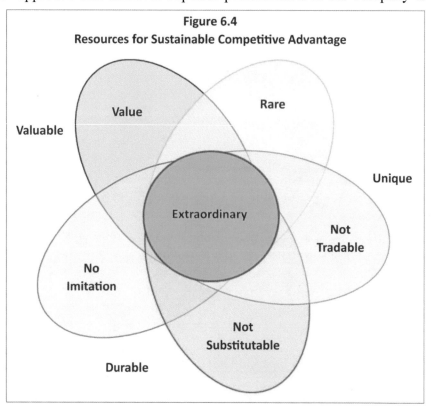

Figure 6.4
Resources for Sustainable Competitive Advantage

inimitable, non-tradable, and non-substitutable, but not valuable relative to competition, then no

193

economic advantage can be garnered. Figure 6.4 illustrates that the five critical dimensions of extraordinary resources, if fulfilled, create conditions – *valuable*, *unique*, and *durable* – that together confer sustainable competitive advantage.

The identification and creation of value, in part, depends upon differences in expectations about how resources may be utilized. In the real estate example mentioned earlier, Peery and Arrillaga purchased land that was thought by most investors to be useful only for farming. The real estate entrepreneurs had a different concept in mind about possible uses for the land and the significantly higher revenue potential that the land appeared to present. Think about almost any successful new venture that you happen to follow or whose business you subscribe to: Facebook; Instagram; Red Bull energy drinks; Under Armour clothing; or others. All of these services and products originated from founders who saw new opportunities to use existing materials in novel ways.

One of the central premises of this text is that both value creation and opportunity recognition are strategic imperatives for all companies in the twenty-first century (Chapter 1). The notion of differing expectations about value creation potential illustrates precisely where these two imperatives come together. Superior and sustainable performance requires more than luck in happening to come upon a new idea that builds on resources exhibiting the five VRIST criteria. Strategic management today involves anticipating markets, and then creatively using new and already developed resources to take advantage of emergent trends. The next step involves structuring the organization and its internal processes to regularly generate new business ideas and new resource possibilities that can create future value. Managing growth will be covered later on in Chapter 8, and structuring the organization will be covered in Chapter 11.

The identification of extraordinary resources should guide any business in its investments and strategic development. To reiterate, those resources and capabilities that are ordinary must be done well, but they need not be done any better than the average for the industry. Having stunning office chairs may be nice, but it is not going to create strategic value for the company. However, extraordinary resources should receive attention and investment by the management team. These become the core foundation upon which to develop competitive advantage. Over-investment in the ordinary dimensions of the business will distract attention needed at the critical strategic core, and have the potential to siphon much-needed funding and time into areas that are not capable of yielding superior economic returns. These ideas allow students and managers to see that strategic management is a balancing act: using the financial and human capital available to develop ordinary resources that must be in place just to conduct business, while dedicating as much funding and attention as possible to extraordinary resources that can deliver competitive advantage.

Types of Extraordinary Resources

The earliest writings in economics and strategy discussed three basic types of resources that firms might rely upon in their development of strategy: physical capital, financial capital, and human capital. The word "capital" in these categories was an extension of even earlier economic thinking about the "factors of production" used by manufacturing firms. Strategic management theory and analysis have since evolved considerably, increasingly recognizing service-based enterprises and the importance of knowledge in all types of business. Strategists now recognize an expanded list of resource categories (Figure 6.5). As we move forward into the analysis of resources, it is helpful to keep these categories in mind as a guide.

Figure 6.5	
Categories of Resources	
Resources	**Examples**
Knowledge	Unique knowledge about a potential opportunity
	Prior industry experience
	Prior new venture startup experience
	Entrepreneurial orientation
Social	Informal networks to gain business and startup knowledge
	Formal industry and value chain networks- industry leaders, suppliers, customers
Human	Prior relevant management experience
	Credibility, reputation
	Functional area expertise
Financial	Access to seed stage and growth capital
	Access to institutional capital for later stage development
	Relationships to support cash flow management
Organizational	Ability to organize complexity: administrative systems, task systems, policies
	Coordination expertise and combining expertise
	Methods to articulate complex resources and capabilities
	Ability to share and routinize capabilities in other parts of the new venture
Technology	Intellectual property claims
	Unique/special manufacturing process or physical equipment
Physical	Manufacturing facilities and location
	Unique access to suppliers
	Unique access to customers

RESOURCES AND CAPABILITIES

So far in this chapter we have referred solely to the idea of "resources." Many strategy professors and people in business, however, often refer to "capabilities" as well as resources. Having presented the five VRIST criteria that help determine if resources are extraordinary, we are now in a position to more carefully examine the difference between these two frequently used concepts. Extraordinary resources represent the raw materials of a business, a core foundation upon which the sustainable advantage of the business may be built. As can be seen from the Apple iPad example, exciting new products are really the result of intermediate level capabilities that exist between extraordinary resources and the products actually sold in the marketplace. Capabilities may be thought of as sets of tightly integrated activities, organizational skills, and internally developed routines that rely on extraordinary resources and that allow the company to create value in a fashion superior to other companies.[9] In the Apple case the intermediate level includes a new product development process that works extremely well. The new product development capability, however, is a result of extraordinary resources of the firm at a deeper foundational level – such as their recruiting process for engineers, a culture that emphasizes design and technical excellence, and the cross-functional coordination that occurs early on in the development process. Each of these extraordinary resources meets all of the VRIST criteria.

This development process capability might be leveraged in multiple ways, such as creating multiple types of new products (e.g., Apple TV, iPod Nano, MacPro, iWatch) or by working with various types of customers (consumers, schools, government, business). Thus we see that resources and combinations of resources lead to the development of firm capabilities, which in turn provide a platform from which multiple approaches to the marketplace may be pursued.[10] In this case Apple intends to leverage its resource-based capabilities to produce additional products and entertainment gadgets that will enable the company to "colonize rooms throughout the home."[11]

Figure 6.6 captures the sense of this relationship between resources, capabilities, and business performance. The figure shows that extraordinary resources are the foundation upon which capabilities are built, and that together these enable the business to introduce products or services in order to generate superior performance. Interestingly, this perspective also reiterates that ordinary resources are important only if they are built on a proper strategic foundation of extraordinary resources and capabilities. This idea can be extended further by suggesting that the accumulation of ordinary resources and the development of products or services are often not even possible unless the proper strategic foundation has been laid. For example, investors and venture capital firms are often unwilling to support a new venture unless there has been some very

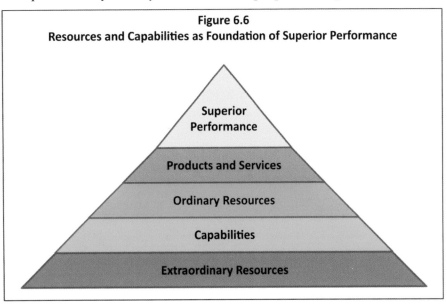

clear thinking about the sources of sustainable competitive advantage. The foundational levels of extraordinary resources and capabilities are critical. Similarly, top management teams and boards of directors of established firms would be remiss in their shareholder responsibilities if they decided to embark on a major new direction without significant attention devoted to the question of sustainability and its foundation.

The combination of resources and capabilities at the base of a business again prompts us to return to the value chain model explored in Chapter 5. The value chain discussion highlighted the critical importance of the coordination of activities across both the internal and external value chains of the business. A product development process, such as that which existed for the iPod and iTunes, is a capability involving an entire coordinated set of value adding activities. In this instance, research and development worked closely with both procurement and operations internally, as well as with upstream suppliers of components. The legal staff developed relations with artists and music labels, and worked carefully

with programmers to create digital music protocols that would protect copyrighted material. The marketing team developed plans for selling iPods through new channels of distribution. These types of connections and coordination in the value chain are valuable, unique, and durable, giving rise to a sustainable competitive advantage. For this reason Apple continues to dominate the paid music download market even in 2016 with a 64% percent market share. Even more consequentially, the company leveraged these iPod development capability facets into iPads and iPhones which contributed mightily to the company's profits, stock price, and shareholder returns over time. The ability to understand and manage these connections, once developed or learned, has also become a valuable capability for the business that should continue to generate superior returns.[12]

Starbucks, Part 2

Everywhere Starbucks looked in 2008, they were being attacked. McDonald's announced that they would be putting in the same coffee drink machines that Starbucks had used for the past few years and would be offering drinks for substantially lower prices. Neighborhood coffee businesses were sprouting up wherever there was a Starbucks, and the economic recession prompted consumers to think twice about high-priced goods. Starbucks was not growing as it wished.

Facing this situation, Howard Schultz wrote an open letter to the entire organization about the commoditization of coffee and the need to again make Starbucks unique in the market. He acknowledged that most of the recent decisions the company had made to handle growth had been for the right reasons in isolation, but that the sum of the decisions was a dilution of Starbucks cachet. They had moved to automated machines, vacuum-packed coffee, and cookie-cutter store designs. While he didn't specifically mention it, the company had also started providing hot breakfast and lunch sandwiches, which put them in direct competition with fast food restaurants.

He told the employees, "I have said for 20 years that our success is not an entitlement and now it's proving to be a reality. Let's be smarter about how we are spending our time, money and resources. Let's get back to the core. Push for innovation and do the things necessary to once again differentiate Starbucks from all others."

QUESTIONS

1. What did Starbucks do to counter the trend toward commoditization? Do you think they have succeeded?

2. What are their resources and capabilities, and based on these, what new avenues would you suggest for Starbucks?

CONDUCTING A RESOURCE ANALYSIS

Although a few company illustrations of the ideas about resources and capabilities in this chapter have been provided, the treatment of this important strategic concept often stays at a very conceptual level in most classroom discussions, and in the executive suite of most companies as well. In the final section of this chapter we want to bring the ideas closer to practice so that they can be easily used by students of strategic management.

A resource-based analysis approach allows each resource or capability to be examined for its potential to provide the business with a competitive advantage. We seek to identify extraordinary resources or capabilities that will provide a focus for the business. Resource-based analysis is a tool providing management with a practical method for discerning the core foundation for sustainable competitive advantage. This methodology has five basic steps that should be proceeded through sequentially:

1. Develop a listing of all resources and capabilities, including those that are tangible and those that are intangible;

2. Divide those resources and capabilities into the categories of ordinary and extraordinary for the industry in which the company competes. Ordinary resources are those that must be developed, but no better than the standard for the industry.

3. For those resources and capabilities that appear to be extraordinary, use the five-point VRIST framework to determine which are truly extraordinary:

   - Valuable
   - Rare
   - Difficult to imitate
   - Cannot be substituted for
   - Cannot be traded for

4. For those resources and capabilities that pass the VRIST test, develop the means to leverage these extraordinary positions.

5. Evaluate the relevance of extraordinary resources for the Key Success Factors required for success in the industry. If there is a mismatch, consider how to develop appropriate resources that address the KSFs.

The following discussion walks through each step of this process.

Develop a resource and capability list. The best method to accomplish this task involves gathering together the key decision makers in the organization. This group will develop a complete list of all the tangible and intangible resources that the company has at that particular point in time.

While this inventory process may seem a bit mundane, it is absolutely critical to the process of identifying potential resources or capabilities that may provide a sustainable competitive advantage for the organization. As this is the first step in the process, it is important to develop as complete a list as possible encompassing the entire breadth of knowledge within the management team. The developed list may be quite long and should include everything that the company possesses now if it is already in business or, in the case of a new venture that it may possess at the time it begins to conduct business.

Identifying the intangibles often presents the greatest challenge for managers and their key advisors or employees. We tend to think of our companies in terms of the products or services they provide or the customers they serve. This is because this is what we experience on a day-to-day basis. On the one hand, this natural orientation is positive because it reflects a fundamental customer and value-creation orientation. On the other hand, we need to recognize that products, services, and satisfied customers are simply a manifestation of a set of underlying organizational resources and capabilities that the business is built upon (refer back to Figure 6.6). Remember also our Chapter 5 insights on the importance of support activities in the value chain and coordinating activities across the value chain. Together these argue for an examination that goes deeper than mere products or services. In identifying the intangibles it is important to continue to ask questions that drill down to the essential core of what the company is really all about and what it does particularly well. In our experience by repeatedly asking a single penetrating question to probe deeper and deeper, the core resources of a firm can be revealed. That question is: "What is the cause of this outcome?"

Figure 6.7 Process to Identify Intangible Resources		
Question	**Management Response**	
What is one of your competitive advantages?	Our products uniquely fill important needs of our customer.	
What is the cause of this outcome?	Our product development team is very good.	
What is the cause of this outcome?	The team is able to respond quickly to new customer needs we identify.	
What is the cause of this outcome?	They work extremely well together as a team.	
What is the cause of this outcome?	We recruited people who each had previous experience in high performing new product teams.	They have developed a system and protocols on what works in product development.
What is the cause of this outcome?	Our recruiting network is quite strong.	A knowledge database provides guidance on what to pursue in new products.
	We have HR expertise in hiring in this industry.	Senior manager with development team coordination experience and expertise.
		Culture that encourages ideas and experimentation.

Figure 6.7 provides a relatively straightforward illustration of the probing process that identifies important intangible resources. In this example, the management team has now identified a number of important, extraordinary resources that they believe ultimately contribute to superior performance in the marketplace. Here they see that their capability (the routines created by the new product development team) depends fundamentally upon their recruiting network that enables them to hire strong managers, a knowledge database they have developed over time, a particular manager with knowledge about managing fast-cycle teams, and a culture that rewards ideation. These intangibles, then, might be added to the company's developing list, which might resemble the list in Figure 6.8.

Figure 6.8 List of Identified Resources	
Tangible Resources	**Intangible Resources**
Building location	Industry experience
Equipment	Contacts and networks
Initial financing	Previous experience in same type of business
Inventory	Education
Patents and patents pending	Unique knowledge of the industry (from previous research)
Software and systems for business	Skills sets of founder and managers (innovation, team
Renovations and improvements to facility	coordination, presence with stakeholders, etc.)
	Name and branding
	Recruiting network
	New product development knowledge database
	Organizational culture

Identify potentially ordinary and extraordinary resources and capabilities. The lists of resources of the organization now serve as a foundation for the next step in the process. Management should further divide the list of tangible and intangible resources into either ordinary or extraordinary resources. This will usually result in a list of ordinary resources or capabilities that is very long and a much smaller list of extraordinary items. As stated earlier, each of the ordinary resources or capabilities should be evaluated very simply to determine if the company is meeting the median expectation in the industry.

Use the VRIST framework. Each of the potentially extraordinary resources should be individually evaluated using the five-point VRIST framework to determine if it is truly extraordinary. Those that fail to pass all five steps should be re-categorized as ordinary. Those that pass through all five steps are the unique resources and capabilities that the company should plan to leverage. The ordinary resources that are identified should be managed well, but since they are customary in the industry and provide no basis for advantage or sustainability, they need only the amount of effort and time necessary to achieve parity with other competitors in the industry.

Leverage extraordinary resources. The result of this effort is the creation of a short list of truly extraordinary characteristics for the business. This process moves beyond the question of "why would a customer purchase from us?" Now the business can narrow its strategic focus to those areas that are most important to creating a sustainable advantage. These areas should receive the time, investment, development attention, and focus of the firm. Leveraging the extraordinary resource positions may be accomplished in one of three ways, which include the following:

1. *Extending the current business model into additional products or customer segments*. After building its unique method for selling books online, Amazon.com leveraged its developed internet capabilities into other product segments. In 2013 it leveraged its superior online retailing environment into fine art, and has since gone further into music, video, food and more. As it further developed its back end computing and database operations, it recognized that these capabilities provided a platform for additional segments of business. So by 2016 one of Amazon's biggest growth segments – and one of its most profitable – is "cloud computing" offered to other businesses.

2. *Replicating the resource or capability elsewhere in the organization to enhance the performance of the business.* United Technologies is a multi-national diversified corporation. In its Otis Elevator subsidiary it developed a program designed to enhance productivity and quality simultaneously, nicknamed ACE for "achieving competitive excellence." Management replicated the ACE program in other divisions of the corporation, making a significant difference in their business and relationships with suppliers.[13]

3. *Developing complementary resources.* Inmar Enterprises came into existence as a manufacturers' coupon clearinghouse, processing millions of coupons received by retail stores for manufacturers' products. They processed payments for the retailers and billed the manufacturers. Originally organized using low-cost labor in other countries, Inmar has since made technology investments to economize on processing fees, and the technology now provides superior competitive market and user information reports and service to its retail and manufacturer clients.

Evaluate relevance of extraordinary resources for KSFs. Extraordinary resources should be relevant for the Key Success Factors that have previously been identified as important in the company's industry. If they are relevant and pivotal, then the company is well-positioned to succeed in the industry on a sustainable basis.

However, occasionally the previously developed extraordinary resources have become obsolete as an industry has evolved (for example, Blockbuster's retail presence when DVD-by-mail and video streaming became popular). Or perhaps through the resource-based analysis the company has discovered it does not have any relevant extraordinary resources at all. This will then prompt an effort to determine how to develop a resource base that will enable the company to compete more effectively. This could mean enhancing an existing ordinary resource so that it becomes extraordinary and a point of strategic differentiation. Or it could trigger the development of an entirely new resource that will match well with the industry's demands.

The VRIST evaluation process may also yield insight on *other* industries that a company might consider entering. Consider, for example, Samsung's historical presence in flat screen TVs and cellphones. It was not a major leap for the company to redirect their resources and capabilities in these markets into tablets, as well. E*Trade started life as an online equities investment service. Yet their core strengths in backroom processing of electronic transactions prompted them to broaden their services into online banking.

An Illustration of the Process

A fairly high-end web design business was formed in the late 1990s around three very talented and personable individuals. In short order the company hired many more people and grew to thirty employees. They offered quality web design, hosting, and customer relationship tracking services at a premium price and in an industry that was in its infancy. After five years in business the company hit a point where their business seemed to stall. During the next nine months they noticed a slow, gradual but steady decline in new business. Discussions with clients and others in the business failed to point out any particular problem with the operation.

They decided to take a break and held a two-day retreat to think through the business. They began by asking everyone to talk about every aspect of their business that served as a resource enabling them to compete in the industry. After a slow start the ideas started to flow more rapidly and a very, very long list was developed. A small part of that list is recreated in Figure 6.9 as an example.

Figure 6.9
Web Page Design Company Resources and Capabilities

Nice office space, desks, chairs, telephones, cubicals
Computers for each employee
Computer servers for client hosting
Attractive reception area
Break area for employees with free soft drinks, coffee
Real-time web host tracking and reporting capability
Web design expertise including creative designers
Accounting, cost, budget and time management systems

Customer relationship experts on staff
Internet marketing experts on staff
Payroll system
Project management systems and staff expertise
Experienced account executives
Business cards, letterhead, logo
Strong web presence

The shock in the meeting room was palpable as they realized that many of the areas listed, which had been unique to them just a few short years earlier, were now just standard fare in their industry. This company had started out with three individuals working out of a rented house with two computers, one telephone, no letterhead, and just a plan for designing web pages. Creating and hosting websites had developed as a result of a client's request for the service. As is the case in many industries, this industry had benefited from upward trajectory and sophistication of readily available software and hardware technology. So as the internet became increasingly ubiquitous into the 2000s, and as the barriers to entry to web designing became relatively inconsequential (a PC and widely available software), the supply of competing firms grew dramatically. Pricing for similar services dropped precipitously, as an increasing number of firms competed for what was essentially moving toward a commodity type of service. Figure 6.10 illustrates the changes occurring in this industry during a time when the supply of web design firms expanded significantly.

A careful examination by the company found that they were relying upon resources or capabilities which had since become commonplace and standard in the industry. This being the case, they had become simply average in their competitive space and were being outcompeted by new businesses offering comparable services at a lower price. This reflects the lesson that durability is not forever. What was extraordinary at one time will become ordinary at some point, as competitors continue efforts to imitate, substitute, and invent their own value-creating practices. As durable advantages dissipate, uniqueness declines, opening the door for competitors to create the same value in the same ways or equal value in different ways.

The most important list to create and regularly update is the list of extraordinary resources or capabilities at the foundation of the business. This list is usually quite small, but in it are the seeds of success. The web design management group carefully considered what was at the root of their ability to attract business, and developed the new list in Figure 6.11

Figure 6.11
Potentially Extraordinary Resources and Capabilities

Strong client base of fortune 500 firms
Well known brand name – winner of several national awards
Located in a very desirable location with relatively low cost of living
Unique web development system that saved 70% of the time needed when
      compared to standard web development
History of successful web page designs
Talented team that worked as a cohesive unit

Each of these potentially extraordinary resources or capabilities was then subjected to the resource-based analysis, using the VRIST framework. While one can disagree with their analysis, the important lesson here is that there is both art and science involved in determining key sources of competitive advantage. The science of the process involves: 1) understanding which resources are tangible and which are intangible; 2) using the VRIST framework to divide those resources and capabilities into ordinary and extraordinary for the industry in which the company competes; and 3) deciding to focus attention on extraordinary resources, and investing only as necessary in ordinary resources to maintain competitive parity. The art of the process is a matter of judgment of degree, discretion, and experience. The company's final chart appears in Figure 6.12.

During this retreat the team decided that just two of their potentially extraordinary resources or capabilities were truly a foundation for developing their competitive advantage. And so the company set about the process of developing a strategic approach that focused on these areas. In turn, this approach prompted them to redefine the industry segment they were targeting as client firms that required high-quality designs quickly. It also prompted a refocusing internally on advanced development of these targeted capabilities, and a shifting of time and investment away from practices that merely supported ordinary web design efforts.

Figure 6.12
VRIST Evaluationof Resources

Resource	Valuable	Rare	Difficult to Imitate	Difficult to Substitute	Difficult to Trade
Strong client base of Fortune 500 firms	Yes	Yes	No	Yes	Yes
Well known brand name	Yes	Yes	Yes	Yes	Yes
Desirable location with low cost of living	Yes	Yes	No	No	Yes
Unique development system saving 70% of time	Yes	Yes	Yes	Yes	Yes
History of successful designs	Yes	No	No	No	Yes
Talented team that works as a cohesive unit	Yes	No	No	No	Yes

CHAPTER SUMMARY

This chapter examined the nature of the resources and capabilities of businesses that provide the opportunity to earn superior returns on a sustainable basis. The resource-based view of competitive advantage is an important supplement to value chain analysis because it enables any business to consider the uniqueness and the sustainability of its position. A process was described that incorporated the following items: 1) develop a listing of all resources and capabilities; 2) divide those resources and capabilities into categories of ordinary and potentially extraordinary for the industry in which the company competes; 3) evaluate those that appear to be extraordinary based upon the VRIST framework as follows:

- Valuable
- Rare
- Imitation
- Substitution
- Tradable

4) determine ways to leverage extraordinary resources that pass the VRIST test, and 5) assess the relevance of extraordinary resources for addressing key success factors in the industry. Extraordinary resources and capabilities provide the foundation for entering markets with products and services, and for earning superior returns versus competition on a sustainable basis.

There are additional issues for businesses to consider in using the resource-based framework for developing its strategy. We highlight a few of these here:

1. How do businesses develop a resource position to begin with? Almost without exception, every new venture begins as simply an idea about a potential opportunity, and the prospective entrepreneur possesses no assets or resources that can be claimed by the new venture he or she might start up. Thus a very real dilemma for the prospective entrepreneur is how to create something out of nothing.

2. What kinds of resources should be developed or invested in? At any stage of a business's development, managers face choices about the application of their time and the limited financial capital they may have backing their efforts. So what should be the priority of focus in the resource development process?

3. All businesses confront specific and identifiable types of strategic challenges over time as they develop through stages. Is there a resource development path that businesses should follow to respond to these widely experienced strategic challenges?

4. Like any kind of organizational asset, resources and capabilities can become obsolete over time. How should businesses respond in their resource development efforts to dynamic changes in industry conditions, evolving competition, and the general obsolescence of previously developed resource positions?

We will explore some of these critical issues in Chapter 8.

Learning Objectives Review

1. *Demonstrate how to compare the types of company resources, and show which can generate competitive advantage.*

- Two types of resources are used by companies in the design and execution of their strategy: ordinary and extraordinary.

- Ordinary resources are those which the company must possess and utilize roughly at parity with its competitors in an industry. Ordinary resources are not a source of competitive advantage. The lack of ordinary resources may put a company at a competitive disadvantage.

- Extraordinary resources are those which exhibit the VRIST dimensions: valuable, rare, cannot be imitated, cannot be substituted for, and cannot be traded for. These are the foundation of sustainable competitive advantage because they confer the qualities of value, uniqueness and durability.

2. *Explain the difference between resources and capabilities.*

- Extraordinary resources are the foundation of sustainable competitive advantage.

- Capabilities are sets of tightly integrated activities, organizational skills, and internally developed routines that are based on and configured out of extraordinary resources. Capabilities provide a platform from which a variety of new products or services may be developed and multiple customer types pursued.

3. *List the categories of resources that companies may draw upon to develop competitive advantage.*

- Knowledge; social; human; financial; organizational; technology; physical.

4. *Outline a practical model for analyzing which resources and capabilities will work to deliver competitive advantage.*

- Develop a list of all resources and capabilities, including those which are tangible and intangible.

- Divide the list into those you believe are ordinary resources and those you believe may be extraordinary resources.

- Use the 5-point VRIST framework to determine which are truly extraordinary resources.

- Leverage the identified extraordinary resources: 1) extend into new products, services and/or customer segments; 2) replicate the resource elsewhere in the company to enhance performance; or 3) develop complementary resources.

- Assess the relevance of extraordinary resources for the Key Success Factors important in the industry.

Key Terms

Capabilities - Sets of tightly integrated activities, organizational skills, and internally developed routines that build upon extraordinary resources and allow the company to create value in a fashion superior to other companies.

Casual ambiguity - A condition that exists when the link between a business's resources and its competitive advantage are poorly understood.

Extraordinary resources - Those resources or capabilities that simultaneously exhibit the characteristics of: valuable, rare, durable, relatively non-substitutable, and non-tradable.

Historical conditions - The ability to develop unique resources often depends on the time and place in which the business began operations.

Intangible resources - Those resources and capabilities that are not physical in nature. They including relationships with key suppliers/businesses, the culture of the organization, the history of the business to date, and perhaps most importantly, the skills of the founders.

Intellectual property protection - A legal means of protecting tangible and intangible assets that are unique to the organization. This is accomplished through patents, copyrights, trademarks, and trade secrets.

Ordinary resources - Those resources or capabilities that are necessary to operate in an industry, but which do not confer competitive advantage.

Resource-based analysis - A method that examines the extent to which a company possesses resources that will allow it to achieve sustainable competitive advantage.

Social complexity - Resources that may result from a socially complex phenomenon, something which cannot be systematically managed or influenced.

Tangible resources - Physical assets such as equipment, buildings, land, furniture, human resources, money, and patents.

Short Answer Review Questions

1. How are tangible resources used in business?
2. How do ordinary resources impact the competitive advantage of a business?
3. What are the ways that extraordinary resources can create value for a business?
4. Explain which resources should be processed through the lens of resource-based analysis.
5. How is the VRIST framework used to the advantage of a business?
6. Ordinary resources must meet what criteria for the organization to be successful?

7. Broadly defined, what are the types of resources that may be employed by a business?

8. What is your conclusion about a resource/capability that meets all five criteria in the VRIST framework?

Group Exercises

1. Your group has decided to start a new business. You see an opportunity to open up a drive-in movie theater. With the dramatic rise in gas prices, people are not traveling very far and they are looking for a great bargain. You plan to charge only $8 per car. What ordinary resources will you need? What might you add to this business that could be extraordinary?

2. Using the VRIST framework, evaluate the extraordinary resources and capabilities that you listed in Question # 1. Which resources and capabilities provide the company with a real opportunity for a sustainable competitive advantage? Why?

3. Have the group do an Internet search on Walmart. What elements of the business does the group believe make Walmart unique? Process those items through the VRIST framework. Which ones hold up as potentially providing Walmart with a sustainable competitive advantage?

References

[1] Green, J. H. 2015. 6 reasons why the future of wine is looking bright, Wall Street Journal, December 9, p. D1; Pierson, D. 2014. Wine cork makers seek to put a stop to declining sales, Los Angeles Times, December 7, p. C1; Aeppel, T. 2010. Show stopper: How plastic popped the cork monopoly, Wall Street Journal, May 1, p. A1. www.nomacorc.com.

[2] Alvarez, S. A., and Busenitz, L. W. 2001. The entrepreneurship of resource-based theory. Journal of Management 27(6): 755–775; Barney, J. B. 1991. Firm resources and sustained competitive advantage. Journal of Management 17(1): 99–120; Grant, R. M. 1991. The resource-based theory of competitive advantage: Implications for strategy formulation. California Management Review 33: 114–135; Penrose, E. T. 1959. The theory of the growth of the firm. New York: John Wiley & Sons; Peteraf, M. A. 1993. The cornerstones of competitive advantage: A resource-based view. Strategic Management Journal 14: 179–191.

[3] Ghemahat, P. 1991. Commitment. New York: Free Press.

[4] Hall, R. 1993. A framework linking intangible resources and capabilities to sustainable competitive advantage. Strategic Management Journal 14(8): 607–619.

[5] Barney, J. B. 1991. Firm resources and sustained competitive advantage. Journal of Management 17(1): 99–120.

[6] Mangalindan, J. P. 2014. The secretive billionaire who built Silicon Valley, Fortune, July 7; http://www.forbes.com/2003/02/26/billionaireland.html.

[7] Polanyi, M. 1967. The tacit dimension. Garden City, NJ: Anchor Books.

[8] Kogut, B., and U. Zander. 1992. Knowledge of the firm, combinative capabilities, and the replication of technology. Management Science 3(3): 383–396.

[9] Quinn, J. B. 2005. Leveraging intellect. Academy of Management Executive 19(4): 78–94.

[10] There has been much discussion in the strategy literature about the relationship between resources, capabilities, and core competence. The definitions of these terms are somewhat different depending on the authors. The argument that resources lead to capabilities, which can be leveraged in multiple ways, captures the sense of the collection of authors. Coyne, K. P., S. J. D. Hall, and P. G. Clifford. 1997. Is your core competence a mirage? McKinsey Quarterly 1: 41–55; Porter, M. 1996. What is strategy? Harvard Business Review. Nov–Dec: 61–78; Prahalad, C. K., and G. Hamel. 1990. The core competence of the corporation. Harvard Business Review. May–June: 79–91.

[11] Wingfield, N. 2008. Apple daydreaming: Report predicts move toward home devices. Wall Street Journal. May 22: D1.

[12] Teece, D. J., G. Pisano, and A. Shuen. 1997. Dynamic capabilities and strategic management. Strategic Management Journal 18: 509–533.

[13] Roth, G. L. 2013. An uncommonly-cohesive conglomerate. Strategy+Business, 72 (Autumn).

Chapter 7: Business-Level Strategy

LEARNING OBJECTIVES

1. Compare and contrast business-level strategies available to organizations, and describe how they create competitive advantage.

2. Examine the underlying drivers that enable a company's choice of business-level strategy to be successful.

3. Analyze when outsourcing makes strategic sense.

Cementing Its Position[1]

Eagle Materials is the 5th largest producer of construction cement in the U.S., competing against larger multinational public corporations. In this commodity-type business, where all cement pretty much looks and acts the same, having a cost structure to ensure competitive pricing is a key to success. Eagle is the low cost producer. They have gained this position by carefully managing all aspects of their operations, so that they have a cost advantage versus the industry on multiple dimensions: raw materials cost, natural gas usage, production and construction waste, administrative overhead, inbound and outbound transportation expenses. Because their operations use less energy and result in less waste, they also are aligned with superior environmental sustainability goals. Since they charge competitive prices but their delivered cost to the market is lower, Eagle earns superior returns. In 2016 they produced an industry-leading 19.2% EBITDA. Their 3-year return on equity of 15% is twice as high as their closest competitor and they outperform all companies in the industry on this key performance metric.

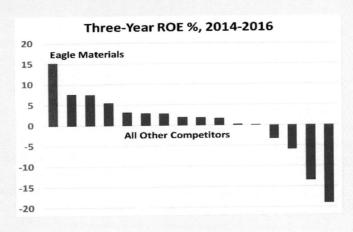

Bowing to the Masters

In a sun-drenched studio outside Boston, Benoit Rolland's personal touch and mastery of his craft has resulted in customers populating a who's who of the world's leading violin, viola and cello musicians. Rolland makes bows for the masters to use when they play their Stradivaria, Guarneri, and other remarkable stringed instruments. Before beginning a bow for any client, he listens to them play to get a feeling for their fingerings and style. "After a while, I'm able to guess their bowings. And then the fingerings. And the fingerings are very important, because they are linked to the bowings." He then creates a design to accommodate the strengths and the weaknesses specific to the musician. He uses a Brazilian wood called Pernambuco, which is celebrated for its tone, strength and longevity. The wood is now hard to come by, but years ago Rolland stockpiled it so he would have enough to last his lifetime. He then sculpts each bow, according to his design, by carving and shaving it. He taps each bow regularly as he progresses to listen to its tone. He determines precisely when it is complete by what he hears and what he feels with his hands. To see a video of the craftsman at work, click the following link: Benoit Rolland.

More than 450 musicians have collected Rolland bows. Because he only produces roughly 30 each year, selling for $15,000 each, a secondary market for the bows has been created. They are often auctioned by companies such as Sotheby's, and have appreciated in value over time.

QUESTIONS

1. How do sets of activities required for a low cost strategic approach differ from activities required for a differentiated approach that enhances benefits but costs more?
2. What is similar in these two approaches?

Danger Out There

On April 24th, 2013, an eight-story complex of clothing factories called Rana Plaza, near Dhaka, Bangladesh, collapsed. As the site was gradually cleared, the final toll counted over 1100 people killed, mainly young women. The building was not designed for industrial use and its owners had illegally added three floors. In the previous decade 800 more people have died in factories in Bangladesh, mainly through fires. It illustrates the dangerous nature of work in garment factories in low-wage Asian nations.

Over the past decade major players in the clothing industry have flocked to Bangladesh, where an average wage of $38 per month has helped control costs in a global industry worth $1 trillion annually. But outsourcing production presents challenges that may offset cost benefits:

coordination and communication issues, quality control, factory safety procedures, warehousing and inventory complications, extended lead times, and more.

Clothing is made in Bangladesh for many famous world brands - including Benetton, Walt Disney, Walmart, German clothing company Kik. None of these companies had authorized factories in Rana Plaza for outsourced manufacturing, although remnants of their brands were discovered in the rubble. UK company Primark and Canada's Loblaw (owns Joe Fresh clothing line) acknowledged production at Rana Plaza and promised compensation to families of the victims.

QUESTIONS

1. Under what circumstances should a company outsource some parts of its value chain activities?
2. How would you organize an internal effort to monitor and control outsourced activity?
3. How can a company recover from the damage to its reputation through involvement in tragedies such as Rana Plaza?

LOGIC OF BUSINESS-LEVEL STRATEGIES

It is now time to step back a bit and look at strategy from a broader perspective. In this book so far we have developed a set of techniques for evaluating the conditions and foundations for creating a sustainable competitive advantage. Starting with an examination of the external environment in which a business operates (Chapter 4), we used the five forces, key success factors, and strategic maps to identify the conditions in which the business must operate. Next, two very effective and practical techniques for completing an internal analysis were examined – value chain (Chapter 5) and resource-based analysis (Chapter 6).

The significant part of the logic we have developed that has yet to be discussed is the overarching question of *how* to coherently put all this together so a company can compete successfully. Over the years a popular framework has developed suggesting that successful companies must use one of five types of business-level strategy approaches. Any company not pursuing some form of these types of strategies is not likely to develop competitive advantage or achieve above-average returns.

These five strategy types lay out a high level organizing approach to business. While they are extremely valuable as communication tools and a useful framework for making decisions, they are nonetheless significantly rich, quite complex, and very much a challenge to manage effectively. Basic business-level strategies have been the bedrock component of many companies. They are used as a rallying point for consistency and coordination among value chain activities and for evaluating sustainability using resource-based analysis. The decision to embrace a particular business-level strategy, in combination with a mission statement, enables management to get everyone in the organization moving in the same direction. Companies may be tempted to vary what they do from time to time in the marketplace in reaction to other competitors, the shifting environment, the beliefs of new top management team members, stakeholders, and/or recent financial performance. However the consistent pursuit of a business-level strategy approach over a longer period of time is usually a recipe for strong performance. A good deal of strategic management research has confirmed that selecting and following a distinct, overarching business-level strategy improves company performance.[2] Your ability to understand and apply this framework, and also to be able to explain its optimal uses and limitations, will put you in a stronger position in whatever company you go to work for following graduation.

In the 1980s our understanding of strategy was given a significant boost as a means for systematically enhancing performance, through the work of Michael Porter and his initial description of a set of "generic" strategies: "Competitive advantage grows fundamentally out of value a firm is able to create for its buyers that exceeds the firm's cost of creating it. Value is what buyers are willing to pay, and superior value stems from offering lower prices than competitors for equivalent benefits or providing unique benefits that more than offset a higher price."[3] These generic approaches have been applied at the business-unit level and have thus come to be referred to as business-level strategies.

Reflecting these ideas, the most prevalent framework used by strategists suggests that competitive advantage can be achieved when firms employ one of two basic approaches: low cost or differentiation. Ordinarily we think of these approaches as polar opposites from each other, such as what Figure 7.1 suggests. Either a company seeks to cut costs versus competitors while offering a competitive level of benefits to customers, or it seeks to enhance the benefits it provides to customers versus competitors while maintaining a competitive level of cost. Within many industries, however, we recognize that there are often several competitors appearing to pursue a low cost strategic approach. However, only one company will, in fact, occupy THE **low cost leadership** position, and there is usually intense competition among those seeking to own this position.

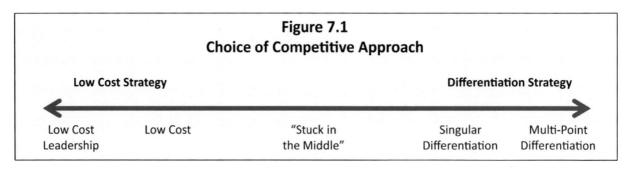

Figure 7.1
Choice of Competitive Approach

Low Cost Strategy | Differentiation Strategy

| Low Cost Leadership | Low Cost | "Stuck in the Middle" | Singular Differentiation | Multi-Point Differentiation |

Dell, the computer giant headquartered in Texas, had developed a competitive advantage by focusing on being the low cost leader in their market space. After Michael Dell dropped out of college to start his company, he completely reinvented the value chain for personal computers and squeezed costs out of every conceivable area in the company. The most visible of these efforts to consumers was their direct sales model, which first used only the telephone and then subsequently combined that approach with the internet to bypass the traditional retail distribution system. This not only had the advantage of enhanced personal contact and avoidance of retailer markups, but allowed Dell to change the flow of goods through the primary activities part of the value chain by allowing customers to customize their computers rather than buying stock computers on the shelf at a store. Dell also pressed its suppliers of parts and components to locate and operate their own supply distribution centers adjacent to Dell's assembly facilities. This way Dell was not required to incur the costs of carrying raw materials inventories. Subsequently in 2002 Hewlett Packard acquired Compaq and sought a low cost leadership position based largely on manufacturing efficiency through large scale, which involved a very different set of activities and method compared to Dell. Then between 2008-2015 Asia-based manufacturers of PCs (e.g. Lenovo, Asus, Acer) have grown market share based on the use of inexpensive assembly labor costs abroad. As these competitors developed lower cost positions for essentially-identical PC models, Dell first announced that they believed both their supply chain and manufacturing areas could be further improved. Michael Dell stated, "I think you are going to see a more streamlined organization, with a much clearer strategy."[4] Dell strayed from its direct sales focus during this period with a decision to begin selling PCs in Walmart and other retailers, just as competitors enabled consumers to order online directly. Amidst this intense industry competition, Dell lost its mojo (i.e. its low cost leadership). Its market share declined (2nd in U.S. share and 3rd in global share by 2016), its stock price had declined by 31% by 2013, and in that year Michael Dell bought out the company to take it private.

Just as low cost competition is fierce, there are usually several companies competing in the differentiation spectrum. Sometimes a competitor's success can be created by a single point of competitive differentiation, such as Qualcomm's targeted research and development resulting in its patented CDMA cell-phone transmission technology. Other competitors seek to develop multiple points of differentiated competitive advantage, in order to make competitive imitation less likely. Apple's i-devices product platform (iPod, iPad, iPhone, iWatch) combines elegant product design, proprietary copy protection software that inhibits piracy and file sharing, a slick Web interface for any type of computer, and an unparalleled digital music catalog. Any one of these features present significant challenges to competitors, while the combination affords Apple a huge, sustainable competitive advantage.

In Figure 7.1 we see a wide space between the low cost and differentiation approaches. This has long been believed to be a sort of strategic "no man's land." Companies that find themselves simultaneously doing a bit of low cost and a bit of differentiation have often been called "stuck in the middle"[5] This is because they are trying to compete in multiple ways against companies that more single-mindedly dedicate resources and manage their value chains toward one of the "pure" strategic approaches. In 2013 Dell's revenue was 1/3 the size of Apple's but their R&D spending was only 1/10 that of Apple's. If Dell were to challenge Apple computer as an innovator (differentiator), for example, it would also need to invest large sums in research and development. This would further reduce its ability to compete for a low cost position. This type of change would be both difficult and expensive, possibly leading Dell to a position of being stuck in the middle.[6]

Another important decision that companies must make when they select their business-level strategic approach is about the scope that they intend to compete in. As suggested by Figure 7.2, a company can either compete broadly or narrowly.[7] Broad strategic approaches are pursued across multiple customer segments, broad geographical territories (even global; e.g., Staples in office supplies retailing and distribution or Arcelor-Mittal in steel), and often involve providing a variety of products or services to meet multiple needs or desires. In contrast, narrow strategic approaches tailor offerings of specific products or services to particular customer segments or

Figure 7.2
Choice of Competitive Scope

Broad Scope — Many customer segments; geographic breadth & scale; product & service variety

Narrow Scope — Tailoring to specific customer segments; local geography; limited product & service

limited geographic territories, and do so to the exclusion of a broader approach.[8] Regal

Entertainment Group and Cinemark Holdings are national companies, operating theaters across the United States that show movies appealing to all ages and demographics. In contrast, Cinema Latino operates theaters in only four cities and focuses exclusively on Hispanic populations, showing first-run movies subtitled or dubbed in Spanish and serving Hispanic foods at the concession stands. Ryanair provides low cost passenger airline travel throughout Europe, while Wizz Air focuses on low cost air travel primarily in and out of Eastern European countries.

When the choice about competitive approach is combined with the choice about competitive scope, the result is the simple array of business-level strategies illustrated in Figure 7.3. Across the top are the broad low cost and differentiation strategies. The approaches that pursue a narrow scope – whether low cost or differentiation – are commonly referred to as *focused* strategies.

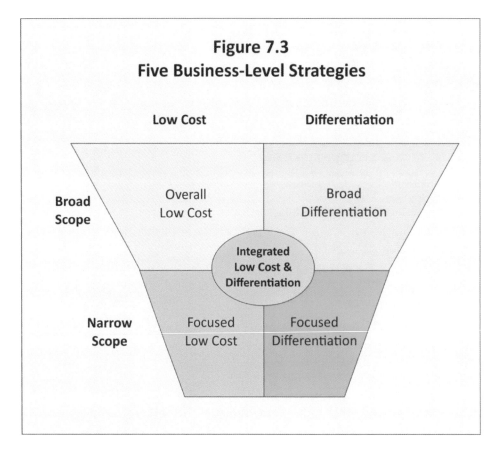

You will notice that a fifth business-level strategy, called the "integrated low cost and differentiation" strategy, has been added in the center of Figure 7.3. This approach is reflected in companies that seek to provide exceptional benefits while at the same time using a reasonably competitive cost structure. Though we mentioned the possibility of getting stuck in the middle when pursuing both low cost and differentiation simultaneously, there have been some recent developments in the field and evidence from industries which suggest that combinations are plausible under certain circumstances. It is a higher risk approach, and we will return to discuss this later in this chapter.

Connecting Business-Level Strategies with Superior Performance

The point of employing a business-level strategy is that it is generative of competitive advantage, and competitive advantage is supposed to result in above average returns or superior performance. We can see why this is the case by referring to Figure 7.4 and comparing each strategy to an average performing company in an industry. The average competitor in the industry earns a level of profits based upon an average cost structure and an average level of pricing charged for the benefits provided by its goods or services. The company pursuing the low cost strategy seeks to lower its costs while providing roughly the same level of benefits as the average competitor and charging roughly the same prices. In Figure 7.4 the low cost strategy (in red) shows that superior profitability is achieved when the company successfully reduces its cost structure. The company pursuing the differentiation strategy seeks to provide enhanced benefits to its customers while maintaining roughly the same cost structure as the average competitor. With enhanced benefits that are valued in the market, it should be able to charge higher prices than the average competitor, and thus earn higher profits (in blue). While not shown in the figure, the integrated low cost/ differentiation strategy seeks to earn higher profits by slightly lowering its costs while slightly elevating the benefits provided and its prices.

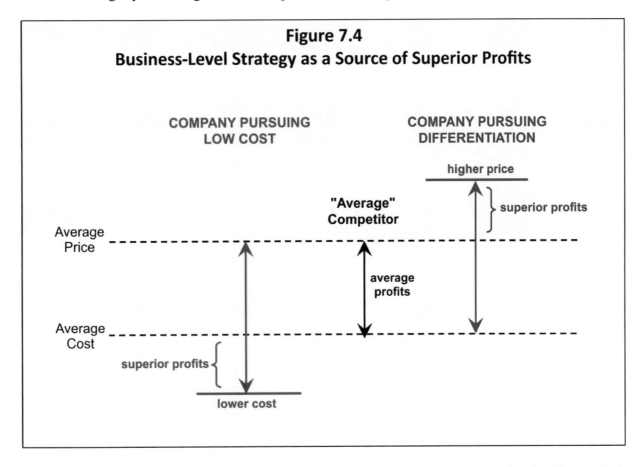

Figure 7.4
Business-Level Strategy as a Source of Superior Profits

If the diagram in Figure 7.4 reminds you of Figure 5.12 on value creation in Chapter 5, it is not a coincidence. As we have already suggested, business-level strategies are closely tied to the value chain and value creation. Consistency of purpose across value chain activities can result in either the lowering of costs (and possibly prices) or the enhancement of benefits with the possibility of charging higher prices. Achieving this consistency of purpose requires strong understanding of the resources and integrated sets of value chain activities that contribute to cost reduction or value enhancement so that they can be proactively managed.

A business-level strategy can best be thought of as the overarching philosophy of value creation within the company. Each element of the value chain displayed in Figure 7.5, along with each of the interrelationships between value chain elements will yield more value if they are coordinated toward a singular approach. Similarly, resource-based investments that are all geared toward one type of strategy allow the firm to take advantage of both the organizational learning cycle and consistent application approach that is possible with a steady message to all employees. In contrast, companies that are inconsistent within their value chains or resource-based investments will find themselves working at cross-purposes internally, presenting themselves to the marketplace with conflicting approaches, and will likely find themselves moving toward a "stuck in the middle" position – doing neither one particularly well. Friendster was the first social networking site, starting up in 2002, predating both MySpace and Facebook, yet the business flamed out early in the United States due to internally inconsistent approaches to the marketplace. According to founder Jonathan Abrams, each of the top executives hired by the company "came to Friendster with strong ideas about how to make the company as big as possible as fast as possible... 'Everybody had their own agenda.' The result was a kind of corporate schizophrenia."[9] Management of the company lost sight of what values social networking site users sought and became involved in several competing initiatives that were based upon entirely different and incompatible strategic differentiation approaches, while competitors honed in carefully and consistently on these dimensions and succeeded wildly.

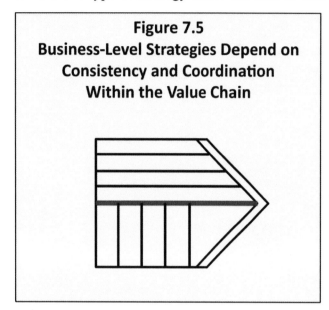

Figure 7.5
Business-Level Strategies Depend on Consistency and Coordination Within the Value Chain

Business-level strategies rely on internal consistency in activities across the company's value chain, in order to successfully pursue a single approach. Once the decision on a strategic approach has been made, then it should be applied with rigor *all* across the organization. In the next sections we explore important drivers of each of the business-level strategies, and draw attention to the relationship between each strategy and the value chain.

Important Caveats!

There are three really important cautions that need to be understood before we go on to examine each of the business-level strategies in detail. Each of these cautions reflects crucial conditions upon which the success of a strategy rests.

1. **Parity conditions**. All of the efforts made to pursue a business-level strategy will be wasted effort if the company does not achieve parity on other conditions that are valued by the marketplace. Differentiation on some dimension is an advantage only if other expected values are also delivered, and only if costs are roughly equivalent with those of competitors. It is very difficult to claim that your business is a five-star restaurant if the health rating on your

establishment is a "C." The expectation in the industry is now an "A" rating, and your competitors will all be seeking to accomplish this rating. If the only way to achieve this five-star status is to spend exorbitantly on location, fixtures, salaries and wages, and advertising, then above-average profits may not materialize. Costs that are significantly more as a result of differentiation must be countered with a price that exceeds the cost differential, so long as the market values the additional points of differentiation and consumers are willing to pay the price.

Cost leadership is an advantage only if there is comparability amongst the products/services with its competitors. Remember the old axiom "you get what you pay for." Many companies have come and gone over the years by providing a product or service at a significantly reduced price based on a low cost structure that resulted from skimping on essential features or quality that customers had come to expect. Packard Bell, a now-defunct manufacturing company that sold inexpensive PCs, was renowned for its poor customer service. In the 1990s "as the market moved from novice buyers to second-time buyers, many experienced consumers shied away from Packard Bell, citing its reputation for shoddy quality and indifferent service and support."[10] The effectiveness of each strategy assumes that all of the ordinary aspects expected of competitors in the industry are adequately delivered by the company.

2. **Evolution of customer expectations**. Pursuing one business-level strategy does not mean ignoring the positive aspects of other approaches. Importantly, as time goes by, customer expectations about valued product or service characteristics will tend to escalate. Therefore, pursuit of a business-level strategy requires the company to continually refine its own approach as well as ensure it maintains parity on other evolving conditions. "A firm should always aggressively pursue all cost reduction opportunities that do not sacrifice differentiation. [Similarly] a firm should also pursue all differentiation opportunities that are not costly."[11]

3. **Evolution of competition**. A business that operates in an environment where competitors are slow to react allows the well-designed and well-funded business to thrive until such time as competitors wake up or move to catch up. Formerly unsophisticated industries - such as dry cleaning, lawn care, and veterinary services - left large openings for single well-designed competitors. Banfield, The Pet Hospital, was founded in 1955 in Portland, Oregon, and developed a reputation for bringing human-quality medical practice to pets. In 1990 PetSmart, recognizing an opportunity to bring consistency of practice to a nationwide scale, asked Banfield to join with them to build veterinary clinics in its store. Today there are over 500, and Banfield was adding pet hospitals to PetSmart stores at the rate of 80 per year.[12]

In intensely competitive industries the efforts of other companies may cause obsolescence of a company's competitive position more quickly, will push the envelope of customer expectations, and will escalate parity conditions. Netflix helped obsolete the Blockbuster physical store model for video rental. But then along came Amazon's streaming services, Redbox Instant by Verizon, HBO-to-Go, and of course movies on demand through local cable providers.

Parity conditions and their evolution – either through normal customer growth or through competitive dynamics – make the management of a business-level strategic approach more complex.

Wendy's International, Part 1[13]

Wendy's International was founded in 1969 and now has more than 6,600 outlets worldwide. The company has always sought to differentiate itself from the rest of the industry with customization of sandwiches, unique offerings (the square hamburger and the Frosty), as well as their stated focus on some of the highest-quality food products in the fast food industry. But the corporate offices felt that Wendy's was suffering a sales loss because cash strapped consumers were avoiding their stores. They invested in a 99¢ Super Value Menu and pushed franchisees to continually increase the number of such offerings on the menu to draw in traffic. One franchisee laid out the problem. "The differentiation of Wendy's from the other [fast-food] concepts was the fact that we were recognized as being the quality player," said Dave Norman, chief financial officer of Crofton, Maryland-based DavCo Restaurants Inc., which operates 161 Wendy's. "For us to compete at that 99-cent threshold, we either have to give away food . . . or we have to damage our quality image because we cannot purchase the quality commodities."

QUESTIONS

1. Should Wendy's continue as a differentiator or try to pursue a low cost approach?
2. What would switching to a low cost approach mean for activities in the value chain and how they are coordinated?

LOW COST STRATEGY

Creating and maintaining a low cost position requires the organization to systematically lower its costs throughout its operations, such that the margins for that business exceed those of its competitors. The Vanguard Group was founded in 1974 as an investment company that single-mindedly focused on a low cost position. Founder John C. Bogle reasoned that if his asset managers matched market investment performance in the long term with the lowest costs and the lowest charges to his clients, then the company's returns would consistently exceed the market

averages. Their initial Vanguard 500 Index has risen to the 2nd largest mutual fund in the United States by 2016 with assets of over $229 billion. Vanguard runs seven out of the ten largest mutual funds with assets exceeding $100 billion. In every facet of the business, they concentrate on lowering costs: returns are distributed directly to individual investors rather than through intermediary brokers, they advertise very little, have pleasant but not elegant offices, and formalize cost containment as a key component of the annual bonus. In 2016 the company's average annual fund expenses are 0.18%, compared with the industry average of 1.01%.[14]

There are several conditions under which the pursuit of a low cost strategy may be more appropriate and hold a greater potential for success. One way to think about these conditions is to refer back to the five forces analysis (Chapter 4) to understand how each industry force might impact the low cost approach.

- **Rivalry**. When there are few opportunities to differentiate one's product or service offering (because such values are not appreciated by buyers), then standardization of product/service features is accompanied by highly competitive pricing. When there is standardization of products or services among competitive rivals, the low cost competitor will tend to fare better because the company with the low cost structure will enjoy a higher profit margin.

- **Buyers and Suppliers**. When buyers and suppliers have strong bargaining power and are able to exact economic concessions from competitors, the company with the lowest cost structure is able to fare better. In addition, if buyers experience low switching costs, the low cost competitor has the greatest flexibility to reduce pricing in order to keep and attract buyers.

- **New Entrants and Substitutes**. Other companies outside the industry may seek to offer products and services that provide a challenging price/value relationship. Given a set of values the company currently provides buyers, a low cost position offers flexibility to reduce prices and offset any perceived advantages that other companies may offer.

There are several factors that can lead to a low cost position. These include: 1) economies of scale; 2) capacity utilization; 3) experience curve; 4) product/service design; 5) process innovation (value chain design); and 6) internal value chain coordination. We discuss each of these below.

Economies of scale. Economies of scale are realized as unit costs drop while quantities produced each period grow larger, as illustrated in Figure 7.6. As firms increase their production (whether a product or service), many are able to attain significant cost savings as a result of being able to spread fixed and indirect costs over a greater number of units. This is especially important for companies competing in industries in which significant fixed investment is necessary, such as steel and automobile manufacturing or for a fuel refinery. Cost reductions through scale often occur because of the specialization of activities and the efficiency of assembly lines that are possible when seeking to produce large quantities in a given time frame.

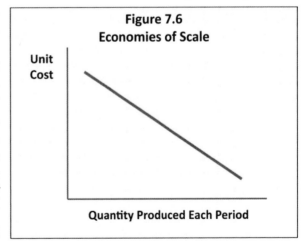

Capacity utilization. Capacity utilization is closely related to economies of scale. Scale economies result from the cost savings associated with production through large facilities;

however, those costs are particularly sensitive to the ability of companies with large facilities to fully utilize them. If they are not fully utilized, then the fixed-cost burden of the facilities is spread across fewer units produced and any possible scale benefits are lost. It is difficult in the short run to exactly match capacity to projected sales. However, companies that pursue a low cost strategy as their overarching approach constantly evaluate this area in order to maximize their investment. There are many industries where fixed costs are significant and profits are highly dependent upon small fluctuations in demand. The dramatic turnaround in the airline industry in 2006–2007 was a direct result of a reduction in the number of available seat miles (the standard measure of capacity in the industry) at the same time that airline passenger traffic was increasing. The result was much higher fleet utilization. Capacity of the big three domestic automobile manufacturers (GM, Ford, Chrysler) far exceeded demand for their vehicles during the recent recession, creating significant cost and competitive pricing problems. Each sought to shed capacity in order to reduce unused fixed costs, while each also offered multi-year interest free loans on new cars in order to generate immediate sales and keep factories operating.

Experience curve. As organizations gain greater experience over the years in producing a product or a service – called the **experience curve** – employees usually learn how to perform many functions quicker, cheaper, and with fewer mistakes. A company that takes this general tendency and translates it into a systematic approach to improvement can yield significant gains. The whole

Figure 7.7
Experience Curve

Unit Cost

Cumulative Production Over Time

movement toward a Six-Sigma approach has been aimed at systematically looking at every facet of the organization, reducing redundancies, eliminating variation, and sharing best practices. It is one of a number of systems used to increase the capability and improve the communication within organizations. The experience curve, illustrated in Figure 7.7, has been observed in a wide variety of industries (e.g., bottle caps, refrigerators, long distance calls, insurance policies[15]), and is a well-understood process by which companies achieve significant cost savings associated with their internal abilities to do things better and better over time.

Product/service design. The fundamental design of a product or service may be the single most important area in developing cost savings. Rather than looking for uniqueness from a customer perspective, a low cost strategic approach can also benefit from design simplicity, easy manufacturing, simple sourcing of raw materials, and inexpensive packaging. The product/service low cost approach must be both systematic and systemic. That is, the company must carefully examine every available aspect of the product or service element, taking absolutely nothing as given and fixed. Simultaneously the company must engineer the process across the value chain, from input to delivery, in a manner that keeps costs as low as possible. Kodak entered the inkjet printer business a few years ago, in competition with HP. HP's replacement ink cartridges are expensive because each contains a chip that determines how ink is dispensed onto the paper. Kodak re-engineered this product, putting the chip in the printer and eliminating this costly element from

220

their cartridges. The cartridges were cheaper and faster to manufacture, and could be priced lower at office supply stores.

Process innovation (value chain design). A new process that radically speeds up assembly, design, or delivery can yield dramatic cost savings that are not enjoyed by competitors. The ability of an individual firm to change those processes in a manner that creates new efficiencies can be a key to great cuts in costs. In its development of the long-range 777 aircraft, Boeing scrapped the traditional design/build process and completely reinvented it. Moving entirely to an electronic process, the 777 was designed digitally in virtual space, and all 3 million parts for each $150 million airplane were sourced electronically among 3,000 suppliers worldwide. Then-CEO Phil Condit claimed that they bet the company on this bold new initiative, which shaved eighteen months and more than $1 billion off the new plane's development, and which is now being used in next-generation aircraft design projects. In 2016 both Boeing and Airbus are introducing increased use of robotics and mechanization to their assembly lines to increase their annual output in the face of huge customer demand for aircraft.[16]

As a new entrant in the very tough airline business many years ago now, Southwest Airlines sought to provide a true low-price alternative to the major airlines. Their approach demanded that they be the lowest cost operation in the business. Every aspect of the business was examined individually for cost savings, and the whole organization was examined to ensure a consistent fit and approach throughout the enterprise. The company purchased only one style of Boeing aircraft. This, by itself, made gate operations and mechanical servicing more consistent and faster because ground crew had to deal with only one type of aircraft. In addition, every pilot was capable of flying virtually every airplane They historically avoided reserved seating in order to speed up passenger boarding. Their employees accepted a lower wage to work at a fun organization that didn't lay people off, in part made possible because senior managers of the company did not collect obscene salaries or work in plush offices. A low cost approach to design permeates every part of the business. And amidst this all, the competitive parity condition of positive customer flying experience was not diminished.

The ability to outmaneuver competitors by the use of speed in a business can provide significant cost savings while providing customers with something of value. France's automaker Renault determined it needed to rapidly produce a new car for a market that was demanding a compact, fuel-efficient car. The company put all the functions in automobile development under one roof, reporting to one leader, and slashed the development time in half. The Twingo was delivered in eighteen months, well ahead of their competition, at a sharply reduced developmental cost.[17]

Internal value chain coordination. Regardless of how costs are wrung out of the individual activities and functions within a company, the ability to reduce costs through the interrelationships between value chain activities is another crucial element in a low cost strategy. For example, when Human Resources is able to staff individual positions within activity areas that create best fit within those units, costs are reduced for the whole company because productivity is enhanced. Earlier we mentioned efforts made by Boeing to reduce costs. Boeing staffed "design-build" teams for the new 777 airplane, putting together pilots, mechanics, assembly plant supervisors, and computer designers with both customers and suppliers. Companies that involve all parts of the organization in parallel to improve the development and handoff of products or services can speed up the whole process, avoid later-stage technical problems, and wring costs out of the system in both the short and long run.

With recycling of products moving to center stage in society, some companies have utilized their R&D, production, distribution, and customer service operations to jointly develop products that can be easily recycled. This has actually led to significant cost savings and has put those companies well ahead of their competitors who might be forced into heavy investments to catch up. HP has spent considerable effort designing their PCs and their ink cartridges for easier recycling and reuse. The result has been a dramatic lowering of production costs, which allowed them to develop a customer service from something that has traditionally been the purview of production. "We're making it easier for customers to reduce waste by designing easily recyclable products. Where feasible, we use common fasteners and snap-in features to avoid applying glues, adhesives, or welds. This makes it easier for recyclers to dismantle, separate, and identify different plastics. Most HP PCs, printers, and servers are more than 90% recyclable by weight. Through our "closed loop" recycling process, Original HP ink and LaserJet toner cartridges are reduced to raw materials that can then be used to make new cartridges as well as other metal and plastic products."[18] Over the past years, HP has shipped over 3 billion Inkjet cartridges containing recycled plastic from this process, and in 2015 alone the company recycled 1.5 million tons of hardware and supplies.

Value Chain and Low Cost Strategy

The low cost business-level strategy can be an extremely effective means of achieving superior profits. How might it be put into place and what are the interrelationships that are involved? Using the value chain, let's look at a detailed example. Ryanair is the dominant low cost carrier in Europe today. They enjoy the largest available seat mile (ASM) capacity among Europe's discount airlines. In 2016 they earned 18.5% operating margins, the highest among all European airlines and nearly four percentage points better than the second-ranked discount flyer Easyjet.[19] Founded in 1985, it almost died within the first five years by trying to provide a range of services, including a business class and a frequent flyer program, using a variety of small aircraft flown to and from Ireland. The airline accumulated over £20 million in losses. The company was recapitalized in 1990 with a new mantra to be THE low cost airline, and they made no apologies for their rigorous approach to the revised strategic direction. Figure 7.8 diagrams their value chain and highlights key low cost-producing activities in each cell.[20] Because of their efforts across the entire value chain, Ryanair enjoys a low cost advantage in Europe that is larger than the advantage that Southwest Airlines enjoys in the United States.[21]

Risks Associated with Low Cost Strategy

No business-level strategy is without risks. This is because each involves significant investments, learning, development, and refinement across the company's entire value chain - a complex and time-consuming management undertaking. Here we outline several risks associated with the pursuit of a low cost strategy.

Low cost strategy versus low cost leadership. As suggested by Figure 7.1, in most industries there may be a number of companies pursuing a low cost leadership strategy. It may be that some companies pursuing this strategy can, in fact, generate returns that are superior to the industry averages because they have managed to create cost structures that are superior to average competition. However, in any market there can be one – and only one – low cost *leader*.

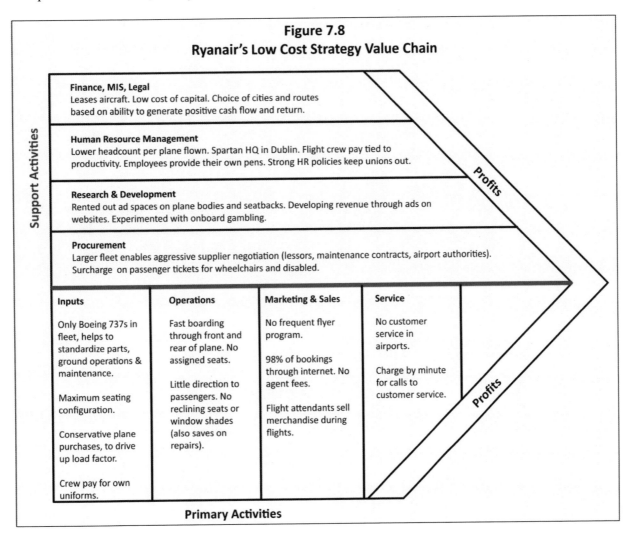

Figure 7.8
Ryanair's Low Cost Strategy Value Chain

Low cost leadership is at the endpoint of the continuum in Figure 7.1 and represents the most powerful competitive position among companies pursuing a low cost approach. Every other business is simply a wannabe low cost leader, chasing the well-heeled, well-focused, low cost leader. This can be a recipe for failure over the long run. Witness the rise of Walmart in discount retailing during the 1980s. Its low cost structure often allowed it to *price* lower than Kmart's *costs*, so that in markets where the two companies were competing head-to-head, Walmart could price low and still earn profits while Kmart would lose money on every sale.[22] Walmart's low cost structure helped drive Kmart into bankruptcy in the 1990s.

This should not be confused with the ongoing and important need to lower costs in the regular course of business. In many (but not all) cases, the effort to lower costs may be a very appropriate approach. If you are operating a very high-end restaurant and are approached with the "opportunity" to lower your costs by using paper napkins rather than cloth napkins, you are wise to forgo that savings as it would negatively impact the customers you are trying to attract. On the other hand, if you could find a means to clean the napkins at half the current costs, you would be unwise not to take advantage of the opportunity. We point this out because the intent and drive is at least as important as the action. Employees as a whole make thousands of decisions every day and they should always be encouraged to consider which of their actions will be the best fit given the company's strategic approach. A focus on low cost as a strategic approach is quite different from the cost savings that allow for parity in the customers' perception.

Price is not a strategy. A low-price approach is often confused with a low cost strategic approach. Price by itself is not a strategic factor, since prices can be changed instantaneously without strategic investments. It is relatively easy for any competitor to try and use low price as way to attract customers, or to instantly match another company's price. Yet without actually having the low cost operation to back it up, low price is a certain means of achieving lower returns. Pricing is tactical, while managing to a low cost position is very strategic requiring investments in facilities, practices, and more.

Customers do not value the benefits derived from low costs. Often a company will use its low cost position to reduce prices in order to make its products or services more attractive and drive up sales volume. However, in some situations and at some points in time customers may not be interested in cost- and price-based benefits, but instead may have significantly greater appreciation for other product or service characteristics and the benefits they convey. Many low cost companies introduced MP3 players into the marketplace in the early 2000s, yet the market continued to embrace the Apple iPod despite its higher price.

Cost positions can be imitated over time. Technology, greater access to global markets, and the greater ease of forming alliances and joint ventures make it possible for competitors to more easily imitate the cost structure of low cost companies. Companies pursuing a low cost position must be constantly on guard against the evolution of competitive positions, and must continue to reinvest resources to further protect low cost positions.

Wendy's International, Part 2[23]

Wendy's continued to push their value meal offerings and then decided to roll out a breakfast offering to half their operating units within the next year. In addition they announced that they would drive sales by pushing four areas of the business; 1) emphasizing stronger marketing; 2) more new products; 3) sharper store operations; and 4) better relationships with franchisees. With the addition of an activist investor on their board, the company began pursuing the idea of selling the company. The investor had little faith that the company executives had a coherent strategy for the firm and were just reaching out using the same methods as their competitors.

QUESTIONS

1. How would selling the company improve its strategy?
2. Which strategic initiatives should Wendy's pursue and which should they drop?
3. What are the implications of offering a breakfast menu for a low cost generic strategy?

DIFFERENTIATION STRATEGY

Differentiation is perhaps the most widely utilized business-level strategic approach. This is because there are virtually unlimited methods by which a company can attempt to uniquely create value for customers. As with the low cost strategy, effective differentiation requires a company to systematically organize its activities throughout its value chain in order to deliver superior value and thus command higher prices. Ferrari has always held out a reputation for extraordinary performance vehicles that have a standard twelve-to-eighteen-month waiting list. While Porsche produced more than 230,000 cars in 2016, Ferrari produced fewer than 9,000. The

  company carefully manages its activities in order to create the value that customers prefer. In research and development the company applies Formula 1 technology to production cars, and has conducted advanced aerodynamic studies in its own wind tunnels. It does not rely on competitive market suppliers for key components such as aluminum, but instead operates its own specialist aluminum production arm. Every vehicle is assembled and customized by a staff that is required to spend years in training before being "allowed" to join the production line.[24] Employees are so dedicated to the company and its culture that it was named in both 2003 and 2007 as one of the 100 best places to work in Europe.[25] The price premium Ferrari commands is directly related to the operation of its value chain. Neither speed nor standardization is a critical component in an industry where both are valued on an almost religious level.

There are several conditions under which the pursuit of a differentiation strategy may be more appropriate and hold a greater potential for success. We again refer back to the five forces analysis to understand how each industry force might impact this strategic approach. The key point for each of these forces is that downstream customer markets must embrace variety within the industry for a differentiation strategy to be successful.

- **Rivalry**. When diversity and variety exists among customers and their needs, then strategic variety is possible within an industry. So long as all buyers do not uniformly demand a common or standardized set of features or benefits, differentiation is a realistic and practical option for competitors.

- **Buyers**. If buyer concentration does not exist and consequently buyers have little power, then cost/price relationships may become less influential in the buying process.

- **Suppliers**. Suppliers may still exert bargaining power on competitors, but as long as diversity of needs exists among buyers and there is no standardization or commoditization occurring within the industry, higher costs from suppliers may be offset by higher prices charged that support the kind of value chain investments in differentiation.

- **New entrants and substitutes**. Effective differentiation often shields competitors from new competition presented by new entrants and possible substitutes. Unique value chain and resource investments designed to create differentiated value should be difficult to imitate.

There are several drivers of an effective differentiation strategy. These include: 1) product and service features; 2) psychographic and cognitive benefits; 3) process innovation (value chain design); and 4) internal value chain coordination. Here we briefly explore each of these drivers.

Product and service features. Most products and services are clearly delineated by their unique features relative to the competition. These features create the opportunity to attract new customers, make existing customers more loyal, and provide the foundation for charging a premium price that offsets the costs of differentiation. There are three dimensions of product/service features that help create an effective differentiated strategic position:

1. **Characteristics that respond to customer needs**. People buy products and services to fulfill their needs and desires, and they will balance the "performance" of their purchases against the prices they pay. The price/performance relationship – between the higher prices paid for products or services and their performance – is the basis upon which customers will judge value and respond to company efforts to differentiate. Performance dimensions that are judged by customers tend to be the kinds listed in Figure 7.9.

CarMax made the process of car buying and selling easy, allowing consumers to avoid the hated car salesman rat race at most car dealerships. Their no-haggle system allows consumers to buy and sell cars in a very objective process without having to negotiate.

Many travel agencies found their business plummeting as online reservation systems became popular and convenient. Now some agencies not only book airlines, but also book hotels, arrange tours, set up restaurant reservations, arrange for child sitters and guarantee an entire trip against unforeseen weather or sickness. The packaging of formerly separate services has allowed them to survive and charge a premium price compared to the single-function agencies.

> **Figure 7.9**
> **Product & Service Performance Dimensions**
>
> - Effectiveness in intended use
> - Physical characteristics (e.g. color, size, shape, etc.)
> - Variety
> - Quality
> - Safety
> - Consistency
> - Convenience (location, ease of access)
> - Immediacy
> - Complementarity with other products (e.g. cellphone synching with computer)
> - Speed
> - On the cutting edge

In Chapter 1 we described the opportunity recognition and value creation imperatives that drive today's strategy. Attempting to stay on the cutting edge of product and service characteristics is one manifestation of these imperatives that we regularly observe. For example, in 2006 Lexus designed a system that allowed a car to automatically perform a parallel park. In 2007 Microsoft introduced Surface, a 30-inch display in a table-like form factor, which uses cameras to sense objects, hand gestures, and touch to turn an ordinary tabletop into a vibrant, interactive computer screen. The 2010 Kinect for Xbox 360 for the first time cut the umbilical wire between the gamer and her machine, allowing free motion to dictate commands.

2. **Integrity of the product or service**. Before they purchase, customers increasingly evaluate the prospects of long-term satisfaction with a company's product or service.

Historical defect ratings and repair histories factor into automobile and other purchase decisions. Automobile manufacturers go to great lengths to assure prospective buyers about these important dimensions. Intuit guarantees the integrity of its TurboTax software, agreeing to pay for any tax bills resulting from errors in its program. Research firm Nielsen's 2015 report titled "Global Trust in Advertising" reveals that 2/3 of consumers act upon posted online reviews of products and services, and these are especially meaningful to Millennials.

3. **The use of quality inputs.** Many of the performance dimensions mentioned previously can be achieved, in part, through sourcing quality inputs from suppliers. This could mean the use of Intel chips in the assembly of laptops, or the staffing of biotech company R&D departments by hiring top Ph.D. candidates from premier university biochemistry programs. In contrast, inferior quality inputs can contribute to poor performance characteristics as well as loss of product integrity. The highly successful Motorola Razr cellphone was hobbled early in its introduction by a faulty component from one of its suppliers, prompting the company to recall many phones and suspend sales until the problem could be corrected.[26] In 2007 pet food manufacturers in the United States discovered that Chinese suppliers of the ingredient wheat gluten were spiking its protein count by adding melamine, a poisonous chemical, which resulted in the deaths of hundreds of pets. Once reputation has been sullied, it requires heroic efforts to recover it.

Psychographic and cognitive benefits. Customers gain value from companies that go beyond physical or operational characteristics of the products and services they buy. Psychographic and cognitive identification with a company and its products or services is difficult to create, but can be extremely valuable once the connection is made. One of the reasons that Chrysler was so successful in its 1980s introduction of the first minivan was that it used psychographic consumer research to better understand the image that young mothers had of themselves and their needs. Traditional demographic research could not reveal the developing market for a new type of vehicle, nor could the usual trends in sedan or truck sales.[27] There appear to be three sources of this type of value creation:

1. **Marketing and advertising**. One of the significant means by which companies can differentiate themselves in a visible and unique manner is with an effective advertising campaign. There is perhaps no other single item of as much importance in differentiation as that of brand. The ability to create a brand that has instant recognition and instant reference to the product/service sold allows the business to draw in customers more easily than their competitors as well as charge more. Google, Target, Outback Steakhouse, Apple, WD-40, and Sony are among the most recognized brands in the world. Each is well embedded in their customers' minds and connotes an exacting message as to what may be obtained. Earlier in its corporate life the famous Macintosh ad titled "1984," which aired only once during Super Bowl XVIII, permanently established Apple computers as leading-edge, break-the-rules machines. Your professors in marketing and strategy will help you understand that the "cola wars" fought for years between Coca-Cola and Pepsi have hinged almost exclusively on "lifestyle" advertising as a means of developing very different images about the two arch-competitors.

2. **Responsiveness to customers**. How many times have you been put on hold when you call a toll-free airline reservation number, or find that the customer service agent you finally reach is unable to help you because of "company policy"? We can whistle George Gershwin's *Rhapsody in Blue* from memory because we have heard it so many times while waiting on the United Airlines phone lines. Responsiveness to customers can make or break a company's image, as well as the desirability of buying or recommending its products or services. Some companies have engineered the customer interface to actually enhance the perceived benefit, presenting alternatives and ideas in advance to customers before they are even requested. Amazon.com presents book and music recommendations to customers who return to their website, based upon their automated analysis of the customer's previous buying patterns. Target analyzes your shopping data, and then matching that with your store or credit card, mails flyers to your home with special deals personalized just for you.

3. **Corporate reputation**. Beyond the immediate experiences that customers have with a company's products and services, advertising, and customer service, a company's corporate reputation can facilitate or impede the creation of differentiated value to the customer. Mentioned earlier in this book in the chapter on value chain, Newman's Own enhances its relationship with customers who buy its food products through its sponsorship of camps for terminally ill children and its support of other charitable causes. Trust in the abilities of a company can be an important factor in the purchase decision, and enables some organizations to outperform others in their industry. The Betty Ford Clinic has developed a powerful reputation as a premier facility not only for the breaking of addictions, but also for its ambiance and confidentiality. Reputations are built on skills and experience, and they can lead to extraordinary returns for the business. In contrast, when British Petroleum's oil spilled into the Gulf of Mexico and all over the world's TV screens, the company's reputation was badly damaged and many customers now refuse to buy gas through BP's retail gas stations.

Process innovation (value chain design). The drivers of differentiation mentioned previously demonstrate that this strategic approach, like the low cost approach, depends upon supportive activities within each cell of the value chain (see Figure 7.10). In addition, reconfiguring the value chain in a manner that differs from the competition has the ability to provide unique value. In confronting the growing trend to dine away from home at restaurants, competitors in the supermarket industry have reconfigured their value chains to better meet the needs of their customers. This includes preparation of fully cooked meals in their deli operations, so that customers on their way home from work can conveniently pick up high-quality meals ready to just heat up and eat at home. Many chains have also developed online ordering systems, where store personnel select and bag the desired groceries and deliver them to the customer curbside at an appointed time. The extremely competitive child care business has usually been considered a commodity business where companies seek to drive down costs, provide basic services, and minimally meet state licensing requirements. Bright Horizons discovered gold when they forged relationships with Fortune 500 employers, set up child care centers in or next to corporate headquarter office buildings, paid higher salaries, and incorporated learning centers within their facilities.[28]

Internal value chain coordination. The ability to achieve effective differentiation relies not only on consistency of activities within the value chain toward the intended point(s) of

228

differentiation, but also on continuous coordination of these activities across the company. Figure 7.10 demonstrates that many of the drivers of differentiation rely on combinations of value chain activities. This recognizes, as is the case with the low cost strategy, that an action taken in one department or function of a company can have a ripple effect throughout the company. A substitution of ingredients brought in by purchasing can dramatically effect whether consumers like the taste of a product. A change in package size by marketing to accommodate more information will impact production line machinery and how packages might fit into cases for shipping. A change in administrative policy about repairs and defects can reshape how customers view a company when they talk to customer service agents. We could go on with many such descriptions of coordination effects at a very specific and practical level. What examples can you think of that illustrate the critical connections between parts of the value chain?

On a grander scale, consistency and coordination of activities, in fact, define whether the differentiated approach that a company takes can succeed. Kodak fought for its life as the film industry moved to a largely digital environment. A company that traditionally earned returns through its imaging, photographic paper and processing businesses, Kodak had to dramatically remake itself and find a new approach that distinguished it from competitors who embraced digital media much earlier on. Within the last decade Kodak had developed cameras, printers, and internet-based printing services for consumers. A tremendous effort in research and product development resulted in a new line of products, while the sales department needed to forge new relationships with electronics retailers and marketing needed to reshape what Kodak stood for in the minds of consumers. Unfortunately, there was still resistance internally to moves toward all things digital among long term employees. Every aspect of the company's value chain needs to be tightly integrated for the company to survive the death of film. Where consistency of approach does not occur, the chances of failure escalate. These internal inconsistency and coordination issues led to the demise of Kodak as we knew it.

Figure 7.10
Differentiation Strategy

Differentiation based on	Requires value chain excellence in
Product or service characteristics	Marketing research, R&D, Operations
Product or service Integrity control	Operations, Manufacturing
Quality inputs	R & D, Procurement
Marketing & advertising	Marketing research, Creative marketing
Responsiveness to customers	Customer service, Administration
Corporate reputation	Administration

Value Chain and Differentiation Strategy

For the differentiation strategy to succeed, we have again stressed the importance of the value chain perspective. Let's look at another comprehensive example to see how it might be put into place and the interrelationships that are involved. Starbucks started business in 1971 as a roaster and seller of whole coffee beans in the Pike Place Market in Seattle.[29] Purchased by one of their former employees, Howard Schultz re-imagined the business along the designs of the Italian coffee shops he visited. Selling premium coffee in a relaxing setting where the coffee barista would know your name and your preferences would allow the business to charge premium prices and differentiate it from the vast number of competitors (including at that time mostly home brewing). Their consistent approach to a differentiation strategy throughout the value chain becomes obvious when we look at what they have done. Figure 7.11 diagrams their value chain and highlights key differentiation activities in each cell. The company has grown to 12,500 U.S. locations and another 10,500 stores in seventy foreign countries; its revenue of almost $19 billion in 2015 increased by 17 percent over the previous year.

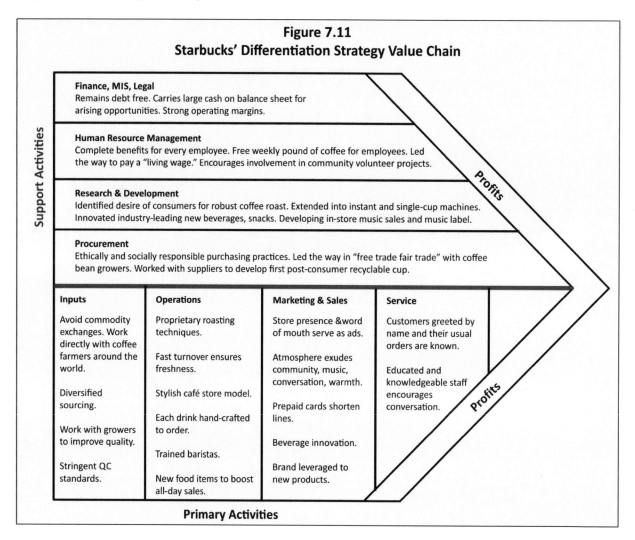

Figure 7.11
Starbucks' Differentiation Strategy Value Chain

Support Activities

Finance, MIS, Legal
Remains debt free. Carries large cash on balance sheet for arising opportunities. Strong operating margins.

Human Resource Management
Complete benefits for every employee. Free weekly pound of coffee for employees. Led the way to pay a "living wage." Encourages involvement in community volunteer projects.

Research & Development
Identified desire of consumers for robust coffee roast. Extended into instant and single-cup machines. Innovated industry-leading new beverages, snacks. Developing in-store music sales and music label.

Procurement
Ethically and socially responsible purchasing practices. Led the way in "free trade fair trade" with coffee bean growers. Worked with suppliers to develop first post-consumer recyclable cup.

Inputs	Operations	Marketing & Sales	Service
Avoid commodity exchanges. Work directly with coffee farmers around the world.	Proprietary roasting techniques.	Store presence & word of mouth serve as ads.	Customers greeted by name and their usual orders are known.
Diversified sourcing.	Fast turnover ensures freshness.	Atmosphere exudes community, music, conversation, warmth.	Educated and knowledgeable staff encourages conversation.
Work with growers to improve quality.	Stylish café store model. Each drink hand-crafted to order.	Prepaid cards shorten lines.	
Stringent QC standards.	Trained baristas.	Beverage innovation.	
	New food items to boost all-day sales.	Brand leveraged to new products.	

Profits

Primary Activities

In the past two chapters we have talked extensively about extraordinary resources and the critical importance of intangible resources and capabilities. One of those crucial intangibles is the means by which organizations coordinate activities across elements of the company. Another is the overall fit that the company achieves between activities within the organization's value chain. Starbucks began losing this fit by failing to see the interrelationships.

After observing that lines and wait times had increased in their stores, the company began a systematic effort in the early 2000s to find ways to address growing demand. They installed machines capable of automatically grinding and brewing almost any coffee combination. This move made the process faster and more consistent, but at the cost of the sight, sound, and aroma (of grinding beans and working the knobs on the machine) so crucial to the original personalized

Starbucks experience. The new machines were also so tall that they blocked the line of sight between the barista and the customer, cutting off conversation and loosening the bond between them. Other moves included the offering of hot lunch sandwiches and pre-packaging coffee beans in sealed bags. Microwaved breakfast sandwiches interfered with the coffee aromas floating around. These decisions to streamline operations and generate additional revenue negatively impacted the customer in-store experience, which had been central to Starbucks' value creation efforts for years. Alignment between the functions of the organization is often much more critical than specific choices made in some departments of most organizations. Something that makes perfect sense in isolation may be a crushing hit to the armor of the company.

Risks Associated with Differentiation Strategy

Like the low cost strategy, the differentiation strategy is subject to several risks. In addition to the parity caution offered earlier, several of the risks associated with a differentiation strategy are outlined as follows.

Product differentiation is not a strategy. In your marketing classes you have probably learned about product differentiation as an effective marketing tool – new sizes, flavors, colors, varieties, hours of operation, and so on. From the strategy point of view, however, mere product or service differences are not the basis for competitive advantage since these types of characteristics can generally be easily duplicated or imitated. Effective strategic differentiation has to do with the *activity* sets within and across the value chain. In this view product differentiation is a manifestation of something deeper within the organization. The *strategic* view of differentiation places a premium on processes that identify emerging customer needs and desires, and how a company organizes its activities in order to deliver the values that customers appreciate. Companies that focus their greatest attention on mere product differentiation may perform poorly over the long run.

Customers do not value the benefits derived from differentiation. Do you use all the functions that are embedded in your cell phone? In some situations and at some points in time customers may not be interested in differentiation activities that result in product and service features, but instead may have significantly greater appreciation for other dimensions. For example, in the desktop and laptop computer industry customers are most interested in standardization at a competitive price. Standardization is important for software compatibility, the use of "plug and play" peripheral devices, and ease of repair if a machine crashes. Price is important because the nature of technology trends have led customers to come to expect falling prices over time. While engineers and technical developers may value aesthetic and multifunctional designs, the technology-push capabilities of machines often exceed the desires and needs of customers.[30]

Differentiation positions can be imitated over time. When a company has developed a valued differentiation position that is insulated from competition, it enjoys an advantage over competitors and can earn superior profits. Competitors will not be unaware of what's going on, however, and will seek to imitate the value(s) that the company is creating and delivering to customers. Once again, with the advent of technology, greater access to global markets, greater access to financial capital, and the ability to more easily form alliances and joint ventures, in time competition will usually discover ways to become more competitive once again. Companies pursuing a differentiation approach must be constantly on guard against the evolution of competitors, and must continue to invest resources to extend and deepen their positions.

OTHER STRATEGIC APPROACHES

Focus Strategies

A variation on the two primary business-level strategies of low cost and differentiation is based on the breadth of the approach. Whereas a low cost or a differentiation approach is a broad market strategy, a focus strategy takes each into a unique segment of the market. Segmentation possibilities are virtually unlimited, but each is usually aimed at a very small part of a larger market. Within the focus approach, companies can pursue either a low cost or a differentiation strategy, thus in practice this is referred to as a cost focus or a differentiation focus. The obvious implication here is that by segmenting the market, a company is able to exploit an inconsistency between the needs of that particular market segment and the overall market.

In-N-Out Burger has longed reigned supreme in the fast-food burger market of the western United States, catering to a clientele that loves fast food but wants the highest quality product they can get. At In-N-Out everything is made fresh to order. There are no microwaves or freezers. Customers can watch french fries being made from hand-diced, fresh, whole potatoes and the shakes being made from real ice cream.[31] They have narrowed their focus both geographically and by customer group. Their food is neither inexpensive nor fast when compared to the traditional fast food competitor.

Focus strategies are most appropriate under a limited set of circumstances. First, the segment in which the company seeks to focus is not as important to other companies pursuing broad strategic approaches. Pursuing a focused strategy is best accomplished by avoiding head-to-head competition with a larger company that usually possesses deep pockets and great resolve to succeed. This can occur either because the segment is too small for the larger competitor to pay attention to, or the incremental investment by the large competitor to tailor its approach sufficiently to address the segment is greater than the estimated return it might earn. Second, the segment or niche is large enough and presents sufficient growth opportunity for the focused strategy company. The possibility for organic growth within a company's market niche is more attractive than having to leverage value-chain and resource investments into unfamiliar territory. Finally, the pursuit of a focus strategy is most appropriate for companies with constrained resources that cannot effectively operate on a broad-strategy scope.

It may not surprise you that start-up companies, young companies, and family businesses usually pursue focus strategies. Why do you suppose this is true? These types of companies ordinarily do not have the depth and breadth of resources that allow them to pursue broad markets. Instead, they rely on a very narrow set of resources, which in turn are the foundation for a relatively specific capability or set of value-creating activities. Broadening into different markets or segments usually requires access to fairly significant financial resources, which many of these types of companies do not enjoy. We will return to this topic of strategic challenges of growth and expansion that many companies experience in Chapter 8.

The biggest risk to the focus strategy is that competitors pursuing a broad strategy will decide to drill down into this more narrow market space. Narrow markets or segments are places where larger, broad-strategy competitors can find additional sources of growth while at the same time leveraging their existing value chains and developed resources. In addition, the growth of the more-focused strategy company may entail ultimately confronting broader markets or segments more directly.

Integrated Low Cost/Differentiation Strategy

A great deal of attention has been paid lately to a variation on these business-level strategies where companies purport to borrow elements from both the low cost and differentiation approaches. Yet this strategy runs a great risk of leaving the company that employs it "stuck in the middle." Let's examine the approach in two ways.

First, imagine three equally resource-endowed companies competing in an industry in which there exists strategic variety (i.e., in which both low cost and differentiation strategic approaches may succeed). In Figure 7.12 we plot the estimated trajectories of companies X, Y, and Z as they seek to reach the "value frontier" (the boundary of optimal possibilities combining both low cost and high differentiation). Company X, which pursues the integrated strategy, faithfully applies its resources and is able to accomplish level m in the low cost spectrum and level p in the differentiation spectrum. Yet company Y is single-mindedly focused on low cost, applies all its resources in that pursuit, and accomplishes level n in lowering its costs.

This makes sense, because they are applying all of their resources and efforts against lowering costs. Similarly, company Z is pursuing differentiation with single-minded focus and accomplishes level q. Unless company X has somehow uniquely identified a special market that appreciates the combination of moderately low cost and moderate differentiation, all else being equal the company will be outcompeted by companies that pursue the pure business-level strategies. Management of X is following an integrated strategy right into a stuck-in-the-middle position, from which it may be difficult to recover.

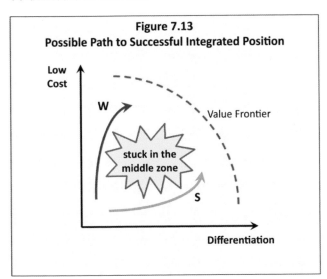

How is it possible for companies to successfully pursue an integrated strategy, then? One possibility is that a company single-mindedly pursues a pure business-level strategy, develops competitive advantage, generates superior returns, and then uses those superior returns to develop the integrated strategy with a secondary competitive position. This is illustrated in Figure 7.13, where a company avoids the zone of being stuck in the middle by moving away from a pure strategy only after it has sufficiently developed its position. Here company W has fully developed its low cost position, and is now using its superior returns to develop a differentiated position as well. Company S has moved out the differentiation path, and is now seeking to lower its costs as an added source of competitive advantage.

It looks simple on paper to move from one successful strategy into new terrain. However, the problem of developing competitive advantage based upon two different approaches simultaneously can be severe, even for highly successful companies. In 2006–2007, for example, Walmart sought to bring more fashionable clothing lines into its discount retail stores. The clothing lines did not sell well, causing huge inventory overstocks throughout the company's U.S. stores, and resulted in lower store sales growth than expected. This prompted write-offs from their income statement, and caused problems for suppliers upstream when the company cut subsequent orders. Walmart has long been known for its low cost strategy, which is supported throughout every activity in its value chain. To succeed in differentiating itself, in addition to low cost, the company would need to significantly enhance capabilities across its value chain that would support this new approach. The new approach requires: marketing research that identifies and understands fashion trends, buyers who can source goods on dimensions other than low cost and acceptable quality, new (usually more expensive) methods of display and merchandising in stores, the attraction of different types of customers who are interested in more fashionable clothing, and more. When a company has been consistently and successfully operating in one mind-set for decades, it is very difficult to begin operating differently throughout its value chain. Like any strategic initiative, embarking on a strategy takes time using appropriate resource development.

The same comments can be made about attempts to move from a highly differentiated position toward a position that also embraces lower costs - company S in Figure 7.13. As we mentioned earlier, during 2005–2006 Starbucks sought to increase the speed and efficiency of its store operations by moving away from handcrafted beverage preparations to machine-assisted preparations. In their stores machines were installed that automatically ground the beans and brewed the coffee for their lattés and other specialty coffees. On February 14, 2007, founder Howard Schultz wrote an impassioned letter to all Starbucks employees about their recent shift in strategy, titling the letter "The Commoditization of the Starbucks Experience," something which he claimed had resulted in declining performance and opened the door to competitive threats:

> "Over the past ten years, in order to achieve the growth, development, and scale necessary to go from less than 1,000 stores to 13,000 stores and beyond, we have had to make a series of decisions that, in retrospect, have led to the watering down of the Starbucks experience, and, what some might call the commoditization of our brand.
>
> Many of these decisions were probably right at the time, and on their own merit would not have created the dilution of the experience; but in this case, the sum is much greater and, unfortunately, much more damaging than the individual pieces. For example, when we went to automatic espresso machines, we solved a major problem in terms of speed of service and efficiency. At the same time, we overlooked the fact that we would remove much of the romance and theatre that was in play with the use of the La Marzocca machines. This specific decision became even more damaging when the height of the machines, which are now in thousands of stores, blocked the visual sight line the customer previously had to watch the drink being made, and for the intimate experience with the barista. This, coupled with the need for fresh roasted coffee in every North America city and every international market, moved us toward the decision and the need for flavor locked packaging. Again, the right decision at the right time, and once again I believe we overlooked the cause and the affect of flavor lock in our stores. We achieved

234

fresh roasted bagged coffee, but at what cost? The loss of aroma - perhaps the most powerful nonverbal signal we had in our stores; the loss of our people scooping fresh coffee from the bins and grinding it fresh in front of the customer, and once again stripping the store of tradition and our heritage?"

Having provided sufficient warning about the dangers of the integrated low cost/differentiation approach, we should also recognize that there are some shining examples of companies that have successfully gone down this path. Toyota is a company that readily comes to mind. It has not only achieved tremendous success through differentiation in design, development, and manufacturing of a range of vehicles that deliver value to customers. It has also achieved a singularly lower cost structure than its chief competitors, enabling the company to price lower and still earn healthy returns. No wonder Ford, GM, and Chrysler continue to struggle!

OUTSOURCING, STRATEGY, AND THE VALUE CHAIN

The connections we have made throughout this chapter between business-level strategies and the value chain allow us to gain further insight on the process of outsourcing, which has become prevalent among all kinds of businesses over the last twenty years. In Chapter 5, you will recall, we mentioned that outsourcing possibilities are occasionally identified through the value chain analysis. Outsourcing is a process through which a company depends on another organization to perform activities in its own value chain. For example, Nike outsources manufacturing of its athletic shoes to production companies in the Far East that have lower labor costs and can produce shoes less expensively than in the United States. Walmart relies on other companies to manage the stocking and restocking of certain kinds of specialty merchandise within its own stores, instead of having that merchandise flow through its sophisticated distribution system. Why would a company outsource any of its activities? How does outsourcing work to improve a company's strategic approach to its industry? Under what conditions should a company refrain from outsourcing? We tackle these important questions in this section.

From a competitive strategy perspective there are two primary reasons that a company might decide to outsource some activity or set of activities: 1) to enhance strategic position in the marketplace, and 2) to offload activities in which they do not have any special competence and which do not contribute to its strategic position. Generally there are fairly straightforward situations that may fall into the first category. Small pharmaceutical companies often form joint ventures with larger companies in order to take advantage of their well-developed sales and marketing operations. In this case the outsourcing of marketing and sales can contribute to significantly greater buyer awareness and perceived legitimacy for the company. Toshiba discovered that their customers value extremely fast turnaround times when their Toshiba computers break down and require authorized repairs. The company farmed out repair operations to trained UPS employees at the Kentucky hub of United Parcel Service, which also picked up and redelivered the machine. Avoiding the extra steps of delivery and pickup to Toshiba itself, Toshiba customers received repairs at least two days sooner and Toshiba's relationship with customers was strengthened.[32]

The second reason – offloading nonessential activities – is much more complicated for companies to determine. As we have illustrated in this chapter and in the earlier chapter on the value chain, management of the value chain to the internally consistent pursuit of a business-level strategic approach is a complex undertaking. If we simply look at the variety of activities occurring in each cell of the value chain, as well as the coordination required among cells and the connections made upstream and downstream with suppliers and customers (Figures 7.8 and 7.11), we begin to see how monumental a challenge this can be. For this reason, not every company is capable of managing and performing every one of the activities in its value chain. Our discussion in Chapter 6 on resource-based analysis helps us arrive at the same conclusion. Most companies develop and pursue unique resources and competitive excellence in a limited number of arenas; it is what they become especially good at, and what they become known for doing well. If in addition they attempt to manage and perform activities in which they have no unique capabilities or that do not leverage their resource positions, then they may be overextending themselves into activities that do not contribute to developing competitive advantage.

It is simple to see that this is the case in some examples, but more difficult in others. For example, every business generates volumes of garbage each day (even in this digital age). Part of conducting business effectively requires that they "take out the garbage;" however, few companies will actually haul their waste to the landfill. Instead, they outsource this to a local company. It makes sense, since hauling garbage is generally not central to what companies do. However when activities become more central to what a company does strategically, the challenge of deciding whether to outsource or not becomes much greater. On what basis does Nike decide to have other companies manufacture its shoes, and why would Walmart entertain having other companies manage what happens within their own retail stores?

It may be easier to tackle this question from the other side – that is, when is it *inappropriate* to outsource activities? There appear to be several conditions that describe when outsourcing may damage or hinder a company's strategic efforts:

Loss of control over costs or differentiation values. Having another organization perform important value chain activities can damage the company's strategic efforts if the company loses control over key values that are central to its strategy. In 2000 toy retailer Toys"R"Us signed a ten-year agreement that made Amazon.com the exclusive online retail outlet for Toys"R"Us toys, games, and baby products. Unfortunately, Toys"R"Us was unable to control the "look" of its merchandise on the Amazon site, nor prevent the introduction of other toys through Amazon's zShops partners.[33]

In contrast, Ryanair outsources aircraft maintenance to another company. Ryanair does not possess an internal set of resources or capabilities to actually perform aircraft maintenance; the company's expertise is in managing such areas as route selection, flight operations, customer-centric employee hiring, on a low cost basis. Yet through long-term contracts they achieve low cost maintenance performed by the other organization, while still retaining the rights to review and make changes to how maintenance is performed. So in this case outsourcing to a low cost third party supports their strategy of low cost, but does so without the company having to relinquish control over that important dimension of the business.

Disruption of coordination and linkages in the value chain. Earlier we argued that the coordination and linkages that exist among elements in a company's value chain are the greatest sources of competitive advantage. This is because they are intangible and extremely difficult to imitate. When outsourcing breaks one of these important coordinating bonds, the company may be less well-insulated from competition.

Hollowing out the core. In the 1990s "business process reengineering" became the latest business fad to talk about in the classroom. Much of the reengineering had to do with outsourcing, and some companies were so enamored with the perceived benefits that they outsourced many of their activities. Individually, each activity may not seem strategically important. Yet often combinations of activities, and especially the coordinating linkages that exist between them, may be central to what a company does well. So any attempts to outsource should consider not only the activities by themselves, but the system and context in which those activities exist.

Competitive learning. In some instances, a competitor may gain greater insight into a company's internal value chain by observing which activities have been outsourced. Not only might the competitor learn more about the outsourced operation, because it will be more visible to outsiders, but they may be able to develop insights about what activities remain inside the company as constituting its strategic core.

Figure 7.14 presents a decision tree for outsourcing activity that summarizes the preceding discussion. In order to gain the benefits of outsourcing without incurring some of the problems that can accompany these efforts, companies will occasionally engage in either vertical or horizontal acquisitions in order to own another company that can perform an important set of activities. Acquiring another company can ensure control over the process and minimize competitive learning; however, acquisitions present their own sets of issues. We will cover mergers and acquisitions more completely in Chapter 10.

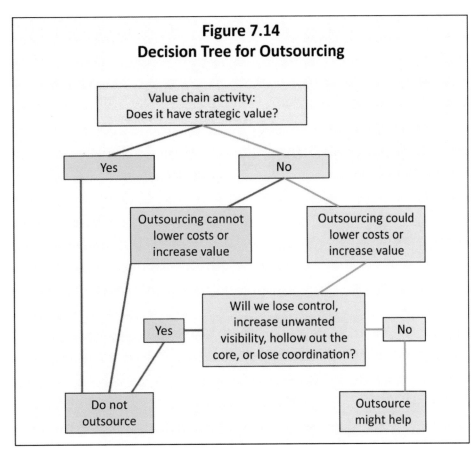

CHAPTER SUMMARY

In this chapter we have examined the business-level (sometimes referred to as generic) strategies of low cost and differentiation as well as the variations of both focus strategy and integrated cost/differentiation strategy. These types lay out the highest-level approach to a business and are extremely valuable as communication and coordination tools and in the process of making important decisions and managing the business. They are used as a rallying point for organizations and as a means to evaluate consistency in various approaches when using value chain and resource-based analysis.

Although several companies in an industry may attempt a low cost approach, there can really be only one low cost leader in a market. The low cost leader has the opportunity to make significant returns by taking advantage of its relative cost structure. All others may find themselves undercut by the leader and discover that it is difficult to prosper when market circumstances are challenging. On the other hand, a differentiation strategy has virtually unlimited variations in approach. Multipoint differentiators inherently enjoy greater security in their strategic positions than do single-point differentiators. For both the low cost and differentiation approaches, it is essential for companies to achieve parity on other competitive dimensions that are valued in the market.

Finally, a focus approach takes advantage of segmentation in the market or geographical differences that can lead to a low cost focus or a differentiation focus. The integrated low cost/differentiation strategy is intuitively appealing, yet it appears to be a risky approach that even very successful companies find difficult to balance. By attempting to compete against other companies that are more single-mindedly concentrating on a pure low cost or differentiation approach, the integrated strategy company risks getting stuck in the middle.

The value chain plays a central role in understanding how business-level strategies are put into practice. A business-level strategy represents a philosophy of competing that should translate to mutually supportive activities in every cell of the company's value chain, producing a consistent approach to the market across the company. Assessing whether or not a value chain activity is central to strategy, and whether third-party organizations can perform the activity at a lower cost or higher value-added, provides a guideline for companies on outsourcing.

Learning Objectives Review

1. Compare and contrast business-level strategies available to organizations, and describe how they create competitive advantage.

- There are two basic types of business-level strategy, low cost leadership and differentiation.

- Either of these types can be pursued on a broad scope or narrow scope. The combination of two types and two scopes results in four different business-level strategies.

- A fifth version, known as the "integrated low cost and differentiation" approach, combines elements of the basic two types (but can be especially risky).

- Competitive advantage is a position in which a company earns above-average profits in its industry. The low cost leader earns superior profits by increasing its profit margin as a function of having a lower cost structure. A successful differentiation strategy earns superior profits because the company is able to more than offset higher costs associated with value-creation through higher revenues charged.

- Each business-level strategy is subject to three critical conditions, upon which its success rests: parity conditions on other dimensions valued in the marketplace, the evolution of customer expectations, and the evolution of competition itself.

2. *Examine the underlying drivers that enable a company's choice of business-level strategy to be successful.*

- A business-level strategy can be successful to the extent that it addresses existing or emerging key success factors in an industry.

- A business-level strategy can be successful to the extent that the company's value chain achieves coordination and consistency of activities that individually and in combination support the adopted approach.

- Drivers of the low cost strategy include: economies of scale, capacity utilization, benefitting from the experience curve, supportive product/service design decisions, value chain design that affects internal process, and internal value chain coordination.

- Drivers of the differentiation strategy include: responsiveness to existing and emerging customer needs, integrity of products and services, quality, psychographics and cognitive benefits to customers, value chain design that affects internal process, and internal value chain coordination.

3. *Analyze when outsourcing makes strategic sense.*

- Outsourcing activity can make sense under the following conditions:
- The activity does not have strategic value.
- Outsourcing can lower costs or increase value.
- The company does not lose control, increase unwanted visibility to what is at its core, or lose coordination benefits in its internal value chain.

Key Terms

Business-level strategies - A term for strategic approaches at a high, overarching level. Often referred to as "generic strategies." Business-level strategy is appropriate for a single line of business with related products or services. It is not appropriate as a means of organizing a diversified corporation with many lines of business.

Differentiation - One type of business-level strategy. It implies a broad market approach where activities performed by the company provide sufficiently differentiated value to allow the company to generate superior economic returns, generally through higher pricing.

Experience curve - Reductions in cost per unit that are achieved through the learning that occurs in cumulative production over time (in contrast to economies of scale, in which unit cost reductions are associated with volume during a fixed time interval).

Focus - A narrow scope for either of the two types of business-level strategies of differentiation and low cost. The company pursues a narrow targeted market, geographic area, and/or particular customer group.

Low cost - One type of business-level strategy. It implies a broad market approach where a company can earn superior economic returns by rigorously reducing costs and expenses below its competitors, while simultaneously maintaining parity pricing.

Low cost leadership - Of the companies that pursue a low cost strategy, one company will enjoy the lowest cost structure. This company has the strongest competitive position among low cost seekers, since it enjoys greater pricing flexibility and can more easily weather industry conditions that compress profit margins.

Outsourcing - When another outside organization is contracted to perform a business process or service.

Parity - Though companies compete on cost or some dimensions of differentiation, they must maintain relative equality on other dimensions that are valued in the marketplace. Without reasonable parity on other valued conditions, the lowest-cost competitor or most-effective differentiator on some dimension may not succeed.

Scope - The degree to which a company competes broadly or narrowly within an industry. Differences in geography, customer segments, and user needs can describe broad versus narrow scope.

Stuck in the middle - A condition where a company simultaneously pursues both a differentiation and a low cost strategy. The result is often that such companies are out-competed by competitors which pursue "pure" business-level strategies more single-mindedly.

Short Answer Review Questions

1. What are the three important conditions that must be kept in mind when considering any of the business-level strategies?

2. What are the five business-level strategies that businesses might employ?

3. Under what circumstances would a low cost approach be most likely to allow a business to achieve extraordinary returns?

4. Under what circumstances would a differentiation approach be most likely to allow a business to achieve extraordinary returns?

5. Under what circumstances would a focused, low cost approach be most likely to allow a business to achieve extraordinary returns?

6. Under what circumstances would a focused, differentiation approach be most likely to allow a business to achieve extraordinary returns?

7. What issues must businesses keep in mind as they consider simultaneously pursuing an integrated low cost and differentiation position?

8. How does a firm become "stuck in the middle"?

9. How are business-level strategies put into practice in the day-to-day running of a business?

10. What strategy would you recommend for a new business being started by a small team of entrepreneurs?

11. Under what conditions would a company be at risk by pursuing a focused business-level strategy?

12. How does consistency of effort across the value chain play a role in attaining extraordinary returns?

Group Exercises

1. Take two companies in the same industry that compete with each other in seemingly different ways. For example, take Netflix and Redbox, or try Nordstrom and Kohl's. Using information from their annual reports and business stories that you can find on the internet, attempt to identify the type and scope of their business-level strategies and how their value chains support that approach.

   a. Do they appear to be consistent across their value chain activities?

   b. What unique resources do they seem to be using to separate themselves from their competitors?

2. Take a single industry such as the grocery store industry. Map out where the top ten competitors are using the Five Business- Level Strategies chart shown in Figure 7.3.

   a. Are all five approaches being utilized in the industry?

   b. Compare each of these firms based upon their five-year ROE performance. How are they doing? Why?

3. Periodically companies attempt to change their business-level strategy (usually due to significant changes in the environment). What cautions would you advise a business contemplating such a move? Can you name a company that has done just such a thing in the past five years?

References

[1] Eagle Materials: Low Cost Producer. 2013, Spring. www.eaglematerials.com; Rivera, M. 2002. In a modern world, a violin bow maker keeps his craft alive, November 23, www.nbcnews.com/business/modern-world-violin-bow-maker-keeps-his-craft-alive-1C7206756; www.benoitrolland.com/; Taplin, I. M. 2013. Who is to blame? A re-examination of fast fashion after the 2013 factory disaster in Bangladesh, in Critical Perspectives on International Business. Johnson, K. 2013. Brands risk image in varying Bangladesh building collapse responses, Concord Monitor, May 7, www.concordmonitor.com.

[2] Porter, M. E. 1985. Competitive Advantage. New York: Free Press; Porter, M. E. 1996. What is strategy? Harvard Business Review 74(6): 61–78. Veliyath, R., & E. Fitzgerald. 2000. Firm capabilities, business strategies, customer preferences, and hypercompetitive arenas: The sustainability of competitive advantages with implications for firm competitiveness. Competitiveness Review 20(1): 56–83. Thirnhill, S., & R. E. White. 2007. Strategic purity: A multi-industry evaluation of a pure vs. hybrid business strategies. Strategic Management Journal 28(5): 553–561.

[3] Porter, M. E. 1980. Competitive strategy. New York: Free Press; Porter, M. E. 1985. Competitive advantage. New York: Free Press.

[4] Lee, L., & P. Burrows. 2007. Is Dell too big for Michael Dell? BusinessWeek. February 12: 33.

[5] Porter, M. E. 1985. Competitive strategy. New York: Free Press.
[6] Lee, L. 2006. It's Dell vs. the Dell way. BusinessWeek Online. February 23, 17.

[7] Porter, M. E. 1985. Competitive strategy. New York: Free Press.

[8] Porter, M. E. 1996. What is strategy? Harvard Business Review 74(6): 61–78.

[9] Chafkin, M. 2007. How to kill a great idea. Inc. June: 85–91.

[10] Armstrong, L. 1996. The numbers are crunching Packard Bell. BusinessWeek. December 30: 46.

[11] Porter, M. E. 1985. Competitive advantage. New York: Free Press, 20.

[12] www.petsmart.com/banfield/index.shtml.

[13] Arndt, M. 2006. Out, damned trans fats. BusinessWeek. July 31: 12. Adamy, J. 2007. Why no. 3 Wendy's finds vanilla so exciting. Wall Street Journal. April 6: B1.

[14] Perold, A. F. 1998. The Vanguard Group, Inc. - 1998 Boston: Harvard Business School Publishing. 9-299-002. https://flagship.vanguard.com. Lim, P. 2007. How the biggest funds fared. U.S. News & World Report. January 15, 142 (2): 73. Maiello, M. 2005. The un-Vanguard. Forbes. September 19, 176(5): 182–186.

[15] Grant, R. M. 2005. Contemporary strategy analysis. Malden: Blackwell Publishing.

[16] The development of the Boeing 777. 1998. Public Broadcasting System; Wall, R. & J. Ostrower, 2016. Jet makers step on the gas, Wall Street Journal, July 19, p. B4.

[17] Capell, K. 2007. Glaxo mimics carmaker to speed vaccine. BusinessWeek Online. April 5: 16.

[18] HP 2012 Global Citizenship Report.

[19] Walmart with wings. BusinessWeek Online, November 17: 13. Sullivan, W. 2007. Flying on the cheap. U.S. News and World Report. March 6: 47.

[20] www.ryanair.com/site/EN/about.php. Walmart with wings. BusinessWeek Online. November 17: 13. Sullivan, W. 2007. Flying on the cheap. U.S. News and World Report. March 6: 47. Davy. 2004. Fare wars: A history lesson. European Transport and Leisure. February 16, Davy: Dublin.

[21] Serpen, E. 2006. Key performance measures. Presentation at 3rd annual Managing Airline Operating Costs Conference, London.

[22] Ghemwat, P. 1986. Walmart stores' discount operations. Boston: Harvard Business School Publishing, 9-387-018.

[23] Arndt, M. 2006. Out, damned trans fats. BusinessWeek. July 31: 12. Adamy, J. 2007. Wendy's to discuss strategic review with investors. Wall Street Journal. May 16: B17. Adamy, J. 2007. Wendy's considers possible sale. Wall Street Journal. April 26: A2.

[24] Kahn, G. 2007. How to slow down a Ferrari: Buy it. Wall Street Journal. May 8.

[25] www.greatplacetowork-europe.com/best/lists.

[26] Motorola moves beyond RAZR glitch. 2006. Forbes. May 31.

[27] West G. P., & J. O. deCastro. 2001. The Achilles heel of firm strategy. Journal of Management Studies, 38(3): 417–442.

[28] Brown, R. 2001. How we built a strong company in a weak industry. Harvard Business Review, 79(2): 51–57.

[29] Adamy, J. 2007. Starbucks chairman says trouble may be brewing. Wall Street Journal. February 24: A4. Text of Starbucks memo. 2007. Wall Street Journal Online. February 24.

[30] Christensen, C. M. The innovator's dilemma. Boston: Harvard Business School Publishing.

[31] www.in-n-out.com/history.aspx.

[32] Friedman, T. L. 2005. The world is flat. New York: Farrar, Straus, and Giroux.

[33] M. Wolk. 2006. Toys R Us wins suit against Amazon.com. MSNBC., March 2.

Section C: Strategy in the Marketplace

Competition today operates in rough-and-tumble, dynamically changing environments in which companies face a continuously changing set of circumstances. This is why we referred in Chapter 1 to the need for opportunity recognition and value creation capabilities. This next section of the textbook takes us deep into the actual practice of strategy in this kind of dynamically changing marketplace.

Competing today can be like getting onto a rollercoaster – moving from slow to fast very quickly, with rapid rises and possibly precipitous descents. When dynamic changes occur in the marketplace in the form of an evolving industry, they have an impact on types of value creation that can be successful and on the need to continuously embrace new opportunities for future growth. Companies also evolve through stages, and must address unique strategic challenges that parallel their evolution. Once again there are implications for building resources and for configuring the company's value chain in order to succeed. In Chapter 8 we will explore how industry life cycles and company life cycles offer context and insight for the formulation and implementation of strategy. As companies evolve they inevitably confront the possibility of operating internationally. This chapter also explores dimensions of international strategy.

Many executives refer to today's business climate as hypercompetition, which we will discuss in greater depth in Chapter 9. Here, competitive dynamics play a central role in the success of a company's strategy. Competing successfully in markets today is akin to performing well in the Xbox Halo game series: it requires performing well on straightforward executional aspects, anticipating and preempting "metagaming" patterns that competitors employ, and cooperating with other important players in the environment. Chapter 9 deals with competitive actions and responses, and how these impact the formulation and implementation of a company's strategy.

Many companies today view the growth challenge as one that necessitates moving beyond the existing business into other types of businesses. They do this through mergers and acquisitions, which is the subject of Chapter 10. The chapter provides perspective on why it is so difficult to engineer successful diversification of this sort – meaning why it is a challenge to provide positive returns to shareholders. Managing a diversified company that operates in multiple industries presents its own unique strategic management challenges and decisions. So this chapter considers the nature of strategic management from a different perspective, that of senior executives at corporate headquarters.

Welcome to the real world, as we explore Strategy in the Marketplace!

Chapter 8: Strategy Issues in Industries, Life Cycle Stages, and International Strategy

> LEARNING OBJECTIVES
>
> 1. Explain the stages of an industry life cycle and their impact on business strategy.
>
> 2. Analyze the strategy implications of competing in fragmented or consolidated industries.
>
> 3. Utilize organizational life cycle stages and the kinds of problems and resources issues that businesses experience in each to proactively recommend value creation activities.
>
> 4. Explain the risks associated with being a first mover.
>
> 5. Explain when a company should expand internationally and what approach it should take for doing so.

"When the Music's Over, Turn Out of the Light"[1]

On July 27, 1997, an event occurred that changed your life, and it dramatically changed the trajectories of several industries that you know so well. On that day Don Katz invented a gadget to play "Motion Picture Experts Group Audio Layer 3" files, now commonly known as MP3 music files. His company, Audible, sold a few thousand of the gadgets. By 2010 nearly 45 percent of U.S. households owned devices that play MP3 music files. And then the smartphone revolution hit, enabling millions to easily carry their tunes with them anywhere.

The introduction of the MP3 changed the course of music history and the nature of the commercial music industry value chain. Though the U.S. household population continues to grow at a steady pace, the advent of MP3 technology led to the start-up and rapid growth of an entirely new industry around digital music and players. Whereas Sony had long been associated with portable music players through its Walkman franchise, new companies entered this market space often for many different reasons. Samsung entered to leverage its capabilities in electronic entertainment devices, as did Diamond Multimedia with its Rio player. SanDisk introduced its Sansa line of players in order to occupy product space where its flash drive technology could be applied. The iPod represented an elegant next step in the evolution of Apple's innovative approach to digital technology for the consumer. Microsoft introduced the Zune because the company wanted to occupy a central position in the digital home. Figure 8.1 shows the rise of digital music.[2]

Paralleling the start-up and growth of MP3 music has been the devastating decline of the recorded music industry. Compact disks replaced LPs way back in the 1980s as a consequence of new technology introduced at the time. CD sales peaked at over $13 billion annually in 2000, just after the first MP3 player was introduced, but have been in steep decline ever since. Music labels such as Warner, EMI, Sony, and Universal find it more difficult to support musicians, as the economics of producing and marketing a new CD has grown worse. In the prosperous years it would not be uncommon for a number 1 CD to sell 500,000–600,000 copies each week, but now the best CDs sell only 15,000-20,000 per week, prompting agents for musicians to claim that "CDs have become little more than advertisements for more-lucrative goods like concert tickets and T-shirts."

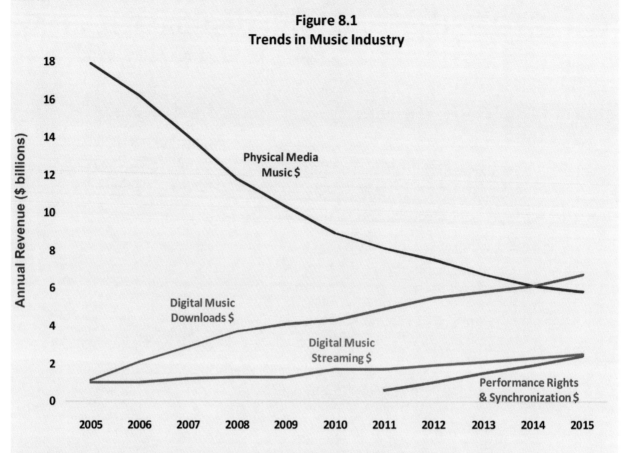

Figure 8.1
Trends in Music Industry

The decline in CDs has also had a cascading effect on other related industries, too. Longtime music retailer Tower Records, which had been in business for forty-six years and at one point had 800 stores nationwide, was liquidated in 2006. With the loss of independent music retailers, more powerful retailers like Walmart now represent roughly 65 percent of music retail sales and are putting more price and margin pressure on music labels. Whereas Tower Records used to stock 100,000 titles, big box stores like Walmart and Best Buy carry only 2-3,000 titles, emphasizing only the fast-selling hits. Walmart cut back the size of its CD department in order to make room for other fast-selling merchandise. Genres of music such as classical, jazz, and hip-hop now experience even greater challenges in reaching consumers effectively.

Musical artists have also been impacted by the digital conversion. The reduced power of music labels in the industry value chain make direct connections with consumers more important. So concert tours have become central to the artists' ability to generate income. Performance rights (songs used at public venues and by broadcasters) and synchronization (songs used in advertising, games, and on TV) have grown in importance. Most artists receive royalties of between 10-20% on music sales, but since less costly single-song downloads and streaming now dominate the market their take has declined. Superstars like Adele and Taylor Swift have exerted star power by preventing streaming sales until CD sales are maximized, but this is unusual among artists.[3]

What's next for this industry? Sales of MP3 players, which peaked in 2010, have been falling at double-digit rates ever since. Because of the viability of other products like smartphones, tablets, and streaming, an ongoing and inevitable decline for MP3 players is unfolding, including

246

even the successful iPod product series. Big retailers like Best Buy, Walmart, and Amazon started music download sites to participate in this increasingly-virtual market.

QUESTIONS

1. What steps would you take to address decline if you were in charge of strategy at a music label company such as EMI?
2. If you were a musician, what steps could you take to increase revenue for your music?
3. What do you expect the next big shakeup to be in the music industry, and how could your company prepare for this?

INDUSTRY LIFE CYCLES

One of the most exciting facets of the study of business and strategy is the nature of industry change. Many years ago the Austrian economist Joseph Schumpeter described "creative destruction" as a process that every industry experiences: they start up often based on some new entrepreneurial insight or innovation, attract new entrants, grow, begin to mature, and then a shakeup occurs that either launches renewed growth or thrusts the industry into decline. It's a "life cycle" that has been observed time and time again across dozens of types of industries.

Life Cycle Stages

An industry's evolution through a complete life cycle is fundamentally driven by two factors: new knowledge about how to create value and growth in demand (Figure 8.2). New knowledge about creating value forms the basis for any new industry to begin with – whether it be the application of modular manufacturing and assembly to democratize the automobile (Henry Ford), the use of durable-stitched material to sell the first pair of "blue jeans" (Levi Strauss), the creation of a new low-cost distribution method for retailing general merchandise (Sam Walton), or figuring out how to encode and play music digitally. However, new knowledge alone, without growth in demand, would lead only to faddish products and services and short-lived industry categories such as Beanie Babies, Pet Rocks, Pogs, Cabbage Patch dolls, or disco music.

> **Figure 8.2**
> **Determinants of industry evolution**
>
> New knowledge about value creation
> Growth in demand

Growth in demand occurs because the sort of value creation resulting from an innovation is substantive and has long-lasting appeal to a wide audience of potential users. The potential for broad appeal attracts new entrants to an industry because they see the possibilities of earning profits, and they remain there to compete because of continued growth in demand. But the growth of companies and the entrance of new competitors eventually leads to a saturation of demand. At this point an industry will experience one of two possible paths. Either there will be a renewed burst of growth because new, innovative knowledge developed within the industry provides the opportunity to create even greater value and attract new customers. Or new knowledge that leads to innovation in some other economic sector will enhance the power of substitutes to draw off customers because of compelling price/value propositions, leading to the industry's decline. The evolution of most industries therefore follows a familiar pattern involving four stages, such as those illustrated in Figure 8.3. We typically describe the stages as the introduction, growth, maturity, and decline (or renewal). Each stage of the industry life cycle tends to exhibit its own defining characteristics that have implications for the type of strategic approach that might be successful.

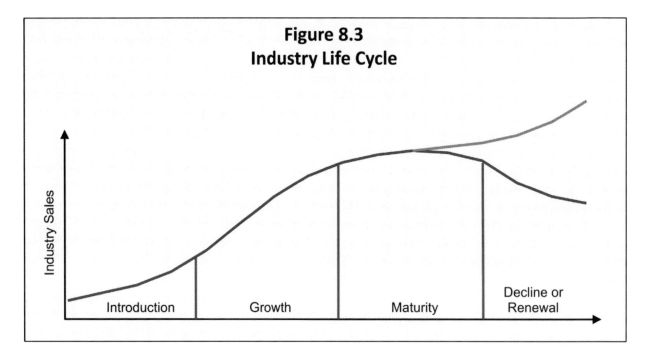

Introduction stage. You would not expect to see a lot of competitors populating an industry at its infancy. Almost by definition, in the introduction stage of an industry there will typically be a very small number of companies dipping their toes in the waters of a type of business that has never been tried before. Sometimes there is just one such "new entrant," often referred to as a first mover. First-mover advantage refers to a sustainable competitive advantage that is achieved by being the first company to enter a new industry or industry segment, and we'll address it in more depth later in this chapter. Companies that are these first movers have the widest possible strategic choice. Innovation results in a wide variety of products or services being offered, primarily because early entrants are trying to determine which bundle of characteristics or approaches will create the greatest perceived value for the customer. These companies are not only figuring out if customers will buy their offerings and which segments of customers might buy, but also which suppliers present the best opportunity for success. Consequently, value creation in the introduction stage is often occurring internally through product design as well as externally in relationship-building both upstream and downstream.

Growth stage. Industries move into a growth stage when the kind of value created begins to engender broader demand. Still experiencing the entrance of new companies seeking to profit from the potential, most industries will also begin to experience some corporate exiting by companies that are unable to successfully adapt to what is usually a growing degree of standardization of products or services. Although Sony essentially created the home VCR market in the 1980s with its Betamax technology, VHS technology became the industry standard and Sony finally withdrew the Betamax from the market (albeit stubbornly). As demand continues to increase, competitors focus on achieving scale to serve a broad swath of customers or markets while reliably and consistently delivering what customers value. There is still an opportunity for innovation and an effective differentiation strategic approach during the growth stage; however, increasing standardization opens the door for a low-cost leadership strategic approach. Because of the focus on standardization and achieving scale and scope, value can be created internally through process as well as externally by working to develop broad downstream customer relationships. Some consolidation begins to occur among industry participants, enabling a small number of competitors to more rapidly increase size and scale.

Maturity stage. Industries mature when demand begins to slow down. In contrast to the 1970s and 1980s when soft drink per capita consumption grew by 50 percent in a fifteen year period, moving into the 1990s per capita consumption remained relatively flat. Maturity is also experienced when a high level of customer saturation is reached, meaning there are relatively few new customers to bring into the industry. The U.S. cell phone market is beginning to experience this now (Figure 8.4)[4] as the industry is approaching 95 percent penetration among U.S. households. When these conditions occur, competition becomes fierce since one of the only routes to growth is to take market share away from other companies. We observe in 2016 that there is now vicious competition among cellphone service providers in the deals they offer to attract consumers in their networks to step up to smartphones. Smartphone penetration can still grow, and they present significant revenue opportunities through the data usage they generate.

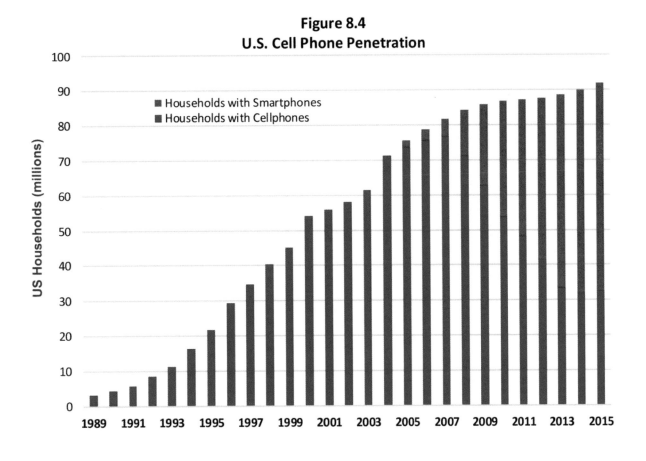

Figure 8.4
U.S. Cell Phone Penetration

Commoditization typically occurs in mature industries, when customers no longer really value innovation and new doohickeys but instead expect a standard set of features that increasingly incorporates the best of the market-tested capabilities. In turn this leads to less opportunity for differentiation-based advantage and more-intense cost competition among companies, often resulting in a shake-up among competitors and exits from the industry by those who are unable to compete effectively under such onerous conditions. Value creation at this stage is largely focused internally on cost efficiency. The availability of low-cost labor in other countries has led to outsourcing production by many U.S. companies in order to remain cost-competitive, as well as to large numbers of exits of U.S. companies from some industries such as furniture and textiles. Many of the exits occur through mergers and acquisitions when businesses are sold to competitors and other corporate buyers, and the result is a smaller number of large industry powerhouses.[5]

Decline stage. At some point an industry will evolve beyond the maturity stage, and one possible direction is decline. An industry will begin to decline either because other substitute industries provide a more compelling combination of price and value, but ordinarily decline occurs because innovation in some other sector has made obsolete the value proposition that the industry had historically created. Figure 8.5 provides examples of industries thrust into decline because of innovations elsewhere. As end users flee to products and services offered in other industries, the declining industry experiences overcapacity. Companies seek to shed assets and engage in cost cutting in order to survive, and this often involves greater consolidation through horizontal mergers and acquisitions in order to gain greater control over remaining productive capacity, costs, and pricing. The value chain focus of companies in declining industries is primarily on internal operations in order to achieve cost control.

Figure 8.5
Declining Industries and Their Causes

Declining Industry	Innovation Elsewhere
Passenger trains	Automobile, airplane
Photo finishing	Digital camera
Network television	Cable broadcasting
Door-to-door sales	Internet
Public libraries	Online book sellers
Tobacco	Medical research
VHS tapes	DVDs
Video rental stores	Internet streaming video
Rivets	Welding

Renewal stage. The alternative to decline is renewal, where innovation *within* the mature industry leads to the opportunity to once again acquire new customers, new markets, and additional business from existing customers. Although one or two competitors in a mature industry might find ways to pump sales by courting niche arenas within the industry, renewal of the entire industry really depends on reconfiguring the industry value chain in one of several ways (Figure 8.6).

Methods for reconfiguring the industry value chain include the following:

Figure 8.6
Reconfiguring Industry Value Chain

Redefine industry boundaries
Disaggregate blocks of industry activity
Redefine value
Shift to complements

- **Redefine industry boundaries.** Broadening the definition of the boundaries to an industry enables its participants to generate new business by developing new sets of value-adding activities. In the 1950s the railroad freight industry was at a mature stage. Companies that survived the shakeout and participated in the industry's renewed growth broadened their industry definitions beyond purely "railroad freight" to "freight," which caused them to focus more carefully on how trucking companies and barge freighters operated. The broader industry focus resulted in the definition of a new set of key success factors that the railroad companies paid attention to, which in turn prompted a reconfiguration of their value-adding activities.[6] You have probably noticed, for example, that freight trains now load detachable trailers from highway semi-trucks directly onto railcars, instead of using traditional freight cars.

Approaching saturation in the cell phone market (Figure 8.4), cell phone companies are broadening their industry definition by enabling their users to surf the Web, take pictures, download music, instant message, check their e-mails and a variety of other services, no matter where they are or what they are doing. These kinds of efforts require companies to develop new supply-side relationships, develop new internal capabilities, and cultivate new customer user groups – essentially reconfiguring the industry value chain from end-to-end.

- **Disaggregate blocks of value chain activity**. By considering how and where value is actually created in an industry value chain, companies may identify new opportunities through disaggregating sets of activities usually combined together that represent "how things are done." In the mature dry cleaning industry, for example, the typical retail store combines three value chain activities - management, operations, and customer service. New opportunities are being created, however, when dry cleaning chains unbundle this typical suite of activities and place customer service desks remotely in the lobbies of corporate office buildings, where customers can conveniently drop off and pick up their laundry. Placing the customer interface closer to the customer by separating it from operations helps change the usual configuration of value-creating activities in the industry. Similarly, supermarkets have unbundled their customary deli operations (mix, cook, serve) to allow customers to pick up fully assembled, prepackaged dinners made with fresh ingredients that need only be heated up at home. Instead of fully cooking meal items in advance and keeping them warm until the shopper is in the store, this new unbundling of activities captures customers who want freshly cooked meals but not the guilt of going out to restaurants.

- **Redefine value**. Redefining industry boundaries leads to the identification of new key success factors and therefore to new value chain activities, and disaggregating blocks of activities can also lead to new ways to create value. A third possibility is to redefine an existing value that is at the heart of the industry, leading to a new configuration of activities. Locked in fierce competition with Coca-Cola in the 1990s, Pepsi embarked on a program that centrally redefined its low-cost approach; its "10X" program changed the focus of the business from "cost per can of soda produced" to "cost per satisfied customer." The new cost concept not only included the manufacturing cost of the product, but also its retail delivery truck schedules to ensure no out-of-stocks occurred, its vending machine technology to provide transmitted data alerts when cans in the machine were running low, enhancing its customer service center operations, and other activities that were part of the customer value creation effort.

- **Shift to complements**. Complements are products or services that have a positive effect on the value of a company's own products or services. Apple's iPod business complements its iTunes business. Video games sold by Microsoft, Nintendo, and Sony all complement the value of the base game unit offered by each company, since the value of the base unit is zilch unless there are a variety of game applications that can be played on it. Disney became successful in theme parks, and more recently in cruise vacations, because of its studio creativity and film success. As these examples suggest, generating renewal in a mature industry through a shift to complementary products or services relies on core characteristics of the companies involved but also requires new configurations of value chain activities to extend these core characteristics into related (but different) industries.

Figure 8.7 summarizes the characteristics of industry life cycle stages we have just discussed.

Figure 8.7
Industry Life Cycle Stage Characteristics

Stage	Introduction	Growth	Maturity	Decline	Renewal
Type of demand	Experimenters, early adopters	Broad penetration	Mass market	Traditionalists, loyal core	New customers, new segments
Competition	Few new entrants	Entrants & exits, consolidation	Shakeout, exits	Overcapacity, exits	
Strategy	Differentiation	Differentiation, low cost appearing	Low cost, focused differentiation	Low cost	New differentiation
Value creation	Innovation, variety	Scale & access to markets Process: standardization, consistency & reliability	Commoditization, cost efficiency	Cost cutting, asset reduction	Leverage core value chain capabilities
Value chain focus	Choices: internal & upstream or downstream	Extend & refine: internal, downstream	Survival: internal	Survival: internal	Reconfigure: redefine industry, redefine value, disaggregate, complements

Length of Industry Life Cycle Stages

Lately it appears as if the business world has sped up, suggesting that industries evolve through at least the earlier life cycle stages fairly rapidly. Rapid progress has been the norm for consumer technology-based industries that we're more familiar with, such as compact disks or video cassette recorders and tapes, each of which moved from inception to peak to significant decline within a period of less than twenty years. Yet this is not always the case. Figure 8.8 illustrates the time periods associated with the rise and maturity of four different technologies that are central to our lives today.[7] The internet and the personal computer are being adopted sooner after each was invented, but surprisingly not at a steeper rate of adoption than was television or even electricity in the home.

It is still true that not all new industries grow up as quickly as some of these recent trends. Biotechnology, for example, has been around for nearly thirty years, has received considerable venture capital and corporate funding. Yet biotech industry sales are still considered in their infancy. Three factors work to stretch out the time it takes for a new industry to evolve beyond an introductory stage into growth: speed of commercialization, affordability, and the existence of complementary infrastructures. Biotech is a case where commercialization takes a long time due to complex research and government regulation, and where each new biotech application can cost tens of millions of dollars to develop. Cable television was developed in the 1960s, but until the physical infrastructure of cable lines strung through communities was developed, there was no way to deliver the signal broadly.

Best Buy, Part 1

Best Buy's founder and long-time CEO, Richard Schulze, worked in the home electronics retailing business for over forty years. Following a tornado's destruction of one of his small audio components stores in Minnesota in 1981, he accidentally discovered that a larger market existed for electronics retailing when he ran a "tornado sale" in 1981 to liquidate vast quantities of merchandise. Taking advantage of the increased disposable income of "baby boomers" who loved rock and roll and could now afford to buy stereo equipment, and of skyrocketing demand for home VCRs, in 1983 Schulz changed his chain's name to Best Buy. Commissioned sales people "took a more proactive role" in assisting shoppers in the store, and retail prices often reflected the desire of the sales staff to earn high commissions. The chain expanded to twenty-four stores by 1987 and generated $240 million in revenue. By 1989 Best Buy had grown to nearly 100 stores.

Expansion of the consumer electronics retailing industry continued to be driven by new technology coming to market, such as innovative waves of personal computers and peripherals, compact disks, and larger televisions. Like Best Buy, other chains were also growing larger. In 1989 Best Buy nearly went bankrupt after a price war initiated by one of its large competitors. Schulz decided to modify his retail store model by increasing its square footage to generate more floor selling space, providing wider aisles, displaying a wider variety of merchandise; ending commissioned sales to take pressure off the salesperson-shopper relationship; and focusing on a low-margin high-turnover economic model. As the first "big box" discount electronics retailer, the combination was a hit with consumers and suppliers.

QUESTIONS

1. Describe how Best Buy's moves reflected changes in the industry's developments.
2. As the electronics retailing industry matures and competition becomes especially fierce, what methods of creating value would you recommend they pursue?
3. How does a company know what stage of its life cycle the industry is in?

FRAGMENTED AND CONSOLIDATED INDUSTRIES

Industry life cycle models ordinarily portray consolidation beginning to occur during the growth stage and then gaining in prominence as an industry moves into and through the mature stage. This is because standardization – and then commoditization – become valued competitive dimensions as an industry evolves. It is often true that larger companies with scale can achieve better standardization of features at lower costs and therefore compete more successfully. This is not always how the story goes, however, and we briefly mention here two other strategic possibilities in industry evolution. The first is how to compete in consolidated industries without benefiting from scale and a low-cost structure. The second is how to compete when industries mature without consolidation ever occurring, that is, in fragmented industries.

Consolidated Industries

Focused differentiation is one strategic approach that can succeed in a consolidated industry where the values of standardization and low cost tend to prevail. The department store industry is in a mature phase, now dominated by a small number of national chains, for example when Federated and May merged and then rebranded nearly all the combined stores as Macy's (Figure 8.9). The increased size of Macy's provides improved buying power with suppliers, achieves economies of scale in managing operations, and results in greater consistency in retail execution from store to store across the chain – values on which most department stores compete. Yet Saks Fifth Avenue and Neiman Marcus each occupy highly focused differentiated positions in this market, by carrying high-end merchandise, investing in expensive store fixtures, pampering customers, and (no fooling) charging higher prices to pay for these luxurious value chain enhancements.

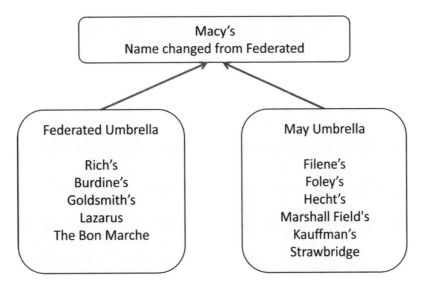

Figure 8.9
Origins of Macy's Department Stores

Macy's
Name changed from Federated

Federated Umbrella

Rich's
Burdine's
Goldsmith's
Lazarus
The Bon Marche

May Umbrella

Filene's
Foley's
Hecht's
Marshall Field's
Kauffman's
Strawbridge

For competitors to succeed in consolidated industries without following the standardization and low-cost recipe, one of several conditions must exist (Figure 8.10). Although size confers the previously mentioned advantages of scale and efficiency, it also creates mobility barriers. For large companies with a portfolio of dedicated resources targeted at one type of competition, it is difficult to go after another business segment that would require a different set of resources and capabilities that are difficult to develop or imitate. Size may also present potential anti-trust concerns, since as we read in Chapter 4 the regulatory authorities are keen on preventing any one company from commanding too much market power. Dedicated sets of resources and traditional ways of doing business also cause large competitors to be blind to new opportunities afforded by niche positions within their industries, allowing other companies to gain traction and develop defensible positions. IBM considered, but then rejected, the opportunity to get into the personal computer business in the 1970s. Its entire value creation system was designed for mainframes and customized corporate software applications, and management could not imagine computing occurring in any way other than how it had traditionally been done. Of

Figure 8.10
Consolidated Industry Conditions Allowing Nonstandard Competition

Mobility barriers of large companies
Anti-trust concerns
Blindness to niche opportunities
Financial resources access

course, this opened the door for Apple. Finally, because consolidated industries are often characterized by cost/price competition, it suggests that many companies may be experiencing profit margin pressure along with low growth. This is especially the risk for those that do not in fact own the low-cost leadership position. Such companies can be short on financial resources (cash on hand, access to inexpensive capital), which can prevent them from going after another more differentiated competitor.

The brewing industry provides an interesting example of how to compete successfully in a consolidated industry. Through the 1970s and 1980s the domestic beer industry experienced increasing consolidation with only three major domestic breweries remaining: Anheuser Busch, Adolph Coors, and Miller Brewing. Along the way, though, came the microbrews that have been so successful over the last twenty years (e.g., Sam Adams, Fat Tire, Saranac), defined as breweries with less than 15,000 barrel brewing capacity per year. Microbrews involve higher-cost ingredients, shorter production runs, longer aging, more expensive packaging, lower sales volume unsuitable for mass distribution – all characteristics that the major breweries were ill equipped to pursue because of their focus on the high-volume, low-cost method of competing with each other. The big three were blind to this new niche market emerging within the industry, and their resource investments and capabilities prevented them from pursuing it. In the 2000s the major brewers have consolidated even further, and have now begun acquiring microbreweries. In Chapter 10 we will discuss the challenges of making and managing acquisitions.

Fragmented Industries

Fragmented industries present an entirely different picture. These are industries in which few large companies have emerged, and consequently where the HHI index or concentration ratio (see Figure 4.13) is extremely low. In the 1990s, for example, there were 33,000 retail stores offering dry cleaning services in the United States, yet the two largest companies in the industry had only 360 stores and 180 stores, respectively. Industries remain fragmented because either 1) there are no mobility or entry barriers to insulate a company from competitive duplication, enabling easy entrance to the industry, or 2) value creation is largely dependent on local labor or conditions for a significant portion of its cost and competitive market position. These two reasons illustrate that fragmentation is the antithesis of consolidation, which depends on barriers to forestall competition and on advantages gained through scalable dimensions of the value chain. Because they behave much more like perfectly competitive markets, in fragmented industries the opportunity to earn superior profits is very small.

A successful strategic approach will involve reconfiguring the industry value chain, usually by unbundling or disaggregating its normally combined parts, into a new system that creates added value and cannot be easily imitated. For example the day-care industry has long been characterized by small neighborhood facilities, low-wage staff, poor benefits, high turnover and thus "barely adequate" child care services.[8] Bright Horizons, which solved the fragmentation problem to become the world's leading provider of child care, hired quality employees and developed rich experience programs, then used the quality care value to seek corporations as customers. By establishing child care

centers in corporate office buildings and staffing them with quality staff, the company created value for corporations that are viewed as better supporting their own employees who have young children. Staples, Office Depot, and Office Max all participated in the industry roll-up of the highly fragmented office supplies market, previously populated by thousands of small independent shops across the country. Each chain unbundled the combined value chain activities at each individual store, and created new value through specialized investments at the corporate level in information systems, procurement expertise, large stores, and retail location modeling.

These examples might suggest that fragmented industries largely exist downstream at the "retail" level, but this is not always the case. Fragmentation can characterize the upstream supply side, as well. As the automobile manufacturing industry grew, for example, suppliers of parts and subsystems that were assembled into finished cars remained fairly fragmented. Other than minor design differences among competing automobile brands, a piston is a piston is a piston, and many machine shops manufactured pistons that were then incorporated into engines. An opportunity existed to create more consistent quality and provide better control and governance over the supply chain, and thus original equipment manufacturers (OEMs) came into being.[9] OEM companies acquired and consolidated many smaller contract manufacturers, as well as managed additional outsourced manufacturing, creating organizational and quality control values needed by the end users (Figure 8.11).

Figure 8.11
OEM Solves Supply Side Fragmentation

ORGANIZATIONAL LIFE CYCLES

In addition to the industry life cycles, firms also face challenges associated with what is known as the organizational life cycle. Like the industries in which they compete, companies also go through stages of development. As a company starts up, it first goes through a conception stage where the idea for the new business is further fleshed out and the strategic approach to the market is developed. Then the company actually "goes to market" in the commercialization stage, developing a customer base and achieving initial sales. If things go well, the company enters the growth stage as the customer base and geographic nature of the business expand. At some point a maturity stage will be reached, at which time the company's business growth rate begins to flatten out. The pattern of growth in sales that typically illustrates a company's stage of development (Figure 8.12) is familiar because it has been witnessed over and over again, so much

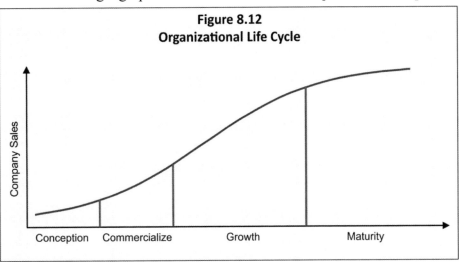

Figure 8.12
Organizational Life Cycle

so that venture capitalists often refer to it as the "hockey stick" curve.

The organizational life cycle concept is useful because it highlights two separate but related issues. Each stage of the organizational life cycle tends to exhibit its own characteristic problems and issues that have implications for the focus of management attention, the development of functional areas of the company, and the development of strategic resources appropriate for the problems encountered. These are the more pressing, shorter-term dimensions that determine a company's success in its present circumstances. But there are also strategy issues that are crucial to the longer-term success of the company, and these manifest themselves at different parts of the cycle.

Life Cycle Stages and Functional Area Issues

Conception. This first stage of a company's development is marked by a focus of the founders on three important elements that the business will require to move forward. First they must have a product or service that works, and so an intense effort is put behind the research and development function. This is often informal and experimental, usually involving a small number of product developers or engineers who have been recruited specifically for this task. Second, the founders must develop a clear articulation of their market entry strategy. This is where some of the insight about both industry analysis and the previous discussion in this chapter about industry stages can come in handy. Entering a mature market populated by large incumbent competitors presents a considerably different strategic problem than entering an early-growth industry where strategic variety exists and no company has achieved a dominant position. The strategic approach selected can have an impact on the product/ service development effort, for example including more bells and whistles if the industry analysis indicates these could be effective strategically. Third, the founders must seek financial capital so that they are able to support the business appropriately when they do enter the market. Raising capital depends on having both an effective product or service and a clearly articulated market entry strategy. Few sophisticated investors would support a new venture unless a clear understanding of the competitive set and the strategic positioning had been developed, even if the product or service was phenomenal.

The key problems for companies in the conception stage are putting the right people with the right knowledge in place. Completion of the product or service development requires specialized technical knowledge. Science-based companies (such as biotech or medical device manufacturers) must also develop scientific procedures and protocols at this stage, so some formalization of the research and development process may be required. The articulation of strategy requires bringing in people who understand the market and the type of business, and raising capital requires tapping into social networks through which knowledgeable financial partners can be recruited. From a strategic resources point of view, the success of the company at this stage depends on the extent to which the founders can leverage their own knowledge about a market opportunity into these kinds of technical knowledge, human, and social resources.

Commercialization. Having invented something, the company must figure out how to consistently make it or provide it in some quantity. New food product companies are often based on a recipe cooked on a stove, but translating the stovetop recipe to a manufacturing quantity of, say, 15,000 pounds at a time is a challenge that must be met. Then, it makes no sense to manufacture 15,000 pounds or more unless the company has customers to sell it to, so marketing and sales programs now need to be developed. Of course, these efforts should be consistent with the overall strategic approach that the company has previously developed. When manufacturing begins and sales are generated, a need develops for administrative systems of reporting and control.

The key problems that commercialization-stage companies confront have to do with these production and market start-up issues. Discrete organizational functions like manufacturing, marketing, sales, and finance ordinarily come into being at this point. The existence of "departments" containing these functions requires an organizational structure with lines of authority and the allocation of decision-making authority. Hiring the right people for the new functional areas becomes important, so that at this point a human resources position or department is also created. Greater complexity results from the combination of resources that have now been assembled to conduct business.

The company's performance at this stage depends on its ability to attend carefully to the myriad of organizational and operational details that make market entry efforts a success. Manufacturing procedures, marketing efforts, and effective selling approaches should be documented and reviewed, so that the company can make corrections that are needed or amplify on methods that are working. So in the face of greater organizational complexity at this early stage, it is important for companies to articulate carefully what works so that it can be reproduced.

Growth. With market acceptance and the existence of demand for the kind of value the company has created, it will experience a period of growth. This is an exciting time for any company; however, it can also be a time when great pains are experienced because growth exposes flaws in the system the business has so far developed. For example, to sell in vast quantities requires production in vast quantities. So the scale-up issue from the previous stage is compounded: instead of how to go from 0 to 15,000 pounds, now the challenge is how to go from 15,000 to 150,000 pounds (or more). Often this type of scale-up requires significant investment in physical facilities. The addition of facilities generates additional manufacturing process and efficiency issues, because the effective integration of large new production capacity does not magically happen overnight. Sales and marketing take on a much more central role in most organizations at this stage, since growth is often driven by the efforts of these functions. Internal conflict may arise, because sales and marketing are focused on selling more while manufacturing is having problems scaling up to produce more without sacrificing quality. Usually manufacturing wants to go slower, while sales and marketing have the pedal to the metal – often promising more than manufacturing can consistently produce and deliver. This is precisely what occurred during late 2007 when Nintendo's manufacturing division could not keep up with the demand created by the company's marketing efforts for the Wii, resulting in significant out-of-stocks at retailers across the United States during the peak holiday sales period. Nintendo encouraged retailers to provide prospective buyers with "rain checks" for when manufacturing would have stock back in stores in February. One CNN news commentator noted, "There is nothing like the squeal on Christmas morning when the kid opens up the box and finds an IOU."[10]

Growth-stage companies are often constrained on all types of resources, so organization and planning take on added importance. Growth can be developed through a number of ways - existing customers buying more frequently, new customers added, and new territories opened up for sale. Management needs to make decisions about focusing limited resources on the best opportunities, not fragmenting efforts across many directions. The resource problem facing companies at this stage is how to coordinate what has become very complex very quickly. Whereas in the previous stage the advice for the company was to make all the steps and procedures explicit so that best practices could easily be repeated throughout the company, now companies need to routinize activities so that employees tacitly understand what to do and can execute best practices without close direction or supervision. Now companies also need to achieve greater cross-department coordination that does not require constant senior management involvement.

Maturity. At some point following tremendous growth, the maturity stage sets in. It happens to nearly every business. This is not necessarily connected with industry maturity; it may be that the particular products or services provided by the company have achieved customer saturation even though the industry is still growing, or that the kind of value appreciated by customers in an evolving industry no longer match the kind of value created by the company. As growth in revenue slows down, growth in profitability will depend upon greater efficiencies and cost reduction. Internal controls become more important, and the roles of the accounting and finance functions become more central to managing for enhanced financial performance. The company at this stage must also find ways to maintain previous growth momentum and market position, which typically involves developing extensions to the product/ service or introducing a second-generation line of products/services.

Most companies in the maturity stage have become highly organized using a functional structure, and are characterized by bureaucratic operating principles. These structural characteristics are useful for monitoring and exerting cost control over operations, in order to improve the profitability of the existing business. But the challenge of developing new business will often require building additional resources and competencies. So the essential resource challenge for companies in the mature stage is to develop secondary or complementary resource positions, beyond those that led to their initial path of success.

Figure 8.13 **Organizational Life Cycle Stage Characteristics**				
Stage	**Conception**	**Commercialization**	**Growth**	**Maturity**
Dominant problems	Innovation effort Strategy design Raising capital	Startup production Hiring Systems	Scale-up production Marketing & sales Chaos & pace Loss of culture Organization	Profitability Internal controls Future growth
Functions important to address problems	R & D	Manufacturing Information Systems	Manufacturing Marketing Sales	Finance Accounting
Resources development challenge	Leveraging founders' knowledge to develop additional resources	Combining resources; Making explicit the processes that work so everyone understands	Coordinating resources; Making routine the processes that work so they can be performed without direction	Developing secondary or complementary resources
Important resources	Knowledge Human Social capital Technology	Human Organizational	Financial Organizational Physical	Knowledge Technology

Figure 8.13 summarizes the characteristics of organizational life cycle stages we have just discussed, including the problems encountered in each stage, the importance of functional areas of the company, and the resource challenges.

Best Buy, Part 2

With added competition from Circuit City and Walmart, and with the U.S. economy falling into a recession in 2001–2002, Best Buy experienced a slowdown in its internal sales growth rate. In 2000 they reported that "same-store sales" (sales in stores open at least one year) had increased 11.1 percent, but in 2001 this had dropped to 4.9 percent and then to only 1.9 percent in 2002. In 2003 CEO Richard Schulz introduced a new customer-focused concept known as "Customer-Centricity." The new customer-centric approach involved: 1) careful customer segmentation research to better understand who were their most profitable customers and the purchasing behaviors of this group; 2) careful geographic and demographic research to better understand specifics of customers living near their stores; and then 3) creating store merchandise and marketing programs tailored at the local level to these specific customer targets. The types of merchandise stocked in stores therefore varied by location, and customers of each store began to receive personalized marketing and promotional mailings. This was in stark contrast to the models used by their competitors, which involved stocking the same merchandise in every store while employing broad-based general advertising. These new efforts enabled Best Buy to increase same-store sales rates, and to enhance gross profit margins through opportunistically charging higher prices.

QUESTIONS

1. Do you think Best Buy's initiatives were in response to industry life cycle or organizational life cycle issues? Why?
2. Since Best Buy moved first into this new way of cultivating the customer, would there have been any advantage for Circuit City to try the same thing then?

STRATEGY ISSUES IN STAGES

There are a few strategy issues that do not fit neatly into the box of generic business-level strategies (Chapter 7), but instead are more appropriately considered in the context of the organizational life cycle. These are "special situations" in strategy. They include first-mover strategy in the earlier stage, managing fast growth in the growth stage, and in the later stage the renewal strategies for the existing business.

First-Mover Strategy
A first-mover strategy describes the decision to enter a new market or industry space before any other company has done so. It is about creating a brand new business in a brand new market,

so it is really about a particular strategic approach for the earliest stage of a business at the earliest stage of an industry.

In our experience students tend to believe there is a positive cachet associated with being first into a new market space, as if getting there first is always the ticket to a sustainable strategic position. Let's be clear that this is not always the case. There are plenty of examples illustrating that the company that moved first into a new market space was not the eventual "winner" in the ensuing competition (Figure 8.14).[11] So we need to be clear about both the advantages and disadvantages of pursuing a first-mover strategy.

Figure 8.14
First Mover Winners & Losers

Industry	First Mover	Winner
Disposable diaper	Procter & Gamble	Procter & Gamble
Instant camera	Polaroid	Kodak
Jet airline	De Haviland	Boeing
MP3 player	Diamond Multimedia	Apple
Personal computer	Xerox	Dell or HP
VCR	Sony	Matsushita
Web browser	Netscape	Microsoft

There are two kinds of advantage that can accrue to first movers: timing advantage and size advantage. Any kind of sustainable competitive advantage rests on the ability of the company's to use timing or size to create barriers to entry to the industry, or barriers to mobility when other companies enter the industry.

Possible advantages due to timing can be a consequence of any of the following four dimensions:

- **Standard setting**. The company hopes to be able to set an industry standard as a result of entering first, thereby requiring other companies to follow design specifications that are created by the company. This is risky, because user tastes and preferences are difficult to predict before they have had a chance to spend time with a product. Superior quality products are not always the standard that emerges (e.g., Betamax versus VHS tapes).

- **Installed base and buyer switching costs**. By entering first, the company expects to develop a large base of users who become functionally and/or emotionally attached to their product or service, "locking them in" and making it difficult for them to switch to competitors. Sony and Microsoft have each been pursuing this approach with their game platforms, which have installed user bases significantly exceeding Nintendo. Programmers want to write game software for the platform that will deliver the greatest economic rewards. This feeds back on consumers who want to buy game platforms that have the most (and coolest) games written for it.

- **Reputation**. Where product performance or quality is difficult to determine prior to buying and there are no major price differences, customers will defer to the company with the strongest reputation. The first mover has a chance to build reputation before others gain traction. This is an approach that e*Trade Securities adopted early in its entry into the discount online trading industry, in which the technological trading capabilities of competitors were perceived as being nearly identical but where trust in handling personal investments is paramount.

262

- **Preemption**. First movers can lock in sources of supply and thus lock out competitors. The clearest example is when McDonald's is first to locate on the busiest corner of a high-traffic intersection; once it owns the land, no other company can occupy that spot. For a period of time in the 1980s Pepsi had an exclusive supply relationship with the popular artificial sweetener NutraSweet, which enabled Pepsi to develop a consumer franchise for its diet soda before Coca-Cola was able to.

It is possible to develop competitive superiority due to size advantages that can accruc to first movers. These include:

- **Scale**. When cost per unit declines with larger production volumes in each period, the company that generates a higher volume of business sooner can enjoy cost – and presumably pricing – advantages. See Figure 7.6 and discussion.

- **Experience curve**. The longer it has done something, the more efficient a company becomes because it has the chance to apply its learning to improve its methods of operation. See Figure 7.7 and discussion.

- **Scope**. If a first mover is able to broaden its procurement of goods and services faster than other competitors, it should be able to develop stronger bargaining power with suppliers and lower costs more quickly as a result.

- **Network**. When a company can more quickly achieve size, its buyers may derive greater value as a result of the presence of other buyers. AOL Instant Messenger and Facebook are only as strong as their networks of users (imagine how often you would visit Facebook if its network had only 1,000,000 active users instead of 1.7 billion in 2016).

Figure 8.15		
First Mover Advantages & Disadvantages		
Timing Advantages	**Size Advantages**	**Disadvantages**
Standard setting	Scale	Pioneering costs
Installed base & user switching costs	Experience curve	Technology uncertainty
Reputation	Scope	Demand uncertainty
Pre-emption	Network	Inertia

This is a fairly compelling list of advantages (Figure 8.15). But there are also some significant disadvantages from pursuing a first-mover strategy, and these challenge the conventional wisdom that first-mover status confers sustainable advantage over the long run:

- **Pioneering costs**. It is expensive to carve out a new business in a new industry space. The costs of pioneering include the R&D, building new infrastructure, and educating customers about what the heck you're trying to do. After all, it is a new business in a new industry, so no one has seen it before. Competitors coming in to the market space later on can build on the knowledge gained from your company's efforts, and can generally effect a market entry at a lower cost. The economic benefits to being first must somehow overcome the economic costs of getting there first, and this usually cannot be evaluated up front. Therefore, there is greater risk involved for the first mover.

- **Technological uncertainty**. As is illustrated by the Betamax story and other examples from Figure 8.14, "it ain't over til it's over."[12] You may be first in to the market with sweet technology that is superior on many fronts, but customers are unpredictable. In fact, it is often the case that pioneers in a market are banking on advanced technology of some sort. However, the early consumers are usually the "innovators" and "early adopters," and are in many respects not comparable to the mass market that will eventually follow (see Figure 8.16).

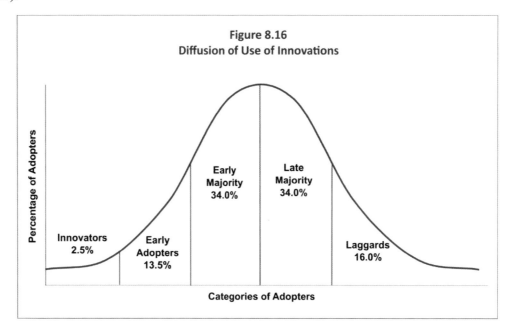

Figure 8.16
Diffusion of Use of Innovations

- **Demand uncertainty**. First movers typically have to make significant investments in specific manufacturing methods and other aspects of infrastructure, long before they know if sufficient demand will exist or even if the technology and standards are what will be preferred over the long run.

- **Inertia**. Having entered the market first and then discovered that different standards or technologies are taking off, many companies are still reluctant to modify their approaches. Sometimes this is based on a "sunk cost" argument that extols continuing on because of past spending, and sometimes it is based on the naïve belief that things will get better if they simply "try harder" and do "more of the same." Managers and product developers are often emotionally attached to their ideas, resistant to change even in the face of evidence that other approaches are preferred.

Fast Growth

Imagine the challenges you would face if your college workload (credit hours, amount of reading and homework) increased by 15 to 20 percent or more in every year! The volume and pace of activity picks up dramatically in any fast-growing organization, and it is not uncommon to find middle level managers putting in sixty- to seventy-hour weeks just to keep on top of current activity. During fast growth the company experiences a dramatic increase in customer volume, requirements from suppliers, extended operations, and more internal paperwork flow. It also attracts attention from competitors who observe what is going on and who likely have vested interests in forestalling further growth. It is often tempting to "throw bodies" at the problems of work overload, so that some of the chaos that typically reigns can be balanced across more people. Most organizations experience a loss of "culture" during this phase because in the midst of pressure to grow and frenetic activity, employees often lose sight of what it was that bound them together in the first place. The real possibility exists that employees will spend inordinate amounts of time putting out the most immediate "fires" as opposed to focusing on the best long-term moves for the company.

This is why fast-growth organizations need to ensure consistency with the original strategy, vision, and mission. Vision and mission – which we discussed in Chapter 3 – become critical during times when other forces try to pull the company in many different directions simultaneously. Refocusing on the business-level strategy that first propelled the fast-growth company into its current "predicament" is also called for. Here the importance of coordination across the value chain is critical, so that despite frenetic activity, each functional area of the company is pulling in the same direction and mutually supporting each other.

Fast-growth companies often find themselves challenged to implement the right kind of organizational structure to support their strategic approach. What works for companies that are mature or even growing at a normal rate, however, often does not work in fast-growth situations. Earthlink founder Sky Dayton had planned to sign up twenty to thirty new users a week to his new "dial-up" internet service back in 1995, but found this new internet offering was so popular that his company was fielding calls from thousands of interested users a week. He claims it was impossible to create an organizational structure that worked effectively, since the structure created one day was inundated within weeks. Therefore, he cycled between organizing and coping, organizing and coping, but made sure that he and his team considered organization on a regular basis as the company continued to grow. We'll talk more about structure in Chapter 11, where we will emphasize the point that structure goes hand in hand with strategy.

Renewal Strategies

We turn now to one of the special situations that a company encounters after it has entered the mature stage of the organizational life cycle. In today's dynamic markets it is seldom the case that a mature company can continue on indefinitely without its base business beginning to erode away. Once again, this type of erosion could be occurring - not because the entire industry is in a state of decline – but because other industry and competitive conditions are obsoleting the value the company's business was originally designed to deliver. At first the mature stage presents itself as a decelerating rate of growth, then growth flattens out, then finally it begins to actually decline year over year. Some kind of renewal effort is called for.

Occasionally some will discuss renewal as the reinvigoration of an existing line of business within the company, such as developing new customers or markets for the products or by encouraging existing customers to buy more frequently. These are actually steps that companies take during the company's growth stage, in order to prolong growth and lengthen the entire life for a particular line of products or services.

But here we are referring to the renewal of the company, and the goal of renewal in the *organizational* life cycle is to regenerate growth of the company. Organizational renewal can happen in one of two ways: 1) expansion through the development and introduction of new businesses, or 2) expansion through the acquisition of other businesses. Because an entire chapter of this textbook is devoted to corporate strategy and the acquisitions of other companies (Chapter 10), we comment here on factors that impact the ability of a company to successfully expand by diversifying into internally developed new businesses. There are four critical factors that organizational renewal efforts depend upon:

- **Opportunity recognition capabilities**. One of the resources that companies in the twenty-first century need to develop is foresight about new market opportunities to move into, which matches up with one of the two strategic imperatives we mentioned in Chapter 1 of this textbook. Better anticipation of emerging market trends usually calls for a set of internal organization processes, research methods, and communication that are different from what hierarchy and bureaucracy tend to produce. Being able to rapidly take advantage of new opportunities identified also calls for "speed-to-market" capabilities that are different from those needed for managing an existing line of business. We mentioned earlier the need for mature-stage companies to develop secondary or complementary resources so that they can effectively identify emerging opportunities.

- **Platform innovation**. Instead of focusing on a series of discrete new business opportunities, many companies today – especially those in industries where research and development costs can skyrocket – seek to focus on platform innovations. A platform represents a base upon which several promising new lines of business can be developed. For example one nanotechnology research group is focusing on the integration of nanostructures into devices for light gathering, a platform that can be developed into high-performance lighting systems for the home, office, and transportation sector uses. When a company such as Microsoft introduces a "developer application toolkit" for its Xbox game hardware (specifications for developers to use in writing applications to work with the hardware), the toolkit essentially represents a kind of platform off which dozens and dozens of new products can be developed. Platform development represents a more efficient way of making R&D investments, since it promises multiple possible outcomes from a singular direction.

- **Optioned investments in innovation**. There has been great debate over the years about the type of innovation effort that is more fruitful for companies - incremental or radical innovation. Innovation that is incremental tends to build slowly on previously developed technical knowledge about products or services. This type of approach can be useful in lengthening a product's life and forestalling organizational decline, but in a maturing business it does not usually present a solution to aggressively build company sales growth. In contrast, radical innovation is the type characterized by tremendous departures from existing technical knowledge, with potentially highly advanced results and payoffs. The flip side of radical innovation is high risk and greater volatility of results from research and development efforts: bigger potential payoffs, but bigger opportunities for failure as well. The solution for many companies has been to adopt an options approach, making small investments in a series of internal new business development initiatives and then evaluating whether further funding is warranted for each based upon the development milestones each effort achieves. Management that makes such option investments essentially adopts a portfolio approach to managing innovation, and the portfolio can include both radical and incremental efforts.

266

- **Culture and incentives**. In mature-stage companies, bureaucracy and formalization often reign. These are not organizational characteristics that support a culture of innovation. Some time ago Rosabeth Moss Kanter described "rules for stifling entrepreneurial efforts" inside an organization (Figure 8.17).[13] Senior management must reengineer the organizational structure and incentive systems to encourage experimentation and innovation and to avoid punishing such efforts that do not succeed. Chapter 11 will offer greater insight on structure and systems that provide the appropriate kind of environment for encouraging innovation.

Figure 8.17
Rules For Stifling Entrepreneurial Efforts Inside A Company

1. Regard any new idea from below with suspicion – because it's new, and because it's from below.
2. Insist that people who need your approval to act first go through several other levels of management to get their signatures.
3. Ask departments or individuals to challenge and criticize each other's proposals. That saves you the job of deciding; you just pick the survivor.
4. Express your criticisms freely, and withhold your praise. Let them know they can be fired at any time.
5. Control everything carefully. Make sure people count anything that can be counted, frequently.
6. Assign to lower level managers, in the name of delegation and participation, responsibility for figuring out how to cut back, lay off, move people around, or otherwise implement threatening decisions you have already made. And get them to do it quickly.
7. Above all, never forget that you (the higher ups) already know everything important about this business.

INTERNATIONAL STRATEGY

Throughout this textbook we have regularly referenced how globalization impacts the kind of dynamic competitive environment that companies face in the twenty-first century. Globalization affects companies in many ways, some positively and some negatively. The fact that we now live in a "global village" makes it easier for foreign competitors to compete against us, since they now have significantly better access to information, technology, financial capital, and alliance partners. This makes nearly every industry more perfectly competitive, since barriers to entry are more easily skirted and new entrants make themselves known and felt. These conditions also create more varied competition, so that the type of "strategic space" that we evaluate when we use strategy maps (Chapter 4) is populated with many types of companies competing on a variety of strategic dimensions.

Domestic companies with deep pockets can also more easily form alliances abroad, resulting in downward-spiraling cost structures and prices – creating less margin for error (and less margin for profit!). In addition, your company can more easily outsource to save costs or focus on core activities, and can therefore more easily manage outsourced efforts using advanced technologies. So competition has thus become more complex, and it has become increasingly difficult to "own" or control a sustainable space on the playing board. But globalization can also work for us, since this dynamic presents opportunities for our business to expand internationally, too, in the same ways.

For these reasons the potential for growth through an international strategy draws significant attention from management, and from strategy professors. However, we want to be very clear that international expansion does not automatically follow from the fact that the world is now a global marketplace. International expansion is but one method of growth or renewal for a company, among others we have already identified in this chapter. As with any new strategic initiative the decision to expand internationally must be made for the right reasons, at the right stage of development, must account for the value creation capabilities and resources that a company has developed and can leverage, and must fit with conditions present in the targeted countries.

There are entire courses in business schools that are devoted to international strategy or management, and we could devote many pages to this broad topic. We will focus our discussion of international strategy on the following important dimensions in this section: motivations for international expansion, leveraging resources and the value chain, assessing fit and risk, and practicalities any company confronts in such expansion.

Motivations to Expand Internationally

Among the many reasons for companies deciding to expand internationally, five stand out as the most traditional from a strategic point of view (Figure 8.18). Seeking new revenue growth, or achieving synergies with existing value chain and capabilities, reflect the kind of rationale discussed earlier in this chapter about growth and progress during stages of a company's organizational life cycle. Seeking revenue growth is usually the most obvious reason suggested. But the decision to expand into international markets must be compared to expanding in domestic markets, or to introducing new products or services into existing or new domestic markets. The unique challenges presented by international markets – for example political, economic, and cultural risks – make this type of expansion more uncertain than simple domestic expansion.

> **Figure 8.18**
> **Reasons for International Expansion**
>
> Traditional Motivations
> - New geographic revenue opportunities
> - Leveraging existing value chain & resources
> - Spreading risk
> - Overcoming trade barriers
> - Achieving location advantages
>
> Emerging Motivations
> - Financial pressure for global integration
> - Technology facilitates achieving greater scale
> - Competitive counter-response

Yet it is often the case that international markets experience more favorable economic conditions than domestic – such as higher growth rates, very large potential customer base, and stronger economies with better customer purchasing power. See Figure 8.19 for international market comparisons. These are very good reasons for considering such expansion, and are central to why so many companies today are especially evaluating the growing BRICS markets (especially China), whose share of world GDP grew four percentage points between 2013 and 2015.

Similarly, growth is easier to come by if the methods used to generate that

> **Figure 8.19**
> **2015 Regional Economic Comparisons**
>
> | | United States | European Union | BRICS* |
> |---|---|---|---|
> | Population (millions) | 321 | 510 | 3,094 |
> | Share of World GDP | 24.4% | 22.1% | 22.3% |
>
> * Brazil, Russia, India, China, South Africa
> Source: World Bank

growth are identical to existing methods. If expansion into international markets can take advantage of a company's internal value chain, or build easily upon its foundation of extraordinary resources and capabilities (Figure 6.6), then the risks of such expansion are significantly reduced. Leveraging the value chain and capabilities may lead to greater efficiencies through increased manufacturing scale or market scope, or may simply extend a proven differentiated strategic position from the domestic market, such as quality or reputation, with minimal risk. Nomacorc, which we profiled at the beginning of Chapter 6, moved from the United States domestic market into other countries because they presented a large untapped market and the move could build on the company's resource foundation (of knowledge about wines and wine enclosures). In contrast, in its international expansion plans Walmart has repeatedly discovered that the local conditions encountered in other countries (e.g., Brazil, Germany, Japan) do not always allow the company to perfectly translate its successful U.S. business model elsewhere.

A third traditional reason to consider expanding internationally is to spread risk. When a company's revenue base is significantly related to the status of the domestic economy, then its entire business is subject to a systematic risk that it cannot manage. Different countries, of course, experience different economic conditions, rates of growth and cycles, and so expansion can help smooth out revenues and earnings. Especially if a company that sells only domestically procures raw its materials or other supply inputs from abroad, then it could fall prey to exchange rate fluctuations when its home market currency declines on the international exchange. In this case it might make sense to expand in order to generate sales revenue abroad, and thus take advantage of the increased value of foreign currencies. The U.S. domestic automobile manufacturers (e.g. GM and Ford) have found profitable growth in markets outside North America over the last few years. We will return to the question of spreading risk in Chapter 10 when we discuss diversification.

The first three reasons have essentially dealt with reasons to expand revenue-generating efforts into other international markets. But it is sometimes the case that such efforts encounter trade barriers of various sorts. Although NAFTA and the 2016 Trans-Pacific Partnership Agreement are intended to promote more open borders and freer flow of goods and services, foreign governments often place other trade restrictions on companies with no physical presence in country. By locating new offices or production facilities in a country, companies can sometimes navigate around such burdens.

The final traditional reason listed in Figure 8.18 has to do with the process of value creation, that is where and how does a company produce its products or services? Establishing production operations in international markets can make sense when such efforts take advantage of local conditions that enhance a company's value creation efforts. For this reason apparel and shoe companies establish facilities or outsource manufacturing in countries in which wage rates are much lower than those paid domestically. They hopefully do this without sacrificing either quality or company image, since it is critical to maintain parity on other competitive dimensions that are valued. The Maytag division of Whirlpool Corporation sources standardized motors from China and Mexican-manufactured wiring harnesses for its dishwashers, but then assembles the final products in Tennessee. They say they want to build cost-competitive machines but also "stay as close as possible to the end market and avoid shedding American jobs."[14] Some steel companies mine iron ore in Brazil and then ship it to Trinidad to convert to iron carbide, since Trinidad has inexpensive natural gas to run their blast furnaces.

More recently an emerging set of motivations have played a more prominent role in why companies extend their international presence. Any company with a globally-integrated presence will have better access to financial resources worldwide, since financial markets often view globally-active companies as managing country-specific risks. Advanced technologies also encourage a more global approach. This is because technologies today have overcome what used to be the challenges of managing far-flung enterprises. Both of these dimensions also reflect the third emergent motivation for expanding internationally, and this is that competition is driving it. Competitors are taking advantage of global financial resources and of advancing technology, so often companies believe they cannot afford to be left behind. More importantly, competition from around the world increasingly shows up on your company's doorstep. According to a UPS strategy vice president speaking about his retailing clients, "if they stay only within their country boundaries, other merchants will compete from outside their country boundaries."[15] Taking the battle to another country may prompt competitors to defend their turf at home rather than expand. Recall the Sun Tzu advice from Chapter 1 on "vacuity and substance," where the recommendation was to show them potential harm in order to keep them from coming forth!

Best Buy, Part 3

By 2001 Best Buy achieved $15 billion in revenue and net income of $396 million through 419 stores open in the United States. Over the next few years CEO Richard Schulze took the company into international markets through a combination of acquisitions and opening new stores abroad. The first market the company entered outside the United States was Canada, where they acquired an existing chain (Future Shop) and began opening Best Buy stores. Future Shop gave the company an immediate presence in the Canadian market and allowed them to leverage their U.S.-based capabilities such as their supply chain and administrative functions. The new Best Buy Canada stores they built then took advantage of their proven merchandising techniques and advertising prowess.

In 2007 Best Buy acquired a 75 percent interest in Five Star, one of China's largest appliance and electronics retailers, with a contractual option to acquire the remaining 25 percent in several years (subject to Chinese government approval). This initial foray into a very different consumer market was designed "to increase our knowledge of Chinese customers and obtain immediate retail presence" in the market. The company opened its first Best Buy store in Shanghai in 2007, and planned to open eight more by 2009.

But China is a very tough market to break into. By 2013 the company had shuttered its own Best Buy branded stories in the country because of significant competition from entrenched Chinese retailers. Instead, it was focusing on expanding its business through Five Star's 184 stores in 20 Chinese cities. Nevertheless, in 2014 Best Buy sold out its interests in Five Star to its minority Chinese partner, and completely exited the country. During the same year it also divested its interests in its European partners.

QUESTIONS

1. With overall company sales continuing to grow so quickly, why did Best Buy decide to expand into international markets?
2. Why did they choose Canada, China, Mexico, and Turkey as markets to expand into?
3. What are the challenges in gaining acceptance and creating a successful business in other countries?

Leveraging Value Chain and Resources

As suggested by the preceding discussion and the Best Buy vignette, a central consideration in international strategy is if and how the company's value chain and resource position might be leveraged. This issue becomes of increasing importance as companies seek to expand further and further into international markets. Should the company adopt the same approach in South Africa as in Brazil? Should the company establish new manufacturing facilities abroad at the same time it establishes new sales offices? How much coordination is needed between operations in different countries? How does senior management ensure that such coordination is occurring? As we can see, the decision to expand abroad raises a number of questions that are materially different from the decision to expand our reach from Baltimore to Denver.

To answer these fundamental questions we can refer back to value creation once again. Here we ask two value chain questions that are related to the two basic business-level strategies of differentiation and low cost:

1. Where in the value chain is value created?

2. What is the pressure for efficiency in the value chain?

The answers to these questions help us determine the type of international strategy the company should seek to develop, and there are four types that are revealed. Figure 8.20 provides a useful visual guide for this discussion.

We will start at the upper right of Figure 8.20, and move counterclockwise looking at each type. When value is created upstream, closer to manufacturing or the supply side of a business, it is far less important for companies to make a series of discrete investments in each country in which it seeks to do business. Those types of in-country investments are not necessary, since they do not dramatically impact value creation. When there is significant pressure in the competitive market for efficiency, such as when pricing is competitive and low costs can be generated by manufacturing scale or scope, then the company should pursue a *global strategy*. Here the company produces a similar product or service for

Figure 8.20
Value Chain and International Strategy

all international markets, and seeks to do so through a combination of facilities investments that optimize costs. Steel is a marvelous example of this type of approach. The location decisions for steel manufacturing plants seek to optimize the inbound transportation costs of raw materials and the outbound transportation costs of finished products. Arcelor-Mittal and other global steel companies have created networks of strategically located facilities to accomplish this goal in a cost-competitive commodity industry. This example demonstrates how a global strategy approach requires significant and complex integration and coordination capabilities by the corporation.

Many automobile manufacturers have been searching for decades for a "world car," one that could be sold in all nations without being modified to local conditions. Ford has been going after this for decades, first with the Taurus, then finally in 2008 with the Fiesta. Hope springs eternal! Unfortunately, automobile manufacturing is quite unlike steel or other commodities; consumer variation in preferences across countries and cultures is significant.

Where there is significant pressure on value chain efficiency, but where value creation must also account for local contexts, then a company is apt to follow a *transnational strategy*. As the name implies, the company's efforts are geared toward producing in a way that bridges across national boundaries in order to gain the efficiencies dictated by the competitive market. However, the pressure to deliver values that are appreciated differentially by local market customers necessitates flexible manufacturing or production – the kind that can tailor aspects of the product or service to local cultures. Many food manufacturing firms follow this type of approach: basic brand research and development is centralized at headquarters, but then brand flavor and size adjustments, packages printed in foreign languages, production, and specialized distribution arrangements are tailored to local countries and cultures. Most automobile manufacturers are actually closer to this type of strategic approach today, seeking as much efficiency and low cost as possible by centralized, scale-efficient manufacturing facilities. But such facilities are still able to respond to local, or at least regional, differences around the world.

A *multi-domestic strategy* is appropriate when there is little pressure for efficiency in value creation and where value creation occurs very close to the customer. In this approach a company sets up an operation in each country it enters, so that it can respond directly to the specific needs of customers in that country. While there will always exist competitive pressure to reduce costs and garner efficiencies, these conditions do not represent critical facets for successfully competing. There is little strategic coordination across borders with this type of strategic approach, since each country places its own unique demands on the company. Any type of strategic decision authority centralized at headquarters may in fact hinder quick response to emerging in-market situations. Therefore you would ordinarily find that companies pursuing a multi domestic approach would set up offices in each country with fully staffed functions across the board. Multi-domestic strategy has historically emerged where there are significant differences in countries presented by culture or government regulation. This used to be the case across Western Europe, but with the advent of the European Union and the euro currency, such barriers to transnational or global approaches have been somewhat dissipated.

The three types of international strategic approaches we have discussed are the most prevalent. The fourth type – what we call *centralized single country strategy* – does not occur very often anymore in the twenty-first century. Here a company essentially produces and sells out of just one centralized operation for the entire world. It would make sense when there is little need to respond to local conditions and when there is little competitive pressure to wring efficiencies out of the value chain. Although these conditions may have described global competition in the 1950s and 1960s, before modern globalization and global competitive dynamics took hold, there are few instances today when this approach can make sense. Specialized pharmaceutical drug manufacturing is one example, where a company's small niche product is patent protected. Here there is no need to set up more than one manufacturing facility and competition is effectively eliminated because of the patent. French wine used to represent this type of approach, but now we can buy very high-quality cabernets and merlots from California, Australia, and many other wine-growing regions. Moreover, customers today are typically demanding greater customization, and competitors are always putting pressure on efficiency. It is for this reason that we put this type in a cloud in the figure; today it is only a type of international situation that companies could dream about encountering!

Figure 8.21 provides a summary of the characteristics of these four international strategy approaches.

Figure 8.21 Four International Strategy Approaches		
Strategy	Characteristics	Example
Global	Value added in upstream activities Efficiency through scale and scope is competitively important Only minor country-to-country variations Requires strong integration and coordination Location decisions important	Arcelor-Mittal steel
Transnational	Value added downstream near customer or user Efficiency through scale and scope is competitively important Variations across countries are meaningful Headquarters involved in strategy formulation, country offices in implementation and tactics	Kellogg's cereals McDonald's
Multi-Domestic	Value added downstream near customer or user Little or no pressure on efficiency Variations across countries are significant Country offices responsible for strategy formulation, implementation, and tactics	MTV in Europe
Centralized Single Country	Value added in upstream activities Little or no pressure on efficiency Occurs mainly where markets are protected or government controlled	Specialized pharmaceuticals Hollywood movie studios

Assessing Strategic Fit with Country Expansion

It may well be that the motivations are sound for a company to expand internationally, and that the company has determined that a particular international strategy approach makes the most sense. But before embarking on a cruise to another country, an assessment of the fit with that country should be made. To move into another country is brutally expensive, time consuming, and a distraction from the company's existing business. Examples mentioned above – such as Best Buy in China, Walmart in Germany – show that much time and valuable resources can be wasted away if the fit with a country is not right.

The first method is to evaluate the potential fit between the target country, the industry environment, and the company's endowments of resources and capabilities. In earlier chapters we showed that when resources and capabilities match up well with the key success factors (KSFs) demanded by an industry, the potential is strong to develop competitive advantage and earn superior returns. But to this pairing we must also compare the unique conditions that characterize the target country into which the company contemplates moving. Our friend Michael Porter (value chain, business-level strategies) also wrote about factors affecting national competitiveness, which are important to consider here (Figure 8.22).[16]

Figure 8.22
Evaluating Potential Fit

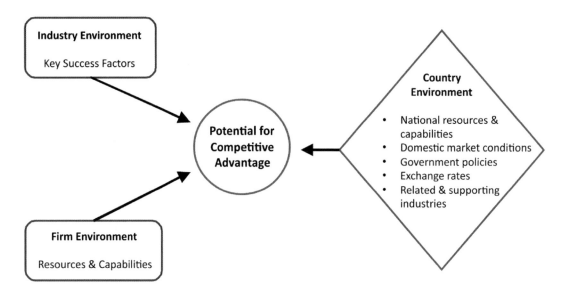

In each country its national resources and capabilities can dramatically impact the potential for successful expansion. These include facets such as the availability of appropriate human resources for needed labor, the transportation and communication infastructures, the availability of or access to suitable raw materials for manufacturing, and whether the legal system provides protections and the rule of law to ensure that credible commitments can be made. The presence of other local industries that complement the company's business may be important, for example shoe producers and leather manufacturers near each other in Northern Italy. Their proximity and resource sharing has been shown to improve innovation and competitive performance. The domestic economy and the country's market conditions can impact growth, just as the interaction between a country's economy and the rest of the world can affect exchange rates, interest rates and other factors.

A second fit assessment considers the risks involved in doing business that is distant from the company's headquarters. Typically, we would think of distance in physical terms: how many thousands of miles away is this new country? This is certainly one important dimension. But here we refer to the CAGE distance framework used to assess the risk of distance along a number of dimensions (Figure 8.23).[17] These dimensions include cultural, administrative and political, geographic, and economic. We offer examples to illustrate each distance dimension:

- **Culture distance**. Culturally, how different is the local company from the sort of culture in which the company's business does well. Krispy Kreme has done exceedingly well in the United Kingdom with its yeast-raised doughnuts. However, the prospects of success across the channel in France would be remote because French culture embraces fresh-baked breads in local shops.

- **Administrative and political distance**. Sweden's Ikea wants to sell its products in India, since their inexpensive design and manufacturing matches up well with a growing Indian middle class. Yet their inability to identify local sources of supply has run afoul of Indian law about requisite levels of domestic manufacturing. Trying to administer procurement and supply chain relationships in a new territory has proven very complicated.

- **Geographic distance**. Here we are talking about pure physical distance. JLR, the Tata division that manufactures Jaguar automobiles, has established a production facility in China. Thousands of miles from the UK where superior-quality manufacturing can be easily observed and tweaked, it is proving a challenge to reproduce the same dynamic so far away.

- **Economic distance**. Like many U.S.-based multi-nationals, Procter & Gamble seeks to develop its business in new markets. But the maker of Tide detergent finds this a challenge in parts of the world where tap water is uncommon and the wash cycle is less frequent than in the west. Developing a robust business is a challenge where the economic distance between existing customers and new customers is so vast.

Figure 8.23
CAGE Distance Framework

Evaluative Dimension		Contemporary Example
C	Cultural distance	Krispy Kreme in France
A	Administrative and Political distance	Ikea in India
G	Geographic distance	Jaguar Land Rover in China
E	Economic distance	Procter & Gamble in Bangladesh

Practical Dimensions of International Expansion

Finally we mention practical considerations in expanding into other countries. We first draw attention to the different ways in which internationalization efforts might take shape.[18] These range from more transactional relationships with little commitment and risk, to heavy resource commitments and risk through significant foreign direct investment. Paralleling this dimension is the level of ownership and control a company will have over its business in another country (Figure 8.24). Many companies will move internationally at first through pure export. With minimal commitment other than lining up sales channels of distribution (possibly through local agents in the country), this approach entails the least risk to the company. It provides an opportunity to "test the waters," although it may not be a true test of the ultimate potential in the country since the investment into the market has been limited by choice. Agents often handle multiple lines, including competitors, so less attention is devoted to the company's business in this very hands-off approach.

Licensing and franchising represent a greater investment and commitment by the expanding company. Typically licenses or franchises are relationships created to last for some time, and thus the company will make an investment in identifying the best partners in the country with which to do business. Agreements will usually specify ways in which licensees and franchisees must conduct business, in order to protect the reputation of the company. Through both methods the company is able to exert greater control over its business in the country. On the other hand, such efforts require a greater level of monitoring the behavior of foreign licensees and franchisees. So the greater dedicated attention one receives through this mode of entry is offset by the greater costs involved in setting it up and managing it.

Figure 8.24
Modes of International Expansion

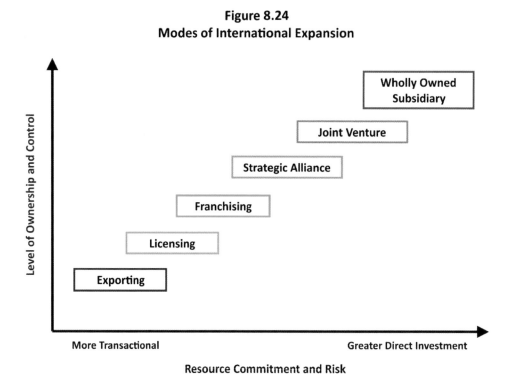

Strategic alliances and joint ventures solidify much stronger, more compelling long term relationships with foreign entities, and enable the company to exert much greater ownership and control over what happens. These sorts of partnerships go beyond arms-length licensing and franchising arrangements. Here the company and its foreign partner both make strategic commitments designed to accomplish goals over the long run that are of mutual interest. VF Corporation – the North Carolina based corporate parent of brands such as Wrangler, North Face, and Vans – has engineered joint venture manufacturing relationships with Far East clothing manufacturers. Here VF invests its own patented technology in foreign-owned plants, enabling them to make top quality clothing while at the same time enjoying the benefits of low wage labor. The foreign entities are able to learn about new manufacturing techniques invented by VF, and to apply these to businesses that do not compete with VF.

Of course, the mode of entering foreign markets which retains the greatest ownership and control is establishing a wholly-owned subsidiary in the country. This also entails the greatest investment of strategic resources. Usually this step is taken after the company has already conducted business in the country for some time, learned about its market, culture, and government, and had developed a deep knowledge base about how to compete there successfully. Minimizing the risk of this approach also usually entails the hiring of managers from within the country. In Chapter 11 we will provide further discussion of how a foreign subsidiary might be organized within the structure of the corporation.

No discussion of international strategy is complete without mentioning at least briefly the political and ethical risks that become more prevalent when moving offshore. Political risks occur in both western cultures and emerging nations. One of our former colleagues was involved with Pepsico's international sales in the 1970s, and was setting up agreements in Nigeria that would allow the company to begin selling soft drinks there. On the morning of his meeting with country's president, he received a call in his hotel room that a coup had occurred removing the president from office, and that his meeting had been cancelled. It was not until the late 1990s that an era of military coups in the country ceased to regularly occur. The 2016 United Kingdom "Brexit" decision, where UK citizens voted for their country leave the European Union, resulted in the rapid decline of the British pound in foreign exchange markets and much greater volatility across European markets. For those companies doing business in Europe, and especially those with UK-based subsidiaries where their revenue was denominated in pounds, this had clear effects on annual performance.

We also encourage interested students to think carefully about ethical issues which manifest themselves as companies expand internationally.[19] Cultural norms of business conduct can be extremely different in other countries, compared to what we are used to. It is not unusual in many countries for company executives to be discretely encouraged – or forthrightly asked – to make "contributions" to indigenous officials in order to accomplish an important business goal for the company. Be forewarned! In 1977 the United States passed the Foreign Corrupt Practices Act (FCPA), which makes this sort of behavior illegal under U.S. law. The law applies to both individuals and companies, and can result in significant fines or imprisonment. In 2014 Alcoa paid more than $200 million in fines and was forced to give up $175 million in revenue previously-booked, because the company was found to have bribed Australian officials. Walmart underwent an exhaustive 3-year investigation by the Department of Justice for its activities in Mexico; DOJ found little in the way of major offenses, but the investigation was a drain on executive resources and a public relations nightmare for years. Other countries have passed laws similar to FCPA.

So what advice can be offered when ethically-challenging situations arise, as they inevitably will? The easiest and clearest advice is to be aware of company policy, be aware of the laws (both domestic and foreign), and – though it sounds corny – "do the right thing." More practically, international managers might view these sorts of situations as opportunities for negotiating better ways to deliver value to local interests and economies. In the U.S., for example, it is not uncommon for companies to seek economic incentives from local authorities in order to establish a new office or manufacturing facility. Local authorities ask for and usually receive some promise about future employment to be generated by the business. So a "win-win" arrangement is created. Created is the right word to use here, since the creativity involved in opportunity recognition and value creation can help companies wend their way through such situations.

CHAPTER SUMMARY

In this chapter we have explored the defining characteristics of industry life cycle stages, and assessed their potential impact on company strategy. The five stages are introduction, growth, maturity, decline, and renewal. Strategic variety can exist in an industry in its earlier stages. But increasingly as the industry grows toward maturity, standardization and then commoditization privilege low-cost strategic approaches. When an industry enters decline, renewal efforts are largely focused on either redefining the boundaries of the industry, reconfiguring industry activities, or redefining values that have been important in the industry. All three directions prompt the creation of new value chain activity sets.

Strategy effectiveness is also dependent on the organizational life cycle context. Organizations experience four different stages of development: conception, commercialization, growth, and maturity. Companies experience different kinds of problems at different organizational life cycle stages, and consequently have different strategic resource needs for each.

Unique strategic issues are highlighted by considering the organizational life cycle. These include the nature of first-mover advantage in the early stage of an industry's development. There are both advantages and disadvantages from moving first into a market, and business history provides evidence of both successes and failures by companies adopting this approach. Fast growth presents a unique context that emphasizes the importance of vision, mission, and strong coordination across the internal value chain. The mature stage of company development highlights the need for renewal, which can occur by diversifying either new through internally developed businesses or through acquisition. Internal new business development depends on opportunity recognition capabilities and a series of structural and incentive system departures from how mature companies typically operate.

Finally, we considered important dimensions of international strategy. Moving into international markets is not a foregone conclusion; it is a decision to grow or expand that should be considered against other alternatives for growth. Often there are good reasons to expand internationally, especially if foreign markets present significant revenue enhancing possibilities or opportunities to leverage the company's value chain and the resources. Four types of international strategy are described, where each depends on where value is actually created in the value chain and the extent to which there is competitive pressure on the value chain to be efficient. These four types include global strategy, transnational strategy, multi-domestic strategy, and centralized single-country strategy.

Companies contemplating international expansion should assess their fit to do so. There are two ways to assess fit. The first method assesses how well the country conditions match up with the company's own resources and capabilities and with the key success factors demanded by the industry. The second method uses the CAGE distance framework to assess cultural, administrative and political, geographic, and economic distance of the target country from the company's home country.

Companies must also carefully plan their mode of entry into other countries. A continuum of choices, from pure export to wholly owned subsidiary, requires increasing resources investment but also promises greater ownership and control over foreign operations. Company representative may encounter ethical challenges when doing business abroad, usually resulting from differences in norms and culture. The laws are very clear that bribery is illegal. Creative approaches to negotiating value creation may present ways to more easily open up new markets.

Learning Objectives Review

1. *Explain the stages of an industry life cycle and their impact on business strategy.*

- There are four basic stages of an industry's life cycle. Every industry goes through its introduction, growth, and then maturity. In the fourth stage an industry can either enter into decline or be subject to renewal. Often renewal efforts occur after an industry has passed into early symptoms of decline, when industry participants finally recognize that change is called for.

- Differentiation strategies are particularly appropriate for industries in the introduction and growth stages. This is because standards have not yet been set in the industry and there are shades of variety that appear to be possible.

- Low cost strategies become more important in maturing and declining industries. Here standardization and commoditization of products and services often appear. Therefore cost efficiency, and cost-cutting to maintain profitability or have greater pricing flexibility, become paramount.

- Industry value chain reconfiguration is most appropriate for a renewal stage. This can involve redefining the industry's boundaries to focus on new key success factors, disaggregating blocks of value chain activity, redefining value itself, or shifting to complement products and services.

2. *Analyze the strategy implications of competing in fragmented or consolidated industries.*

- Consolidated industries often privilege scale and scope which confers cost efficiencies and the low cost strategy. However, large scale companies are slow to move because they are so complex, may be blind to new niche opportunities, must be careful about getting too large for antitrust reasons, and may have constrained financial resources because of their focus on efficient operations. These all present mobility barriers enabling smaller, more agile companies to do well.

- Fragmented industries are usually more perfectly competitive, experiencing a high level of new entry. Companies in these industries can be successful by reconfiguring the industry value chain, disaggregating usually-combined operations or finding ways to aggregate usually-fragmented operations.

3. *Utilize organizational life cycle stages and the kinds of problems and resources issues that businesses experience in each to proactively recommend value creation activities.*

- There are four organizational life cycle stages: conception, commercialization, growth, and maturity.

- Companies in the conception stage face innovation, strategy design, and raising capital as the key challenges. These require the development and use of knowledge, human, social capital, and technology resources.

- Commercialization stage companies face the problems of startup production, hiring, and systematizing production of what had been ad hoc experimentation in the R&D phase. This requires strong organizational and human resources.

- In the growth stage companies must scale up production, develop sophisticated marketing and sales, and deal with a frenetic pace of activity which can lead to loss of culture. Physical and financial resources assist in operations, and organizational resources can address the people and culture issues.

- Mature companies often experience profit pressures and worry about future growth. Developing a process to gain insight on emerging trends can be especially helpful, and technology resources can assist in providing information and internal controls on existing operations.

4. Explain the risks associated with being a first mover.

- The first mover into a new industry or product category often receives great attention and becomes popular to the untrained eye. But there can be risks to this approach. These include:

- Pioneering costs, where it is very expensive to be first in. Others can come along later at a lower cost.

- Technological uncertainty, where it is unclear at the beginning what sort of standard will ultimately be most-highly valued by customers.

- Demand uncertainty, where it is unclear at the beginning whether a segment will grow sufficiently large.

- Inertia, where once in a new segment with a developed product or service, it is usually difficult for a company to make changes even when things are not going as expected. Here the mindset is to dig in and try harder doing more of the same.

5. Explain when a company should expand internationally and what approach it should take for doing so.

- The decision to expand internationally should be made after careful evaluation of other growth opportunities domestically. International expansion raises added sets of complexities for companies, including legal and cultural issues, which do not exist in domestic growth initiatives.

- The type of international strategy should be determined by two questions:

- Where in the value chain is value created? A different approach is called for if value is created downstream close to the customer versus upstream in manufacturing.

- What is the pressure for efficiency in the value chain? Where efficiency is prized, the strategy will usually call for some sort of centralized manufacturing or production that affords scale.

Key Terms

Commoditization - An industry condition in which a standard set of features and benefits is required for any serious competitor, and in which such features and benefits are readily available from a variety of suppliers. These conditions lead to low-cost competition.

Complements - Products or services that have a correlation relationship with, and can affect the value of, a company's own products or services. For example, iTunes and iPod.

First-mover advantage - The sustainable competitive advantage that is sought by being the first company to enter a new industry or industry segment.

Industry roll-up - The consolidation of an industry when many small fragmented competitors are combined into a larger company.

Mobility barriers - Strategic actions and resource investments that prevent competitors in the industry from imitating the company.

Options - An investment approach that places a small initial bet on an initiative, with the opportunity to invest further if the initiative makes favorable progress and reaches positive milestones.

Perfect Competition – A marketplace in which there is perfect information, zero transactions costs and costless entry, so that all firms become virtually identical and no firm earns any profit.

Reconfiguring the industry value chain - A strategic approach that calls for changing the usual sets of relationships across the industry value chain.

Size advantage - One of the possible benefits of first-mover status when entering a new industry. Size advantages tend to produce favorable cost structures and network effects.

Standardization - An industry condition in which customers begin to appreciate a standard set of features and benefits or products or services.

Timing advantage - One of the possible benefits of first-mover status when entering a new industry. Timing advantages tend to build customer loyalty through setting standards, building reputation, and achieving customer lock-in.

Short Answer Questions

1. How do life cycle stages affect the decision process of businesses?

2. Explain why a new product tends to follow a life cycle.

3. Where are the value creation opportunities in a consolidating industry?

4. Why do industries consolidate?

5. How does a fragmented industry offer opportunities for expansion?

6. Explain why a first mover is so successful.

7. How is being a first mover also dangerous for an organization?

8. How do companies initiate a pattern of continuous renewal?

9. Why is renewal so difficult to achieve for established organizations?

10. What unique issues does fast growth require management to address?

11. Why do companies seek to grow internationally?

12. International value creation opportunities are best under what circumstances?

Group Exercises

1. Using your knowledge of the latest and greatest gadgets to hit the market, map out the life cycle of a particular product. How fast will it traverse the entire cycle? How many competitors do you predict will enter the market and when? What would you recommend to management knowing that this cycle will most likely play out? What should the company do when the product moves into decline?

2. Over the years a number of formerly fragmented industries have gone through a rapid period of consolidation that changed the dynamics of the industry. Select at least two industries that you and your group believe are ripe for consolidation. What avenues do you think are available for the current players in this industry? How will consolidation change the business model they use? Will consolidation open other opportunities in the industry?

3. You have recently been hired as the head of strategy for a rapidly growing chain of computer repair shops. The company provides on-site service for all laptop and desktop computers, guaranteeing all repairs within a twenty-four-hour period. The CEO has announced a decision to expand internationally and has asked you to develop the best methodology for making this a reality. How will you organize the company going forward? What critical issues seem to have the highest potential for derailing the expansion? What industries would you look to for examples?

References

[1] The Doors. 1967. When the music's over. Strange Days. Elektra Records: New York.

[2] Data based on Mintel Reports, Recording Industry Association of America (RIAA), IFPI, Statista.com, U.S. Department of Commerce, and authors' estimates.

[3] Smith, E. 2007. Sales of music, long in decline, plunge sharply. Wall Street Journal. March 21, A1; Karp, H. 2014. Artists press for their share, Wall Street Journal, Jul 21, p. B4.

[4] Mintel Reports and authors' estimates.

[5] Deanes, G. K., F. Kroeger, and S. Zeisel, S. 2002. The consolidation curve. Harvard Business Review. December: 20–21.

[6] Barr, P. S., J. L. Stimpert, and A. S. Huff. 1997. Cognitive change, strategic action, and organization renewal. Strategic Management Journal 13(5): 15–36.

[7] Cox, W. M., and R. Alm. 1996. The economy at light speed: Technology and growth in the information age and beyond. 1996 Annual Report, Dallas Federal Reserve Bank. Dallas: Federal Reserve Bank

[8] U.S. Department of Labor. http://www.doleta.gov/SGA/sga/99-006sga.htm.

[9] Bitran, G. R., S. Gurumurthi, and S. L. Sam, 2006. Emerging trends in supply chain governance. Massachusetts Institute of Technology working paper. Cambridge, MA.

[10] CNN Headline News. 2007. December 18.

[11] Teece, D. 1987. The competitive challenge: Strategies for industrial innovation and renewal. Cambridge, MA: Ballinger.

[12] Attributed to Yogi Berra. Who else!?

[13] Kanter, R. M. 1985. The change masters. New York: Free Press.

[14] Aeppel, T. 2003. Three countries, one dishwasher. Wall Street Journal. October 6: C5.

[15] Berman, D. K. 2014. My jacket from China and what it portends. Wall Street Journal, December 19, p. B1.

[16] Porter, Michael E. 1990. The competitive advantage of nations. New York: Free Press; Bartlett, C. A., and S. Ghosal. 1998. Managing across borders: The transnational solution. Boston: Harvard Business School Press.

[17] Ghemawat, P. 2001. Distance still matters. Harvard Business Review, September.

[18] Westhead, P., M. Wright, and D. Ucbasaran. 2001. The internationalization of new and small firms. Journal of Business Venturing 16: 333–358; Jacques, L. L., and P. M. Vaaler. 2001. The international control conundrum with exchange risk: An EVA approach. Journal of International Business Studies 32: 813–832; Arnold, D. J., and J. A. Quelch. 1998. New strategies in emerging markets. Sloan Management Review 40(1): 7–20; Prahalad, C. K. 2005. The fortune at the bottom of the pyramid. Upper Saddle River, NJ: Wharton.

[19] Kolk, A., and R. V. Tulder. 2004. Ethics in international business: Multinational approaches to child labor. Journal of World Business 39: 49–60; Rodriguez, P., K. Uhlenbruck, and L. Eden. 2005. Government corruption and entry strategies of multinationals. Academy of Management Review 30(2): 383–396.

Chapter 9: Competitive Dynamics

LEARNING OBJECTIVES

1. Describe how to use industry and company trajectories to evaluate an industry environment.

2. Select and evaluate the appropriate techniques for producing competitor intelligence.

3. Describe the differences between tactical and strategic methods for responding to competitors.

4. Discuss the conditions under which cooperation can be an effective competitive approach.

Will One of U Play?[1]

Nearly fifty years old, console-based video gaming is a $27 billion dollar worldwide industry dominated by three main competitors: Sony, Nintendo, and Microsoft. Over the years these competitors have released system after system aimed at the same hard-core gaming market of boys and young men.

The pace of competitive pressure has intensified in this industry. By any measure, game console manufacturers have stepped up the frequency with which they introduce new consoles that take advantage of newer technology such as memory, chipsets, and networked computing. In the first fifteen years following the 1972 introduction of the very first console game system, the Magnavox Odyssey, 6 major new consoles were introduced by a handful of competitors. Nintendo's NES system was introduced during this period. But in the last fifteen years, fifteen major new consoles have come out as the industry has moved rapidly from fourth to eighth generation platforms using more highly advanced technology. As the three major competitors continue to upgrade their systems, each jockeys for the privileged position of coming to market first and trying to lock up consumers. In 2012 Nintendo led with its Wii U, with Microsoft and Sony following in 2013 with their new upgraded systems.

Each company has stretched beyond mere games in the technology it employs in updated hardware. Microsoft seeks to further integrate its Kinect peripheral, provide live television, a built-in Skype client, and cloud-based gaming. Nintendo's controller includes an LCD touch screen, web browser and video chat capability. Sony sports many of these same features and also adds remote play to its lineup.

The competitive focus in the industry is also on the suppliers of game software as much as it is on attracting customers to the consoles themselves. A highly successful game launch, netting hundreds of millions for the successful video game producer, also attracts and retains console customers. And so when competitors introduce new game consoles, they also introduce new games that take advantage of the technological capabilities of new consoles. In 2013 Microsoft announced its new Xbox One with a suite of games re-developed for this new machine (Halo; Ryse - Son of Rome; FIFA 14; Metal Gear Solid V - The Phantom Pain; and Titanfall). When Sony announced its PS4, it had three big exclusives scheduled for launch (Killzone: Shadow Fall, Knack, and Drive Club).

In 2016 Nintendo's partner companies introduced the new Pokemon Go mobile game app, downloaded over 15 million times worldwide in the first few days. This is the first major game from one of the big three that has moved onto the mobile platform.

QUESTIONS

1. How can any of these companies predict what its competitors will do next, and when?
2. Will the intensity and pace of competition increase in this industry? How?
3. Could the advent of mobile game apps be ruinous to the game console industry, and how should Microsoft and Sony respond?

A Galaxy Far From Google[2]

Samsung, the Korean company that excels in electronics, introduced its Galaxy phone in 2009. The phone utilizes the Android operating system, which was developed by Google. By 2012 Samsung had the leading worldwide market share of smart phones, with a 31% share compared to only 20% for Apple's popular iPhone.

In 2013 Samsung introduced its S4 smart phone, but significantly downplayed its involvement with Google and its reliance on the Android operating system. The Android "ecosystem" is similar to the PC ecosystem, which combined Windows and Intel chips into what was known as the "Wintel" standard. Samsung cooperated with Google in the development of its phones, in order to ensure that the hardware and software were not only compatible, but mutually reinforcing in a way that presented competitive product benefits in the marketplace.

Cooperation presents an interesting dilemma for both parties. Google developed Android as an alternative to Windows and Apple's iOS system in anticipation of a growing market for mobile computing. They were right: by 2016 over 80% of devices shipped relied on Android. But in the cell phone market Samsung is the 500-pound canary, three times larger than its closest Android phone manufacturing competitor.

Google needs Samsung, or does it? Google was worried that Samsung would develop its own version of Android that relied much less on other Google-provided services like maps and search. This is precisely what Amazon did with its Android-powered Kindle Fire. So in 2012 Google acquired the cell phone division of Motorola, solidifying an installed based of its own phones that utilized Android. But then in 2014 Google sold the Motorola phone business to Lenovo, a world leader in low cost hardware manufacturing. But then in 2016 Lenovo struck a deal with Microsoft to produce new phones using the Windows 10 mobile operating system. So now Lenovo's presence balances the competition between Samsung, Apple and Microsoft, while continuing to ensure a large Android operating system user base.

QUESTIONS

1. Does Lenovo need Google? Does Google need Lenovo?
2. What are the benefits and risks of cooperation?

COMPETITOR INTELLIGENCE

Through the first eight chapters of this text we have focused on developing a sound foundation for strategy development. That foundation included: 1) knowledge of the relationship between strategy and performance; 2) recognition of the need for vision and mission for the organization; 3) a deep understanding of the competitive environment; and 4) understanding how to use value chain and resource-based analysis to develop sustainable competitive advantage. In addition we have discussed how these relate to the choice of a fundamental business level strategy approach, and then most recently how strategies might be modified given varying conditions in the marketplace.

As we pointed out in Chapter 8, strategy is not developed in a vacuum and its actual execution is most certainly not executed in a vacuum. It is incumbent upon business executives to not only react to competitors, but much more importantly to anticipate how those same competitors might react to moves that their business initiates. The dynamism of competition creates tremendous uncertainty for the strategist, which amplifies the importance of thinking through the intentions and estimated moves of competitors. This chapter is about the development of competitive intelligence, as well as the application of techniques to predict, respond to, and even preempt competitor moves.

This chapter is much more about tactics than about strategy. Recall from Chapter 1 that strategy is about longer-term moves, significant resource investments that play out and pay out over time, a focus on sustainability and long-term performance. Subsequently in Chapters 2 and 4

we explored how financial statement analysis and industry analysis can reveal patterns of financial resource investments, strategic positions, and intentions of competitors. In contrast when we take up the topic of competitive dynamics, we are interested in the more immediate moves, countermoves, and responses of competitors to both changes in the industry environment as well as our own company's initiatives. Grand master chess players are known to think strategically about how their opponents will move eight to ten turns from now; in this chapter we want to think tactically about how they will move over the next one to three turns. Short-term tactics will (or should) be consistent with long-term strategy, so the previous work we have done in understanding strategic dimensions of competitors is certainly helpful here.

INDUSTRY CHARACTERISTICS AND TRAJECTORIES

Prior to examining the individual attributes of companies, it is important to recognize that competitive dynamics fundamentally relate to the types of conclusions we draw from industry analyses in our discussion in Chapter 4. One important characteristic of an industry is how benign or hostile it is. While it is generally acknowledged that a benign environment provides companies with significant opportunity primarily because of less intense competition, many companies operate in intensely competitive environments and must therefore figure out how to prosper in hostile conditions. We will briefly examine the characteristics of each and then tie that analysis to approaches that appear to provide the best opportunity for sustainable advantage.

Benign Environments

Benign environments are usually characterized by conditions among the following: 1) market demand exceeds market supply; 2) high gross profit margins; 3) low competitive intensity, meaning no one competitor controls a high proportion of the market; 4) strong customer loyalty; and 5) a customer tolerance of occasional management miscues.

Studies have suggested that benign environments reward differentiators. As you may remember from our discussion of business level strategies in Chapter 7, differentiation exists on one end of the business level strategy continuum. In benign environments customers are looking for unique product or service characteristics, high levels of product or service quality, and often rely on a substantial amount of educationally oriented advertising in order to make purchase decisions.[3] Once a company secures a customer base in this type of industry environment, customers tend to remain loyal, and competitors do not vigorously attack established positions. In this type of environment, therefore, we would not generally expect competition to directly assail our company's product or market position.

But stop for a minute, before reading on, and try to think of an industry today which could be characterized as operating in a benign environment. It is tough to think of many (any?). Competition in the 21st century often occurs in more hostile environments.

Hostile Environments

Hostile environments are usually characterized by conditions among the following: 1) slow growth, flat or even declining revenue; 2) frequent price wars; 3) high competitive intensity, meaning that one or a few competitors control a substantial portion of the market; 4) rapid pace of product or service obsolescence; or 5) active efforts targeted at cost containment by competitors. Hostile environments also occur where technological change is rapid, coming either from developments outside the industry or from suppliers or internal R&D. This is certainly the case in video gaming, where advances in memory, chip design, and software programming have led to increasingly more frequent introductions of new platforms and games.

Whereas benign environments tend to exist at the earlier stages in an industry life cycle, hostile environments seem to emerge once an industry approaches maturity. Referring back to Chapter 8, a low cost strategic approach seems to provide organizations the best opportunity for a sustainable advantage in maturing situations. In hostile environments, companies that seem to perform best have product lines that leverage a core set of resources and capabilities (so that they can concentrate on a tight fit within their organization), a broad market approach to maximize their geographic reach, sophisticated process technology, and purchasing advantages relative to their competitors.[4] These factors tend to support the low cost management dimension that is elevated in importance under these conditions.

The term "hypercompetition" was coined to describe a perceived new reality in competitive dynamics. This view of the competitive environment argues that traditional competitive responses are insufficient when the new realities of the marketplace – better information, global reach, access to technology and capital – mean that the dynamic of competition is speeding up. This view suggests that the only real competitive advantage is that of speed. The rapid creation of new competitive advantages that either neutralize or make obsolete the advantages of competitors is the new core capability of successful organizations.[5] Sun Tzu would have certainly agreed with this approach to dealing with competitors, as he found virtually no advantage to measured responses and saw only positive consequences to the use of speed. Apple released the iPod in October 2001, and it rapidly became the gold standard for audio players. As industry competitors scrambled to match the capability of the original iPod, Apple successively released various versions aimed at specific points in the consumer market. iPod Nano, iPod Mini, iPod Touch, and iPod Shuffle all crushed the competitors' ability to respond, because before competitors could match the existing product, Apple had released the next version. In hypercompetitive markets companies seek to stay ahead of their competitors by constantly destroying the old fabric (including their own products) and creating new rules of the game.

In these types of hostile or hypercompetitive environments we might, therefore, predict that key competitors will make a couple different types of moves. First, we can expect them to continue working on their own cost structures, in order to be price competitive or to offensively engage further in price wars. This means our company must continue its efforts to manage to lower costs, and often we will need to carefully benchmark how we are doing relative to competitors on this dimension. Secondly, we might anticipate that competitors will tend to introduce new products and services into larger customer and geographic segments, in order to gain efficiencies and disrupt the status quo.

Industry Trajectories

We learned in Chapter 4 how strategy maps can be useful in bringing together information about competitors in a compelling visual format. Competitive maps take a variety of forms, but the most popular strategy execution maps compare primary competitors on each of the key success factors in an industry. A rigorously maintained set of maps showing current relative positions as well as historical trending for each company can be especially useful for analyzing competitive moves. In that discussion we noted how historical trajectories in "strategic space" on a strategy map are an excellent indicator of future intention. Referring back to Figure 4.22, for example, if we were to predict the kinds of competitive moves that Dell might make in the future – based purely upon its past positions using a map that compares innovation versus unit cost – we would expect the company to continue to make investments that would lower its unit costs further (and not so much work an innovation agenda). This was the trajectory the company had historically followed, and its resources and capabilities were tied into this approach. So its future efforts might include pressing suppliers further, reorganizing its assembly operations, and possibly seeking additional distribution outlets for its existing products in order to increase scale. It comes as no surprise, then, that between 2013-15 Dell's PC business level strategy involved exactly these steps.[6]

A second kind of industry trajectory prediction can also be extremely useful in anticipating possible new moves by competitors. In this case what we are interested in is not so much what competitors will do based upon past historical trends, but what all competitors must do based on the evolution of customer preferences and supplier technologies. In 1965 Intel co-founder Gordon Moore predicted that the number of transistors which could be inexpensively placed on a circuit board would double roughly every two years. From that prediction, which has actually been observed in practice to occur roughly every eighteen months ever since, many have been able to predict the advent of new devices that utilize advancing technological capability. StorageTek was started up by three IBM employers who followed "Moore's Law" in the tape disk storage industry; it rapidly became a Fortune 500 company. Figure 9.1 shows a Moore's Law projection for memory and logic technologies, which many technology companies have used to predict when they (and their competitors) might be able to introduce new products incorporating advanced technology.

Figure 9.1
Technology Predictions in Logic and Memory

General predictions can also be made by carefully evaluating the evolution of customer preferences and demands. As we have stated throughout this textbook, a better understanding of what sort of value will need to be created in the future provides a company with an important roadmap of areas it might invest in, and likely presages what competitors will also be thinking about. Figure 9.2 shows the evolution of customer preferences in the cell phone handset market.[7] This type of mapping should have enabled competition to predict that the "ultra-premium" segment would emerge and that Apple would be expected to drop its price to below the "expected" price line – both of which actually occurred.

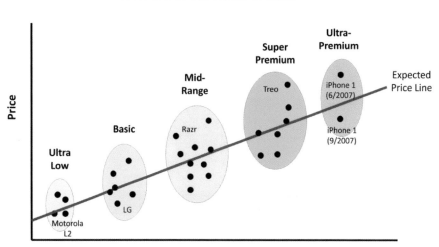

Figure 9.2
Evolution of Cell Phone Benefits

PREDICTING COMPETITIVE MOVES

As we can gather from the previous discussion, general characterizations about the industry environment can help us make general predictions about what competitors might be contemplating. We can, however, develop more specific and detailed information about key competitors in our industry. Competitive intelligence and the knowledge that such intelligence provides is the first step available for dealing with the competitive dynamism inherent in a hostile industry environment. Fortunately, we have a number of tools available that allow for effective classification and use for competitor prediction. These include: 1) classifying organizations based upon their behavioral styles; 2) examining internal competitor characteristics; and 3) scenario analysis.

Classifying Organizations

The first technique available for examining potential competitor moves is to attempt classifying organizations based on their past styles of behavior. In many ways past behavior is one the best predictors of future actions and reactions, whether we are talking about organizations or individuals in our own lives. There are many techniques available to classify organizations such that we can better understand and predict their intentions and likely reactions to moves by other companies. One of the more popular and best developed techniques is a classifying system developed some years ago by Raymond Miles and Charles Snow.[8] This system suggests that every company in an industry can be classified into one of four categories: 1) Prospector, 2) Defender, 3) Analyzer, or 4) Reactor (Figure 9.3). The first three are each sustainable and viable postures for a company to take in an industry. The fourth type (Reactor) is unsustainable and companies that do not move from a reactor position are likely to under-perform or even fail as independent organizations. It is generally acknowledged that each type is present in most industries.

Figure 9.3
Four Ways to Classify Companies

Prospector
Defender
Analyzer
Reactor

Most companies do not fall cleanly into any one category, but are most likely to predominantly fall within one category. The lines between the categories are a bit fuzzy, so we look for overarching patterns in behavior to assist us in classifying the company's style. Let's take a look at each position.

Prospector. A prospector organization is one that tends to view the industry from its own internal perspective and that of its customer base rather than being concerned with the competition. Prospectors are usually leaders of change in the industry with little concern for the effects or impacts of other organizations. They are generally willing to cannibalize their own market position with something new and are thorough collectors of detailed information about customers and customer needs. A prospector organization is relatively inefficient primarily because it views control and cost-cutting efforts as counter to its primary objectives of organic growth and the opportunity to change the industry.

Apple is the epitome of the frame-breaking prospector organization, especially during the times that Steve Jobs served as its CEO. The introduction of the Apple II PC, the Macintosh, the iPod, iTunes, the MacAir and the iPhone, just to name a few groundbreaking products and services, virtually changed the nature of each industry that the company entered. Google created a platform that was simple to use and very intuitive for the user by means of a new algorithm for ranking website importance. Their approach to this segment of the internet fundamentally changed the way in which internet searches occurred and forced other companies to develop better methods.

We mention these two well-regarded companies here as exemplars of prospector organizations. However, it is important to recognize that it is not technology or technology-based businesses alone that occupy these positions. Prospector organizations are those which have embedded behaviors internally, across their value chains, which enable them to identify new opportunities and move on them with dispatch. Recall the two strategic imperatives we mentioned way back in Chapter 1.

Prospector businesses pursue an aggressive stance aimed at identifying new ways to satisfy customers, new means to extend their reach, and a creative desire to lead rather than follow. A prospector organization is unlikely to directly react to a move by a competitor. It will release its latest product or service on its own schedule and simply presume that it is what the market was looking for. These organizations rarely lower prices or make new market entries as a result of moves by a competitor.

Defender. At the opposite end of the continuum is a defender organization. Defender organizations are intensive rather than extensive. That is, they usually focus on a limited number of key criteria, analyze their costs, and rigorously defend their competitive position against all competitors or potential competitors. A defender is geared toward protecting its current position and maximizing market share. This type of organization spends very little on new product or service development, is highly efficient, and is structured in its policies and procedures.

The retailing icon Sears was once a prospector as it spread across the United States and became a one-stop shop for middle America. However, with the advent of other large specialized retailers it changed into a defender model as it sought to focus its efforts and protect what it perceived as its turf. Cereal companies, such as Kellogg's and General Mills, while exhibiting vital new business development behavior, are at their core defender organizations. Everything they do works to protect a brand's franchise, shelf position and presence in supermarkets, and market share. When competitors introduce similar products or flavors into new markets, cereal companies will often flood those markets with exceptionally high levels of promotional coupons or spot television buys in order to wreck the results of the newcomers. Defender organizations will react swiftly and with an intensive attack to any move by a competitor that it deems threatening or even potentially threatening. They will lower prices, offer coupons, change formulas, add new extensions to existing product lines, pressure suppliers, run attack ads, and more to counter the move by a competitor. Recall that one of the attributes within the threat of new entrants dimension of the five forces analysis (Chapter 4) was potential competitive retaliation.

Analyzer. Somewhere in between these two more extreme forms of organizations are analyzers. In analyzer organizations parts of the company behave like a defender while other parts of the company behave like a prospector. Usually an artifact of the way the organization formed and grew over time, this two-part stance within a company is quite difficult to manage and maintain. While one part of the company performs the sophisticated customer analysis and develops products or services that will directly address the customer regardless of whether it cannibalizes its current product offering, another part of the organization is intensively examining competitors and trying to milk every dollar out of its current product or service portfolio. The risk for analyzer organizations, of course, is that they may become stuck in the middle from a business-level strategy perspective.

It is more difficult to predict exactly how analyzer organizations will respond to significant changes in the market. Because they have in the past demonstrated dual propensities, to both step out innovatively but also defend their turf vigorously, they deserve greater attention by the strategist.

Reactor. Reactor organizations perform as the name implies, by essentially reacting (often very slowly) to emerging conditions in the competitive environment. This is usually an unstable form of organization and one that is not destined to last very long, because it tends to be buffeted by the forces in the environment rather than making proactive moves. It then has a choice: either to adapt and move to one of the other three models, or collapse as an independent entity. Defunct organizations such as Eastern Airlines, Montgomery Ward, and Gino's are classic examples of what happens to reactor organizations that refuse to change. Who are these companies, you may ask? Exactly!

Starting in the late 1990s McDonald's (a company we generally praise for their incredible strategy execution capability today) had fallen into this mode. They were under attack from health groups, suffering from the consequences of a film documentary called *Super Size Me* (where one man ate super-sized meals at McDonalds morning, noon, and night for a month), were ineffectively responding to growth by their competitors, and had lost perspective on their own competitive resources and capabilities. Same-store sales were dropping. But to the company's credit they sensed that they might soon be in a precarious strategic position. A new management team shook up the organization and moved them into a more defined analyzer role, where utilizing the combination of prospector and defender they flourished once again. Portions of the company had always exhibited prospector aspects – the first fast food operation to serve breakfast, the introduction of the Happy Meal for children, and the creation and funding of the Ronald McDonald House charity. More recently, though, they have exhibited defender characteristics – for example, the move into premium coffee service to bring back customers lost to Starbucks' U.S. stores, a rigorous value meal selection, advertising aggressively, and seeking to buy up and hold potential real estate sites for future store growth.

It is important to understand the value and use of this Prospector, Defender, Analyzer, Reactor classification system as a means to gain important insight into competitive dynamics. The ability to effectively classify organizations allows us to make relatively accurate predictions about how specific companies will respond to changes in the industry. This classification system also provides insight into how competitors view the industry. This systemization can augment the general kinds of predictions we make based upon industry characteristics, discussed previously. As an example, we might be preparing to release a brand new product that we believe has the potential to change the market. In the competitive analysis we would not be very concerned about the reactions to our new product release from prospector organizations, since they are usually focused on their own initiatives. Defender competitors are a significant concern, since they might view a new introduction as a competitive threat and therefore may actively work to defeat it. The company should then consider devising effective tactics to deal with predicted competitor response. Analyzer companies are a bit of a wild card; each must be examined for its history and current position. We would be far less concerned about a potential response from reactor organizations, which have previously demonstrated non-threatening responsive behavior in the market.

The Four Walls Have Become Porous[9]

Access to technology, global reach, better information: these present hypercompetitive challenges to today's retailers - in the form of "showrooming." Two years ago a 25-year old shopper in Best Buy spotted the perfect gift for his girlfriend, a $185 Garmin GPS. But he first took out his Android phone and used Amazon's price comparison app, only to discover the same item for only $107 online (plus no tax). He bought it from Amazon right on the spot. Last holiday season another shopper at Walmart considered buying a 2 Gb memory stick for $11.99, but her shopping app found it elsewhere for $2 less.

In 2009 mobile devices accounted for just 0.1% of visits to retail sites. One year later in 2010 they accounted for 5.6%, a fifty-fold increase. By 2016 over 85% of shoppers are using mobile devices in doing research for retail shopping.

QUESTION

1. How should traditional "bricks and mortar" retailers respond to mobile shopping?

Internal Characteristics of Competitors

Classifying organizations as Prospector, Defender, Analyzer, or Reactor allows us to narrow the list of organizations that need closer scrutiny. A more detailed means of evaluating competitor moves is now in order. In this analysis we will consider a number of internal competitor characteristics and how they might impact our organization. These include: 1) understanding their management outlook and patterns; 2) conducting our own internal strategy analysis of competitors; 3) analyzing their financial situation; and 4) gathering competitor intelligence.

Understanding management patterns. One effective technique in the analysis of competitive dynamics is the observation and evaluation of patterns by competitor CEOs and their top management teams. Sun Tzu would argue that the general who never changes his pattern of battle is highly susceptible to a crushing defeat. All of us have patterns in our behavior. In fact, much research demonstrates that in times of challenging circumstances or crisis, people tend to rely on "automatic" behaviors as a response and coping mechanism. When those patterns become predictable, management exposes its company to potential harm. Some CEOs are aware of this problem and work diligently to address it by changing up approaches and seeking new solutions. However, when times get tough, there is a tendency to return to base patterns of behavior. Those patterns, when accurately observed, provide useful competitive insight.

"Chainsaw" Al Dunlap became famous as a CEO for his single-minded approach to corporate profit. He took the helm at several troubled companies with the same approach each time: fire thousands of employees, dramatically cut back on new spending and rigorously attack all current spending. This was his system at companies including Scott Paper, Crown-Zellerbach, and Sunbeam. Knowing his approach to business and his

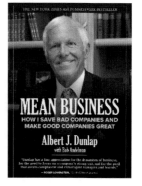

293

universal "game plan" for success, competitors were able to take advantage of the turmoil it created within his companies. Some top management teams have standardized reactions to new competitive threats, making them easier to predict and therefore easier to work around.

On the other hand, companies that find themselves in a strong competitive position in a market will often ignore widely available information and miss opportunities that end up costing them their business. DEC was the king of minicomputers in the late 1970s and early 1980s, posting astounding returns in their industry. They held so strongly to the notion that minicomputers were their competitive advantage that they simply missed the PC revolution. The CEO at the time (Ken Olsen) noted the failure later when he observed that "we had 6 PCs in-house that we could have launched in the late '70s. But we were selling so many [minicomputers], it would have been immoral to chase a new market."[10]

The difference we see between these two examples has to do with the attitude of management of the company about the kind of business it is in, its "ownership" of a market, or its beliefs about effective ways of managing its business.

Strategy analysis of competition. Although much of this textbook has so far been devoted to tools and frameworks that you can use to develop strategy for your own company, the same tools and frameworks can be useful for understanding your competitors' strategies. Having your most recent industry analysis results in hand, which has identified current and emerging key success factors, now you might conduct a value chain analysis and a resource analysis of each competitor. What are their value chains, and how are these fundamentally different from your company's? Use the resource analysis method to deconstruct the sources and causes of capabilities that your competitors are particularly good at.

A colleague of ours was a brand manager for one of the major cereal companies. Her brand was being seriously challenged by a competitor's brand, and her brand's market share was sliding slightly. In 2016 the breakfast cereal market generated over $35 billion sales globally and $11 billion in sales in the U.S.; so slipping just 1/10th of one percentage point of U.S. market share would represent a loss of nearly $11 million in revenue! She spent nearly three months digging deep into her competitor's business: understanding its supply chain, its marketing tendencies, the history of the decisions that the managers behind the business had made, and more. What resulted was an in-depth, highly detailed view of what her competition was very good at, and where there were holes in their armor. She used this information to exploit the weaknesses, effectively restaged her brand and reversed the trend in market share. She was subsequently promoted to marketing director. Her work was good for the company, and good for her career path.

The Baltimore Orioles baseball team won six division titles, 3 pennants and the World Series under the leadership of its successful manager Earl Weaver. The organization developed resources and a process to assiduously study the tendencies of opposing managers. Weaver pored over this data and committed their tendencies to memory so that he could rely on it tactically in everyday game situations. He knew in advance when they would steal bases, put on hit and run plays, substitute pinch hitters, and employ other facets of the game. He was then able to preempt such actions with his own moves on the field. There are only nineteen managers who have ever been inducted into the Baseball Hall of Fame, and Earl Weaver is among them.

Many organizations maintain business analysis units that have as their task the job of developing competitor profiles. For some companies, these units have in fact become a resource exhibiting the VRIST characteristics, helping to confer sustainable advantage. Changes in the market and competitor responses are regularly tracked, to build an effective "map" of past and predicted moves. Much like playing chess with someone over and over, it then becomes much easier to predict his or her response to certain moves and therefore to use that information to beat that person in the game.

Financial situation. Firms that find themselves in a situation where their returns are not as they anticipated are more likely to react in unpredictable ways. As long as a company is growing and making reasonable returns or better, it is likely to maintain its current competitive approach, believing that it will continue to deliver results. Unfortunately, if these returns slip or go negative, then predicting their actions becomes more difficult. Sun Tzu reminds us that an army with no retreat available will fight to the last and fight with everything available. Competitors that get into this situation need to be closely watched for industry-damaging behaviors. The sort of financial analysis we examined in Chapter 2 – connecting strategy to patterns of financial investments – can again be very revealing about what competitors are doing and the financial strengths of their organizations.

We can observe interesting behavior occurring periodically in industries with heavy financial investment in fixed assets. The "big three" automobile manufacturers each lost money during the late 2000s recession. Their initial reaction to declining sales was to cut prices in order to move unsold cars off dealer lots and keep assembly operations going. Unfortunately, it is the rare organization that can cut its way to success. Price wars generally damage the market by removing future customers, generating the need for even greater cost savings, and opening the door for better-organized foreign competitors who have lower cost structures. The prudent strategist would have looked at this damaged economy, examined the financial situation of its key competitors, and been able to predict with probably great accuracy just what sorts of promotional tactics they would soon be engaging in.

Gathering competitive intelligence. Having classified each competitor as Prospector, Defender, Analyzer, or Reactor and having dug deeper into these organizations by evaluating their internal processes, we should also mention how detailed competitor information can be gathered. Sun Tzu wrote more than 2,000 years ago that "The means by which enlightened rulers and sagacious generals moved and conquered others, that their achievements surpassed the masses, was advance knowledge."[11] Foresight can be an extraordinary resource, because there are few means that improve performance better than knowing in advance what a competitor is planning to do. In virtually every sport or competitive activity, being able to predict how a competitor might react or how they will act can dramatically change the outcome. General George Patton was a prolific reader of military history and military strategy. He understood not only that there were patterns to success, but that particular generals had their own approach to victory. Having studied the tactical battle books written by General Rommel and used by most German tank commanders, Patton would set up his battle plans to take advantage of the patterns laid out in Rommel's books. The same type of intelligence is often just as easily available in business.

In 2001 Hewlett Packard announced its intention to acquire Compaq Computer, and at the time then-CEO Carly Fiorini acknowledged that combining the two companies into a single organization would take at least three years. Knowing this, other computer companies took advantage of HP's distraction to profit from their relative positions in the PC industry. HP performance suffered during this time period.

It is relatively rare to have books written by a competitor or to have such a clear announcement of distraction as that made by HP available to guide the direction of your company.

Annual reports are often characterized by what is termed "impression management," designed to glowingly discuss a company's past year, and 10K reports filed with the SEC reveal little of strategic substance. Fortunately, there are a number of other techniques for gathering specific competitor intelligence (Figure 9.4). These include: 1) using media evaluation services; 2) conducting research among suppliers; and 3) examining competitor comments from public conferences and speeches.

Figure 9.4
Methods of Gathering Competitive Intelligence

Media stories evaluation
Research among suppliers
Conferences and speeches

Each of these techniques allows us to drill down from the higher-level analysis performed in Chapters 2 and 4 as well as the overarching classifications we have talked about earlier in this chapter. For instance, utilizing our STEEPG approach we may have already drawn conclusions about the nature of an industry we wish to enter. The five forces analysis provided us with insight into the key characteristics of that industry, and an analysis of a specific competitor's financial statements allowed us to reconcile their actual strategy with their stated strategy. We then classified each competitor into its strategic posture (Prospector, Defender, Analyzer, or Reactor) and determined its patterns of behavior. We now wish to delve more deeply into those competitors that seem most likely to impact any new strategic move we would make.

Media stories evaluation services. For as long as news has been reported, there have been businesses that accumulate and report on that information. Competitive intelligence consulting organizations, known as clipping services, can provide a complete, detailed record of all available public information about any particular company, area, person, or situation. Much of this information is publicly available and could therefore be collected by anyone. In a few short years since the advent of the internet, the sheer volume of such material is beyond the scope of the typical company manager to deal with. For example, if you are interested in the fashion business a recent Google search turns up 262 million hits for Zara and 74 million hits for DKNY! So news gathering or clipping services companies, which have developed their own resources and capabilities to sift through and synthesize such a volume of information, will provide a more complete examination of a particular subject or company.

Hiring a clipping service to maintain information on a particular competitor is a common practice. The costs of these services are usually based upon the level of detail that the client desires, the breadth of outlets that need to be researched, and the type of media that the client would like to review. In the not-too-distant past, these services would develop binders full of newspaper articles, magazine reference, videotapes from local news reports, audio tapes of speeches or radio broadcasts, and any press releases from the target company. Today this is all provided online with a secure website provided to the client.

Suppliers. A tremendous source of information is often available from suppliers that would like to conduct business with your company. Just as the supply chain is often a great source of information and inspiration for new ideas and materials, suppliers will often discuss what competitors are doing. They possess greater insight into their own industry and competition that can aid your company. There may be many reasons for providing information on what competitors may be up to, and these can include: 1) share cutting-edge technology or raw materials that can be useful to buying companies, 2) demonstrate a willingness to work with a customer, or 3) create a more competitive group of customers seeking to buy so that combined demand exceeds supply.

Start-up company Championship Foods, mentioned earlier in Chapter 4, learned how to reduce its cost of putting chili into glass jars by engaging in lengthy conversations with one of the country's major glass manufacturers. In the quest to seek glass jar cost reductions, the company learned who supplied glass jars for Ragu spaghetti sauce and how it might incrementally add its requirements on to Ragu jar production runs. In this case Ragu was not a direct competitor, and the glass company found a way to increase its own production volume. But during the same conversation the company had learned that its chief canned product competitor had previously explored, but rejected, getting into a glass jarred product. Good news for investors in Championship Foods!

We should be careful to note here that competitive intelligence with a supplier may be a two-way street. Just as your company learns about competition from your suppliers, so too will they learn about you through the same channels.

It is important to note that there are significant ethical considerations in seeking competitor information through suppliers. On the one hand merely discussing publically-available information seems well within the framework of acceptable corporate behavior. But careful discussion should occur internally before asking a supplier (or anyone else) to "look into" the nature of another company's business. You should discuss the boundaries and acceptable limits of such requests in your study teams and with your professor.

Conferences and speeches. CEOs and senior managers are regularly asked to give speeches at various events and will often participate in presentations at conferences. While the text of a speech can be viewed with the assistance of a good clipping service, the context, the Q&A session that typically follows a talk, and any other interaction or interviews after a speech can be particularly revealing. The value of conferences is much the same. Senior managers present new ideas, serve on panels, and provide after-meal comments on developments within their companies or on how their companies view markets and emerging opportunities. Even though these are generally open forums, the level and detail of thought provided can sometimes be quite insightful.

Scenario Analysis

The previous sections help all companies deal with the competitive nature or their industries as they exist today and in the near-term future. A final consideration for dealing with the competitive nature of an industry is the utilization of long-range planning tools.

A very interesting predictive approach developed over the past thirty years is scenario analysis. The technique requires an organization to consider potentially dramatic shifts in the business environment over a longer time frame, and to then map out a set of actions that it can begin to take if the warning signs of those shifts start to appear.

Consider Figure 9.5, which shows oil price increases over the previous decades. To the shock of many organizations, oil went from less than $25 per barrel to over $125 per barrel, and then back to under $50 per barrel. Just two year ago, who could have predicted that oil prices would drop by $50 per barrel? What if oil were to skyrocket to $200 per barrel? What would the impact of $200 oil have on an organization's transportation infrastructure, cost of goods, and the ability of customers to buy a product? Scenario analysis allows companies to plan out potential vectors for their organization as the environment changes, to have considered those actions long before they arrive, and to identify markers along the way that signal that a particular path is coming true to prediction. Response scenarios are dramatically improved if organizations have had the opportunity to consider and prepare for potential futures.

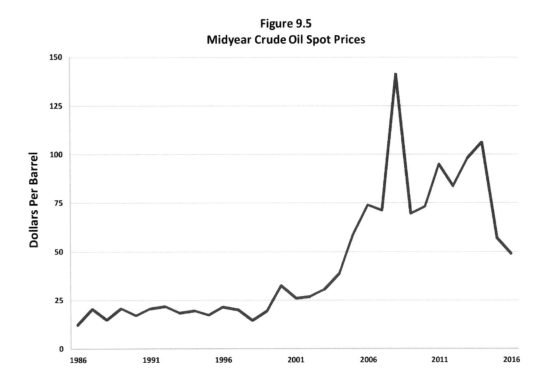

Figure 9.5
Midyear Crude Oil Spot Prices

Turmoil can trigger crisis in the life of any organization. In his 2007 book *The Age of Turbulence* Alan Greenspan recalled his concerns for the stability of the banking system in the hours after September 11, 2001. Stuck on an airplane being forced to return to Zurich as all U.S. airspace was closed to civilian air traffic, he knew that there were well-developed plans in place that would be engaged if a scenario like this one played out. Arriving back in Zurich, he was relieved to hear that all the emergency plans had already been enacted and the Federal Reserve banking system was stabilized.[12]

Crisis scenarios are certainly a part of this planning process, as is consideration of more logically unfolding changes of significance that may transpire in the decades. Indeed, scenario planning usually uses a time frame that goes from ten to twenty-five years. Not yet knowing exactly how an industry will reach the next plateau does not mean that planning will be useless. In the airline industry it seems relatively easy to predict that at some point in the future all passengers will be able to stay connected with the internet and make phone calls before, during, and at the end of a flight (whether or not the rest of us abhor the thought when we are stuck on a four-hour flight next to Bill the Salesman). This scenario has been forecast for the past decade or more. Knowing this might lead some airlines to build in a capability for all future airframe purchases or develop an effective system for charging new fees for the service. It might lead airlines to invest in systems that broadcast signals from the ground or utilize satellite-based technologies. As the day of reckoning approaches (and partial systems are now being installed), those airlines that had planned out their paths would be checking off the milestones and would have developed an effective set of tactical maneuvers to take advantage of the coming capability.

The result of this type of thoughtful analysis process should be a holistic look at the environment, competitors, and potential paths that might appear. Within each path, the company should consider how to apply its unique resources - or what new resources may be necessary to develop - in order to take action to ensure its competitive position.

Dumpster Diving for Diamonds

DeBeers is renowned for its beautiful diamonds. But it also competes in industrial markets where diamonds are used as cutting tools. One of their chief competitors is the abrasives division of General Electric. Recently the General Electric division general manager scratched his head and wondered how DeBeers was managing to price its industrial diamonds so low. GE was having difficulty even manufacturing them at that price. They needed to figure this out. One day some folks from the GE plant followed a trash truck leaving a nearby DeBeers plant to the local public landfill. They paid the customary fee for anyone to enter the landfill and searched through the debris left by the truck, discovering pieces of molds used by DeBeers in its manufacturing. The molds were of a completely different size and material than anything GE had possibly imagined, and provided significant insight on the sources of DeBeers cost and pricing advantage.

QUESTIONS

2. What ethical considerations are raised by this story?
3. What are the ethical limits to gathering competitive intelligence?

TACTICAL AND STRATEGIC RESPONSES

Companies establish their *strategic* position by considering the value chains and unique resources they employ relative to the industry in which they compete. While we have examined the patterns of resource investments and value-creating activities that a company should engage in given its vision and strategy, we must also recognize that there are a set of *tactical* actions that may be more or less appropriate when taking into account the moves of a competitor. Competitors will react to our company's activities, and we need to be prepared to react in the short run to competitive activities.

Tactical

Tactical responses are those that organizations pursue as a matter of course in dealing with regulators, stakeholders, and their direct competitors. Organizations respond to competitor moves with varying degrees of aggression based upon history, personality, or position in the market. These tactical approaches can be described as part of a response style to an immediate threat and include, from most passive to most active: 1) Acquiesce, 2) Compromise, 3) Avoid, 4) Defy, and 5) Manipulate.[13]

Figure 9.6
Response Styles and Tactics

Response Styles	Tactics	Descriptions
Most passive (Acquiesce)	Habit Imitate Comply	Following invisible, taken-for granted norms Mimicking institutional models Obeying rules and accepting norms
Passive (Compromise)	Balance Pacify Bargain	Balancing the expectations of multiple constituents Placating and accommodating institutional players Negotiating with stakeholders
Neutral (Avoid)	Conceal Buffer Escape	Disguising nonconformity Disengaging Changing goals, activities, or playing fields
Active (Defy)	Dismiss Challenge Attack	Ignoring explicit norms and values Contesting rules and requirements Assaulting the sources of pressure
Most active (Manipulate)	Co-opt Influence Control	Importing influential constituents Shaping values and criteria Dominating constituents and processes

Figure 9.6 outlines the tactics associated with each of these response styles. The Acquiesce and Compromise styles are sort of the "jujitsu" approach, in which your company avoids direct confrontation against an aggressive opponent. Here the force of the competitor is redirected, or at least deflected, so as not to damage your company's position and strength. Often "going with the flow" or placating and accommodating affected stakeholders can be a particularly effective way of dealing with a competitive thrust. And these approaches draw from your company's existing strengths and probably cost less to put into practice immediately.

The Avoid style is apt to come into play when the competitive move threatens some dimension of your company's position or business that is not worth an expensive immediate fight. Disengaging from the battle buffers and conserves resources for another time when fighting may be more meaningful. Deciding to change goals, activities, and even the field of play – for this particular dimension of your company's business – may be prudent for the short term, until more favorable circumstances are developed which would allow you the greater chance to win. Avoidance does not mean "give up the business," just that at this moment it is not wise to engage in a competitive joust.

But some competitive moves cannot be disregarded, even in the short run. Under these circumstances a company may choose to actively Defy the threat or Manipulate the players and conditions. Defiance tends to be activities directed at the competitor, while Manipulation is associated with moves to coopt, influence and control other stakeholders and influential constituents in the industry. Companies tend to be tactically active or most active when a key business segment that is central to its market position is threatened.

Strategic

A more complex set of approaches is called for when a threat is truly strategic and may impact the long-term performance of a company. When faced with a significant strategic threat, strategy research suggests that there are five fairly effective response types that are available (Figure 9.7).[14] Much of the capacity to engage in these responses falls upon each company's ability to spot a threat early.

Figure 9.7
Competitive Responses to Strategic Threats

Containment
Shaping
Absorption
Neutralization
Annulment

Containment is an approach that is best engaged in at the earliest stages of a competitor's entry into a market with a game-changing product or service. Existing companies will engage in a series of moves, including: locking in customers, raising switching costs, filling distribution channels to eliminate unused capacity, launching blocking brands, and making announcements that de-legitimize the company or its approach. Early in the MP3 revolution, for example, established record labels attempted many of these approaches in an effort to slow down the adoption of this new music standard.

Shaping is undertaken as the competitive threat develops and the containment strategies are no longer providing sufficient protection for the established organization. Here a threatened company will engage in moves that include co-opting the threat by organizing a group to influence the market through setting broad standards and creating acceptable practices within the industry. Another method used is to become involved with the threatening organization, such as through a strategic alliance, in order to have influence over its development. Shaping has also been called competitive cooperation, which we will address in the final section below.

Absorption is when it is clear that the competitive threat is likely to succeed and the prior approaches have not allowed the threatened company to control the process. Threatened companies in this situation turn to responses that usually involve some sort of acquisition of the new competitor. Microsoft has engaged this approach on numerous occasions, as the control of the desktop and the development of applications software has moved increasingly to mobile computing and the internet. In addition to internal new product development for devices and software, Microsoft has also specifically turned to acquiring new companies in many areas related to mobile communications. Since 2008 they have acquired almost 75 companies such as Powerset, YaData, Danger, Skype Communications, Yammer, Talko and more, spending in excess of $10 billion.[15] Chapter 10 will be devoted to the challenges and opportunities associated with mergers and acquisitions.

Neutralization is generally engaged in when the competitive threat had not been truly appreciated earlier on, but has now spread too widely to be contained, shaped, or absorbed. In this instance, threatened companies turn to very aggressive means of attack, including: 1) using legal action, 2) giving away the benefits offered by the new competitor for free, or 3) engaging in a process of continuously improving existing products. The Recording Industry Association of

America used the courts to shut down the renegade Napster, which was seriously (and illegally) impacting the industry sales model. This successful effort forced other Napster-like companies to cease operations or try to stay so small that the RIAA would not seek sanctions against them. In confronting the onslaught of Netscape in the late 1990s Microsoft developed and gave away its Internet Explorer browser software at no charge. Why buy Netscape when you could get another effective browser for free? Netscape Communications did not last long as an independent company. Since then Microsoft has also engaged in serious and sustained upgrades to its Windows operating system – with embedded applications such as music and video players as well as other digital media management tools, and now an app-based tablet-like desktop appearance. Through these moves they are hoping to neutralize the competitive impact of independent application development competitors and other device manufacturers who are moving away from the Windows operating system.

Annulment is the last response left when all the other techniques have failed and the threatened company is in danger of being swamped by the new approaches. Threatened companies are left with only two responses. They can attempt to leapfrog the new company's approach or they can attempt to sidestep the new approach by changing the fundamentals of the industry.

Gillette has a long history of leapfrogging its competition with the release of newer and more technologically advanced razors. PayPal was originally envisioned as a cryptography company, and then later as a means of transmitting money via PDAs. After several years of trial and error did PayPal find its sweet spot as the leading online payment system for millions of customers.

COOPERATION

A final category of competitive response that has received a substantial amount of attention most recently is the concept of cooperation with competitors. Both tactically and strategically, there are two occasions when cooperation between competitors may be useful. The first is when competition is unusually destructive. We mentioned earlier the very destructive price wars that are often in vogue in the automobile industry. This has been experienced many times before in many different industries: prices are lowered by one manufacturer, triggering the lowering of prices by other competitors, resulting in the same volume of business for each competitor but now at a lower price (and lower profits). Fare wars in the airline industry have been rampant for nearly thirty years since deregulation of the industry. The problem for competitors is that it is illegal to collude on competitive tactics such as pricing and markets. This is the classic Prisoner's Dilemma problem you have probably heard about in previous courses. If all companies refrain from engaging in destructive tactics, then all companies are better off; but if one company fails to refrain, then all must jump into the fray.

The real solution to this type of problem where cooperation is needed is not easy, though. In some cases it never occurs, and competitors continue on in their mutually destructive ways. In some cases the competitors intuitively try to adopt a "multiple period" perspective, which deflects attention from the immediate need to generate added business volume through short-term tactics. Where industries are populated by companies that adopt this latter approach, there tends to emerge one or two companies who become "price leaders" or leaders in some other tactical dimension. Their behavior then "signals" what is acceptable to the rest of the industry.

Signaling is not just important in making tactical moves that other competitors will then follow. It also represents a means through which a company can *prevent* competitors from initiating destructive tactics. When a company repeatedly matches its competitor's tactics, action for action, time and time again, it sends a signal to the competitor and the rest of the industry that destructive tactical behavior will always be met with opposing force. In this way a company tacitly creates a cooperative situation in an industry, without formally cooperating.

The second type of occasion when cooperation with a competitor has advantages is when this type of collaboration can lead to developments that exceed the capacity of any one company. This situation results in the formation of strategic alliances with competing companies. Some time ago the automobile makers foresaw the need to have truly revolutionary battery technology. They did not want to leave this effort to chance, they did not want to embark on a development path where their direction would not become the accepted industry standard, and they did not want to deal with one powerful supplier that could control one of the most significant cost items in a car of the future. So they formed the Advanced Battery Consortium (ABC) to cooperatively develop this critical component. New opportunity recognition in many industries will therefore involve the use of cooperation for the development of new technologies or new capabilities that can be beneficial to all competitors.

Strategic alliances should not be lightly entered into. Each party to an alliance must have a clear understanding of what its resource investment obligation to the alliance is to be, as well as what its estimated benefit will be. In this way, it can more accurately assess whether participation in the alliance makes sense. Far too many alliances have been entered into over the years where participating companies have not fully appreciated what their investments would need to be or what they would get out of the results produced by the allied effort. Alliances will usually require the development of a new set of resources or capabilities to be properly managed and to derive the greatest value from the relationship. An effective alliance involves more than simply managing the effort as if it is the same as an internally managed department or project. Typically, the fullest value of an alliance is realized when multiple functions within a company are involved. We discovered earlier that achieving consistency and coordination across the internal value chain is one of the most difficult facets of strategic management, and this makes effective alliance management a real challenge. Management must therefore carefully consider the dedication of time and commitment to resource-building that such efforts will inevitably involve.

CHAPTER SUMMARY

This chapter aimed to examine the intricacies of strategy in the context of real competitors and the environment in which they operate. The ability to understand competitors, track their efforts and predict competitive moves (both proactively and reactively) are essential capabilities in the running of a successful business. We first examined the industry conditions under which companies must make their strategic moves. Industries may generally be classified as either benign or hostile, and can often be characterized as hypercompetitive. We looked at the conditions that describe each characterization, and the unique approaches that research has suggested are successful in these circumstances.

We next observed that improving our ability to predict competitive moves relies upon our ability to drill down more carefully into the nature of specific organizations. To do this we can classify organizations into one of four categories: Prospectors, Defenders, Analyzers, or Reactors. We also looked at internal competitive company characteristics that offer insights into their potential actions and reactions. These included: management team behavior patterns, relative market positions, and financial conditions. Information sources of competitive intelligence include: 1) media reports through evaluative clipping services, 2) suppliers, 3) former employees, and 4) conferences or speeches by key executives of competitors. Scenario analysis presents another tool for companies to map out strategic moves over a very long period of time based on alternative possible scenarios for the future.

We examined competitive responses and actions based upon ordinary and strategic threats to the organization. Ordinary threats are traditionally addressed with one of five tactical approaches including: 1) Acquiesce; 2) Compromise; 3) Avoid; 4) Defy; and 5) Manipulate. Strategic threats are addressed with different approaches that are categorized as: 1) Containment; 2) Shaping; 3) Absorption; 4) Neutralization; and 5) Annulment.

Finally, we took a look at cooperation and strategic alliances as an increasingly important component of strategy in the twenty-first century.

Learning Objectives Review

1. *Describe how to use industry and company trajectories to evaluate an industry environment.*

   - Examine whether the industry is benign or hostile, and analyze its trajectories using strategy maps and historical industry information.

   - Classify competitors according to their behavioral patterns as Prospectors, Defenders, Analyzers, or Reactors.

2. *Select and evaluate the appropriate techniques for producing competitor intelligence.*

   - Examine patterns of CEO and senior management's previous decision making.

   - Conduct an "internal" value chain and resource analysis of the competitor.

   - Analyze the competitor's financial statements.

   - Synthesize publically-available information about the competitor using a clipping services consulting organization.

   - Discuss industry and competitor developments with suppliers, with ethical considerations in mind.

   - Examine public speeches given by competitor employees.

3. *Describe the differences between tactical and strategic methods for responding to competitors.*

   - Tactical responses to competitors are appropriate for dealing with immediate challenges that might compromise short-term position of business. In a range from more passive to more active, these include: Acquiesce, Compromise, Avoid, Defy, Manipulate.

   - Strategic responses to competitors are appropriate for dealing with emerging challenges that could impact the long term position and viability of the business. These include Containment, Shaping, Absorption, Neutralization, and Annulment.

4. *Discuss the conditions under which cooperation can be an effective competitive approach.*

- Cooperation is appropriate when passive agreement avoids destructive competitive behavior. This is usually a Prisoner's Dilemma type of situation, and often appears when it is illegal for companies to strike active agreements with one another.

- Active cooperation between companies takes the form of strategic alliances and joint partnerships. Such ventures are beneficial when the challenges are greater than any one company can afford, or when mutually beneficial industry standards can be developed.

Key Terms

Analyzer - A company that combines both Prospector and Defender behaviors. Parts of the company behave like a defender and parts behave like a prospector.

Benchmark - A process through which a company compares its own process and structure to that of other organizations. Companies most often benchmark directly against competitors. Occasionally, benchmarking will be done against other unrelated companies that have a "best in class" process. For example, General Mills examined how NASCAR pit crews organize for pit stops in order to better understand how to implement rapid cereal production line changes.

Benign environment - Characterized by: 1) market demand exceeds market supply; 2) generally high gross profit margins; 3) low competitive intensity - meaning no one competitor controls a high proportion of the market; 4) strong customer loyalty; and 5) a tolerance for occasional management miscues.

Clipping service - Provides a detailed, synthesized analysis of all available public information about any particular company, area, person, or situation.

Defender - A company that is intensive rather than extensive. That is, they usually focus on a limited number of key criteria, analyze their costs, and rigorously defend their competitive position against all competitors.

Hostile environment - Characterized by: 1) slow growth; 2) continuous price wars; 3) high competitive intensity - meaning that one or a few competitors control a substantial portion of the market; and 4) a focus on cost containment by competitors.

Prospector - A company that tends to view the industry from their own perspective and that of the customer rather, and less concerned with the actions of competition. They are usually leaders of change in the industry.

Reactor - A company that reacts (often slowly) to conditions in the competitive environment. This is an unstable form of organization.

Scenario analysis - A technique allowing organizations to consider dramatic shifts in their business model. The organization maps out a set of actions that it can start to take if warning signs begin to appear along the path of a particular scenario.

Strategic alliance - A joint venture or partnership formed with other companies (sometimes competitors) in order to develop a new technology, process, or other type of strategically important resource.

Tactics - Dealing with short-term competitive moves and countermoves, as opposed to long-term direction, investments, and performance.

Short Answer Review Questions

1. How would a benign environment impact the strategic choices of an organization?

2. How would you characterize a hostile environment?

3. Provide an example of a Prospector organization (separate from the examples in the text) and explain how it reacts to its competitors.

4. Why can't a company remain in a Reactor mode and still be a profit generator?

5. How would you collect competitive intelligence on a group of competitors?

6. How would a scenario analysis assist the airline industry going into 2030?

7. What competitive tactics should Starbucks employ with the encroachment of McDonald's into the premium coffee business?

8. How should absorption be used as a response to an innovative new entry?

9. How does a company's financial position impact its strategic choices?

Group Exercises

1. Select a well-known company in the Fortune 500. Using publicly available information, put together an analysis of the CEO who runs that organization. What are his or her strategic tendencies? How might he or she react to an encroachment by a competitor? Has this CEO been consistent in his or her behavior?

2. Using the same company that you selected in #1, create a strategic map with as many aspects examined as you can locate.

3. Select an example company from the past week in the Wall Street Journal that is under attack from a substantial new competitor or new process. Using the tactics defined in the chapter, what would you recommend as a strategy for that company?

References

[1] Bremner, B. 2007. Nintendo storms the gaming world, BusinessWeek Online, January 29: p. 21. The Economist, 2005, Way beyond the PC, November 26, p. 83. Edwards, C. 2006. Game definitely not over, BusinessWeek Online, November 16: p. 11. Edwards, C. 2006. Nintendo Wii:

One ferocious underdog, BusinessWeek Online, November 26: p. 10. Hall, K. 2007. Nintendo: Calling all players, BusinessWeek Online, October 11: p. 24. Sherr, I. 2013. Microsoft's New Xbox girds for its smartphone battle, Wall Street Journal, May 20, B1. Wingfield, N. 2009. Xbox chief's next play, Wall Street Journal, June 2, B4.

[2] Winkler, R. 2013, A Galaxy far, far away from Google, Wall Street Journal, March 16, B16. Winkler, R. 2014, Google's costly Motorola maneuver may pay dividends, Wall Street Journal, January 31, B6.

[3] Covin, J., D. Slevin, and M. Heeley. 1999. Pioneers and followers: Competitive tactics, environment, and firm growth. Journal of Business Venturing 15: 175–210.

[4] Ibid.

[5] D'Aveni, R. 1994. Hypercompetition: Managing the dynamics of strategic maneuvering. New York: Free Press.

[6] Worthen, B. and Sherr, I. 2012. PC sales show steep decline, Wall Street Journal, October 11, B1. Moorhead, P. 2013. Dell's PC growth strategy - in it to win it. Forbes, June 21.

[7] D'Aveni, R. 2007. Mapping your competitive position. Harvard Business Review. November: 1–10.

[8] Miles, R. E., and C. C. Snow. 1978. Organizational strategy, structure and processes. New York: McGraw-Hill Book Company.

[9] Bustillo, M and Zimmerman, A. 2010. Phone-wielding shoppers strike fear into retailers. Wall Street Journal, December 15, B1.

[10] The dark side of DEC's rebound. 1984. BusinessWeek. January 30: 51–53.

[11] Sun Tzu. The Art of War. 1983 edited translation by James Clavell. New York: Delta.

[12] Greenspan, Alan. 2007. The age of turbulence. New York: Penguin.

[13] Oliver, C. 1990. Determinants of interorganizational relationships: Integrations and future directions. Academy of Management Review 15: 241–265; Oliver, C. 1991. Strategic responses to institutional processes. Academy of Management Review 16: 145–179.

[14] D'Aveni, R. 2002. The empire strikes back: Counterrevolutionary strategies for industry leaders. Harvard Business Review, November, 5–12.

[15] www.microsoft.com.

Chapter 10: Corporate Strategy

Deli Meat Slicers, Car Door Handles, and Plastic Six-Pack Ring Carriers[1]

Illinois Tool Works was founded in 1912 in Chicago as a manufacturer of metal cutting tools. Over the years it branched out into completely unrelated enterprises such as electric switches, screws, fasteners, transmissions, and plastics. The company created and patented the plastic 6-pack can holder, among many other inventions. By the early 1980s the company had forty separate business units, each operating a different type of business in a variety of industries. After several of its business units came under competitive pressure from Japanese manufacturers and a troubled domestic auto industry, CEO John Nichols and his successors accelerated acquisitions. The blistering pace of acquisitions over the last thirty years has resulted in a company that operates 750 separate business units worldwide. In 2016 they are organized into seven SBUs (strategic business units). The ITW headquarter office extols its "portfolio management" capabilities for handling this kind of business diversity.

Mickey Mouse Marries Princess Leia[2]

Walt Disney acquired Lucasfilm Ltd. in 2012 for $4.1 billion. It paid half the acquisition price in cash, and half with Disney shares. Disney CEO Michael Eisner had a clear vision that that Disney's future rested on enduring characters. Building on its previous acquisition of Pixar Animation, the Star Wars movie portfolio gave Disney more material to appeal to a broader range of children and families, especially teenage boys. George Lucas, who produced Star Wars, had initially been worried about giving up control and oversight of the Star Wars franchise and details to another company. However, Disney and Lucasfilm had already collaborated on a Star Wars ride at Walt Disney World Resort, and this has given each company to the chance learn about how the other worked. Lucas commented about the sale of his company: "Disney's reach and experience give Lucasfilm the opportunity to blaze new trails in film, televisions, interactive media, theme parks, live entertainment and consumer products." The six Star Wars movies generated $4.4 billion in worldwide theater revenues over a 31-year period. Disney CEO Robert Iger defended its acquisition price: "We are confident we can earn a return on invested capital well in excess of our cost of capital."

In 2015 Disney released its first major collaboration with Lucasfilm – Star Wars Episode VII: The Force Awakens. By mid-2016 the film's world box office had more than doubled the previous best-selling Star Wars film, achieved the highest domestic box office revenue of all films ever, and achieved the third highest worldwide box office revenue ever.

Breaking Up is Hard to Do[3]

Three years after she took over as CEO of Hewlett-Packard, Meg Whitman announced that the iconic company would rend itself into two separate entities – one selling PCs and printers (HP), and one selling enterprise hardware and systems (HPE). The dynamic of the two businesses were very different in 2014. PCs and printers were a mature industry, where large scale and thin profit margins prevailed amidst ever-increasing global competition. Enterprise hardware and systems (massive servers and cloud computing technology) were fast growth industry segments that required speed and agility. Although operating them as completely separate divisions was possible, markets tended to push down HP's stock and overall growth assessment because of the old, staid PC business. Splitting the company in two, HP's investors would continue to benefit from the cash flow produced by PCs, while allowing for greater management focus on the growth segment.

Breaking up is hard to do. The company planned to spend $1.3 billion in restructuring costs and another $950 million in taxes to accomplish the split. Leadership was reshuffled, and 80% of the company's headcount moved over to the spun-off enterprise business. Whitman herself became CEO of HPE, while retaining the position as non-executive chair at the PC and printer business.

QUESTIONS

1. Although some companies bring together similar businesses (Disney-Lucasfilm), others operate businesses that are completely unrelated to each other (Illinois Tool Works). What does strategy mean for these highly diversified companies?
2. How is success measured when acquisitions are made?
3. On what basis should a corporation decide to divest itself of one of its businesses?

CORPORATE STRATEGY VERSUS BUSINESS STRATEGY

For most of this book we have focused on strategy as it relates to managing a single business. Industry analysis, value chain, generic strategy, life cycles, and competitive moves: all fundamentally relate to how a company formulates its strategy for a particular type of business and competes in an industry with its products or services. When a company operates in only one line of business, the discussion stays in the realm of business strategy. As the opening vignettes to this chapter illustrate, however, companies often move beyond a single business by acquiring other similar or related businesses and by acquiring completely unrelated businesses. When a company owns multiple companies and/or operates in multiple lines of business, then we move into the realm of corporate strategy. Here, senior executives must make decisions about managing sets of businesses. Recall from Chapter 1 that one of our five critical questions defining the field of strategy is: "What is the nature of strategy in a multi-business firm?"

Corporate strategy involves making decisions about issues that rise above – but also take into account – the decisions made at the business strategy level. Corporate strategy decision domains include the areas listed in Figure 10.1.

> **Figure 10.1**
> **Domain of Corporate Strategy**
>
> Deciding which industries to enter and exit
> Defining a strategic business unit
> Establishing business unit investment priorities
> Effecting resources and management transfers
> Structuring the corporation

Deciding which industries to enter and exit. At the corporate strategy level executives contemplating growth through internally developed new businesses or acquisitions will evaluate the industries in which these new businesses would exist. Remember in Chapter 4 we concluded that industry structure can enhance or impede the ability of a participating company to earn above-average returns? It usually makes more sense to enter an industry where prospects for profits are strong. In addition, companies that have previously diversified will periodically reevaluate the wisdom of continuing in a particular industry. Diversified companies often decide to divest a business because they determine that its industry is no longer sufficiently attractive.

Defining a strategic business unit. When a company owns and operates many different lines of business, management must decide how to organize the portfolio of businesses. The concept of the strategic business unit (SBU) captures the idea that a set of businesses that share very similar challenges or strategies can be effectively combined and managed as a single unit. General Electric competes with hundreds of products and services across literally dozens of industries; the company has been doing this for decades. Today, however, they have organized all of their business into seven important groups and within each group are strategic business units. Within a recently-downsized GE Capital group, for example, in 2016 there are five SBUs (e.g. Aviation, Energy, Healthcare, Industrial Finance, and Industrial Finance Foreign), each of which combines multiple lines of business that are different from other SBUs but internally confront similar issues and challenges. Defining strategic business units and which lines of business should be within them can be an extraordinary challenge for corporate strategists, especially in organizations such as GE or Illinois Tool Works that operate hundreds of types of businesses.

Establishing investment priorities. The diversified corporation usually engages in a budgeting process in which divisions or SBUs seek corporate investment to further develop their businesses. Corporate management must decide how to judge the merits of requests for additional capital investment by SBUs and how to allocate available capital among competing requests. The process effectively makes the corporate headquarters operate much like a bank, doling out resources based upon estimated output and return measures. Developing an effective set of evaluative criteria and creating a means of analyzing competing requests is a critical issue for corporate strategy decision makers.

Making resource and management transfers. Many corporations decide to acquire companies that are somewhat related to their existing lines of business. This is done to take advantage of anticipated synergies that might exist between the newly acquired company and the existing business or to establish a foothold in another promising area. When this happens, corporate management needs to determine how best to infuse the new company with the unique resources and learning from its existing business, as well as how to take advantage of what is special about the acquired company within its other existing businesses. Facilitating this sharing of resources can be exceedingly difficult for a variety of reasons, which we will return to in a later discussion about capturing synergies. The corporate office must also implement appropriate management changes to align the new company with the corporation. Such moves may ultimately have the added benefit of developing managers with a broader experience across the entire organization.

How to structure the corporation. To accomplish all of this, corporate management must determine the type of structure that will be most effective for this complex set of businesses. Neither a traditional functional organization nor the hierarchy of a typical single-line business will generally work for a multiple-business corporation. Financial management for helicopter leasing and financial management for Lightspeed computerized tomography scanners (both business lines within GE Capital) are worlds apart and each requires a completely different set of skills! Corporations employ a variety of structures to accomplish coordination, sharing, control, and management. This topic will be discussed in detail in Chapter 11, "Strategy and Structure."

HISTORICAL PERSPECTIVES

Developing a deep understanding of corporate strategy is important for students of strategy because diversified corporations are a significant part of the business landscape in the United States and around the world. Rarely does a week go by that the *Wall Street Journal* does not report on yet another corporate merger or buyout. The diversified company has become increasingly important in the U.S. economy. Figure 10.2 illustrates merger and acquisition (M&A) activity over the last forty-five years in the United States. Until the mid-1980s, although the number of M&A deals rose and fell, the total value of such deals remained fairly constant. Since the early 1990s both the number of transactions and their value has grown dramatically; in 2015 the value of all U.S. mergers and acquisitions exceeded $2.4 trillion.

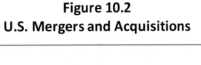

Figure 10.2
U.S. Mergers and Acquisitions

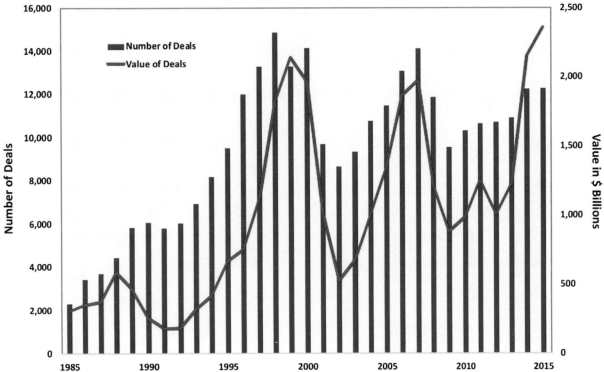

The reasons for M&A activity over the years have changed. Until the 1960s many corporations had grown through internally generated new business within their own industries, or had completed horizontal diversification in order to own and manage other companies that were very similar to their core business. However, by the late 1960s many U.S. corporations found it increasingly difficult to grow because of maturing domestic markets, greater foreign competition in the United States, and concerns about antitrust enforcement since industry concentration ratios had increased in many domestic industries (see discussion in Chapter 4).[4] Therefore they sought to fuel growth by getting into new industries outside their dominant business. The era of conglomerates took shape, during which corporations acquired many types of companies that were completely different from what had originally been their dominant business. If you think of a conglomerate in its usual definition – "rock composed of fragments varying from small pebbles to large boulders in a cement"[5] – then you have a picture of what conglomerate corporations were like. Textron, Gulf+Western, ITT, Litton Industries, and General Electric are corporate names often associated with conglomerates. In fact, during the 1960s GE competed in twenty-three of the twenty-six industries defined and tracked by the Commerce Department,[6] with forty-six different operating divisions and 190 departments.

Conglomeration continued into the early 1970s as the largest corporations grew even larger. One business reporter, believing the trend toward monster-size corporations would not abate until virtually all companies were owned by only a few giant corporations, was prompted to write an article titled "The Day They Couldn't Fill the Fortune 500."[7] By 1974 the complexion of the U.S. economy had changed significantly from twenty-five years earlier. Figure 10.3 shows how diversified the Fortune 500 had become during this period of time. In 1949 over 40 percent of the largest corporations operated in only a single business, and 70 percent operated in a single business or were predominantly in a single industry. By 1974, in contrast, 64 percent of the largest companies were diversified and operating in multiple industries. But by 2014 this level had increased to 90 percent.[8]

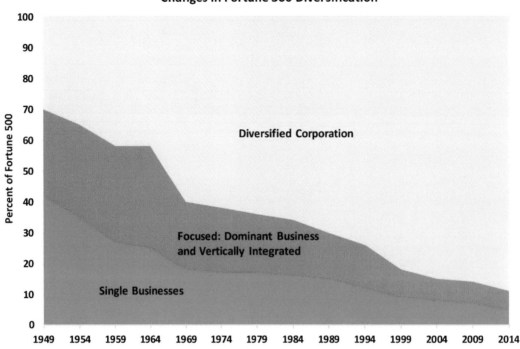

Figure 10.3
Changes in Fortune 500 Diversification

By the 1980s large, widely diversified firms were experiencing significant difficulties in the sound and profitable management of such a breadth of businesses. Conglomerate company stocks started trading in equity markets at a discount in PE ratio to more focused firms (the "conglomerate discount"). What goes up must come down – or so we are led to believe. Corporate activity during the 1980s was characterized by efforts to dismantle conglomerate firms and redeploy their assets more effectively and efficiently. With a more permissive antitrust environment under President Reagan's administration, and with financial innovations such as junk bonds and leveraged buyouts (LBOs), conglomerates began to shed unrelated businesses in order to become more focused in their portfolio of businesses.[9] By 1988, when the value of deals peaked during the decade (Figure 10.2), 63 percent of acquisitions involved cash or debt (as opposed to using equity). LBOs were the talk of the town on Wall Street; the most exciting deal was the frenzied $25 billion LBO of RJR Nabisco in 1988, subsequently chronicled in a popular book titled *Barbarians at the Gate*.[10] If you enjoy corporate finance, backroom politics, soap opera, and drama, this book is a must-read page-turner!

The 1990s witnessed the escalation of M&A activity to a point never before experienced in the U.S. economy. Increasing globalization and more intense competition provided the impetus for firms to grow larger. The soaring stock market and a continuation of the restrained antitrust environment enabled firms to use their own highly valued shares of stock to acquire companies that were related to lines of business they were already in. The confluence of these factors led to a dollar volume of deals that exceeded 20 percent of the U.S. gross national product (Figure 10.4).

313

Figure 10.4
Value of M&A as Percentage of GDP

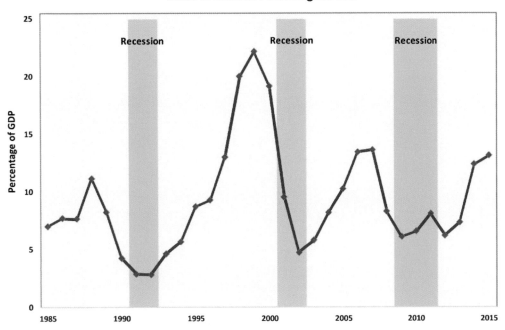

After the "dot-bomb" led recession in the early 2000s and the corresponding decline in diversification activity, M&A activity resumed its rise once again. Before the 2008 financial crisis this activity was assisted by the growth of private equity firms and by the advent of innovative financing methods such as SPACs (special purpose acquisition companies) and CLOs (collateralized loan obligations).[11]

Since 2000 two aspects of conglomeration have become evident. First, within the United States and advanced economies, this sort of broad diversification is not just the province of traditional manufacturing and service companies. Technology firms have been very active in diversifying, led by the likes of Microsoft and Google. Since 2000 Google has acquired over 170 companies, using hoards of cash sitting on its balance sheet. Second, conglomeration appears to be prevalent in many emerging countries. Sometimes dominated by family ownership, conglomerates can often perform well because their internal organization of market-based transactions can overcome the institutional voids and government influence that exist in emerging nations.

One of the Worst Deals Ever? Part 1[12]

On January 17, 2006, Boston Scientific secured a deal to acquire Guidant Corp. In a follow-up investigative report published in Fortune, the deal was characterized as "a roller-coaster tale of bet-the-franchise corporate brinkmanship, miscalculation, and overreaching. It is a stark lesson in how the single-minded pursuit of victory can blind even brilliant execs to the true costs of a deal." Boston's $80 per share bid for Guidant beat out Johnson & Johnson's $71 offer after multiple rounds of bidding in which the "bad blood" that had existed between Boston and J&J manifested itself in "gladiatorial" combat.

J&J had originally bid to acquire Guidant because it saw opportunities for significant growth through Guidant's pacemakers and defibrillators in the medical products industry. J&J competed in this industry and wanted to broaden its product lines. Boston Scientific also saw a similar opportunity for growth through related acquisition. The marriage of Boston's Taxus drug-coated stent business and Guidant's promising new stent products and proprietary stent implantation technology also made a potential merger quite attractive.

Boston's winning bid was the eighth bid entertained by Guidant's board of directors. After earlier J&J bids had been viewed favorably by the Guidant board, Boston's CFO Larry Best is claimed to have announced to his internal team, "We need to make a bid that ends this, to swing for the fences." Best was viewed as a "mercurial street fighter" who "doesn't like to lose." The final Boston bid was $27.2 billion, valuing Guidant at $80.03 per share, representing a PE ratio of 64.6 and a premium of 40+ percent over its share price before the first J&J bid. The bid was paid in part with newly issued Boston shares, which increased its share count by 80 percent and diluted Boston shareholders. Part of the bid price was paid with cash, requiring Boston to borrow $6.5 billion on which was to pay in excess of $300 million annually in interest.

After the deal was consummated, Boston was plagued with poor performance. Guidant was forced to recall stents due to poor quality control; the FDA warned Boston about its manufacturing facilities, preventing approval for new products. Drug-coated stents, in general, also received negative publicity from the health-care community. These factors interfered with Boston's efforts to increase Guidant sales so that, with the interest that Boston paid on the acquisition debt, the Guidant business was contributing nothing to the company's earnings. Boston's share price, which was at $24 when the bid was accepted, dropped 34 percent into the mid-teens. Larry Best insisted the acquisition would pay off and that success should be judged in three to four years, not based upon short-term hiccups. CEO Jim Tobin had "no doubt" that the company would eventually realize the deal's potential.

MOTIVATIONS FOR DIVERSIFICATION

We saw in Chapter 8 that companies experience different stages and strategic considerations in the course of their development. After a company has started up and then gone through the commercialization and growth stages, the challenges of managing a mature business set in. As a company matures and its sales growth starts to flatten out, the strategic option to diversify is often considered by senior management. When a company diversifies by acquiring another company, there is usually a core logic that is operating. The company sees potential competitive advantage that might be attained with the combination. Through the application and sharing of corporate resources, the acquiring company believes that it will be able to assist the acquired company to become much more than it could have been if it had remained independent, or much more than it could have been if it had been acquired by another company. So the core logic of diversification through acquisition is usually that "we can do something special for them, and as a result our overall corporate performance will be significantly improved." It's also often the case that acquiring companies have something to gain from the acquired company, such as new technology or new capabilities. Here the logic is "they can also do something for us."

There tend to be four primary motivations for diversifying a company, which include: 1) seeking growth, 2) market entry, 3) seeking market power, and 4) spreading risk. Within each of these primary motivations are sets of underlying reasons, and we briefly discuss each below.

Growth

The desire to continue growing a company generally heads the list of motivations to diversify, and this motivation to grow through diversification can occur for various offensive or competitively defensive reasons.

GROWTH
- Better external opportunities
- Acquire new capabilities
- Response to intensifying competition
- Avoiding decline & takeover
- Benefits to management & employees
- Managerial capitalism

Better external opportunities. Corporate management will come to believe that they have exhausted their opportunities to sustain strong growth rates through their customary internal development process. They may not see any exciting new products in their development pipeline, they may believe that they have saturated their current channels of distribution, or they may have expanded geographically as far as they possibly can with existing products or services. It may be that large markets or segments no longer exist in their core business that can satisfy the level of growth a company desires (remember that as a company grows in size, it will require larger increments of new revenue in order to sustain a given percentage rate of growth). Or it may be that the cost of expanding further within an existing business domain appears to be prohibitively expensive. To try to change an established organization so that it can generate a significant number of innovative ideas can be difficult, time consuming, and fraught with uncertainties that appear overwhelming. In these cases companies will typically search for external opportunities to fuel growth, and will consider acquiring another business that meets their acquisition criteria.

Acquire new capabilities. Expansion into new products or industries may require new capabilities and resources that the company does not possess. As we discussed in Chapter 9, a company may gain access to new capabilities through alliances or joint ventures with other companies. Yet the acquisition of another business and its inherent capabilities allows the parent company to own and control new resources and capabilities, as well as prevent access to them by competitors.

Oracle is a prime example of these first two reasons for growth through acquisition. The company was known historically for its database software; however it was clear that the industry was maturing. So they began to acquire other companies in business application software, financial services, and telecommunications. Over a three-year time period Oracle acquired more than twenty-five software application companies, as well as major purchases of PeopleSoft and Siebel Systems. Acquisition represented a quick route to maintain Oracle's historical growth rates, but was also required because Oracle systems developers did not possess the skills or capabilities required to enter other software application categories.[13]

Response to intensifying competition. As competitors become larger and more powerful, companies are often prompted to acquire other businesses in order to maintain a competitive position. Acquiring another business can generate benefits of size, reduce the company's dependence on its limited array of products and services, and reduce dependence on specific geographic markets or customer segments. In 2007, organic grocer Whole Foods sought to acquire Wild Oats Markets, another organic grocer, in order to counter the growing competition in organic foods from conventional supermarkets such as Kroger, Supervalu, and Walmart. The argument was that the two organic grocers would save on overhead costs and would allow the combined company to more effectively compete for customers through advertising and retail location.

Avoiding decline and takeover. As internally generated growth of a company begins to slow down, management typically comes under pressure from investors and the stock market to continue generating attractive returns. This kind of slowing growth can occur for any number of reasons: the overall market is maturing, competitors are increasingly effective, the company's strategic approach is increasingly ineffective, or the overall complexity of the corporation makes it difficult to manage effectively. If revenue growth is slowing, improving returns can happen only through cutting costs, and cutting costs can only go so far before interfering with a company's competitive strategy in the marketplace. Lackluster revenue growth and inadequate investor returns paint a target on the backs of senior management, since they are responsible for performance. If the problem of growth in returns is not resolved, the business may become ripe for a takeover, in which another company buys the business and replaces the management team to

317

make necessary changes. Senior managers therefore look at acquisitions and other diversifying moves as an effort to arrest decline and forestall the possibility of any sort of takeover.

Benefits to management and employees. Attempts to grow through acquisition occur for reasons sometimes unrelated to what is actually best for the company itself. Employees and (especially) senior managers derive benefits from working in larger organizations. Compared to smaller companies, in larger organizations there are usually greater opportunities for advancement in position and responsibility while compensation also tends to be higher. For senior management, incentive programs that include bonuses and stock options tend to become more lucrative in larger companies, and can be a powerful inducement to create growth for growth's sake. In this sense, big is beautiful, and getting bigger may be more attractive to employees for personal reasons.

The idea that important strategic decisions for a company might be made in order to personally enhance members of management highlights what is known as the agency issue. Corporate officers and managers are duty bound to act in the interests of shareholders, yet personal incentives may corrupt this straightforward charge. This is one of the reasons that controls are put in place by boards of directors and stockholders. We will return to these issues of governance in Chapter 12.

Managerial capitalism. The last two ideas suggest that something other than the basic economics of a business and its industry can affect whether and how managers pursue growth – that, in fact, managers may pursue growth based on their own personal needs, interests, and aspirations. Building on this idea, Robin Marris long ago suggested that managers trade their desire for growth against fear of takeover.[14] In his model of "managerial capitalism" corporate managers seek growth in ways that go beyond economic justification, until such time as they have assembled more than they can effectively and coherently manage. We will see further evidence of non-rational thinking about mergers and acquisitions in our following discussions.

Market Power

The quest for greater market power is a companion motivation to the quest for growth. Market power refers back to some of the dimensions of industry analysis that we covered in Chapter 4. Here a company seeks to attain a position in the industry that enables it to earn superior returns, through one of several ways.

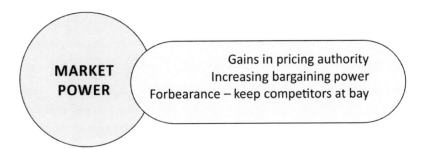

Gains in pricing authority. A company that grows larger in its industry by horizontally acquiring one of its competitors can develop size advantages it previously did not enjoy. These include greater economies of scale in its operations, as well as cost savings through the integration of identical support activities in its value chain (such as combining R&D, purchasing, and human resource functions). Together, these cost savings create greater flexibility in establishing prices for products and services. Most industries have price leaders and price followers; however, the price leaders tend to be the larger companies with the better cost structures.

Increased bargaining power. Because they command a greater percentage of sales in an industry, larger companies will often enjoy enhanced bargaining power when they deal with both suppliers and customers. This is one reason that the Federal Trade Commission originally decided to oppose the Whole Foods – Wild Oats combination mentioned previously, because the combined company would have what is thought to be too much power to demand lower prices from small organic suppliers as well as greater power to command premium prices (without significant competition) with consumer shoppers.

Mutual forbearance – keeping competitors at bay. Mutual forbearance is defined as "the ceding of control of one product or geographic market to a competitor in exchange for that competitor's acquiescence in another market."[15] This means that, in order to keep a competitor out of its industry (or at least less aggressive) and maintain its competitive superiority, a company might acquire a company in another industry in which that same competitor is active. It is sort of a "tit for tat" approach: if you do this to me, I'll do it to you. For example, to slow down Gillette's entry into the disposable pen market, which was BIC's primary market, BIC decided to enter the disposable razor blade market, which was Gillette's hallowed ground. As was pointed out in Chapter 1, this type of "attack" is taken directly from Sun Tzu, who suggested that attacking something of value to the enemy will cause them to reconsider attacking you. Although in this example BIC entered razors through internal development, many examples of mutual forbearance exist through acquisitions into an industry. In 2008 Microsoft bid to acquire Yahoo! to compete more aggressively in the online advertising business. This would likely prompt Google to devote much greater attention and resources to this battle, since it is central to Google's revenue stream, and by doing so draw Google's attention and resources away from its efforts to develop software applications that compete with Microsoft.

Market Entry

Companies often seek to enter industries outside of where they currently operate. They plan to accomplish this type of diversification through acquisition, rather than through internal development, for a number of reasons that relate to cost and speed.

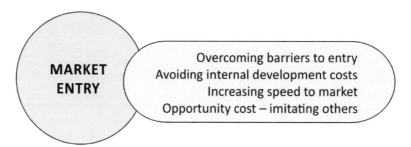

Overcoming barriers to entry. The competitors in most industries seek to raise entry barriers to keep the flow of new entrants to a minimum, thus better preserving their own stakes in the industry's profits. Barriers to entry can be both significant and expensive – whether they involve building scale-efficient manufacturing facilities, developing broad distribution, or creating brand awareness through advertising and promotion. Acquiring an existing company in a new industry does an end-run around the costs of breaking through the entry barriers because the company takes advantage of an existing industry player who already holds the resources needed to be a competitor. Breaking into the sports drink market with a new product line would have been a difficult and slow road for Quaker Oats to pursue; instead they purchased Gatorade (at a somewhat outrageous price) and immediately became an important player in the industry.

Avoiding internal development costs. Similarly, through the acquisition of a going concern in an industry, the acquiring company can avoid the costs and uncertainty of developing products or services internally. Buying a company means taking over an existing business with defined suppliers and a customer base. Therefore most of the uncertainty that is usually associated with any type of new product development effort is also avoided.

Increasing speed to market. If analysis reveals that another industry is attractive, acquiring a company in that industry enables the acquiring firm to begin operating more quickly than would be the case if it developed its own products or services internally. Acquisitions often close within six to twelve months, whereas effective new product development efforts can take many years.

Opportunity cost. Finally, a "bandwagon" effect sometimes happens when a leading company in one industry makes an acquisition in another industry, encouraging competitors to make similar acquisitions. In the 1990s, pharmaceutical manufacturer Merck acquired generic drug distributor Medco, and shortly afterward a number of Merck's competitors also snatched up drug distribution companies. As this suggests we occasionally witness a flurry of similar types of acquisitions in an industry within a short period of time. In these cases the first acquisition prompts other firms to consider the opportunities they might be missing if they stayed on the sidelines. This kind of bandwagon effect usually occurs when the industries involved are undergoing dynamic changes, revealing new possibilities for value creation through a new combination achieved by acquisition.

Spreading Risk

The final motivation for diversification has to do with spreading risk.

Every company experiences two kinds of risk. There is the systematic risk that is associated with macro-economic forces (forces that affect everyone in the economy), and the unsystematic risk that is associated with its particular line of business. You have no doubt run into these terms in finance classes you have taken previously, since both are used to calculate the beta (β) of a company's stock. Companies which diversify can reduce their unsystematic risk by acquiring other companies whose lines of business offset performance variations in the company's own business. In Figure 10.5 Company A's business fluctuates, such as might be the case when A manufactures hot chocolate mix primarily sold in colder months or in mostly northern states. During the warm months A must reduce employment because seasonal sales are low, but may still find that it loses money because of high fixed overhead costs associated with its underutilized plant during that time. So during the summer its revenue and profits decline, as suggested by curved line A. When it files its quarterly reports with the SEC, the investment community responds to unprofitable quarters by selling stock, and its stock price declines. So Company A decides to acquire Company B, which manufactures popsicles sold primarily in the warm months and the southern states. After the acquisition, A combines the two manufacturing operations so that consistent employment and better plant utilization can be maintained. Administrative, marketing and sales efficiencies work to lower other costs as a percentage of revenue. Since revenue and profits do not now fluctuate widely, the company may report more consistently profitable quarters throughout the year. Shareholders of A benefit from the smoothed-out revenues and earnings the company now achieves.

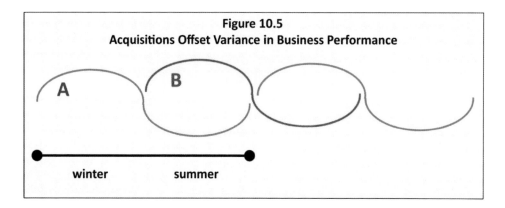

Figure 10.5
Acquisitions Offset Variance in Business Performance

Why couldn't shareholders in Company A simply buy shares of Company B to accomplish the same level of risk spreading? In this case Company B's business also fluctuates considerably during a year and across geographies. So shareholders of A who also invest in B would simply be buying another company with a fair degree of unsystematic risk. However, by putting together the lines of business the fluctuations associated with the combined company are reduced[16] and shareholders thus benefit from a stock price that should be more stable over time.

TYPES OF DIVERSIFICATION

In Chapter 8 we covered a range of options that companies have at their disposal for growing their businesses – including introducing new products within their industry, expanding into new geographic regions or internationally, or forming alliances or joint ventures. Because this chapter deals with corporate strategy (managing multiple lines of business), we have more or less focused on the acquisitions route at this point. We have to recognize, however, that companies may still diversify into new businesses through internal development efforts or through joint ventures and alliances, in addition to acquisition. As discussed in the preceding section, diversifying through acquisition can offer some advantages over these other methods. These advantages relate to control of resources and capabilities, overcoming entry barriers, avoiding internal development costs, and increasing speed of entry.

Regardless of how a company diversifies, there are distinctions in the type of diversification that a company engages in. These distinctions can be described in terms of the combinations of industry similarity and value chain similarity (Figure 10.6). The primary types of diversification fall into two well-known categories: related diversification and unrelated diversification.

Figure 10.6
Types of Diversification and Their Distinctions

Types of Diversification	Variation	Characteristics of	
		Industry	Value Chain
Related	Horizontal	Same Industry	Same Value Chain
	Vertical	Same Industry	Extend Value Chain
	Cross-Sector	Different Industry	Similar Value Chain
Unrelated		Different Industry	Different Value Chain

Related Diversification

As the phrase implies, related diversification means that there is some dimension of similarity between the corporation and the company it seeks to acquire. Related diversification can be divided into three variations: 1) horizontal, 2) vertical, and 3) cross-sector. Horizontal

diversification occurs when a company enters another business in the same industry and essentially employs the exact same value chain as is used in its core business. Earlier we mentioned how Whole Foods acquired Wild Oats Markets during 2007. These two organic foods grocery store chains draw upon the same suppliers, operate in the same fashion at retail, and seek to attract the same types of customers. In 2008 InBev, one of the largest European beer companies, acquired Anheuser-Busch in order to establish a worldwide distributor of beer. Black & Decker, the 100-year-old manufacturer of power tools for homeowners and the construction trade, acquired Vector Products, which manufactures battery chargers, jump-starters, and other equipment for the automotive market. Since many of the Vector products are sold in traditional hardware store channels of distribution, Black & Decker is able to leverage its resources and capabilities in tool manufacturing and sales distribution to significantly expand the presence and impact of the Vector line.

Because horizontal diversification extends a company's influence further into an industry in which it is already operating, acquisitions of this sort tend to draw the attention of regulatory authorities. Acquiring companies in the same industry may lead to significantly enhanced market power, through which the resulting combination may exert undue influence upstream on suppliers or downstream on customers, in the form of pricing demands or other requirements. InBev announced plans to cut $1.5 billion from Anheuser-Busch's cost structure partly by reducing the number of independent distributors and reducing payments to those distributors that remain.[17] From our earlier discussion in Chapter 4 on industry analysis, we know that the Federal Trade Commission and the Department of Justice are interested in preventing combinations that lead to excessive market power for just these reasons. This is why the FTC objected to Whole Foods' acquisition of Wild Oats Markets.

Occasionally companies will engage in vertical diversification, in which they enter new businesses in the same industry but which occupy different positions up or down the value chain. Vertical acquisitions ordinarily occur when a company wants to continue operating in its own industry, where it has deep knowledge and capabilities, but wants to exert greater control over some part of the industry value chain. When Disney decided to enter the cruise line business, it could have simply licensed its name and the use of its characters to another company that already operated in this business. Yet Disney believed that the quality of the customer experience is at the heart of the company, and that delivering an exceptional experience is a critical part of their strategy. Monitoring how another company accomplished this on their behalf would have been incredibly difficult and would have subjected the company to a significant downside risk that the Disney image might be tarnished. So, in entering this business they decided to enter vertically, by building and operating their own cruise ships and cruise line reservation service.

Vertical diversification also occurs when companies seek to gain greater control over sources of supply in their value chains. You have probably been advised by your university to back up your files in case the hard drive on your computer fails and you lose those term papers you have been working on (it's probably more important to you to back up your MP3 and picture files!). Western Digital manufactures internal and external hard drives used for this purpose, and their drives are often sold in electronic stores like Best Buy. In 2007 the company acquired Komag for nearly $1 billion. Komag manufactures the rotating disks that serve as the storage media inside the drive box you buy. The acquisition was made so that Western Digital could better keep pace with technological developments and cost changes in the manufacturing of this important subcomponent, allowing them to be more competitive with Seagate Technology. Said John Coyne, CEO of Western Digital, "This acquisition puts us in a position to be in greater control of our own destiny."[18]

Cross-sector diversification describes the situation when a company enters a completely new industry but intends to utilize a value chain that is very similar to that employed in their core business. The Philip Morris Company decided to apply its branded marketing and sales capabilities for cigarettes to the categories of beer and soft drinks, resulting in the acquisitions of Miller Brewing and the 7-Up Company in the 1970s. Long known for its razor blades, Gillette acquired Duracell in 1996, believing that its value chain capabilities in innovation, marketing, and retail sales management could be effectively brought to bear to improve the Duracell battery business. In a further twist of corporate combinations, Procter & Gamble subsequently acquired Gillette in 2005. Although P&G already operated in many different industries (paper products, personal care items, cleaning agents, etc.), acquiring the Gillette lines of business could also be considered cross-sector diversification because they expected to leverage their existing value chain capabilities by entering new industries. In discussing the acquisition, CEO A. G. Lafley claimed that Gillette was "one of our biggest growth opportunities, and served to provide... a balanced mix of businesses, brands, markets, and customers provide flexibility to deliver results reliably, in good times and challenging times alike."[19] It becomes apparent that P&G viewed the Gillette acquisition not only as a means of generating future growth through entry into new markets, but also as a means to spread risk – three of the motivations for diversification mentioned previously.

Why Related Diversification Is Supposed to Succeed

Corporate performance is expected to improve because diversification takes advantage of synergies that are believed to exist between the corporation and the company it will acquire. Each of the types of diversification discussed previously illustrates how related diversification builds upon or leverages aspects of the corporation's existing value chain (Figure 10.7).

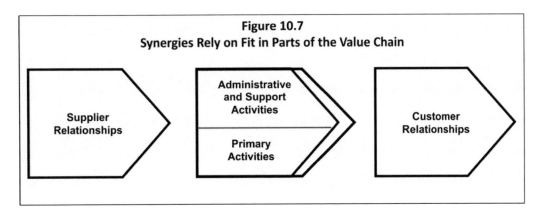

Figure 10.7
Synergies Rely on Fit in Parts of the Value Chain

Supplier Relationships

Administrative and Support Activities

Primary Activities

Customer Relationships

Three forms of "fit" offer the opportunity for synergistic gains from an acquisition. Synergies may spring from market fit, in which the corporation takes advantage of external value chain relationships with customers or suppliers in order to improve the competitive position and business of the acquired company. When Cisco Systems acquires another company, for example, advanced planning allows Cisco to add the acquired company's products onto its own price list the very first day the new company is officially part of the Cisco family. In this way the Cisco sales organization can immediately begin selling the new company's products on a much broader scale. Procter & Gamble expected to significantly expand the Duracell and Gillette product lines throughout their worldwide organizations, selling these products to wholesale and retail accounts that P&G already had relationships with.

Operational fit occurs where the corporation is able to combine similar primary value chain activities, such as manufacturing facilities, transportation systems, or warehousing operations. In 2007 XM Satellite Radio Holdings proposed a merger with Sirius Satellite Radio, its chief competitor. The two companies, competing aggressively with each other and both losing money as a result, would expect to combine significant aspects of their nearly identical broadcasting operations and eliminate duplicate operational activities. E*Trade Financial and TD Ameritrade also engaged in merger talks during 2007, believing that "uniting both company's accounts on a single computer system" would eliminate duplicate computer operations and minimize the cost of adding new customers.[20]

The third type of fit is the kind of management fit that occurs when synergies might be realized in the administrative and support activities of the value chain. Combining procurement and purchasing functions can lead to increased bargaining power with suppliers and with the shippers who deliver raw materials and other inputs to the company's primary activities locations. Research and development efforts can be enhanced either through the streamlining that can occur when redundancies are eliminated or through the access to new types of technical knowledge, processes, or patents that result from combining two companies. Other corporate support functions, such as finance and legal, can also be made available to acquired companies and thereby further reduce redundancies. Perhaps most importantly, the more sophisticated knowledge possessed by management about how to successfully build a business and compete can be leveraged into a newly-acquired division.

Just as there are three fit sources of synergies in related diversification, there are three types of synergistic benefits that related diversification efforts can lead to: scope, economizing, and leverage (Figure 10.8). Scope is created when the corporation is able to broaden its product line or broaden its customer base by virtue of an acquisition. Scope provides immediate performance benefits in the form of higher sales revenue. It also provides immediate opportunity for sales revenue growth, such as the type that Procter & Gamble or Cisco count on, by expanding distribution into existing channels of distribution.

Figure 10.8 Sources and Results of Synergies	
Sources of Synergies	Results of Synergies
Market fit	Scope
Operational fit	Economizing
Management fit	Economizing; Resources Leverage

Many of the merger and acquisition deals announced in the newspapers trumpet the synergies to be gained from economizing. Economizing refers to the cost savings accomplished by operating the combined companies more efficiently. Occasionally efficiencies are created by combining separate manufacturing operations into a large, scale-efficient plant. More often than not, however, efficiencies are realized through layoffs and workforce reduction of redundant and duplicate jobs. This kind of economizing strikes white collar workers in support and administrative activities as often as it does blue collar workers in manufacturing and service jobs in the primary activities sector of the value chain. Arguments for economizing have become so prevalent as justification for acquisitions that *Fortune* magazine offered a wry view about the meaning of synergies.

Media euphemisms for synergy

- Corporate "catch and release" program
- Fueling demand for lottery tickets & malt liquor
- Dissing the gruntled
- Hiring a bunch of people, only backwards

Both scope and economizing present more objective, more obvious benefits of related diversification. Consequently, corporate actions immediately following an acquisition tend to be focused on developing these more immediate economic benefits. However, the cost of making an acquisition in order to diversify is seldom paid back through these types of benefits alone. The return on investment in related diversification will usually occur when the corporation develops the benefits of resources leverage. Leverage does not occur through merely combining; it occurs through the extension and application of corporate resources to the newly acquired company. If we think back to the discussion of resources and the value chain in Chapters 5 and 6, we will recall that the dimensions of the value chain that are most valuable are those that have to do with "the coordination and linkages that exist between and across elements of a company's value chain." This is because they are unobservable to competition and extremely difficult to reproduce. The resource-based arguments of Chapter 6 would call these "extraordinary" resources, ones that provide the opportunity for sustainable advantage. Other intangible resources include management knowledge. The greatest performance benefits that accrue to corporations that diversify relatedly through acquisitions should therefore come from the extension, or leverage, of these extraordinary resources into the newly acquired company. Because coordinating mechanisms within a corporation are often tacit and buried in routines or culture, they are less obvious and more complex, and therefore it can be extremely difficult to leverage them effectively. We will return to this point when we discuss the evidence on diversification performance.

Unrelated Diversification

Unrelated diversification occurs when a corporation enters a new business in a different industry from that in which it currently operates *and* does not expect to achieve any value chain synergies through the combination. Unrelated diversifiers are usually referred to as either *conglomerates* or as holding companies. Conglomerates such as GE operate multiple lines of business under one corporate name. In contrast, holding companies own other companies, or at least own the majority of the voting shares of other companies so that they may control management and operations by influencing or electing their board of directors. On the other hand, they allow the other companies to operate as relatively independent entities. In 2016 Warren Buffet's holding company Berkshire Hathaway owned sixty-two subsidiary operating companies that compete in eighty-one different businesses, and the company continues to aggressively manage its portfolio of companies. Kohlberg Kravis Roberts and other private equity firms also operate as holding companies, owning shares and controlling the companies but not actually participating in the active management of the business of these companies.

If unrelated diversification is not intended to improve corporate performance through capturing synergies, then what is the reason for this type of corporate acquisition behavior? Unrelated diversification is supposed to succeed because of the exceptional financial expertise that the acquiring corporation brings to the table. The senior management in these organizations usually excel in identifying undervalued companies, financially distressed firms with strong business fundamentals, and companies that have significant growth prospects if they can gain access to financial capital. With the injection of corporate financial capital, as well as a strong corporate governance system to ensure effective monitoring of the performance of acquired companies, unrelated diversifiers expect that corporate performance will be buoyed by above-average performance of their acquisitions.

The astute student will recognize that these types of unrelated diversification transactions are apt to occur primarily when there are certain types of financial market imperfections. In some cases financial markets may look unfavorably at an entire industry, in which case the stock price of a company that has particularly strong fundamentals or prospects may get "unfairly" beat down. Corporations that identify these "diamonds in the rough" can provide the financial capital that the companies cannot gain access to through financial markets. Another issue may be that the costs of raising either equity or debt capital is prohibitively expensive in financial markets, whereas the corporate holding company's transactions costs for providing capital are significantly lower.

Parenting Advantage

The above discussion of related and unrelated diversification ordinarily focuses on the extent to which the resources and capabilities that exist within the current portfolio of companies might be applied to a newly-acquired company. A "parenting advantage" framework can offer some additional insight and utility in thinking about how well a newly-acquired company might fare under the corporate umbrella.[21] The idea here is that the headquarters of the corporation has its own capabilities and can influence the outcome of an acquisition simply by virtue of the "parent-child" relationship. Value can be created when the Parent's skills and resource fit well with the needs and opportunities of the company targeted for acquisition.

Figure 10.9
Parenting Advantage Fit

Figure 10.9 provides a matrix to use to assess the parenting advantage fit. Fit is assessed along two axes, and each depends on understanding important characteristics of the parent company. These characteristics include the overarching philosophy HQ management regularly uses, the corporate structure, central functions and services the parent is particularly good at, the experience set of senior management, and the degree of decentralization the HQ office allows. Is there a fit between these characteristics and the sort of headquarter support that is needed by the target acquisition (horizontal axis)? If the fit is high, then this may bode well for the acquisition. But the vertical axis helps us understand if there might be *misfit* between parenting characteristics and the specific key success factors the target company must address in its industry. If there is no misfit on this dimension, then the business is seen as falling into the "heartland" where value can

327

be created by the parent company. This might be the case, for example, when an acquired company wants to expand internationally, and it can take advantage of the corporate parent's structure that is organized with country-level subsidiaries. Often parent companies can provide needed corporate services to acquisitions but are unable to help acquisitions with critical business success factors. These fall into the "value trap" segment in the matrix, where the parent really cannot help the acquired company on factors that are critical to its success in its industry.

By a similar logic, it may be the case that the parent company has fitting experience through its other divisions in the target company's industry but lacks fit between what HQ does well and what the target might need from HQ. Perhaps the parent company is a holding company of independently-operating retailers. In this case, although the acquired company may benefit from resources and learning from within the other subsidiaries, the parent itself has little value it can offer. These potential acquisitions would represent "ballast," something that just weighs the corporate parent down. And then there is "alien territory," where nothing about the target company matches up well with the corporate parent HQ.

DIVERSIFICATION PERFORMANCE

Even though mergers and acquisition activity is a huge economic force, the evidence is mixed as to whether these diversification efforts actually enhance the performance of corporations. Corporations engage in diversification in order to derive corporate benefits from bringing a new business into the corporate family. Ultimately, these moves should provide enhanced returns to shareholders of the corporation.[22] Yet a variety of sophisticated studies over the years conclude that diversification is nearly as likely to destroy shareholder value as it is to create shareholder value. One popular study from the 1990s examined 150 deals that exceeded $500 million, finding that shareholder value was eroded 50 percent of the time, while shareholder value was only created 17 percent of the time. In the rest of the cases (33 percent) there was little change in shareholder value.[23] A more recent study examined the results of dozens of sophisticated analyses and arrived at a similar conclusion. This study finds that shareholders of acquired firms make out exceedingly well. However the benchmark-adjusted return to shareholders of corporations that do the acquiring "is close to zero... [and] the distribution of corporate returns is wide – which means that many buyers in M&A transactions should prepare to be disappointed."[24] Figure 10.10 illustrates this conclusion: negative returns to shareholders are nearly as likely as are positive returns, and the average level of returns is marginally above zero. The conclusion, then, is that acquisitions on average produce slightly positive returns but those efforts subject shareholders to high volatility.

There is some limited evidence that management experience in making acquisitions tends to produce better corporate returns. For corporations that have been down the

Figure 10.10
Distribution of Returns from Diversification

Probability of Occurring

average

negative   0%   positive

Returns to Corporate Shareholders

328

acquisition path at least six times, positive shareholder returns are created 72 percent of the time; zero or negative returns occur only 28 percent of the time.[25] We suppose this is a better story than the 50/50 chance of enhanced performance mentioned previously. However the ability to accomplish even this modest feat may come only over time after the expense of multiple costly business mistakes.

What type of diversification do you think would produce better returns for corporations: related or unrelated? Once more, the story is somewhat mixed. You might think that corporations that diversify relatedly, capturing synergies by taking advantage of similarities in industries and value chains, would tend to perform better than would corporations that acquire completely unrelated companies. One study reports that moderate related diversification can enhance performance versus single-business firms, but that moving into unrelated businesses leads to poor performance.[26] Corporations that move beyond being a single-business firm can better utilize assets through scale and scope advantages, and economize through combining value chain activities. Yet the ability to effectively manage many different types of businesses becomes increasingly difficult as a corporation moves into unrelated businesses. That kind of complexity can contribute to poor performance. The effectiveness of diversification efforts depends on a number of critical factors.

Factors Affecting Acquisition Performance

In speaking about successful diversification through acquisition, someone once declared that it is like having a baby: "easy to conceive, but hard to deliver." It is pretty easy for corporate managers to imagine how great a combination of companies can be. Unfortunately, there are a number of factors that are critical to engineering successful acquisitions, both individually and collectively. Figure 10.11 lists the range of factors that corporate managers must pay attention to if they want to increase the likelihood that their diversification moves will produce positive returns for their shareholders. Some of these are relatively obvious but deserve brief mentioning anyway; some of them are not so obvious.

Attractive industries. In Chapter 4 we learned how various forces can cause a particular industry to be more or less competitively attractive. Less attractive industries are those in which competition begins to resemble perfect competition – where standardization of products or services is highly valued, growth has slowed, profit margins are razor thin, and companies that do well are those that have truly superior cost positions. These conditions often characterize mature industries, as we read about in Chapter 8, and they present tough environments for any company. Some industries may involve onerous conditions like significant government regulation, as in health care or medical products and services. In contrast, more attractive industries are those that are experiencing growth, and where strategic

---

Figure 10.11
Acquisition Performance Depends On

- Selecting attractive industries
- Strategic rationale
- Due diligence
- Capturing synergies
- Acquisition premiums
- Loss of focus of acquiring company
- Accelerating growth of acquired company
- Post-acquisition integration efforts

---

variety can exist. Since industry attractiveness impacts the opportunity to earn above-average returns, it stands to reason that diversification efforts should take advantage of industry context.

Strategic rationale. The more successful acquisitions are those that spring from well-defined acquisition target criteria that relate to the strategy of the corporation or its existing business units. Acquisitions are occasionally pursued because corporate managers concentrate more on the opportunity that a target company presents, rather than its consistency with existing strategy. Establishing criteria for acquisitions that mirror the corporation's strategy narrows the field of potential target companies to those that offer the greatest possibilities for economizing, scope, and leverage.

Cisco Systems, a leading supplier of networking equipment and network management for the Internet, has been particularly successful in its string of acquisitions because it specifies strategic criteria before it ever engages in a search for target companies. These criteria include:

- Must be complementary technology,
- That can be sold using Cisco's existing sales force,
- And serviced by Cisco's existing customer support organization,
- And which leverage Cisco's resource base.

Establishing strategic criteria up front, such as Cisco has done, can avoid costly acquisitions based on speculation about synergies. eBay acquired Skype Technologies in 2005 for $2.6 billion at a time when Skype was only generating $7 million in annual revenue. eBay CEO Meg Whitman claimed this move was central to its strategy of developing significant presence in the three related internet commerce domains of "buy, pay, communicate" (Figure 10.12). Skype was designed to enhance communication in the auction environment between sellers and buyers. Few actually used it, as early adopters of eBay began defaulting back to huge online retailers like Amazon.com or Target.com. The hoped-for synergies never materialized. Four money-losing years later, eBay – having never integrated the service into its auction business – sold 70 percent of Skype to a group of private investors for $2.8 billion.[27]

Figure 10.12
Strategic Rationale for eBay's Acquisitions

| Find | Buy | Pay | Communicate | Entertain |

eBay — # 1 in eCommerce

PayPal — #1 in online payments

skype — #1 in voice communications

Occasionally a corporation discovers it has acquired a company that needs to employ a different strategy in the marketplace. This is what occurred when Gillette purchased the Duracell business. Gillette's core razors and blades business was built on a highly differentiated approach, and they believed they could leverage their differentiation capabilities into the battery business.

However, the battery market was in transition, where what was becoming increasingly valued in the marketplace was low cost and price – a set of strategic management disciplines that Gillette did not possess.

Do the due. Corporate acquisition teams often fail to complete a thorough due diligence process. In due diligence every aspect of a targeted company's external and internal dimensions, as well as its potential fit with the corporation, should be exhaustively investigated. This includes the target company's markets, customers, suppliers and competitors, its internal operations, its people, its culture, and more. Due diligence includes analysis that carefully identifies where and how opportunities for scope and economizing exist through the potential acquisition, and how the management and cultural fits between the two companies can leverage the corporation's resources and competencies.

Acquisitions are plagued by poor due diligence, which manifests itself in two important ways. First, many acquisition efforts simply fail to follow a rigorous process. This leads to statements such as the following by QVC's chairman Barry Diller when he contemplated acquiring CBS in 1994: "Sure there are some (synergies) here for sure. I don't know where they are yet. To say that now would be an idiot's game."[28] When there is poor due diligence, acquiring companies make the mistake of simply assuming that synergies exist and can be easily captured. Second, even when the due diligence process is followed, some acquisition analysis teams focus on the more obvious of the potential economic benefits – scope and economizing – while devoting significantly less effort to the more difficult and complex area of leverage through management, administrative systems, resources, and culture. GE Capital's John Lanier comments on this failure, claiming that errors during the due diligence process are rarely due to faulty technical analysis: "The reason why the prognosticated value fails to appear in many cases is that people fail to pay enough attention to cultural factors. That is why many acquisitions flounder – because of the people side, the soft side. That is the reason for failure in three out of five cases."[29]

Capturing synergies. Identifying potential synergies leading to scope, economizing, and leverage is one thing; actually capturing them is quite another. Combining sales organizations and operations to accomplish scope and economizing is difficult enough. It is often unclear how to leverage the intangibles of the corporation – value creation routines, resources, capabilities – to the advantage of the acquired company.

Integrating cultures usually leads the list of reasons why synergy is so difficult to achieve. Corporations that acquire companies try to avoid a "winners and losers" or "conquerors and conquered" mentality, but often these feelings persist in the post-acquisition phase anyway. In addition, the clashing of very different cultures can make any synergistic effort fail miserably. Perhaps the best known clash of cultures occurred when America Online (AOL) acquired Time Warner in 2001 for $103.5 billion. AOL was a hip, knowledge-based internet company run by freewheeling young people tuned in to the new digital age, whereas Time Warner was a traditional asset-based media company (magazines, books, studios, cable television) run by old school managers who made money the "old-fashioned way." After five years management of the combined company finally gave up trying to push synergy across two such different enterprises.[30]

In an effort to exert control over newly acquired companies, corporations often install new rules and regulations, routines, procedures, and corporate managers in the acquisition. Inadequately communicated as to why these actions are taken, they are either misunderstood by employees of the acquired company or serve to reinforce the "conquered" feeling. It is also difficult to start changing the ways one acts on a day-to-day basis, so the implementation of new systems and procedures often requires the "new" employees to take time away from the business itself in order to attend to the "administrivia" forced on them from the new corporate owners.

In combination, the clash between cultures and the installation of new systems leads to serious problems in achieving the synergies that the corporation had hoped for. One study quantified the negative impact of acquisitions on employees in acquired companies (Figure 10.13).[31] Presumably a corporation acquires a company because it believes the employees of the company have accomplished something worthwhile that the corporation can build upon. When employee morale and productivity suffer, and when employees resign, it is difficult at best to achieve the hoped-for leverage.

Figure 10.13
Workforce Impact of Acquisitions

Decrease in employee productivity	17%
Decrease in employee morale	41%
Increase in unwanted turnover	25%
Increase in desirable turnover	33%
Increase in retirements	25%

Acquisition premiums. Due to the opportunities for scope, economizing, and resources leverage in an acquisition target, corporate executives generally believe a target company is worth more than how financial markets value that company. They are therefore willing to pay more than the current stock price for the target company. Between 1978 and 1990 the average premium paid over a company's stock price immediately preceding an acquisition announcement was 34 percent.[32] After the excesses of the late 1990s stock market Internet bubble, one would think sanity might return to the corporate suite, but in fact in the 2000s acquisition premiums increased to an average of almost 40 percent over a target company's stock price three months prior to acquisition. By early 2014 takeover premiums were down to only 19 percent, due to uncertainty about the economy. But by the middle of 2016 acquisition premiums were back up to 32.4%.[33]

Huge premiums over the market value of the stock of the target acquisition make it very difficult for a corporation to produce a positive return for their shareholders. Students can use a spreadsheet to calculate this very simply: to break even on a 35 percent premium would require the corporation to increase the acquired company's ROE by 10 percentage points (say, from 14 percent to 24 percent) in the second year, and then to maintain that increase for the next seven years. Such increases would call for significant short-term improvement in some combination of the ratios that make up ROE (profitability, asset productivity, or financial leverage – see Chapter 2), all very difficult to pull off.

Figure 10.14
Reasons for Acquisition Premiums

Poor due diligence
Synergy trap
Bidding wars
Hubris & ego of CEO
Bandwagon effects

Why are corporate executives willing to pay so much to acquire other companies? Figure 10.14 lists the most compelling reasons behind this behavior. Poor due diligence is right at the top of the list (literally). Poor due diligence leads to what is known as the "synergy trap," in which executives justify ever-higher acquisition prices because of synergies they think they will be able to find and capture. Then we witness bidding wars occurring with some regularity, such as what happened between Boston Scientific and J&J profiled earlier in this chapter. In 2007 Tom Tom and Garmin, the two leading manufacturers of GPS tracking devices, engaged in a bidding war for electronic mapmaker Tele Atlas. Tom Tom finally bid 41 percent higher than its initial bid earlier in the year, at a level representing an 81 percent premium to Tele Atlas's shares before the initial bid.[34] Executives become emotionally tied to acquiring a particular company, so that in the face of competitive bidding they are willing to increase the stakes. Often the egotistic personalities of corporate executives play a hand in this. Supreme self-confidence – some call it hubris – leads executives to believe that they can accomplish nearly anything. "Almost all of us believe ourselves to be in the top 20 percent of the population when it comes to…managing a business."[35] This tendency is also evident in the Boston Scientific–Guidant acquisition, where CFO Larry Best didn't want to lose and believed that the management team could make the acquisition work at even higher prices. Occasionally, we observe a bandwagon effect happening, where an acquisition is made "because everyone else is doing it" and because "we don't want to get left behind." A rash of internet advertising firm acquisitions during 2007 is an example of this type of corporate behavior, and the herd behavior can easily lead to over-bidding.

Loss of focus. It is not uncommon to find corporate management so caught up in the process of trying to effectively integrate two businesses to capture synergies that they pay less attention to the core business of both the corporation and the acquired company. In 1997, for example, Boeing and McDonnell Douglas merged to create a larger commercial aircraft manufacturer and the largest defense contractor. Unfortunately, the problems of integrating McDonnell Douglas into Boeing led Boeing executives to "take their eyes off the ball," and Boeing soon experienced serious problems in managing its own aircraft assembly operations. In turn this led to a dramatic management shake-up, but more importantly it led to an opportunity for Airbus to gain additional business and challenge Boeing's status as the worldwide leader in the commercial aircraft industry.

Accelerating growth is tough. When companies spend so much energy trying to attain synergies, when they spend so much effort seeking to combine different cultures, when they lose focus on their core businesses, it becomes difficult to accelerate the growth of the acquired company. Employees worry about their jobs and new procedures, suppliers worry about their contracts, and customers become unsettled. Accelerating revenue growth under ordinary conditions is difficult because of competition, but under these circumstances accelerating growth becomes an extraordinary challenge. In fact, the evidence is that most acquiring companies fail to accelerate growth (Figure 10.15).[36]

Figure 10.15 Success in Accelerating Growth	
Change in Revenue Growth	%
Slowed down	19
No change	64
Accelerated	12

As we mentioned before, accelerating growth of the acquired company is one of the most important challenges that management of the corporation faces, since the economic success of acquisitions ordinarily depends more on revenue growth than it does on cost savings. Where there is little revenue growth, then management is under tremendous pressure to cut costs drastically in order to achieve the desired return on the premium price it paid for the acquisition. Cutting costs – often by shedding jobs – can simply complicate further efforts to merge two companies. On the other hand, the pressure to cut costs is significantly reduced where revenue growth has been accelerated, as is suggested in Figure 10.16.[37] While holding costs constant, accelerating revenue growth of the acquired company will deliver enhanced cash flows to the corporation. The most successful acquisitions are those which economize, create scope, and leverage resources in order to accelerate growth and cut costs. These are companies that operate in the upper right corner of Figure 10.16, creating value for their shareholders through the acquisition.

Figure 10.16
Creating Value in Acquisitions

Post-acquisition efforts. A few lessons about post-acquisition efforts have been learned by observing companies that have an enviable track record in making successful acquisitions, such as Cisco Systems and General Electric. Although every acquisition situation offers a unique context, the following steps seem to enhance the odds of success:

- **Immediately establish an integration team**. The team should be jointly formed with members from both the acquiring and the acquired company.

- **Ensure that senior management of both companies are visibly involved**. Involvement by senior management of the corporation signals that the acquisition is important, while involvement by senior management of the acquired company signals that the perspective of the acquired is critical.

- **Give accountability to the integration team, and also provide them authority and resources to effect changes**. Nothing is worse than constituting a team that can only advise and wait for a decision to be rendered. This slows the integration process down, and signals that senior corporate management really holds all the cards after all.

- **Have a human resources transition plan and team in place the day the acquisition becomes official**. In order to avoid the kind of turnover mentioned earlier, it is helpful to make HR resources available to employees of the acquired company to answer questions and calm concerns.

- **Implement a system that provides financial controls and operational indicators.** While strategic responsibility for the integration is shifted to the integration team, it must be clear that financial performance is the overarching goal of the corporation. A system of operational indicators will provide valuable feedback to both the integration team and corporate management if problems are cropping up.

334

- **Communicate early and often**. Employees of both the acquired company and the corporate parent don't want to be left in the dark about what is going on or how things are going. Building on the discussion in Chapter 3 on vision and mission, communicating with employees helps to align their day-to-day actions with the goals of the company. The corporation should also have a proactive plan to communicate with suppliers and customers.

One of the Worst Deals Ever? Part 2[38]

Two-and-a-half years after completing the acquisition of Guidant Corporation, Boston Scientific was continuing to suffer from the deal. On top of massive cuts and continuing restructuring charges related to the deal, the company was also being impacted by the entry of a new, very powerful competitor. Medtronic received approval from the FDA to sell its coated stent in the U.S. market starting in 2008. In the first quarter of its release to the market, Medtronic's share went from zero to 26 percent.

In April 2008, Boston Scientific announced that it was going to divest itself of what it referred to as "noncore" businesses and lay off 2,300 employees in an effort to cut expenses by over $500 million a year. They also announced that the integration of Guidant was complete and the company was poised to move forward.

What has happened since? Boston Scientific has faced a major controversy relating to the concealment of a defibrillator design flaw by Guidant. By 2011 it had paid $234 million in settlements to affected patients and $296 million in fines. This raises concerns about the quality of Boston Scientific's due diligence process. In 2015, nice years after the acquisition, Boston finally settled a lawsuit filed by its original bidding competitor in the Guidant deal – Johnson & Johnson. J&J had sued because it claimed Guidant had breached a prior merger agreement. In addition to this $600 million settlement Boston has written off nearly $9 billion in assets since 2006, mostly related to Guidant. By 2016 Boston's stock price has almost returned to where it was when it originally bid for Guidant 10 years ago.

QUESTION

1. Given the discussion in the earlier section, what pre-acquisition advice would you have given to the Boston Scientific senior managers before they acquired another company?
2. With Guidant completely absorbed into Boston Scientific, how can you determine whether or not the acquisition was a success? For Boston shareholders? For Guidant shareholders?

MANAGING THE CORPORATE PORTFOLIO

The advent of companies that were highly diversified in the 1960s and 1970s created a new management problem that had really not been experienced previously. How do you manage such a variety of different types of businesses? How does corporate management establish investment priorities among subsidiary operations? On what basis does corporate management decide to prune the portfolio, weeding out companies that no longer seem to have real promise to contribute to corporate performance?

Portfolios Management Tools

In response to these evolving challenges, two consulting firms developed methods of evaluation that became very popular tools used by diversified corporations. These include the GE Business Development Matrix developed by McKinsey & Co. and the BCG Growth Share Matrix developed by the Boston Consulting Group. We'll discuss each briefly because you will undoubtedly run into these at some point after you have graduated. However we'll also mention a few of the limitations of portfolio tools, since they do not reflect more contemporary thinking about strategic management.

GE business development matrix. Figure 10.17 presents an example of this matrix developed specifically for General Electric. Each operating division is plotted on the chart using metrics that assess the attractiveness of its industry and the operating division's strength. Market attractiveness is determined by many of the same factors we discussed in Chapter 4 on Industry Analysis. A rating for the strength of the division is developed after assessing factors such as brand strength, market share and market share growth, cost position and margins relative to competitors, innovation strength and technological capability, quality, management strength, and other dimensions. As was the case when we measured key success factors and created strategic groups maps in Chapter 4, one needs to carefully quantify factors and avoid pure judgment or "guesstimates," in order to get an objective picture of the operating divisions. By convention, the size of a circle represents the size of the industry in which the business unit operates, and the "pie slice" within each circle represents the market share of the business unit. The arrows represent the direction the business unit is expected to move in the future.

Figure 10.17
GE Business Development Matrix

The green shaded cells in the figure represent areas of opportunity for the corporation because divisions that are in these cells or headed into these cells are strong business units operating in attractive industries. These are divisions that the corporation would want to invest in. On the other hand, the divisions that are in or headed into the pink shaded cells are those with weaker business strength operating in less attractive markets. These divisions might be candidates for divestiture, since continued investment in them might not pay off.

BCG growth share matrix. By far the most popular tool in the 1970s and 1980s for assessing portfolios of companies under a corporate umbrella was Boston Consulting Group's Growth Share Matrix (Figure 10.18). The BCG matrix contains only four cells, but here the operating divisions are measured and plotted along the dimensions of industry growth rate and relative market share (share relative to largest competitor). One of the reasons the BCG matrix is so well known is because each cell is labeled according to its cash flow characteristics and needs. Where the division has a high relative market share in a growing industry, it is a "star" and merits investment by the corporation. Where the division has a high market share but is in a low-growth industry, it is called a "cash cow"; it should not receive major corporate investment. Instead the corporation should "milk the cash cow," using cash the operating division generates to fund other more promising divisions. A "dog" is a division that is a candidate for divestiture: low share in a low-growth industry. The only way to grow that kind of a business would be to steal share from stronger rivals, which would require a huge investment and is typically a risky move. In the upper right corner is the "question mark," because it is unclear what to do with businesses that fall in this low share-high industry growth quadrant. To gain market share in a growth industry would require growth faster than the rest of the industry, which means taking market share from competitors. Divisions that exist in this quadrant are thus likely to require large injections of capital from the corporation.

Figure 10.18
BCG Growth Share Matrix

Drawbacks of portfolio techniques. While these two methods for arraying a corporation's businesses do provide a comprehensive picture and are relatively easy to understand, there are a number of drawbacks that users of the tools should be aware of. Most importantly, neither method draws upon the dimensions of competitive advantage that have been emphasized throughout this book: value chain, extraordinary resources, capabilities. Earlier in this chapter we described how GE organizes its multiple lines of business into strategic business units, since they acknowledge that there are strategic characteristics that are shared across businesses. The GE and BCG matrices are static, not necessarily accounting for whether or how strategically important resources in one business could be leveraged into others. In addition, if an operating division is in one of the uncolored cells in the GE matrix, or is a cash cow or question mark in the BCG matrix, there is no straightforward advice that corporate managers may take from the analysis. It is not clear whether investment in the question mark businesses will result in market share growth. Even cash cows may be costly to fortify and defend if competition grows more intense (which often happens in low-growth industries).

Finally, the BCG matrix critically depends on an underlying assumption that high market share is always related to superior profitability. Following this assumption, BCG advice has usually been to expand product lines and sales territories in order to develop experience curve economies (see Chapter 7), which would result in lower unit costs and presumably higher profits. We now know that enhanced profitability is *sometimes* related to higher market share, but this relationship is certainly not *always* the case. Market share can be "bought," such as when companies invest in a business at a rate higher than makes economic sense for long periods of time. Additionally, efforts to support larger market shares, such as building additional manufacturing capacity to achieve scale efficiency – especially if pursued by competitors who are also aware of the BCG matrix – may result in industry overcapacity, leading to poor asset utilization, higher unit costs, and lower profitability. The domestic automobile manufacturing industry in the first decade of the 2000s is a dramatic, striking example of the economic dilemma that occurs when a number of competitors build more capacity than they can productively use. Overcapacity, combined with stiff competition from foreign-owned manufacturers, left each of Detroit's "Big 3" struggling for their very survival.

Restructuring

The waves of conglomeration and acquisitions seen in the United States and global economies over the last few decades have ordinarily been followed by periods of restructuring. As in baseball, amusement parks, and life, "what goes up often comes down." Corporations that have diversified too much or too broadly through acquisitions often find they have difficulty managing the resulting complexity and experience performance declines. Such corporations then engage in restructuring, through which they seek to improve performance by divesting undesirable businesses.

Typically, restructuring efforts will involve what is known as downscoping.[39] Through downscoping a corporation reduces its level of diversification and strategically refocuses on core businesses where the synergies of scope, economizing, and leverage are more evident and more easily realized. In 2007, for example, VeriSign announced that it would sell off ten of its fifteen business units. The financial community on Wall Street had criticized the company for poor financial performance due to over-acquiring into fields unrelated to its core internet name registry and e-commerce security businesses. Analysts had seen little synergy among its wide array of technology businesses, beat down the company's share price, and forced the resignation of the CEO who had acquired all these businesses between 2004 and 2006. William Roper Jr., the new CEO, indicated that "with so many divergent businesses and teams fighting for resources, the company had lacked a coherent focus."[40] Pruning out these less-related divisions allowed the company to focus.

Downscoping can also involve selling a part of a company in order to achieve better strategic focus. Nike sold its Starter footwear and apparel brand, removing this line from its Nike-branded items. As part of a new strategic thrust, Nike had acquired Starter in 2004 in order to capture low-end shoe markets, and it sold Starter-branded products primarily at Walmart. Later recognizing that succeeding in the downmarket shoe segment required different strategic capabilities that were inconsistent with the Nike-branded business, the company made the decision to downscope.

Another cause for restructuring is when *some* of the parts are worth more than the whole (which is in contrast to the usual synergistic argument that the *sum* of the parts are worth more than the whole). In 1994 Ralston Purina spun off its breakfast cereals business into a new company named RalCorp. Management of the new company could pay attention strictly to the cereal business and not be distracted by the much larger pet food business, which was Ralston Purina's core focus. Consequently, the RalCorp cereal business performed much better, and the new company's stock price rose from $15 per share to $23 per share in a little over a year.[41] Ralston Purina shareholders who received shares of RalCorp would never have seen this kind of rise with the cereal business buried inside a pet food company.

Similarly, in 2007 General Electric's CEO Jeffrey Immelt discovered that financial markets placed a significantly higher value on the Saudi Basic Industries plastics business it sold than had GE's own management. Realizing $11.6 billion in the sale of the business (which was 45 percent higher than internal valuations placed on the business), it has sparked consideration as to whether GE is too diversified and holds other assets that are also undervalued.[42]

Often restructuring efforts such as those described here are undertaken not only to improve the corporation's performance, but also to smooth relations with large activist shareholders. Activist shareholders – such as T. Boone Pickens, Rupert Murdoch, and Carl Icahn – accumulate large blocks of corporate stock and then command management and board attention when they point out the need to do something about underperforming businesses or divisions. If existing management does not improve the performance of the underperforming business or sell it off, the possibility exists that the large shareholders will persuade other shareholders to join them in an attempt to take over control of the company. This happened in 2013 with Carl Icahn, who challenged Michael Dell's restructuring plans for the PC company.

Deciding What and How to Unload

The idea of gaining more strategic focus through restructuring begs the question of what businesses to divest. Referring back to the BCG Growth Share Matrix (Figure 10.18), we could simply sell off the "dogs." However, as we described in that earlier section, this tool provides insight only on the market share characteristics of businesses and not on their strategic importance. So management needs to develop another set of criteria to help guide decision making on divestitures.

Divestiture, of course, is simply the reverse of acquisition. This simple insight suggests that management can use many of the same decision criteria for divesting that guide their thinking about acquiring:

- Is the industry still attractive?
- Is there a strategic rationale for holding onto a particular business?
- Are there scope, economizing, and leverage synergies that are possible with other businesses in the corporate portfolio?

- Do opportunities still exist to grow the business?
- Will the invested capital that the business requires enhance the corporate ROE?
- Is the value of the business greater as part of the corporate family, as an independent business enterprise, or as part of some other corporation's portfolio of businesses?

If the answer to any of these questions is "No," then the business under scrutiny is a candidate for divestiture.

There are generally three ways to divest a company (Figure 10.19). As HP is doing in 2016 with its enterprise hardware and systems division HPE, the corporation can spin off the business into a new independent company. Corporate shareholders receive shares in the newly formed enterprise, and a new board of directors is created. Spin-offs will generally favor corporate shareholders when the new company has a strong competitive position in its industry and the industry environment is attractive.

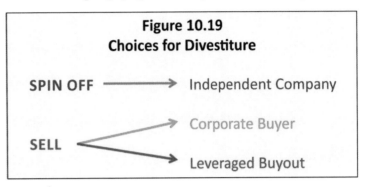

Figure 10.19
Choices for Divestiture

SPIN OFF ⟶ Independent Company

SELL ⟶ Corporate Buyer
SELL ⟶ Leveraged Buyout

The other two ways of divesting are by selling a business, either to another corporate buyer or through a leveraged buyout. Most typically, another corporation will be the buyer for a business that is being sold, and that corporation will entertain the same set of acquisition criteria that we discussed earlier (Figure 10.11). During 2007 Kraft Foods decided to downscope by selling off its Post Cereals business, which would allow Kraft to focus its management attention and resources on faster growing brands. The buyer for Post Cereals was RalCorp, earlier spun out of Ralston Purina; the acquisition would increase RalCorp's sales by 50 percent and create a larger, more credible player in the cereal business.

Leveraged buyouts occur when the management of a company uses debt financing to buy the company from its corporate parent, and then continues to run the company. LBOs occur when management of the business sees greater potential in the business than does the corporate parent, or when the corporate parent is unable or unwilling to provide corporate financial resources that would be necessary to take advantage of the potential that exists. Extremely popular in the United States in the 1980s, LBOs surged in Europe in 2007–08, fed by well-functioning capital markets abroad and the rising purchasing power of the euro. Yet the success of LBOs depends on interest rates, since the "leverage" in the phrase indicates that the companies are purchased using large amounts of debt. High interest rates tend to depress LBO activity and make consummated transactions very risky. The success of LBOs also depends critically on both cutting costs and accelerating revenue growth (Figure 10.16), since interest payments on the debt create onerous conditions for management if the business does not improve.

CHAPTER SUMMARY

Whereas business strategy concerns itself with management of a single business, corporate strategy involves the management of sets of businesses. Corporate strategists must make decisions about which industries to enter and exit, how to combine businesses that are strategically related, how to establish investment priorities among a portfolio of businesses, how to achieve synergies among related businesses, and whether to acquire or divest businesses. These are important decision domains because the economic landscape of the United States has been dominated by diversified corporations for nearly fifty years.

Corporations diversify beyond a single business for a variety of reasons. They seek to grow, to develop market power, to enter new markets more rapidly, and to spread risk—all in an effort to enhance corporate financial performance.

Diversification is either related or unrelated. Unrelated diversification depends on financial market imperfections, in which case corporate financial expertise presents an advantage over market-based transactions. Related diversification depends on similarities in industry and value chain conditions between the corporation and its intended acquisition. Synergies that take advantage of these similarities are of three types: scope, economizing, and leverage. Leverage is the most challenging to achieve, but also the most rewarding if achieved. The parenting advantage matrix can help assess the degree of fit between headquarter capabilities and the needs of the business being considered for acquisition.

Successful acquisitions hinge on the following factors:

- Selecting attractive industries

- Being guided by a well-articulated strategic rationale

- Conducting due diligence, examining in very specific terms where synergies can be captured

- Not paying a huge premium to acquire a company

- Post-acquisition steps that enhance the integration of the companies

Due diligence and a well-articulated plan to capture synergies will help corporations avoid the loss of focus and the difficulty in accelerating growth that often occurs after the acquisition is completed. Refusing to pay outrageous premiums reduces the urgency to cut costs that management often feels is necessary, and instead leads to concentration on creating scope and leverage synergies that accelerate revenue growth.

Corporate strategists also make divestiture decisions in efforts to restructure the corporate portfolio. Downscoping involves divesting a business in order to focus more carefully on the strategically related businesses at the core or the corporation. Divestiture may also unlock economic potential of businesses that might fare better under different ownership.

Portfolio management techniques can help corporate managers decide which business divisions to invest in, which to milk, and which may be ripe for divestiture. The GE Business Development Matrix and the BCG Growth Share matrix are tools that have been popular for decades, although each has limitations.

Learning Objectives Review

1. *Compare and contrast corporate strategy decisions and business strategy decisions.*

- Business strategy ideas and frameworks – e.g. value chain, resource based analysis, low cost leadership or differentiation strategy – are appropriate to use when a company operates largely in in only one line of business.

- Corporate strategy decisions encompass a wider array of issues:
  - Which industries to enter and exit.
  - Defining a strategic business unit (SBU).
  - Establishing SBU investment priorities.
  - Effecting resource and management transfers among SBUs.
  - Structuring the corporation.

2. *Appraise historical acquisition performance and the explanations behind it.*

- Research provides evidence that acquisitions on average produce low positive returns, but that there is wide variance in performance results. Many companies destroy shareholder value through their acquisition efforts.

- Acquisitions are more successful when they involve:
  - entering attractive industries
  - a well-thought out strategic rationale that guides which companies to consider acquiring
  - when strong due diligence is performed in the courtship phase of negotiations.

- Acquisitions are difficult to pull off because:
  - they usually depend on capturing synergies in culture and the softer parts of the value chain.
  - acquirers pay premium prices to buy companies.
  - there is a loss of focus on the core business, and accelerating growth is difficult.
  - post-acquisition efforts are not well-organized.

3. *Create a map explaining why companies diversify.*

- Growth
- Market power
- Market entry
- Spreading risk

4. *Explain the two primary types of diversification: related and unrelated diversification.*

- Related diversification means that there is some dimension of similarity between the corporation and the company it seeks to acquire.

- Variations in the similarities of the industry and value chain determine whether the style of related diversification is horizontal, vertical, or cross-sector.

- Unrelated diversification occurs when a corporation enters a new business in a different industry and does not expect to achieve any value chain synergies through the combination.

5. *Using the types of diversification methods available, support an argument for a conglomerate to utilize each one.*

- A supermarket chain decides to expand the territory in which it operates by acquiring another supermarket chain in a different part of the country. This horizontal acquisition is designed to increase scale and result in cost savings throughout the company's primary value chain.

- The same company acquires a manufacturer of private label food products. This vertical acquisition enables the supermarket to gain control over the supply and costs of products it then sells in its stores.

- The supermarket chain itself is then acquired by a holding company, which also owns other businesses such as insurance services and veterinary clinics. The holding company provides an infusion of cash to the supermarket so it can upgrade its back end technology to become more competitive in the industry.

6. *Apply tools for managing a diversified conglomerate effectively.*

- The GE Business Development Matrix provides a method for evaluating which SBUs to invest in further and which to consider divesting. SBUs with strong market shares in attractive industries deserve further management attention and investment.

- The BCG Growth Share Matrix is a popular tool with four easy-to-understand dimensions based on industry growth rate and relative market share of the SBU. The usual advice is to invest in the Stars, milk the Cash Cows, and get rid of the Dogs.

- There are some important caveats for each of these matrices, since neither fundamentally considers possible strategic resource sharing across SBUS, and each presumes that high market share is associated with strong financial performance.

Key Terms

Agency – Where an individual (such as a corporate officer) acts on behalf of someone else (such as a shareholder).

Business strategy – The types of decisions made and direction created for a single business.

CLO Collateralized Loan Obligation – Large pool of bank loans bundled together by financial services firms and sold off to investors in slices, with the goal to spread default risk "an inch deep and a mile wide."

Conglomerates – A corporation that owns a large number of businesses that are different sizes and operate in different industry sectors.

Corporate strategy – The types of decisions made and direction created for a corporation that operates multiple lines of business.

Cross-sector diversification – Acquisition of a company in a different industry, but which employs a similar value chain.

Dominant business – A company in which 70–95 percent of revenue comes from a single business.

Downscoping – When a corporation reduces its level of diversification and strategically refocuses on core businesses where the synergies of scope, economizing, and leverage are more evident and more easily realized.

Economizing – Cost savings accomplished by operating combined companies more efficiently.

Holding company – Corporation that owns the majority of voting shares of other companies, but that allows the other companies to operate as independent entities.

Horizontal diversification – Acquisition of a company that operates in the same industry using the same value chain.

Junk bond – High-yield debt that is rated below investment grade at the time of purchase. These bonds have a higher risk of default, but typically pay higher yields than better quality bonds in order to make them attractive to investors. Typically issued by businesses that are unable to secure investment grade financing.

Leveraged buyout (LBO) – A process where a company is bought primarily using debt. Typically engineered by management of the company, or by private equity firms.

Management fit – When a corporation can take synergistic advantage of administrative and support activities of the value chain in making an acquisition.

Market fit – When a corporation can take synergistic advantage of relationships with suppliers and/or customers in making an acquisition.

Operational fit – When a corporation is able to combine similar primary value chain activities.

Private equity firm – Private (nonpublic) corporations or partnerships that use their financial resources to engineer buyouts and acquisitions of other companies.

Related diversification – A merger or acquisition where there is some similarity of industry and/or value chain between the corporation and the company it seeks to acquire.

Resources leverage – The benefits that develop through the extension and application of corporate resources to a newly acquired company.

Scope – Ability to broaden a product line or a customer base achieved through an acquisition.

SPAC Special Purpose Acquisition Company – Empty-shell firms that promise to buy businesses with the proceeds of their initial public stock offerings.

Spin-off – Divestiture in which a corporation creates a new company out of one of its businesses. The new company has its own shares of stock and shareholders, and its own board of directors. Typically, shareholders of the corporation will receive newly issued shares out of the spin-off company at its organization.

Strategic business unit (SBU) – The organization of a set of businesses that share identical or very similar strategies or strategic challenges.

Systematic risk – Risk associated with macro-economic forces.

Takeover – A process where a large group of shareholders vote in new members to the board of directors, with the result that the new board can make changes in the company's management.

Unrelated diversification – When a corporation enters a new business in a different industry from that in which it currently operates and does not expect to achieve any value chain synergies through the combination.

Unsystematic risk – Risk associated with a particular business.

Vertical diversification – Acquisition of another company upstream (supplier) or downstream (buyer) in the value chain of the same industry in which the corporation operates.

Short Answer Review Questions

1. Why do companies choose to diversify?

2. What are the critical questions that each company should ask itself before embarking on a course of diversification?

3. How do diversified companies decide which business areas to divest?

4. What issues would you discuss if you were approached about an opportunity to buy a related company?

5. How about an unrelated company?

6. What can management do to improve the odds of success in an acquisition?

7. What information does the BCG Growth Share Matrix provide?

8. How would you use the GE Business Development Matrix?

9. What considerations should a business make prior to divesting a business entity?

10. Discuss the different types of diversification.

Group Exercises

1. Take a look at the Wall Street Journal for the past week. What merger or acquisition has just been announced? Based on your analysis, how successful will this M&A be? What would you recommend they do in the short term?

2. General Electric has announced that they will be divesting businesses over the next few years. Take a look at the companies that they have divested in the past year. How have those businesses performed since leaving the GE fold?

3. One of the more significant functions in a company that is an active acquirer is the analysis of which companies to acquire. Pick a company that actively acquires other companies (e.g., 3M, Intel, Microsoft, GE) and develop a short list of potential target companies for them to approach. How much would you pay for such an acquisition? Why? Where are the opportunities for the acquiring firm?

References

[1] Brat, I. 2007. Turning managers into takeover artists. Wall Street Journal. April 6: A1.

[2] Smith, E. and Orden, E. 2012. Mickey, Darth Vader to join forces. Wall Street Journal, October 31. B1; Leonard, D. 2013, The inside story of how Disney bought Lucasfilm – and its plans for Star Wars, Bloomberg, March 7, www.bloomberg.com/news.

[3] Ovide, S., Lublin, J. S, & Mattioli, D. 2014. Hewlett-Packard set to break up 75-year-old company, Wall Street Journal, October 6, B1; Bort, J. 2015. The HP breakup will happen for real in November, Business Insider, March 19, 1; Anders, G. 2015. After a costly breakup, HP Inc. is ready to have some fun, Forbes, October 14.

[4] Nissan, E., and J. Caveny. 2005. Aggregate concentration in corporate America: The case of the Fortune 500. International Journal of Applied Economics 21(1): 132; Yellen, J. L. 1998. Testimony before Senate Judiciary Committee. June 16. Washington, DC. http://clinton2.nara.gov/WH/EOP/CEA/html/19980616.html.

[5] Definition from Webster's New Collegiate Dictionary. 1974. Springfield, MA: G. and C. Merriam Company.

[6] Using 2-digit industry codes under the Standard Industrial Classification (SIC) system.

[7] Tobias, A. 1976. March 3, 1998: The day they couldn't fill the Fortune 500. New York. December 20: 63. Three weeks after this article was published, New York was acquired by media mogul Rupert Murdoch.

[8] Rumelt, R. P. 1982. Diversification strategy and profitability. Strategic Management Journal 3: 359. The data presented in this article are from a sample of the largest firms listed annually by Fortune. In addition, the author's own research on the Fortune 500 provides update data into 2014.

[9] Markides, C. 1992. The economics of de-diversifying firms. British Journal of Management 3: 91.

[10] Burrough, B., and J. Helyar. 1990. Barbarians at the gate. New York: HarperCollins.

[11] Ng, S., and H. Sender. 2007. Behind buyout surge, a debt market booms. Wall Street Journal. June 26: A1. More than half the loans behind buyouts in 2006 were resold to investors as CLOs. The Economist, 2014, From dodo to phoenix, January 11, 58. The Economist, 2014, The new GE: Google everywhere, January 18, 63.

[12] Burton, T. M. 2006. Boston Scientific faces pivotal test after victory in fight for Guidant. Wall Street Journal. January 26: A1; Hensley, S. 2006. How Boston Scientific beat J&J. Wall Street Journal. January 26: C1; Rappaport, M. 2006. After Guidant deal, a case of seller's remorse. Wall Street Journal. October 23: C3; Tully, S. 2006. The [second] worst deal ever. Fortune. October 16: 102.

[13] Vara, V. 2007. Oracle results reflect successful acquisitions. Wall Street Journal. March 21: B3; Vara, V. 2007. Oracle's profit shows acquisition spree is paying off. Wall Street Journal. June 27: A3.

[14] Marris, R. 1999. Managerial capitalism in retrospect. New York: Palgrave Macmillan.

[15] Golden, B., and H. Ma. 2003. Mutual forbearance: The role of intrafirm integration and rewards. Academy of Management Review. 28(3): 479.

[16] Technically, the covariance between the company's returns and market returns would be reduced, leading to a lower beta.

[17] Foust, D. 2008. Looks like a beer brawl. BusinessWeek. July 28: 52–53.

[18] Clark, D. 2007. Western Digital purchase shows disk-drive dilemma. Wall Street Journal. June 29: B5.

[19] Procter & Gamble 2005 Annual Report.

[20] Craig, S., and D. K. Berman. 2007. TD Ameritrade in merger talks with E*Trade. Wall Street Journal. August 22: A1.

[21] Campbell, A., Goold, M. & M. Alexander. 1995. Corporate strategy: The quest for parenting advantage. Harvard Business Review, March-April, 120.

[22] Returns or the investors in the corporation can be measured in several ways, including the following in increasing order of rigor: 1) Did the share price of the corporation rise after the acquisition? 2) Did the corporation's return exceed a comparable benchmark in which they might otherwise have invested, for example an S&P 500 index? 3) Are corporate shareholders better off after the acquisition than they would have been if it had not occurred? This third test is difficult to assess in practice because there is no way to know what might have happened if a deal was not struck.

[23] Sirower, M. 1997. The synergy trap. New York: Free Press.

[24] Bruner, R. 2004. Where M&A pays and where it strays: A survey of the research. Journal of Applied Corporate Finance 16(4): 63–76.

[25] M. Sirower, op. cit.

[26] Palich, L. E., L. B. Cardinal, and C. C. Miller. 2000. Curvilinearity in the diversification-performance linkage: An examination of over three decades of research. Strategic Management Journal 21(2): 155–174.

[27] Fowler, G. A. 2009. eBay retreats in web retailing. Wall Street Journal, March 12. A1. Mitchell, D. 2011. Skype's long history of owners and also-rans: At an end? Fortune, May 11.

[28] Quoted in Mueller, D. C., and M. L. Sirower. 2003. The causes of mergers: Tests based on the gains to acquiring firms' shareholder and the size of premia. Managerial and Decision Economics 24(5): 373–391.

[29] Knowledge@Wharton. 2001. The right way—and some wrong ways—to make an acquisition. General Electric Corporation. http://www.ge-cef.com.

[30] Karnitschnig, M. 2006. After years of pushing synergy, Time Warner Inc. says enough. Wall Street Journal. June 2: A1.

[31] Towers Perrin. 2004. HR rises to challenge: Unlocking the value of M&A. http://www.towersperrin.com/tp/getwebcachedoc?webc=HRS/USA/2004/200412/TPTrack_MA.pd

[32] Mueller and Sirower, op. cit.

[33] William Blair & Company. 2004. Presentation to the board of directors of Johnson Outdoors. http://www.secinfo.com/d14D5a.166Mw.d.htm. Monga, V. 2013, M&A mystery: Why are takeover price plummeting, Wall Street Journal, November 26, B1.

[34] Singer, J., and A. Ewing. 2007. Tom Tom escalates bid war for digital mapper. Wall Street Journal. November 8: B4.

[35] Lovallo, D. P., and O. Sibony. 2006. Distortions and deceptions in strategic decisions. McKinsey Quarterly. February: 19–29.

[36] Bekier, M. M., A. J. Bogardus, and T. Oldham. 2001. Why mergers fail. McKinsey Quarterly 4: 6–10. Based on a sample of more than 160 acquisitions made during 1995–1996.

[37] Ibid.

[38] Kamp, J. 2008. Boston Scientific net falls hurt by charges, stent sales. Wall Street Journal. July 22: B6; Twitchell, E. 2008. Recovering from heart failure. Smart Money. April: 29; Barron's, 2012. Boston Scientific's Guidant acquisition led to fines, settlements and penalties. March 2; Farrell, M. 2015. Can Boston Scientific finally move on from its Guidant mistake? Wall Street Journal, February 18, B1.

[39] Hoskisson, R. E., and M. A. Hitt. 1994. Downscoping: How to tame the diversified firm. New York: Oxford University Press.

[40] White, B. 2007. VeriSign to slim down, sharpen its focus. Wall Street Journal. November 14: A12.

[41] Forest, S. A., G. Burns, and G. DeGeorge. 1995. The whirlwind of breaking up companies. BusinessWeek. August 14: 44.

[42] Cox, R., and D. Cass. 2007. Placing value on GE's Parts. Wall Street Journal. May 22: C14.

Section D: Strategy Implementation

In this final section of this book we will examine one of the most crucial and yet most difficult areas of the field – managing strategy implementation. In the previous three sections we have laid out the foundations of the field and its importance to organizations, developed a means for analyzing the competitive landscape and developing a strategy, and discussed a number of contextual situations for putting strategy into practice. This included a review of life cycles and organizational stages of development, international strategy, competitive dynamics, and corporate strategy for running multi-divisional companies. The chapters in Section D tackle areas that must be addressed for the organization to successfully implement all of this great effort that you have now formulated. A well-developed strategy that is right for the market and provides a competitive advantage is of little value if it is not executed effectively. In fact, evidence suggests that many failures to achieve competitive advantage are the result of good strategy that is just implemented poorly.

In Chapter 11 we will examine how to structure the organization for success. There is a reason that organizations exist – to accomplish what cannot be accomplished by a single individual. When we have more than one person doing the work, questions immediately arise about who does what, who reports to whom, who makes decisions, who should be getting certain kinds of information, how people elsewhere in the company are to know what is going on, how we know that others are doing what they are supposed to do, and more. Structuring the organization in response to these types of questions is not only crucial to our strategy, it is the means by which we accomplish it. Simply stated, the more effectively the company is organized, the more likely it is that we will meet our expectations for superior performance. As we have done in previous chapters, we will look at this first from a broad level and then dig down deeper into the details. We incorporate some of the best thinking in consulting practices and solid academic research to provide you with a practical understanding and some very useful techniques.

In Chapter 12, we examine the methods for translating the ideas and practices from the preceding chapters into methods through which important strategic activities can be monitored and therefore managed. Developing effective monitoring techniques and measures of performance which can be used by everyone in the organization enables a company to become a learning organization that can respond to changes in the competitive environment and thus outperform its competitors.

Chapter 11: Strategy and Structure

LEARNING OBJECTIVES

1. Explain how strategy is implemented through a company's structure.

2. Construct a map of the types, characteristics, and outcomes of the most common means of structuring organizations.

3. Analyze and explain the type of mechanisms used to coordinate the activities in an organization.

4. Evaluate whether the structure of an organization aligns effectively with its strategy.

Electrolux[1]

Founded in the early 1900s with a single vacuum cleaner, Sweden-headquartered Electrolux today sells more than 60 million products in 150 countries. The company produces and sells appliances such as vacuums, dishwashers, washing machines, and various cookers under such well-known brand names as Electrolux, Eureka, Frigidaire, and Westinghouse. It employs 58,000 people. As can be seen by the following organization chart, in 2016 Electrolux structures the company around the type of products they offer (Major Appliances, Small Appliances, and Professional Products). Furthermore, since their Major Appliances group is the main business, that operation has evolved into four divisions, which are organized by geographic location (Europe and Middle East, Asia Pacific, Latin America, North America). The Latin American division was newly-created in 2012-13 reflecting its growing business in that part of the world.

Beyond the operating divisions, the company has created six head office staff functions under the executive. Three are administrative in nature – Finance, Legal, and Human Resources. A previously fourth executive department of "Communication and Branding" has recently been divided into three separate areas – Marketing, Technology, and Design.

There are many ways to structure a company such that the strategic priorities of the business are supported. In the company's 2016 annual report Electrolux states that they intend to create exceptional value by increasing the pace of innovation in product development, reducing complexity in manufacturing, and optimizing purchasing. These are accomplished through a formal structure called the "Innovation Triangle, whereby the close collaboration between design, R&D and marketing enables new products to reach the market at a faster pace and ensures that these products are preferred by more consumers."

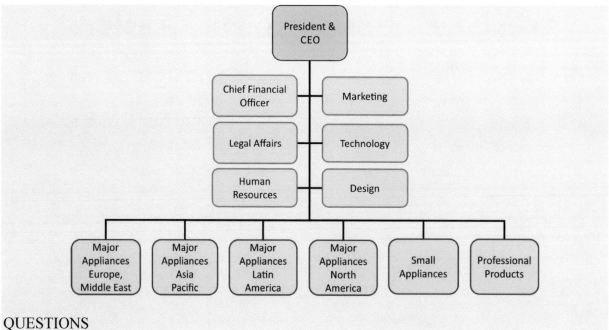

QUESTIONS

1. Why does the company mix geographic divisions with product group divisions?
2. What effects will it have to expand the corporate headquarters branding department into the three new areas?
3. Does their current structure provide them any competitive advantage?

ALIGNING STRATEGY AND STRUCTURE

We have spent a considerable portion of this text learning how to create the optimal strategy for an organization. This has included analyzing the competitive environment, developing the resource base and value chain foundation for competitive business level advantage, and examining what types of businesses we should be involved with. We now turn our attention to implementing our strategy. The topic of structuring an organization is as old as the study of business itself. At its most fundamental level we are faced with an absolutely pivotal question: How do we orchestrate ten people, or ten thousand people, in an organization such that they are all moving in the same direction and that this direction is consistent with the company's strategy? Coordinating the activities of even a few people is challenging. You have probably experienced this on a small scale in team projects in school. However, it gets increasingly difficult as three impactful factors work against the organization. Those are: 1) the number of people working in the company increases; 2) employees are increasingly dispersed geographically; and 3) the business becomes more multidimensional with different products, services, and operating divisions.

Let's actually consider the case of an orchestra as an example of coordination. Each musician has a specific instrument and role to play in providing the audience with the very finest performance. The conductor provides the overall coordination, but cannot and does not play the individual instruments. Instead, each musician is expected to be an expert in playing a particular instrument, reading the music, reacting to the musicians around them, as well as being able to follow the direction of the conductor. The structure employed by a typical orchestra is referred to as a simple structure, as there is only one person to whom all the players "report." Yet there is effective coordination because all the musicians can see the conductor and simultaneously hear all the notes being played by the other musicians. By convention the coordinating mechanism for everyone has been distilled down to a universally understood metric – the musical note on a sheet of paper. What if the conductor was not present, or what would happen if the sheet music was lost by the airline when the orchestra traveled to its next concert site? What if the musicians were dispersed between rooms throughout the building, or were in different buildings and live-streamed their audio in as a broadcast that was then somehow mixed on stage in real time? What if the musical composition called for improvisational playing by certain instruments located in different places? How would you structure an orchestra to accommodate these innovative and eclectic approaches, and what kinds of systems would you need to coordinate geographically distant – and sometimes innovative and improvisational – efforts? These are the kinds of challenges that strategic leaders in every organization face.

UNDERSTANDING THE STRUCTURING IMPERATIVE

Deciding how to structure an organization is perhaps one of the most visible components in effectively implementing a strategy developed for a company. It is much more than deciding who works for whom, although that is a crucial element. Structuring the company formalizes who is responsible and accountable for decision making, how important information is channeled within the company (and where channels may impede information flows), how budgets and resources are provided, how procedures and controls will be implemented, and how the company believes its organization of activities can enable it to outcompete its competition. Together, these characteristics of structure describe how the company's strategy will be implemented.

The answers to these questions become increasingly complicated as organizations expand and grow. Alfred Chandler, who first described "strategy" as it relates to companies (we mentioned him in Chapter 1), observed this complexity in his study of four large U.S. companies.[2] Expansion through new products and new markets pushes organizations to grow larger, with the usual result that individuals with strategic responsibility tend to become increasingly removed from day-to-day operations. At the same time field units and people on the operating level tend to become increasingly specialized and therefore separated from other operational units. This creates a new set of problems: coordinating disparate departments and workgroups, communication between the groups, creating the understanding of a common set of goals across the entire organization, and ensuring that day-to-day operations are actually consistent with overall direction. This is one reason we have emphasized value chain coordination throughout this book.

The complexity that Chandler observed in aligning strategy and structure can be described by three structural facets of organizations: specialization, centralization, and formalization (Figure 11.1). Specialization occurs as companies grow, hire more people for functional areas such as marketing or production, and need to create greater efficiency or effectiveness of activities within these areas. When departmental specialization occurs, then issues of centralization come up – whether important decisions are made centrally by

**Figure 11.1
Structural Facets of Organizations**

Specialization
Centralization
Formalization

the head office or by others in the newly formed departments and divisions. Additionally, the more companies rely upon departments and divisions, the more formalization of rules and procedures usually takes the place of informal "seat of the pants" methods for making sure everyone is on the same page.

The conflicts created by specialization, centralization, and formalization are a major issue in both large and small organizations. When growth necessitates the formation of departments or groups, removed as they are from easily interacting with each other, it is unfortunately not uncommon for individual departments to come to believe that their own activities are the raison d'être of the company and to create their functional-level plans and goals in isolation from the rest of the organization. The accounting department's goal in a manufacturing company is not to create a world-class public accounting operation (however laudable that effort may seem); it is to accurately track and report on the internal activities of the company. Human Resources' goal in the same company is not to demand every employee's participation in semiannual benefit program information sessions; it is to effectively support the hiring, retention, and growth needs of the employees of the company. Sometimes this may require progressive new systems, sometimes not. Engineering's goal is not to create a world-class R&D lab with every cutting-edge device available; it is more likely to be the development of functional products that meet the needs of the company's consumers in the most desirable manner possible. Fragmentation such as this requires attention from management.

So with the advent of departments, divisions, and groups that specialize come both centralization and formalization. Strategic decision making becomes the province of management in the central office to ensure that there is one consistent approach throughout the company, and formal rules and procedures are instituted to make sure all the departments are coordinated with that approach. This sounds good in the sense that the complexities created by growth and expansion may be resolved. Yet the combination of these three facets makes it exceedingly difficult for companies to excel at the two strategic imperatives we have discussed throughout this book: value creation and opportunity recognition. Value creation occurs more easily when various parts of the value chain are more aligned, where their respective activities are well-integrated with the rest of the company. When separate departments are created and formal rules and procedures are instituted, this type of synthesis is more difficult to achieve. Similarly, opportunity recognition capabilities often depend on cross-functional efforts, which also become more difficult with separation, centralization, and formalization. When centralization and formalization are prevalent, the kind of experimentation and flexibility that is important in trying to take advantage of new opportunities is reduced.

Communication, Coordination, Control

These ideas lead us to the fundamental issues that lie at the heart of the alignment of organizational structure with strategy – which are communication, coordination, and control. As we earlier described in Chapter 5 on the Value Chain, a business is nothing more than an organized system of activities that creates value. The structure of the business should be aligned with the strategy in order to support the system of activities. So the

> **Figure 11.2**
> **Three C's of Systems**
>
> **C**ommunication
>
> **C**oordination
>
> **C**ontrol

core structure question is how it can be used to facilitate communication, coordination, and control.

By working to facilitate and improve these three Cs (Figure 11.2), the structure can enhance the system of value-creating activities.

Communication. Effective communication is central to any organization structure. Think about how often it seems that one part of a company has absolutely no idea what another part is doing. Have you ever called an airline to get a fare quote, and then called back again later only to receive a completely different quote? How often have you heard someone say "I didn't get the email"? What's the effect on a company whose differentiation strategy involves new product introductions, if the manufacturing plant manager is only interested in producing the existing products 24/7? What do you suppose employees think and talk about when a new CEO or vice president is hired? How long does it take someone in management to approve a budget request for a new development project, or to OK a special price reduction for an important customer who has been enticed by an aggressive competitor? These questions point out that communication must be effective up, down, and across the organization.

The business strategy lays out the logic of how value will be created (e.g., through low cost or a specific type of differentiation). This logic must be communicated throughout the company, so that employees understand it and their efforts can be coordinated. This is accomplished partly through ongoing efforts to embed the vision and mission (Chapter 3), but this is also accomplished through everyday communications and information that flow through the formal channels created by structure. It is difficult to strike the right balance between overwhelming employees with information: ensuring that they are kept well-informed, keeping them in tune with their areas of specialization, and reinforcing the overall direction that the senior management wants to go. Because communication systems are even more sophisticated than they have ever been and we are in an instantaneous information-rich society (memos, reports, e-mails, text messages, blogs, Twitter, video conferencing, Facebook, etc.), the danger of overwhelming individuals such that they ignore important information is much greater now than in the past.

Organizational communication is more than just downloads from senior management up high. In addition, the organization needs a system through which employees can pass critical information back up to senior decision makers, as well as across departmental boundaries. Upward flows of information can provide better perspective on the sources of core competence within the company, and how activities supporting the strategic logic can be improved upon. Lateral flows between departments or divisions, without having to go up a chain of command and back down again, can improve organizational response to competitive threats and new opportunities.

Coordination. Central to effective strategy is the coordination of activities across the value chain, which achieves consistency of effort throughout the organization. We know quickly when organizations have failed to coordinate their activities. The Boeing 787 launch was repeatedly delayed because the company failed to properly coordinate suppliers with the assembly operation, aggressive sales efforts, and the rigorous testing schedule required by the Federal Aviation Administration. Disaster relief for Hurricane Katrina victims was delayed so long because of inept coordination by the U.S. government's FEMA office that George W. Bush's presidential standing and effectiveness was significantly damaged. We have also witnessed examples of coordination excellence. Recall from the last chapter, for example, how Cisco Systems makes sure that an acquired company's products are listed on the Cisco's price list the day the deal closes so that its salespeople can immediately start selling them.

Control. Creating, maintaining, and managing an effective system of control allows senior management to implement the vision, mission, and strategy as designed. While we will discuss control in significantly more detail in Chapter 12, it is important to note here that structure performs one of the key control functions for strategy implementation. Structure not only provides the means to share certain information in an organized fashion. It also provides the opportunity to identify areas where there are problems, so that corrective action can be taken.

We can see that the issues of coordination, communication, and control are highly related to the decision about how to structure a company. We want to be careful that any structure we put into place provides formal recognition to the kinds of coordination and communication that are most important for the company's strategy to be successful, and to the ways in which control must be exercised. We will see in a few minutes that there are a variety of ways to be thinking about this.

Prior to moving to structure, however, we think that managers should develop a better understanding of what type of activities need to be structured and how they might be coordinated to most effectively support strategy. There are three critical aspects to examine:

1. What are the key organizational components of the company's business?

2. What coordinating mechanisms are available for use with these components?

3. What types of structures might work best for a company's chosen strategy?

KEY ORGANIZATIONAL COMPONENTS

Every part of a business must be coordinated to some extent; however, as much as some people may not want to admit it, there are parts of an organization that are simply more critical to the overall success of a company than others. Understanding the elements of an organization is a crucial first step to structuring. Excluding senior management, in general the parts of any organization may be divided into three components: 1) Core, 2) Techno Structure, and 3) Staff Support.[3] We want to emphasize the universal nature of this part of structuring. Regardless of the type of organization (public or private, profit or nonprofit, domestic or international), the size of the organization or its age, these three parts of the company are central to any structuring or restructuring effort (Figure 11.3).

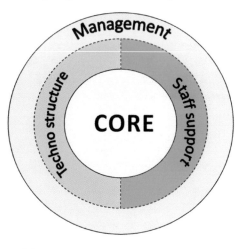

Figure 11.3
Key Organizational Components

The Core

What part of the business is most crucial to its success with consumers? What area or areas of the company are therefore at the strategic core of the business? The core group or groups are those most central to generating the competitive advantage that the firm enjoys. Developed in our earlier chapters on value chain and resource based analyses, the areas of the business that are most responsible for the competitive advantage of the business are the areas that should receive the lion's share of management time, attention, resources, and focus. The activities in other parts of the business, while still important, are then viewed as providing support to and servicing the strategic center of the company in the core.

An example can illustrate what we mean by the core. If we were running an upscale restaurant known for its top-rated cuisine, it would be relatively obvious that the chefs would be the core of the business. This is the primary reason that customers come to eat there. If we mistakenly placed primary focus on the wait staff, then critical decisions might be made in support of the wait function – such as about when the food would be delivered and how it would be presented – that may compromise the efforts of the chefs. This may seem a bit obvious, but it is also a central aspect of competitive advantage.

Some years back Bennigan's restaurant introduced a lunch deal where your meal was free if it took longer than 10 minutes to deliver it to your table from the time of order. In this case, we hope it is obvious that customers were not coming to the restaurant because of its superior quality food; they were coming because of the service promise. Whether consciously or not, Bennigan's placed its wait staff at the strategic core; it was the table-serving process that provided the competitive advantage for the firm. It was the wait staff that had to deliver on the customer promise, both by getting the order to the kitchen and by getting it back to the table. Everything the company did was oriented around the facilitation of rapid order-taking, rapid food preparation, and rapid table-waiting. An acceptable quality of food was assumed to be an orthodox feature, and simply had to meet normal expectations.

Don't assume from this discussion that other areas of the company are not important – they are. They are just not the core reason that customers give the company their business. Reflecting the previous discussion on ordinary resources (Chapter 6) and competitive parity (Chapter 7), all other functions within the organization must be done and done well, but the company need not perform those tasks any better than at parity for its industry. That is, all the other jobs – like the chefs, hostess, table cleaners, dishwashers at Bennigan's – need to be done for the business to function. If any one of these areas fails to perform, then the business can be damaged such that the core cannot deliver on the customer promise. Secondly, they must do their jobs well. That is, they must perform in a manner that does not negatively impact the customer or the core. The dishes must be clean, the food must be satisfactory, and the host or hostess must be pleasant and efficient. But although these noncore activities must be done well, there is no strategic benefit in outperforming the rest of the industry. Since resource allocation is a fundamental decision to make in strategic management, companies must decide where to concentrate their limited resources. Tying together your knowledge of resource-based advantages and the value chain, you can see that any resources applied toward improving an orthodox part of the organization such that it exceeds the industry norm is wasteful and will not lead to superior competitive and financial performance. Similarly, resources not applied to the core are missed opportunities for developing and sustaining competitive advantage.

Noncore Functions

Noncore functions of the business can be classified into two quite distinct areas: techno structure and staff support. The techno structure consists of those groups whose activities provide advice and policy input to the core, while the staff support consists of all other groups (other than the core and the techno structure) who carry out work of the organization. In the earlier example of Bennigan's, where the wait staff was core, the chefs would be categorized as techno structure, since their advice and food preparation policies must still be considered crucial to the operation. For instance, the wait staff may want the burgers put on the plate immediately to meet the 10-minute deadline, but the chefs are required to cook the burgers to a standard temperature prior to serving the customers. The chefs have bounds to their policy making and advice giving. They are bounded by the scope of their operational responsibility; however, their positions put them in a higher "orthodox" category as they have influence on the core.

In contrast, we might categorize the table cleaning crews as staff support because they neither provide advice nor establish any policy that might affect the core. Their job is to effectively and efficiently bus and clean so that the tables can be reset for the next customer. Staff are not in a position to advise the core on how plates should be arranged to make their work easier or set a policy for how long it is before they clean a newly abandoned table.

The relationship between the core and either techno structure or staff support is not a two-way street. While input and advice from the techno structure and staff often establish boundaries within which core activities occur, the demands of the strategic core exert a profound influence that completely shapes both the techno structure and the staff support. In the case of a fast-service restaurant like Bennigan's, the core premise of the business may demand that the kinds of meals prepared by the kitchen are only those that can be prepared quickly. Food ingredients and other supplies may be purchased and delivered in premeasured quantities that facilitate rapid preparation. Fast service also requires a certain amount of support staffing at the lunch hour to ensure that tables are turned around and dirty dishes are washed quickly in order to be ready for the next customers.

This division of activities allows all types of organizations to function more smoothly as everyone more explicitly understands their relative contributions in a system that is focused on a specific method and process of value creation. Effectively developed and communicated, it allows for far fewer disputes that must be resolved by senior management. The operation is more focused on the sustainable competitive advantage of the organization.

Commercial Airlines in the United States, Part 1

Think about the groups that make up a typical commercial airline: pilots, flight attendants, gate agents, maintenance workers, baggage handlers, reservation specialists, not to mention the back office operations of accounting, payroll, IT, policies and procedures, purchasing, human resources, training, etc.

What group do you think group is at a typical airline?

What difference might it make if we defined different parts of an airline as the core? Remembering that the core group is primarily responsible for the areas of the company in which value creation occurs, what if we define the pilots as core? Do you know who your pilots are on a commercial flight? Would it make a difference if you could actually understand the announcement at the beginning of a flight regarding who your pilots are for the flight? Do you choose your airline or flight based upon the pilots for that flight? Would you pay more for a particular pilot team?

The pilots of commercial airlines in the United States are typically in the techno structure of the company. In many ways they personify what it means to be techno structure. They must do their job and do it well; furthermore, they provide advice to the core and help set policies. Pilots can and do decide whether the planes are flight worthy and make hundreds of decisions about how the flight proceeds; however, they make no decisions about the type of plane flown, what gate it will fly out of, what the scheduled departure time is, and what city the flight is headed toward. If you make no decisions about which airline to fly based upon who the pilots are, if suppliers provide resources regardless of who the pilots are, and if management plans flights assuming that they will be able to staff the plane, then the pilots cannot be core to the function of the airline.

QUESTIONS

1. A similar analysis could be applied to every group that was mentioned at the beginning of this vignette. So, what group is responsible for the core in commercial aviation?
2. Does it vary by airline?
3. Why do you fly a particular airline?

COORDINATING MECHANISMS

Once the organization has been divided into the groups of activities that comprise the core, techno structure, and staff support, then decisions must be made about how to coordinate the work of each group. In other words, the first step is to distinguish among critical value adding activities and the next is to decide the most appropriate means of coordinating their activities. There are five relatively common methods for coordinating work, and within virtually every organization we typically find all five in use. Using a combination of coordinating mechanisms gives the organization an opportunity for the best fit, but it may interfere with one of the ultimate goals of good structure design – that of reducing layers of hierarchy to their bare minimum. Fewer layers in a company generally translates into swifter and more accurate transmission of important information both to and from the apex of the business (CEO and top management team), and thus generally leads to higher quality strategic decisions.

Five effective coordinating mechanisms were outlined by Henry Mintzberg some years ago, and they have since been developed and modified over the years to fit the practice of business.[4] They are:

1. Mutual Adjustment
2. Standardization of Work Processes
3. Standardization of Work Skills
4. Standardization of Work Output
5. Direct Supervision

These five mechanisms really represent a continuum from self-direction of the activities of a group to total direction of all aspects of the activities by a single authority within the company (Figure 11.4). Some units are best coordinated by mutual adjustment, while others by work skills. Even within smaller departments, there is sometimes the need to use multiple techniques, as for instance when we have technicians and administrative staff within the same unit.

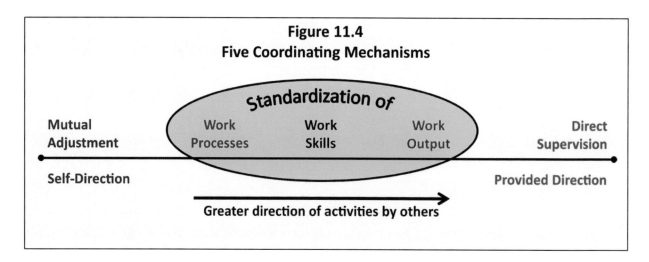

Figure 11.4
Five Coordinating Mechanisms

Standardization of

Mutual
Adjustment

Work
Processes

Work
Skills

Work
Output

Direct
Supervision

Self-Direction

Provided Direction

Greater direction of activities by others

We should point out here that coordinating is not the same as evaluating. Virtually everyone within an organization will have their performance measured and evaluated in some form, and that form usually takes place as some type of output measure. Here we are talking about how to structure and coordinate efforts, not how to measure the effectiveness of those efforts. None of these coordination methods negate the need for effective performance measures that are tied to the overall performance of the organization.

Mutual Adjustment

The best possible coordination method is mutual adjustment because virtually 100 percent of each employee's effort is devoted to moving the company forward. Under mutual adjustment, each person knows everything that is happening in the organization and simply adjusts her or his work patterns for the conditions at hand. When used within departments these groups require a relatively small number of folks, because they all understand the goals and work collaboratively to accomplish those goals.

In a small organization where everyone works within the same room, this type of coordination method can be easily used. Take the packing operation at a typical UPS retail store. Various packages arrive during the day and must all be boxed correctly and prepared for shipping. A group of employees, each of whom is trained in all aspects of the operation, can mutually adjust to one another in order to handle the flow and get what needs to be completed prior to the shipping time. Many entrepreneurial firms use mutual adjustment as their operations begin and every member of the team is expected to do what needs to be done without a "supervisor" to coordinate their movements.

In class, we often use the example from the movie Apollo 13 where a dozen or so engineers were brought into a room to design a carbon dioxide filter out of spare equipment that happened to be in the capsule. There were no supervisors in the room and each person knew that if they didn't get it designed within the next three hours that the astronauts would die in space. They did not have the time to establish a supervisor and have that person coordinate their efforts, nor were they sure

NASA mission control during Apollo 13, 1970

360

exactly how they would even design the unit. These are perfect conditions for using mutual adjustment as a coordination method.

With mutual adjustment, almost no time is wasted in meetings, preparing status reports, or duplicating others' efforts. This coordination method provides the highest percentage of time devoted to work effort available. It seems to work best in the following situations:

1. Where there is a small group of people,

2. Where the tasks are either very well-known such that everyone is cross-trained on all the jobs, or

3. Where the means to success is uncertain and a strong degree of innovation will be required.

Standardization of Work Processes

As the number of employees grows and mutual adjustment is no longer viable as a means of coordination, companies will look to one of three standardization criteria. Using these criteria, literally hundreds or more employees can be effectively managed without reverting all the way to direct supervision. Using standardization of work processes requires a deep understanding of the work involved such that a supervisor can manage the processes rather than the employees. To a certain extent and without impugning the potential that any one employee may have upon an organization, employees are seen as somewhat interchangeable when this coordination method is employed. In an automobile manufacturing plant, engineers have meticulously designed the system so that a frame enters at one end of the plant and a car emerges from the other end. Each process along the way has been designed to be done in a particular order and in a particular way for the overall product to be a success. Supervisors walk the line looking to see if the processes are being followed and trying to improve the processes along the way. The actual employee is evaluated on his or her ability to perform the process as designed.

At virtually every organization of any size, there are parts of the business that can be designed into a process. For those areas, the process itself becomes the focus and the employees are measured against the process. Using this system, the number of employees reporting to a single supervisor can be dramatically increased. Each supervisor can manage larger numbers when the processes are well designed and implemented. Furthermore, this coordination method works for both manufacturing as well as service companies. In most banking operations tellers are expected to follow a very strict protocol for taking deposits and distributing money. Tellers are measured upon their ability to follow the procedures that have been set, and deviation from those procedures – even when no loss occurs – is negative performance.

Blackjack dealers at a casino are another prime example of standardized work processes. Each dealer is required to shuffle in a particular manner (and that method is actually different at different casinos), pay the winners in a particular order, make change with a standard process, and so on. Dealers are evaluated on their adherence to process.

Standardization of Work Skills

Once again, as we move away from our ability to use mutual adjustment and without yet resorting to direct supervision, there are groups within the company where it is simply inappropriate to attempt a routinized process operation. Where possible (and when standardization of work processes is not practical), we can use standardization of work skills as a basis for coordination. This is especially so for groups whose skill sets are well understood in the wider market. Traditionally, this was only done for groups of employees who held valid, well-recognized, national, or international certifications. These might include, for example, CPA (Certified Public Accountant), CMA (Certified Management Accountant), CFA (Certified Financial Analyst), JD (Law, usually with bar exam passage as an additional criteria), MD (Medicine, usually with Board certification), PE (Professional Engineer), Plumber and Electrician (requiring completion of both the exam and journeyman work time), CLU (Chartered Life Underwriter in the insurance industry), among others. Through their organizations and professional associations these groups tend to self-police and typically require ongoing maintenance of education in their professions. These groups of people can be managed in large numbers with the expectation that they have certain fundamental skills.

In practice, this coordination technique has been extended by a number of companies to include detailed training and certification within their organizations. For example, General Electric has been on a campaign since 1995 to certify employees in Six Sigma (an efficiency and management control system) and indeed that certification has become an important criterion for promotion within the company. The level, complexity, and importance to the organization elevated GE's training efforts well above the typical quick-hit training session so prevalent at most organizations.

The value of standardized skills includes a common nomenclature among the members, a common base knowledge set, and an understanding of the responsibilities expected by someone who holds that particular designation. Using this method of coordination, the manager hires only those individuals with the requisite qualifications and leans on the expectations of the certifying organization to provide a baseline for performance. Performance beyond that baseline is what is measured and evaluated within individual company human resources systems.

Standardization of Work Output

For those groups where standardization of work processes or work skills is not applicable, and yet when the group is still too large or scattered to utilize mutual adjustment, one means of coordination exists prior to reverting to direct supervision. Those employees can be coordinated via standardization of work output. There are many groups where the other coordinating techniques are simply not appropriate. How do you coordinate the activities of a sales staff? What makes a great salesperson? There is no standard set of skills, nor any outside society that can certify a salesperson as having achieved any level of sophistication within their profession. Furthermore,

there is simply no one best way to sell something. Companies that have tried to apply a rigorous methodology to a sales call or sales cycle have found themselves marginalized by other players in the market who discover more effective methods.

Working with a large automobile dealer operation on the east coast, we were struck by the complete dissimilarity of the three top salespeople. One was an outgoing, loud, bear of a person who knew very little about cars but loved to talk with people. He turned many people off, but his manner was really loved by others and his sales numbers were the best in the entire multistate operation. The next person (with sales just barely behind the first person) was a quiet, professional woman who would wait and watch potential car buyers looking for clues as to their real needs. The third salesperson (again with numbers barely below the first two) was a bit of a slob who simply knew everything there was to know about cars. He was a classic "car guy." There were no processes that were the same between them and no common background on which to hang a skill set. They each worked in their own manner toward the objective of selling as many cars as possible in a month for as much money as could be made on each sale. The company used a variety of output measures to measure their performance. Output measures that are well crafted allow a manager the ability to track a majority of performance using a spreadsheet or computer.

Care in developing the output measures such that they include the balanced nature of the business is critical. Furthermore, when employees are coordinated through output measures, it is important to have a well-established ethical code of conduct. In this way the company explicitly jettisons any kind of "ends justify the means" mentality. We will further discuss the establishment of important output measures in Chapter 12 on control and performance.

Direct Supervision

Although mutual adjustment may be the preferred means of coordination, some situations move organizations toward direct supervision as a coordination method. The first situation is when the group working together simply gets too big or too scattered for them to be able to effectively mutually adjust. Classic symptoms of this problem situation include products that are miss-shipped, a production line misses its targets, a backlog is created in the operation, or employees voice complaints regularly about lack of coordination. Poor coordination among employees demands that a more directed coordination approach be adopted.

Direct supervision is necessary when standardization of work processes, skills, and outputs are also ineffective in achieving the kind of coordination that is necessary. Direct supervision is called for when an organization's strategic approach requires that work 1) be done in a certain way, 2) be done by employees with specific skills sets, and 3) result in a highly predictable and consistent output. Under these circumstances none of the standardization methods, by themselves, would be sufficient for what the company needs. For example, Johnson & Johnson's Alza pharmaceutical division manufactures implantable and transdermal drug delivery systems for personal use. Manufacturing these devices must follow FDA-approved methods, must be done by certified technicians, and absolutely must result in a consistently safe and effective final product since patients' lives are at risk. This type of business leaves no room for flexibility, and must be subject to direct supervision.

Another situation that may call for direct supervision is when cost control is of paramount competitive concern. The risk in striving to become the low-cost leader is that a company may not actually develop the leadership position; a lower cost rival may outcompete it through aggressive pricing. In the early 2000s Dell achieved the low-cost leadership position in the personal computer business through a variety of value chain activities, including direct supervision of its PC assembly operations. In these types of assembly operations where strict control is required in order to drive down unit costs, information flows and coordination typically run through a supervisor or manager who is able to see the whole picture at once and immediately take any corrective actions needed in case a problem comes up.

Unfortunately, ego is occasionally the driving force behind direct supervision. There are managers and owners who feel they must be "in charge." They demand to be the focal point through which all work flows, and then they become the control point in the operation. Although managing for strategic excellence often requires a delicate balancing effort between coordination and control, these types of managers opt for control as their means of coordination.

These examples illustrate that there are very appropriate times and places for using this traditional method of coordination. In general, this is a default pattern of coordination that should be used as a last resort. In other words, it should be used only if one of the other four coordination methods is ineffective.

Strategy and Coordination

The previous discussion implies that a certain type of coordination is appropriate for a certain type of strategic approach. A deep understanding of the core areas of a company and what means might work best for their coordination provides good insight into an organizational structure that can enhance and support strategy. There are many ways to define the core by combining up groups of employees and then deciding on a set of coordination methods. Remember we stated earlier that a company uses a variety of different forms of coordination for the various groups it has identified. So there is simply no "perfect answer" to this process; it is at least as much art as it is science.

Figure 11.5
Coordination and Generic Strategies

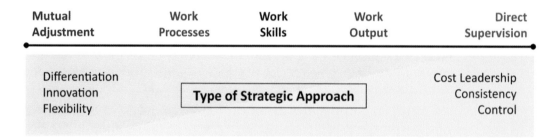

Yet we can offer some general guidelines for the mixture of strategy and coordination (Figure 11.5). Where a company's strategy depends increasingly on cost leadership, consistency of output, or significant control over aspects of the product or service production process, the method of coordination will tend toward the direct supervision end of the spectrum. The company values a strict, disciplined approach to the conduct of its business and discourages employees from acting independently. This is an organization that is more machine-like, with all the parts working tightly in synch. In contrast, where innovation and flexibility are desirable – often hallmarks of a company seeking a differentiation approach – coordination will tend toward the mutual adjustment end of the spectrum. Here employees are increasingly able to investigate new information they receive and respond to new ideas, making decisions on their own for the benefit of the company.

Commercial Airlines in the United States, Part 2

Earlier we considered which groups might constitute the core of a commercial airline. What if senior management decided to make the pilots the core of a new airline? How might this be effectively implemented? If pilots were core, then the company might need to educate customers to make their ticket purchase decisions because of the pilots. Simply claiming that we had the best, most experienced pilots would probably not be sufficient. The strategy of the organization would need to be focused upon the pilots and we would need to structure it appropriately. We could design the web page to highlight the pilots that would be in charge of each flight: their flight experience, a rating provided by passenger feedback (regarding takeoff, landings, information provided in flight, etc.), their pictures on the web, etc. In other words, we would make the pilots not only more accountable to their customers, but more accessible to the customer decision making. If we were right to make them core, then the industry might have to scramble to catch up with an important new criteria of travel. As the industry tried to catch up, we could focus on pilot pay, benefits, scheduling, ego (from the heightened attention), and work conditions to attract the best pilots to our airline. Our company could gain a first-mover advantage by building the reputation as the airline that not only does everything that the other airlines are doing (the orthodox), but we put only the best in the front seats that should matter the most to you.

QUESTIONS

1. How might these pilots be managed and why?
2. Would you use an output-based system, a process system, or a skill-based system? Which would be most appropriate given their new role as the core of the airline?

TYPES OF ORGANIZATIONAL STRUCTURE

Having examined the individual parts of the company and determined which parts of the organization are core, which fit into techno structure, and which are more appropriately staff support, each area needs to be examined to determine the best means of coordinating its activities using the techniques outlined in the previous section. Combining like-oriented groups allows for a common coordination method to be used and improves the patterns of communication and the types of information that are important in managing the strategy of the company. However, we must now specifically examine exactly how we can apply our understanding of components and coordination to the development of an effective structure. It is one thing to be able to state with some clarity which groups are which and how you will coordinate their activity; it is quite another to develop that into a functioning hierarchical structure for the overall management of the company. That is the focus of this section.

While there are many variations on how to structure an organization, most evolve from five basic types. We will examine each of these by building on our understanding of the core and the appropriate methods for coordination. But we should also pay attention to the two strategic imperatives of value creation and opportunity recognition within organizations. The five structures we will discuss below are 1) Simple; 2) Functional; 3) Divisional or Multidivisional; 4) Matrix; and 5) Adhocracy (or what is more-popularly referred to as Holacracy).[5]

Simple Structure

The simple structure appears just as its name implies. In a simple structure all areas of the company report to a single person. It usually develops organically as an organization has grown larger, with many of its "legs" being created originally as individuals or small groups. Each group has now become larger, and the company has reached the stage where it requires more formal coordination. The pure form of the simple structure is referred to as a flat organization structure such as the one in Figure 11.6.

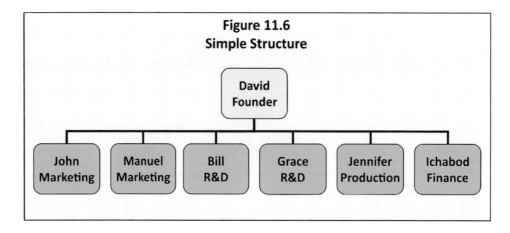

Figure 11.6
Simple Structure

A simple organizational structure provides most of its value in rapid response and leans heavily on the capability of the single head of the organization. The company's business is not really organized by functions, by products, or by geography; as Figure 11.6 illustrates, multiple individuals from the same functional area may report to the leader. There is little to filter information; coordination is straightforward, and involves strong person-to-person managerial abilities. While it requires the leader to be knowledgeable about a variety of functions, the structure is nonetheless easily understood. Since the "distance" is short between operating managers and the location of decision making at the leadership level, this structure allows for rapid opportunity recognition and quick changes to adapt to the market conditions. On the other hand, the company is limited by the capability of the person in charge as well as by the resource constraints of having to manage an increasing number of people and issues. Increasing complexity makes it more difficult to maximize each employee's contribution as the time the manager can spend with each employee is reduced. When a manager has six managers reporting to him or her, there are twenty-one different person-to-person relationships that exist within the group, and over 275,000 possible paths through which information could be communicated between group members!

A simple structure is usually best under one of four situations: 1) single product (or function) organization; 2) a new organization; 3) one trying to maintain an entrepreneurial orientation; and 4) a crisis organization.

The first situation where a simple structure works very effectively is a company that is a single product (or function) organization dealing in a relatively dynamic environment where reaction time is at a premium. Interestingly, this would include many organizations in the retail sector. A typical, locally owned restaurant has all of the employees reporting to a single owner regardless of their function. The ability to make a quick decision to please a customer or react to changing conditions is a hallmark of the simple structure. Value is created in these organizations by having almost instant access to a decision maker. It is said that in retail all profits are made in the moment. A simple structure allows the company to maximize this responsiveness.

A second situation is a new organization. New organizations start with one person or a small number of people and as new people are hired they report directly to the founders. There is no need to complicate the communication system with a structure that negatively impacts the ability of the founders to make quick decisions.

In the third situation a firm is trying to maintain an entrepreneurial orientation tied to the founder or leader of the organization. By flattening the organization, the company is able to rely on the entrepreneurial approach of the founder and his or her unique skills/insights. There are some individuals who possess an amazing capability in this regard, and a simple structure allows this person to use these talents to direct the actions of the organization.

A final situation is when an organization is confronting a crisis. At various times in the life of an organization a crisis may develop that demands swift attention and the focused efforts of everyone in the company. Just such a condition has been faced by companies like Dow Chemical (the Bhopal cyanide leak), Tylenol (the tampering and poisoning of their products), Coors (an investigation by CBS News' *60 Minutes* reporters), and others. A crisis is best handled with a swift response, few or no layers of hierarchy, an ability to quickly respond to the slightest change, and the ability to unilaterally clear communications that come from all points in the organization. The simple structure allows the company to quickly react and deal with a crisis, returning to their former structure after the crisis has passed.

Functional Structure

As organizations develop they generally find that particular functions of the company are becoming either quite large, quite important to the mission of the organization, and often scattered geographically. One means for bringing a measure of control to this situation is to form the organization into functions. This functional structure generally divides up the company based upon their functional areas of expertise such as procurement, accounting/finance, marketing, production, and IT. Often a functional structure will include grouping similar to those areas in the basic value chain diagram (Chapter 5). This can be advantageous when applying various coordination methods, since functional groups can generally have their work coordinated with similar methods. For example, managing the legal department with standardization of work skills is relatively easy. The company can require every employee to have a law degree, and if they wish, can extend the capability by having each attorney also pass the bar exam in that state. The non-lawyers in that area are most likely staff support and can be managed by standardization of work outputs or processes, depending upon the requirements of the organization. Functional structures are effective organizational forms under one of the following three situations: 1) growing business activity or volume; 2) public or governmental organization; 3) large, mass-production organization.

A growing volume of business usually parallels the need for an organization to develop specialization and greater efficiency. These can be accomplished through structure and coordination. Businesses tend to grow because they have developed a unique and inimitable method for creating value; often this method will rely upon sets of specialized functional activities, as well as coordination across functions. At some point the company realizes that they need to have a structure that supports the type of specialization that will lead to an improving strategic position, and management also realizes the need to exert greater control over related processes and procedures that are evolving. As it grows, a company also tends to add employees simply because of the higher volume of transactions and activity. The growth in size and the need to better manage specialization often leads companies to adopt a functional structure.

High-speed internet service provider EarthLink is a marvelous example of just this process of growth and organization. Started up by Sky Dayton in 1994, EarthLink experienced phenomenal growth in the mid-1990s after Netscape's Internet browser software was introduced and consumers became aware that this thing called the internet existed "out there" somewhere.[6] Dayton started off with a simple structure in his company – just himself and three other managers working together.

However, as subscriptions to the internet service skyrocketed, he learned that he needed to move from the chaos of the growing business to greater control afforded by a functional structure that included marketing, engineering, customer service, and finance.

Cheltenham Borough Homes is a not-for-profit management company that manages, maintains, and rents homes in the United Kingdom.[7] This organization developed a functional structure as illustrated in Figure 11.7. In this case the business was split almost directly along the value chain lines for a services organization. Notice that the right side of the chart under the Vice President for Resources consists of the support value chain functions (Finance, Information Systems, HR, and in this case Corporate Governance). The left side of the chart under the Vice President for Service Delivery consists of the primary value chain functions for this organization's value creation (Investment and Asset Management, Property Services, Safer Estates, Neighborhood Services, and Community Involvement). These functional areas are dramatically different in size and are not organized in this manner in order to balance the organization. Rather, this type of organization structure has a number of benefits including a focus upon the strategic approach of the organization. The structure formally elevates services as constituting the core, enabling greater attention on each of these services as well as the flow of important information and resources to support them.

Figure 11.7
Functional Structure of Cheltenham Borough Homes

A second situation in which a functional organization is particularly effective is the typical public service operation of governmental agencies. As control is more important than efficiency, these organizations tend to be molded along lines of specialization. In fact, specialization is prized within a fairly bureaucratic framework. The negative to the functional structure becomes increasingly clear in this scenario, that of communication. Communication between functions then requires endless meetings and groups specifically designed to achieve coordination between the activities of different groups.

The third situation where a functional structure makes strategic sense is in a large mass production organization. Developed for efficiency in producing a product, these organizations tend to form functional specialties in order to tightly manage available skills and resources. As some mass production organizations stagnate in sales growth, they refocus their efforts on efficiency and cost reduction. As long as the company is in a single line of business or a dominant business, then the functional structure provides the company a better opportunity to take advantage of efficiencies and provides the organization some level of sophistication in the development of its expertise within functional areas.

A classic type of functional organization chart is that of the integrated circuit developer Seiko NPC Corporation (Figure 11.8).[8] Each segment is comprised of functional specialists who report to a department head. Each of these department heads reports directly to the president.

Divisional Structure (Multidivisional)
The divisional structure, also known as the multidivisional structure or "M-form," is traditionally used as companies develop and/or acquire completely separate lines of business. That is, as the company diversifies it establishes different operating divisions within the overall company. While it is common for most organizations to initially accommodate diversification through an existing functional structure, as diversification continues and greater complexity arises, most corporations move to some form of a multidivisional structure.[9]

M-Form corporations can be structured in a variety of ways. Figure 11.9 shows one that is organized by lines of business. Quite unlike the functional structure, each operating division is a fully functioning entity in which every area of its value chain is contained within. In turn, the divisions then often structure their individual operations using a functional structure. In most diversified corporations there are also sets of staff functions at the headquarters level; however those are usually responsible for setting overarching company policies and initiatives, for performing financial and accounting analysis for the divisions, and for managing the flow of resources and information between the divisions. The headquarters office of the corporation usually exercises control over divisions using financial performance output measures and comparing each division to the others for resource allocation purposes. In some cases under this structure the headquarters operation might also exercise considerable strategic control. This is apt to occur when a company is pursuing a global strategy, meaning value is created upstream in manufacturing and supply networks (Chapter 8), yet the divisional structure is organized geographically by region so that sales and marketing can be handled locally. Here the regional division offices are clearly important, yet the primary strategic value creation occurs through arrangement and activities orchestrated through the corporate office.

Figure 11.9
Multidivisonal Structure (M-form)

Value creation is found within the capabilities of the structure itself. The individual divisions or companies need capital in order to pursue their markets. This capital is often more easily and more cheaply obtained through the internal corporate headquarters than through external financial markets. Furthermore, as an individual profit center, each entity is constantly seeking to maximize its own division's returns. The entire division is focused on the returns for that division and is in a better position to seek out new opportunities and pursue them with vigor. Communication between the divisions is usually problematic as each is directing its efforts within its division as opposed to pursuing goals of other divisions. An attempted solution to this problem is the creation of strategic business units (SBUs) that combine groups of related divisions or companies under a single office which reports to the corporate headquarters. If interactions between divisions is crucial for success and yet the organization wishes to have each division be nimble within its own market, then an SBU structure improves that coordination with another layer of management. Figure 11.9 illustrates this concept with Strategic Business Unit X.

Other versions of the M-form are possible. The major divisions of Boeing are organized by a combination of product line and customer segment (Figure 11.10). Other companies organize by geographic region. Coca-Cola is largely organized by geographic regions (Africa, Eurasia, European Union, Latin America, North America, Pacific), and within each region are complete capabilities for production of soft drinks, marketing, and sales that can respond adeptly to the region's unique culture and conditions.

Hitachi is a classic multidivisional organization that is almost 100 years old, displaying a mix of functional divisions and SBUs.[10] Developed to effectively handle a broad array of businesses, this M-form structure (Figure 11.11) has functioned well for this company for many years.

> **Figure 11.10**
> **Boeing M-Form Divisions**
>
> Customer
>   Commercial Aircraft
>   Integrated Defense Systems
>   Phantom Works (aerospace)
>
> Product Line
>   Boeing Capital (financial services)
>   Shared Services (design services)

Figure 11.11
Hitachi Organization Structure, 2013

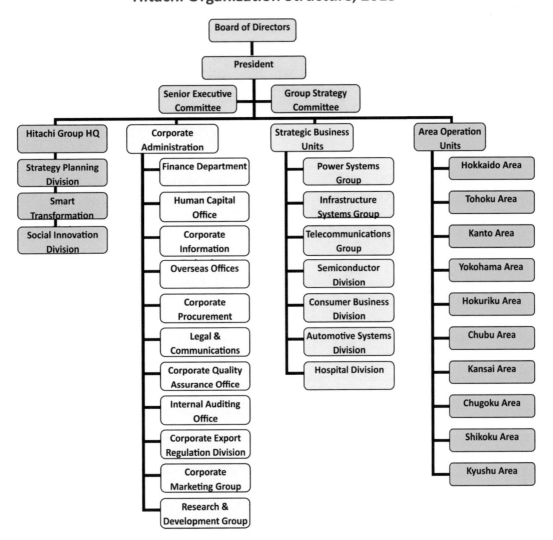

It is important to remind ourselves, however, that "structure follows strategy." So when strategy must change, due to new competitive threats or market-wide changes, then structure may need to change. Structures should evolve with the times. In the case of Hitachi, though quite large and complex, its structure continues to evolve.

Matrix Structure

Dissatisfied with the ineffectiveness of the functional structure for multiple lines of business, but frustrated with decentralizations and the dispersion of control apparent in the multidivisional structure, the matrix structure was developed to attempt to address both efficiency and effectiveness across diverse businesses. This form is no longer quite as fashionable as it once was, and yet there are a number of organizations that continue to use it despite its numerous negatives. The matrix organization has a dual structure such that each employee in the organization has both a functional home as well as a divisional home. The functional home is their area of specialization and their divisional home is the focus of their work flow.

As organizations grow they tend to add functional specialists to handle the increasing volume, complexity, and information needs of the company. In the normal ebb and flow of business, some lines of business end up with functional groups that are too large for the volume of business in that division, while others have significant needs that can't be quickly met through hiring. Furthermore, existing employees develop a knowledge base about a company that helps make them effective more quickly than brand new employees hired from the outside. All of this combines to suggest the matrix organization, in which functional specialists could be reassigned to lines of business where the work was most needed.

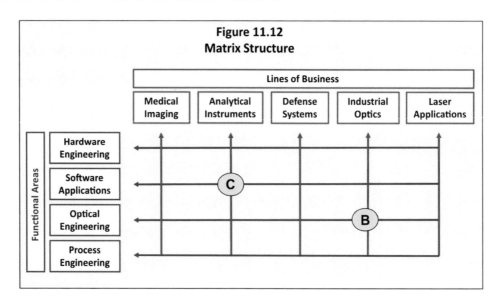

Perkin Elmer was founded in the 1930s based on the interests of its two founders in astronomy and precision optics. Over the years its core optics research led the company into a variety of different lines of businesses, including optical systems for defense applications, lasers, and medical imaging technologies. The company's most famous endeavor was grinding and polishing the primary mirror that is central to the operation of the Hubble telescope. In the 1970s the new leadership of the company implemented a matrix structure, such as that illustrated in Figure 11.12, in order to better manage the portfolio of scientific applications across multiple lines of science-based businesses. In this organization employee B had a reporting relationship to both the manager of Industrial Optics and the head of Optical Engineering, while employee C was responsible to the Analytical Instruments line of business manager as well as the scientist who oversaw software application development.

In theory, the matrix structure would provide a diversified organization with the best of both the functional and divisional forms. But resource allocations and trying to establish annual budgets between lines of business and functions can become a highly politicized process, with negotiated solutions developed through ongoing meetings involving heads of divisions, functions, and senior management. More importantly, the reality of the structure is that reporting to two bosses (their functional head and their line of business head) proves problematic for most people. The conflict that inevitably arises in devoting time to the requirements of each boss reduces an individual's effectiveness. The difficulties in planning and budgeting, together with the natural tendency of employees to please a particular boss or to choose between the wishes of competing bosses, have led to a drastic reduction in the number of companies that use this type of organization structure.

Adhocracy (or Holacracy)

A very special set of organizational circumstances might lead to the creation (or perhaps recognition) of an organizational form with little formal structure that can take advantage of mutual adjustment as a coordinating mechanism. In business organizations that can utilize an adhocracy there are no true supervisors and everyone in these groups function with a single goal in mind (Figure 11.13).

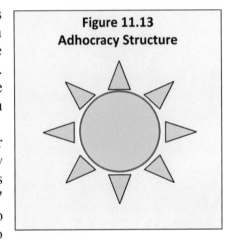

Figure 11.13
Adhocracy Structure

You may have read about the online shoe retailer Zappos, which started up in 1999 but was acquired in 2009 by Amazon, which pretty much lets it operate as an autonomous subsidiary. Zappos CEO Tony Hsieh instituted a "Holacracy" structure in 2015, writing a 15,000-word "constitution" to explain to employees how it would work. There are no managers, no one has titles, and there are no teams. Employees self-organize into "circles" and collectively decide on roles, responsibilities, and business issues. Zappos is a large organization, with 1500 employees, a complicated online retail business model, and has been migrating its software onto Amazon's cloud platform. There has been much criticism of this non-traditional model, although Hsieh believes it will work effectively after 3-5 years.[11]

The adhocracy or holacracy form is most effective and yields the best effect under the following conditions: 1) when the means to task accomplishment is unknown, but the goal is well understood; 2) when the duration of the task is well defined; and 3) when creativity is the most prized outcome.

Means of task accomplishment is unknown. When the methods and outcomes are well known and repeatable, then a process can be developed and taught. In situations that are new to the organization, however, an adhocracy may provide the best structural solution. In this structure there are no supervisors and every person on the team mutually adjusts off of each other in order to attain the goal. Many small project teams are formed to find a way to accomplish some new need of the organization. For instance, a well-known shirt manufacturing company had to decide whether to accept a new order that would double the number of shirts produced during a year, but did not want to sharply increase its staff because they were uncertain as to whether they would get a reorder the following year. The company put together a small team to devise a means of accommodating the order while maintaining staffing at the current levels and not unduly taxing the current staff. They determined that a bonus system dramatically rewarding those employees who could increase their output and were willing to work extra hours in the short term would be a viable solution. The pay system solution, the communication approach to the employees, its impact on the organization, and the schedule for the implementation plan were put together over a two-day period by a team of six people.

Special effects teams that work on a movie are another classic example. The script may call for visuals that have never been previously filmed, and it is the special effects team's charge to bring those visuals to life for the director. These folks are not effectively managed in the same manner as a programmer; instead they are told what the outcome should look like and given free rein to find a means to create the scene for filming.

Duration of task is well defined. A second situation when an adhocracy structure works well is when the amount of time available prior to a decision is very well defined and usually very short. When groups have a very short time frame to accomplish their task, then an adhocracy structure helps to facilitate the best returns for the company. There is an old saying that the task will expand to the time allotted for its completion. Task success can be greatly enhanced with the use of an adhocracy.

Creativity is most prized. When the creativity of the solution is the most important outcome need of a group effort, then the use of an adhocracy structure is most likely to yield the best result. Not relying on any one individual to filter the solutions and having everyone understand the need for a speedy solution lends itself to an approach that eschews bureaucracy.

The most critical components of an adhocracy structure are to: 1) maintain the equality in the group; 2) ensure that all have a complete understanding of the goal and any relevant time frames; 3) isolate the group from the rest of the company to minimize interference from normal structural effects; and 4) free the group from any formal reporting criteria. All four of these criteria can be easily seen in the making of a large budget movie (providing the director and producer are sufficiently accommodating). The Apollo 13 example from earlier in this chapter is an excellent example of an adhocracy in practice.

CHAPTER SUMMARY

In this chapter we looked at the very sensitive and yet critical process of structuring an organization. First we learned that organizational structure must inevitably change as organizations expand, grow, and mature. "Structure follows strategy." Structure can either help or hinder the implementation of strategy, so strategic managers must carefully think through the type of structure that helps the most.

Three facets of structure include specialization, centralization, and formalization. These may present inherent conflicts in effective strategy implementation, and may be especially troublesome for companies seeking to address the two strategic imperatives of opportunity recognition and value creation. The issues presented to managers considering the right type of structure include effective communication, coordination, and control.

We looked at the three areas of any company's organization:

1. The Core: the group or groups primarily responsible for the company's sustainable competitive advantage.

2. The Techno Structure: those groups that are advice givers and policy makers.

3. The Staff Support: those groups that are not core, and not advice givers or policy makers for the organization. These groups are responsible for the orthodox of the company.

Fundamentally these are the three parts of any company that must be organized by senior management to focus the organization on those areas where they have the potential to develop a sustainable competitive advantage.

Once these areas have been identified, then each group of employees needs to be organized by the most appropriate and effective means of coordinating work. The five coordinating methods, which generally exist in every organization, are:

1. Mutual Adjustment

2. Direct Supervision

3. Standardizing Processes

4. Standardizing Skills

5. Standardizing Outputs

We then examined the different types of structures that organizations can use, and how the coordinating mechanisms aligned with those overarching structures. The five most prevalent types of organizational structure are:

1. Simple

2. Functional

3. Divisional or Multidivisional

4. Matrix

5. Adhocracy

Learning Objectives Review

1. *Explain how strategy is implemented through a company's structure.*

- The structure of a company should follow, reflect, and support its strategy.

- Strategies oriented toward cost leadership, consistency and control are more likely to implement structures that call for more direct supervision of employees. Strategies oriented toward differentiation, innovation and flexibility are more likely to implement structures that call for greater mutual adjustment by employees. These represent the ends of a continuum of mechanisms to coordinate work.

375

- Management should define the key organizational components of the core, techno structure, and staff support. Together with mechanisms to coordinate work, identifying these parts will help influence how groups are formed and the resulting structure.

2. Construct a map of the types, characteristics, and outcomes of the most common means of structuring organizations.

- Simple structure. Provides the advantage of rapid response. Depends on responsive leader at the helm.

- Functional structure. Sound structure for growing or geographically-dispersed organizations, and where a particular function is at the core. Cross-functional coordination becomes an issue.

- Multidivisional structure (M-form). Often used by conglomerates and diversified corporations, and can result in strategic business units of related operating divisions. Needs to evolve as markets and competition evolve.

- Matrix structure. A solution for functional deployment across a multi-line business, without the decentralization associated with M-form structure. Very complicated to manage, and subject to internal politics.

- Adhocracy. Little formal structure, appropriate for projects requiring creativity, short time frames to complete a project, or where the means to complete the project is unknown at the outset.

3. Analyze and explain the type of mechanisms used to coordinate the activities in an organization.

- Mutual adjustment. Each individual understand strategy and adjusts their behavior accordingly.

- Standardization of work process. A mechanism to manage large numbers of employees based on the extent to which they follow prescribed process guidelines for doing work.

- Standardization of work skills. Relying upon sets of externally developed professional criteria to ensure that appropriate quality work will be performed.

- Standardization of work output. Mechanism that focuses exclusively on the output of work, because the work process cannot be standardized nor are there validated external criteria available to assess employees.

- Direct supervision. Every employee is directly supervised by another individual.

4. Evaluate whether the structure of an organization aligns effectively with its strategy.

- The structure should include groups formed to emphasize the strategic core.

- The structure should include groups formed to provide consistency between the business level strategy and the work coordinating mechanism most appropriate for that type of strategy.

- The structure should facilitate the two strategic imperatives of value creation and opportunity recognition.

Key Terms

Adhocracy – A method of organizing usually used within portions of the organization rather than the entire organization. There are no supervisors, and everyone in the group operates organically toward a well-defined goal.

Core – The group or groups that are directly responsible for competitive advantages that the firm enjoys.

Direct supervision – Every person is coordinated via a direct supervisor and coordination flows into and from that supervisor.

Divisional (multidivisional, M-form) structure – A method of organizing a company that divides up the organization into discrete companies (or semiautonomous divisions) within the overall company. These divisions generally contain all the elements of an independent company.

Functional structure – A method of organizing a company that divides up the company based upon their functional areas of expertise.

Matrix structure – A method of organizing a company that utilizes a dual structure such that everybody in the organization has both a functional home as well as a divisional home.

Mutual adjustment – A method of coordination where every individual knows everything that is happening in the organization and adjusts his or her work pattern for the conditions at hand.

Simple structure – A method of organizing a company in which all areas of the company report to a single person. The pure form of the simple structure is referred to as a flat organization.

Staff support – All other groups who are not core and not advice givers/policy makers.

Standardization of work output – A method of managing large numbers of employees based upon a well-developed set of output measures that in combination provides insight into the performance of the employee.

Standardization of work processes – A method of managing large numbers of employees based upon the processes that they perform.

Standardization of work skills – A method of managing large numbers of employees based upon their skill sets as established by some externally validated means.

Techno structure – Those groups who are advice givers and policy makers to the core.

Short Answer Review Questions

1. How does structure affect strategy?

2. What groups are core to a company?

377

3. List what groups might constitute the techno structure of a bank.

4. Under what conditions would mutual adjustment be the best system to apply to a particular group?

5. Provide several examples where standardization of work processes might work the best in an organization.

6. Why is direct supervision a structure of last resort?

7. Explain how output measures are used to direct employee efforts.

8. What type of coordination method might you suggest for the payroll group of a large insurance company?

9. Under what circumstances would you suggest that an organization consider a divisional or multidivisional structure?

10. How does a functional structure assist an organization that has grown from an entrepreneurial venture?

11. Faced with a crisis in your organization, what structure might you suggest the company employ? Why?

12. What must you keep in mind if you wish to utilize an adhocracy?

13. What would you suggest to a manager who wants to increase the effectiveness of the communication within the company?

Group Exercises

1. With the exception of new ventures, all businesses are operating under some type of established structure. Select three Fortune 500 companies and, using their Web pages, annual reports, and available public material, attempt to piece together their organizational design.

   a. What do you think of the design that is in place?

   b. Does the structure align with their mission/vision/strategy?

   c. Pick a particular area within the company that you believe needs a change. What would you change and why?

2. Select a local business that you are very familiar with as a customer.

   a. What group or groups constitutes their core? techo structure? staff?

   b. How are these aligned from your perspective?

   c. What do you believe is the company's sustainable competitive advantage?

   d. How does the structure align with your assessment in "c"?

3. Grocery stores are quite varied in their approach to the customer. Select three competitor grocery stores in your area.

a. What are the differences in their competitive approach?

b. Given your answer in "a," how would you structure each company?

c. Create a chart with the grocery stores across the top and the following categories down the side—Core, Techno Structure, Staff, primary organizational form as it exists, suggested organizational form. Evaluate each.

References

[1] 2013 Electrolux Annual Report; Sains, A., and S. Reed. 2006. Electrolux redesigns itself. BusinessWeek. November 27: 13–15; Sains, A., S. Reed, and M. Arndt. 2006. Electrolux cleans up. BusinessWeek. February 27: 42–43.

[2] Chandler, A. D. 1962. Strategy and Structure. Cambridge, MA: MIT Press.

[3] Adapted from Mintzberg, H. 1979. The structuring of organizations. Englewood, NJ: Prentice Hall.

[4] Ibid.

[5] Ibid.

[6] In telling the story of his start-up efforts, Sky Dayton discovered that there were no businesses anywhere in all of Southern California with the word "Internet" in their company names as late as 1993.

[7] www.cheltborohomes.org/

[8] www.npc.co.jp/en/general/chart.html

[9] Chandler, A. D. 1962. Strategy and structure. Cambridge, MA: MIT Press.

[10] www.hitachi.com/about/corporate/organization/index.html.

[11] Silverman, R. E. 2015, Going bossless backfires at Zappos, Wall Street Journal, May 21, A1; Kinni, T. 2015, The audacity of holacracy, Strategy+Business, August 19; Reingold, J. 2016, The Zappos experiment, Fortune, March 15.

Chapter 12: Strategy Implementation: Internal Control and Performance

> LEARNING OBJECTIVES
>
> 1. Translate strategy into functional area goals and activities using the keys to implementation control.
>
> 2. Develop effective metrics for the control and growth of the organization.
>
> 3. Describe the differences between the models used for implementing a strategic plan.
>
> 4. List and describe the core responsibilities of strategic leadership.

McDonald's[1]

McDonald's was a one-store business in San Bernardino, California, run by brothers Dick and Mac McDonald. In 1954 Ray Kroc convinced them to let him open several more restaurants based on their process-based business formula. The astounding success of the company is a testament to tenacity and a striving for perfection in a business that primarily sells hamburgers, sodas, and french fries.

During the subsequent sixty-two years, McDonald's has grown into a worldwide organization employing 420,000 in its corporate-owned operations and another 1.5 million at franchisees in more than 36,000 restaurants in 118 countries. The company was the first fast food chain to have a drive-thru window (1975), offer breakfast (1977), and create whole product categories such as the Happy Meal (1979) and the Chicken McNugget (1983).

The elimination of a corporate program for the evaluation of domestic stores, a focus on international expansion and a lack of focus on the nuts and bolts of the core business set off a terrible decline in competitive advantage in the mid to late 1990s. This was accelerated by a rapid growth in competitors, dramatic improvements in competitors' processes, a set of international crises, the parallel onset of interest in healthy eating, and the release of the film *Super Size Me*, which took direct aim at McDonald's as the purveyor of an unhealthy lifestyle.

In January 2003, McDonald's reported their first-ever quarterly loss of –$343 million. Same-store sales (a critical metric for retail store health), which had been stagnant for the past ten years fell for fourteen straight months through the first quarter of 2003. The company's rating amongst consumers ranked it last among seventy fast food chains measured that same year. McDonald's was in trouble.

Jim Cantalupo (newly re-minted as CEO in 2003) came out of retirement to fix the company, after having been with the company in various capacities for more than twenty-eight years. He developed an approach that was back to basics.

He focused on the McDonald's brand by systematically divesting businesses and reducing the importance of other brands the company had acquired during the years. These included: Chipotle, Boston Market, Fazoli's, Donato Pizzeria, and Pret a Manger. He cancelled big IT initiatives started by his predecessor and virtually halted the new store building program.

His next step was to determine what the key value drivers were for the company. The company looked to its foundation with Ray Kroc, who had restated in his autobiography what a consulting company previously concluded. "The basis of McDonald's success is serving low-priced value oriented product fast and efficiently in clean and pleasant surroundings." Cantalupo said "Those are the greens fees; unless you execute (those basics) you go nowhere." So McDonald's had its marching orders. The only question left was would they be able to execute the strategy? Many analysts were skeptical and openly predicted his ouster in the next eighteen months.

QUESTIONS

1. Do you believe that this approach was the best one for McDonald's to take at the time?
2. How would you organize the company to implement this approach?
3. How would you suggest they measure success?

KEYS TO IMPLEMENTATION CONTROL

Far too much time, money, effort, and goodwill is devoted to the development of an effective strategy for its implementation to be ignored or handed off to lower-level employees as something beneath the attention of senior management. Having worked through the process of strategy design and development, it is time to execute all that has been decided and planned. This can best be done by approaching the issue as a process that simultaneously directs activities throughout the organization, provides monitoring and control, and ensures that the performance of the organization is tied to the mission.

There are a number of methods that exist for coordinating the implementation of strategy. However, monitoring and control begin with metrics. In this chapter we will examine the development of metrics that are helpful in gauging strategic progress, and then discuss three of the most popular implementation approaches: 1) the balanced scorecard, 2) the value-driver-action model, and 3) the 7-S framework.

Prior to that discussion it is important to highlight five overall keys to successful implementation. These should be kept in mind as you read on, and should be the criteria by which implementation efforts are considered.

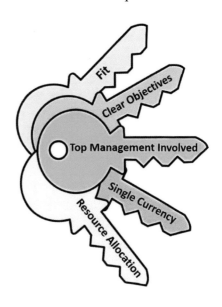

Key #1 – Fit

There is no more important concept to keep in mind than that of fit. The complete alignment of the company's strategy, structure, resources and value chain is crucial to its success. Companies are difficult to align and there are many aspects, both formal and informal, that need to be dealt with in order to attain fit. Imagine a Google where every employee was required to be in his or her cubicle by 8 A.M. and the dress code was a business suit. Or you walk into a bank branch where there is trash on the floor and the tellers don't seem to have a handle on how to do simple math. Have you recently called the 800-number for a company that distinguished itself in the marketplace through its customer service – only to find that you are kept on hold for eight minutes waiting for an agent who ultimately does not have the authority to correct the error the company originally made? How might a company such as Apple perform if it was led by a rigid, bureaucratic leader whose entire goal was organizational efficiency? These simple examples point out the most elementary aspects of the need for fit in everything a company does, from end to end.

Key #2 – Clear and Compelling Objectives

Implementation is a process that depends on everyone in the organization moving in the same direction. It is always quite an effort to focus the energy of the organization toward achieving a set of objectives. But this is far easier to do if the objectives are not only clear to all the employees of the company, but also if every employee feels that he or she has the ability to truly contribute to that achievement. Far too often companies have a very general objective to grow sales or to increase profitability, which are simultaneously uninspiring and remote to most employees. People who not only understand a compelling set of objectives, but also how they can contribute to their success and make a difference themselves, will pour out their energy and ability in an attempt to achieve them. We should break down every high-level objective into definable metrics that are relevant and important to employees, in order to help the company achieve its goals.

Key #3 – A Single Currency

One of the quickest ways to dismantle an effective plan is to provide different employees with different types of performance incentives, resulting in internal conflicts and inconsistent actions. Most reward systems are based upon some metric that would be representative of strong performance, such as bonuses, merit pay increases, stock options, stock grants, ESOP plans, and the list goes on. Virtually every type of "currency" has been tried. However, one tried and true success factor in effective strategy implementation has been for companies to reward as many people as possible in the organization using the same incentive. This keeps everyone focused on the same idea. Jack Welch talked endlessly about his success at General Electric as he shifted more and more people over to a system where they were rewarded with GE stock. Individual bonuses still existed, but they became a very small part of the compensation package as was any reward tied to the particular part of the company that person was working for.[2] The financial rewards were primarily tied to the success of the parent company stock, and it was that single currency system that helped focus employees in a widely disparate conglomerate on a single overarching financial performance goal.

Key #4 – Top-Management Involvement

Implementation has been regarded by some as that dirty business that is "operational" not "strategic," and therefore beneath the role of senior management. Absolutely nothing could be further from the truth. A well-designed strategy that is not effectively executed is useless. In fact, a recent study found that strategies deliver only 63% of expected financial performance because of inconsistent or nonexistent senior management involvement.[3] One of the most important functions of the executive is seeing that strategy is executed well. Larry Bossidy (retired CEO of Honeywell and Allied Signal) and Ram Charan stated in their book (*Execution: The Discipline of Getting Things Done*) that execution is: ".... a central part of a company's strategy and its goals and the major job of any leader in business.... "[4]

Key #5 – Resource Allocation

Strategy implementation is about action and the commitment of resources. A strategic plan that does not include a commitment of resources is doomed from the start. The concept of resources is broad and includes people, finances, plant and equipment, knowledge, time, and support, among others. One of the best ways to see if a company is truly committed to its stated strategic plans is to look at its resource allocations. A mismatch suggests either a lack of consistent follow-through in the management of the strategy, or alternative and competing priorities that are not all aligned with the stated direction. Both situations are a recipe for disaster.

Keep these five keys to successful implementation in mind as you read this chapter. These principles should help in organizing what is inherently a messy and difficult part of strategic management.

The refinement of an overarching strategy into a workable program is a process of continuous improvement and of iteration. Refer back to Figure 1.6 in the very first chapter in which we discussed the "feedback" arrows, suggesting that what managers observe and learn about implementation efforts through structuring and internal control provides guidance for how to go back and modify the strategic approach. Separating Strategy Formulation from Strategy Implementation and Evaluation (Figure 1.6) is something of an artifact arising from how strategy concepts have historically been taught in a logical and sequential fashion. In practice, though, they are combined and continuous, constituting what many refer to as the "learning organization."

METRICS

Strategy implementation is focused on defining what constitutes success, the means to get there, and the ability to measure its progress and ultimate achievement. The development of metrics is a key to that process, but it is at the same time difficult to do. Metrics should be tied to the overall goals of the organization and then translated by management to all of the efforts within the company, down to the most basic levels. Virtually all of the work efforts in a company should be tied to an overarching set of corporate metrics. Metrics can also help identify work effort that is not related directly to goals of the organization, and these can then be minimized, outsourced, or eliminated.

Every company should have a unique mission and a unique means of competing. Therefore it is crucial that the metrics of the company be tied to its mission. ROE is a good general outcome measure of performance, but says precious little about *how* a particular company is achieving its individual mission internally. The mission of the organization is the means by which you hope to draw in increasing numbers of customers returning to you and increasing economic profit.

One of the key challenges in strategic management is the execution of the wide variety of activities that fulfill the mission and constitute the essential value chain. The development of metrics must account for the simple fact that every company must balance its work effort toward the simultaneous and coordinated activities across multiple departments. Effective strategy implementation must build upon and reflect the tenets of value chain and the complexity of the company's resources and capabilities.

A company that merely focuses its metrics on highly-visible outcomes will probably distort the actions of its employees. A "whatever yields financial returns must be good" approach can lead to ethical lapses and debilitating scandals like those at Tyco and Enron. A single focus upon market share can produce excesses that lead to unprofitable distortions where sales are maintained by cannibalizing profit, quality, or other critical areas.

In Chapter 2 we pointed out that companies deal with a multitude of stakeholders who have complex and diverse wants from the organization. Therefore all companies should develop measures of performance that are both quantitative and qualitative. We now want to extend this performance measurement perspective and apply it inside the company as a means of focusing employee effort.

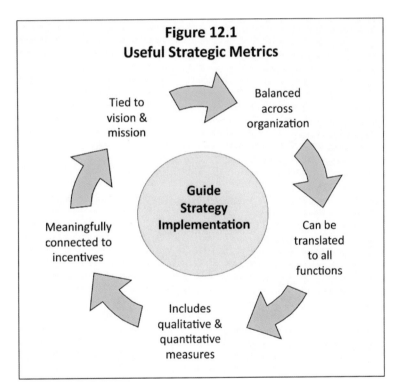

Figure 12.1
Useful Strategic Metrics

With these ideas in mind, implementation metrics should meet the following criteria (Figure 12.1):

1. Are tied to the overall mission/vision of the organization.

2. Are balanced across the organization so that all areas are covered.

3. Can be translated to all value chain functional activities and levels of employees.

4. Are composed of both quantitative and qualitative measures of performance.

5. Can be meaningfully connected to incentives on individual and group behavior.

Metrics Tied to the Mission/Vision

The most fundamental issue regarding the creation of useful metrics is ensuring that they are tied directly to the mission and vision of the company. It is relatively easy for a company to get caught up in the development of easily measured, but generally unhelpful measures of activity and/or performance. The mission statement for the organization should provide the guidance for the kind of value the company seeks to create, and therefore the types of metrics that will provide guidance on how well the company is creating value.

Consider the following points in the mission statement for the Coca-Cola Company:[5]

- To Refresh the World . . . in body, mind, and spirit.
- To Inspire Moments of Optimism . . . through our brands and our actions.
- To Create Value and Make a Difference . . . everywhere we engage.

The Coca-Cola Company

This mission statement suggests that there is a set of values that the company seeks to create in its business. These include the psychological and physical benefits of consuming its beverage products, the creation of a relationship with stakeholders that transcends mere consumption of food products, and a substantive contribution to communities and populations with which the company engages. If these values do indeed reflect the mission of Coca-Cola as a company, then it is incumbent upon the senior management to initiate activities that directly support the accomplishment of these values. In turn, management will need to develop metrics that will allow them to track these activities and evaluate their progress toward achieving the value creation they envision.

The point here is that the metrics a company decides to employ should reflect its mission and the strategic approach it is taking. If the company is pursuing a differentiation approach, then capturing information about efforts to reduce costs will be unproductive in allowing top management to understand whether progress is being made on the true strategic agenda. Unless "brand image" is a key success factor that parallels "low cost" in being able to effectively compete in an industry, then precious management time, attention, and resources might be used up gathering data on the effectiveness of a company's advertising campaign or the reputational effect of its product logo. So the kinds of metrics we refer to for implementation are those that guide the internal activities of the business in order to maintain strategic consistency. These allow senior management to understand whether the company is making positive progress in the pursuit of its strategic goals.

Recall from Chapter 1 that strategic management has to do with making substantive decisions affecting every area of the company, the results of which may not be apparent for a long period of time (in some cases years). Between the time an important strategic decision is made and the time when the results of that decision are clearly apparent in the form of enhanced economic returns, senior management must somehow gain insight as to whether the company is actually making progress. Creating insightful performance metrics allows senior management to assess progress, to enhance initiatives that are working well, and to change those that are not. Thus a set of metrics provides a means for senior management to gauge what is happening and exert strategic control.

Metrics Translated to Functional Levels

The overarching goals for the organization must become the guideposts for everyone in the company. This requires the creation of a set of metrics for every manager and every employee that guides their daily activities, such that the accomplishment of the activities is directly related to the overall organizational value creation objectives. To maximize their usefulness, therefore metrics must have balance, and what is needed is the right metric for the right level of the organization.

Balance. Important metrics may be gathered about production operations, sales effectiveness, employee training, marketing and advertising, and other activities in the company.

This is a key element in implementation as strategy involves coordinated and consistent effort across every area of a company. If a differentiation advantage is sought, this might translate not only to lower defect rates in manufacturing operations, but also the acquiring of raw materials from top-notch suppliers, the creation of superior packaging, the development of a unique advertising campaign, and the cultivation of a special customer segment. For a company to truly succeed in its differentiation strategy, metrics should be developed to indicate how well each of the functional areas or departments responsible for these efforts is succeeding in its support for this approach. As we discussed in earlier chapters on the value chain and business level strategies, the coordination, consistency of approach within and across an organization, and fit is often at the heart of superior performance.

Appropriate for the functional level. The metrics created for each employee or level must be related to activities that are under the control of that employee or level. Each metric is supposed to guide the conduct of certain activities or functions. What sense would it make to establish a metric for an individual or group that in part is determined by activities beyond the control of that individual or group? Not only would this potentially lead to frustration by employees who cannot fully control outcomes they are made responsible for, but it also leads to poor feedback to management regarding the sources of problems if a metric is not progressing as was desired.

Distilling down strategic-level value creation goals into activity-level metrics at the functional, group, or individual level is truly a challenge for management. This essentially challenges management to develop a causal logic about how and why things work the way they do. For example, one manager might believe that quality, as defined by minimizing defective products shipped can be best achieved by ensuring that assembly line workers have undergone training to enhance their production skills and capabilities (standardization of work skills, see Chapter 11). But another manager believes that quality is enhanced when employees are evaluated at their individual stations at a certain piece rate per minute (standardization of work output) in combination with placing personal signatures on products to certify their adherence to quality standards (mutual adjustment). Here are two competing causal logics, so how do we determine which is true? We develop measures to evaluate each logic, and go with the one that works best (or some combination). The same kind of causal logic development can be applied to every area of the company that is mission-critical in pursuing a particular strategic approach.

Establishing appropriate metrics for each functional level fosters greater control over strategy outcomes by creating the opportunity for organizational learning, as well as an understanding of when and where to take corrective actions if something is not working as planned. This is because the company can more closely monitor progress on the critical activities that are tied directly to the strategy of the business, and can make changes more quickly if progress is not apparent. In Figure 12.2 a company has the cause-

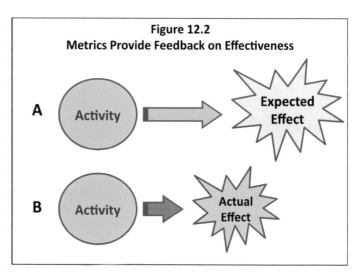

effect logic of A, where a certain activity taken in one of its departments will lead to an expected outcome at the departmental level that supports the company's strategic approach. Yet what the company actually experiences is B, where the outcome is less than stellar. By collecting outcome metrics on this important activity-effect relationship, the company might learn that its causal logic is flawed. The company then responds in one of two ways: either it needs to strengthen the activity in order to achieve the desired outcome, or it needs to engage in a different activity to achieve the outcome. Either way, the early insight the company gains on this very specific activity level increases the likelihood that the company can make necessary changes in order to enhance its strategy. This is a fundamental element in the creation of a learning organization.

Quantitative and Qualitative

Companies should develop a list of performance metrics that are a mix of both quantitative metrics and qualitative metrics. As students of business we are most familiar with the quantitative dimensions – collecting and analyzing the hard, objective data. We are prone to relying on numbers because our ability to use sophisticated programs for statistical analysis makes us feel less uncertain about what's going on.

But qualitative measures are just as important as quantitative measures. Qualitative data collection requires that the management team resist the temptation to distill everything down to a number and discount any "data" that cannot be distilled. Results from surveys, focus groups, call reports from the sales force, input from the customer service lines, trends in complaints or compliments are all ripe for quantification, losing valuable perspective that cannot be captured numerically. Qualitative metrics involve reading between the lines of numerical response data that are gathered, asking open-ended questions, and interpreting responses for which there are no clearly defined categories.

For example, although field sales reports may indicate that physicians are seeing pharmaceutical company representatives on a timely basis, they believe that the sales calls are not particularly helpful. Further interviews may reveal that physicians are not receiving as much

technical detail on new products as they would like. This suggests better training of the salespeople, the provision of more technically oriented literature, or possibly the creation of a company website strictly for physician use. This should lead the company to consider a measure of performance that is not a quantified number, but a perception from a physician's point of view. After changes are made at the pharmaceutical company, follow-up interviews yielded fewer negative, and even positive, comments about the information received in sales calls.

Consumer products companies often use focus group research, engaging small groups of consumers in deep conversations, to better understand how consumers think about and use their products. The results from these explorations provide a much deeper insight into new advertising messages and possible new product extensions. A qualitative evaluation would include the impressions the focus group leaders had while observing the group rather than the number of times that X was said. The "sense" of customers is a key means of guiding a company's actions.

Whether qualitative or quantitative, all performance measures need to account for two aspects: 1) its current state, and 2) its comparability across time and to competitors. The current state establishes where the metric is at the present time, so that we can assess its change going forward. Both absolute increases and relative change calculations can impart valuable insight. If for example, the organization has determined that an important criteria for the success of the company is high quality (when high quality is an effective point of differentiation), then it might measure defect rates. This gives the organization three important issues to deal with. The first is the establishment of the current defect rate. Taking a random sample of products over some period of time (created in a scientific manner that can be consistently replicated in the future), the firm can establish the current average defect rate as well as the range of defects it experiences. Secondly the firm must decide by what denominator it will divide the defect rate, such that it can compare its performance to the industry. Comparing the raw number of defects produced by a small shop versus those in a multinational business is not of much value unless the measure is somehow equalized or common-sized. Defects per thousand products produced, defects per employee, defects per volume shipped are among those that will provide valuable insight into the metric and how it changes over time in response to company actions. Finally, the relative defect rate method should be used to research, estimate, or calculate each of the company's direct competitors.

With quantitative performance metrics, averages are often used, however they are not nearly as important a measure of performance improvement as is range. Assume that the defect rate is 10 for every thousand products produced. After significant efforts at reducing this rate the company is pleased to announce a 20 percent improvement to 8 per thousand. What those numbers don't show is the range of defects, which might also illustrate what customers will experience over time and what will matter to them. If the range per thousand moves from 5 to 50 defects beforehand but now runs from 3 defects to 100 defects, it shows that nominal improvements in the average defect rate have come at the

Figure 12.3
Averages and Ranges in Quantitative Performance Metrics

Before improvement

After improvement

0   5   8 10   15   50   100
Defects per 1000 Produced

expense of greater volatility (Figure 12.3). This subjects the customer – and the company's reputation – to higher risk. A narrowing of the range without an improvement in the average is arguably much better for the organization because consistency is the hallmark expectation of most customers. The variation in a metric is therefore an extraordinarily powerful signal about performance, since it highlights the compelling issue of consistency of effort in strategic execution.

Quantitative metrics that reveal progress toward strategic performance need not be those which can only be measured by observing operations and calculating hard, objective numbers.

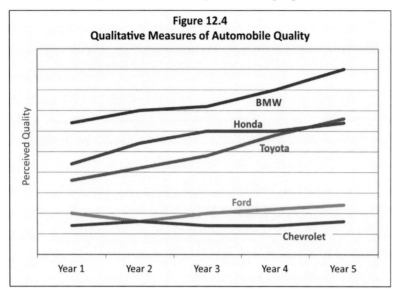

Figure 12.4
Qualitative Measures of Automobile Quality

Perceived quality is an area where this approach can also be used, for example. Rather than a specific quantified measure of quality such as the defect rate, the business decides that an important measure to keep track of is the customer's perception of quality. Their causal logic is that *perceptions* of quality lead to repeat purchase behavior. Utilizing a survey methodology, the company contacts its customers periodically and asks them to rank the quality of the products it produces as well as those of its competitors. There is a relatively simple set of questions that will allow a company to create a comparative chart of perceived quality. This data can then be collected on a regular schedule, such that progress toward particular quality goals can be assessed. Figure 12.4 illustrates precisely these sorts of measures collected by automobile companies.

Metrics Connected to Incentives

Creating a company where everyone is dedicated to the same set of goals is most successful if the organization can connect everyone's pay, bonuses, and incentive rewards to the metrics they are personally responsible for. Sun Tzu advised leaders to distribute the profits of war to everyone involved in order to incentivize their continued efforts. The currency of the business must be available to everyone in the company, not just the senior management team.

One of the most traditional means for public companies to attempt this connection has been to use stock options (the option to purchase x number of shares of stock at a pre-set price with the hope that the stock will be worth substantially more over time). The theory has been that this will focus executive attention on profitability and ROE (which will drive up stock prices), and thereby encourage them execute in ways that will increase the stock price above the option price. Even as some companies have increased the participation in stock option programs to include lower levels of management, its connection with what lower level managers actually do and can control is suspect at best. Stock prices rise and fall for a variety of reasons that may or may not have anything to do with individual actions. Furthermore when stock options are underwater (when option shares are priced substantially above the current market price), there is little to motivate performance.

Since the metrics that are developed to monitor and control performance have a clear connection with the company's strategy, they should also have a clear and discernible effect on the company's financial performance. When metrics are developed, therefore, it should be made clear to employees exactly how their own individual efforts contribute to both strategic objectives and financial performance goals. The best performing organizations are those that connect the efforts of employees to these overarching objectives and goals.

Of course one way to accomplish this is to regularly communicate the company's vision and mission to all employees, to keep it centrally in mind. But here we are suggesting the need to put that connection into daily practice, making sure that when employees successfully perform activities that are mission-critical, they participate in the financial rewards that accrue from that success. If the focus of the company is on quality, then achieving certain stretch quality standards should result in economic rewards for everyone. If corporate success is tied to the simultaneous achievement of three values (as in Coca-Cola), then success in those areas as measured by stretch metrics should enable contributing employees to share in the financial rewards that result.

The causal logic that forms the basis for the selection of metrics is the key to making this practical connection for each and every employee. It is also helpful if employees can become involved in developing the causal logic to begin with, although we recognize this is not always possible. But sharing the rationale for the selection of metrics by which employees will be incentivized, and making the connection to mission and strategy, helps to complete this process.

Ford Motor Company

Founded by Henry Ford and eleven business associates in 1903, Ford Motor Company pioneered the moving assembly line where workers remained in place performing the same job on every automobile that moved down the line. Henry Ford's vision was to produce automobiles that everyone could afford. Over the next 100-plus years, Ford grew its line of automotive labels to include Ford, Jaguar, Lincoln, Mercury, Mazda, and Volvo. Despite this proud heritage, by 2005 it was struggling with multiple issues. These included enormous legacy costs (retirement benefits to former employees), high labor costs (fostered by decades of contentious labor relations with unions), a slow response to changes in the environment (gas price increases and changing consumer desires), and slow responses to new competitive challenges from foreign automakers.

Ford was losing billions of dollars each year. The company announced a new strategic plan dubbed "The Way Forward" in early 2006, which called for dropping models, shutting down some assembly plants, reducing factory jobs, and innovating. "Our goal is simple – to build more of the products that people really want and value. Exciting new products that reflect the needs of today's and tomorrow's customers, with striking designs that are safer, more fuel efficient, and offer even greater value. That includes an expanded commitment to small cars, more crossovers, and more capable and fuel efficient trucks."[6] With this, they have spelled out exactly where they want to go. Developing a set of strategic metrics would be an important first task.

QUESTIONS

1. What metrics would you suggest?
2. If you had to keep it to seven or fewer metrics, which would be most important?
3. Focusing on the qualitative side, how might you measure "exciting new products" or "needs for tomorrow's customers"?

DEVELOPING AN IMPLEMENTATION PLAN

The remainder of this chapter is devoted to examining practical approaches for creating an implementation plan that bridges the divide between lofty strategic objectives and the day-to-day activities of employees. Translating strategy into action is the core of strategy implementation. We will examine three tools available for this purpose: 1) Balanced Scorecard; 2) Value-Driver-Action Model; and 3) 7-S Framework.

Balanced Scorecard Model

Introduced in the 1990s, the balanced scorecard [7] presents one practical (and very visible) approach to connecting strategy to action. This approach allows top management the ability to monitor progress toward overarching organization objectives and identifies those areas that are not meeting expectations. The central notion of the balanced scorecard is that financial measures of performance are the *result* of a variety of activities that people in the company engage in. This is a point we made in the very first chapter of this textbook. Therefore, managers need to examine and manage the activities that will ultimately contribute to financial performance. This central idea is, once again, entirely consistent with the nature of strategic management itself. That is, strategy has to do with sustainable long-term performance. Those that try to connect today's action's to today's financial performance find that the data is quite misleading, and can lead to inappropriate decisions. So one of the main purposes of the balanced scorecard is to connect today's actions and investments with long-term competitive and financial performance.

There are three important dimensions of the balanced scorecard model to understand. The Balanced Scorecard is: 1) driven by strategy, 2) used to address the cause-and-effect logic across four levels of the organization, and 3) used to delineate both lead and lag metrics.

The first dimension reflects the earlier discussion, that every metric developed must fundamentally reflect the strategic approach of the business. If we were to consider two restaurants in the fast food business, one pursuing a low cost leadership approach and one pursuing a differentiation approach, we would expect to see that the metrics used by one would be very different from the metrics used by the other. Not unlike the observation from Chapter 2 that a company's financial statements should reflect the nature of its market strategy, the set of metrics in a balanced scorecard should also mirror the company's strategy.

Figure 12.5
Balanced Scorecard Model

Learning & Growth Perspective	Internal Processes Perspective	Customer Perspective	Financial Perspective
Employee competences Systems Structure Culture	Customer management Operations & logistics Innovation Corporate citizenry	Product/service leadership Operational excellence Customer intimacy	Increase customer value Build franchise Improve cost structure Improve asset use

Second, the model incorporates four different levels of any organization, which are connected in a cause-and-effect fashion (Figure 12.5). Success in one perspective leads to success

391

in the next perspective. In the Learning & Growth Perspective, management considers the skills and competencies that the company develops in employees, as well as the facilitating systems, structure, and culture in which employees do the work of the company. If management provides the right structure, builds the right culture, and provides the right kind of training for employees, this should contribute to strong performance in the Internal Processes Perspective. In turn, excellence in internal processes regarding innovation, production, and customer management systems should enable the company to deliver new and better products or services to customers and to develop strong, enduring relationships in the Customer Perspective. Finally, the successes achieved in the Customer Perspective should roll up into strong performance in the Financial Perspective. The challenge for management is to create a set of metrics that provides insight on the extent to which the company is making positive progress in each of the sub-dimensions of the four perspectives that is specific to their organizational goals. Similar to the cause-effect logic illustrated in Figure 12.6, close ongoing attention to these specific metrics enables management to monitor progress and make changes when necessary.

Figure 12.6
Balanced Scorecard for Non-Profit

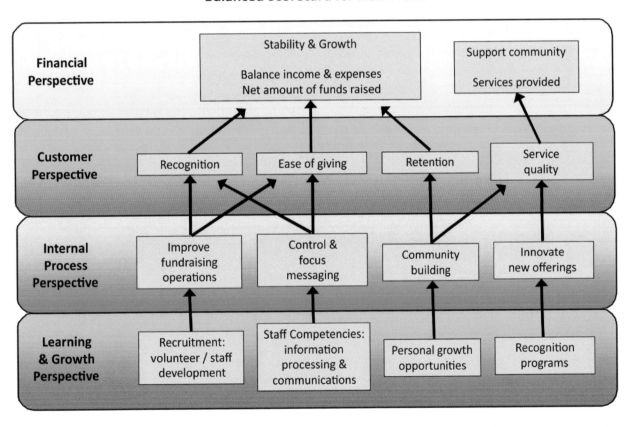

Figure 12.6 provides a semi-detailed example of a balanced scorecard used in a non-profit setting.[8] Typically you would begin at the bottom with the Learning and Growth Perspective, since employees, competencies, culture and incentives are foundational to organizations. Here the right kind of recruitment and proper development of organization-specific competencies at this level are believed to result in successes at the next level up. Better messaging about the nature and goals of the non-profit, together with enhanced fundraising techniques and methods, should then yield improvements in the Customer Perspective. Recognition of contributors and easier methods to

contribute both work toward one of the Financial Perspective goals of financial stability and growth. This example illustrates the causal logic that runs from bottom to top, connecting actions taken in the short run with longer terms strategic goals.

The third dimension of the balanced scorecard model involves the development of both lead metrics and lag metrics. Lag metrics are results that we would hope and expect to observe for each of the sub-dimensions in any one perspective. These are results that we cannot directly change. For example, in the Customer Perspective we may have a goal to acquire new customers, but the decision to buy from our company is up to the customer, not us. Customer acquisition is therefore a lag metric, but there are actions that our company can take that will impact this metric – for example, increasing sales call frequency or increasing the sales training of our salespeople. These are actions that we can directly affect, and they represent lead metrics that we can also measure. Figure 12.7 provides examples of lead and lag metrics in the Customer Perspective.

Figure 12.7
Examples of Lead and Lag Metrics in the Customer Perspective

Lead	Lag
% orders filled immediately	Customer acquisition
% on-time delivery	Customer retention
Customer survey feedback	Share of customer's total purchases
Number of sales calls per period	Ranking by customers vs. competition
Hours of training per sales person	% of sales from new products
Number of special customer requests filled	% of product line carried

---

You might recognize that the balanced scorecard fundamentally reflects an important theme of strategic management that is carried throughout this textbook. Competitive advantage has to do with creating value through sets of well-coordinated activities across the company's entire value chain. Similarly, the balanced scorecard focuses attention on strategically important activity sets and how these, in combination, work toward superior financial performance. Figure 12.8 illustrates a simplified version of a scorecard for a low cost airline.[9]

Figure 12.8
Balanced Scorecard for Low Cost Airline

	Objectives	Metrics	Targets	Strategic Initiatives
Financial	Profitability Fewer planes Increase revenue	Market value Plane lease cost Seat revenue	25% per year 5% per year 20% per year	Optimize routes Standardize planes
Customer	Flight is on time Lowest prices More customers	FAA on time rating Customer ranking Passenger traffic	# 1 in industry 98% satisfaction % change	Quality program Customer loyalty program
Internal	Fast ground turnaround	On-ground time On time departure	< 25 minutes 93%	Cycle optimization program
Learning	Ground crew coordination	% ground crew as stockholders % ground crew trained	Year 1 70% Year 2 90% Year 3 100%	Stock ownership plan Ground crew training program

Value-Driver-Action Model

It is important to recognize the contribution of the balanced scorecard to the ability of organizations to implement their strategy. Forcing organizations to simultaneously consider multiple facets of the organization and to codify those into measurable outcomes has made a significant impact in the ways in which some organizations manage and perform. On the other hand, the balanced scorecard model requires management to think about its organization using the four perspectives, which does not often resemble the way organizations are structured or the way in which managers think about their value chain activities. So for many managers, the balanced scorecard may be like asking a right-handed batter to bat left-handed: you know what to do, but you are definitely not practiced at it and it therefore is difficult to put into use.

An alternative to the balanced scorecard is what we refer to as the value-driver-action model. This model builds more directly off the key ideas that managers use when they consider formulating strategy. Where strategy implementation can more transparently take advantage of strategy formulation ideas and perspectives, the formulation effort can be more easily accomplished. Like the balanced scorecard, this model also focuses on the needs of the individual company and its unique resource-based advantages.

The design of an effective value-driven-action plan has five components:

1. Identifying key value drivers that will lead to a competitive advantage for the business.

2. Outlining the position the company wants to occupy from the perspective of how customers, suppliers, employees, and other stakeholders experience the company.

3. Translating desired stakeholder experience to business/market position.

4. Creating a list of actions to be taken, both short-term and long-term, that answer the question what must we do now to ensure success?

5. Developing metrics (both quantitative and qualitative) that measure progress toward the accomplishment of each value driver.

Key value drivers. The first and most critical element is the identification of the key value drivers for the organization. These can be identified from three sources:

- The list of key success factors (KSFs) developed through industry analysis (Chapter 4)
- The resource-based analysis that pinpoints extraordinary resources (Chapter 6)
- The vision and mission statements (Chapter 3)

One of the goals of industry analysis that we discussed in Chapter 4 was the identification of key success factors – those three to five competitive dimensions that are critical to succeeding in an industry. Through resource-based analysis (Chapter 6) managers should also be able to draw conclusions about the extraordinary, advantage-producing resources that the company possesses. Finally, the aspirations of the company may extend beyond the immediate industry environment and immediate resource endowments, and so critical dimensions for creating value over the long run might be identified with reference to the company's vision and mission statements.

The key value drivers for the company therefore arise out of some combination of current industry demands, current company capabilities, and future company aspirations. It is usually the case that current demands and current organizational capabilities dominate the list of value drivers that management decides upon. There is no absolute "right answer" when it comes to establishing the drivers, but the choice of drivers will make a significant difference in the results of the overall implementation plan.

Earlier in this chapter we noted that the mission elements of Coca-Cola were: 1) to refresh the world in body, mind, and spirit; 2) to inspire moments of optimism through their brands and actions, and 3) to create value and make a difference everywhere they engage. Coca-Cola, which competes in an industry where scale, innovation, and global presence are critical, also has significant and extraordinary resources in brand marketing, international management, and bottler relations, among others. Together this combination of mission elements, industry requirements, and company capabilities should form the basis for identifying the value drivers for the business.

Desired stakeholder experiences. Articulating desired statements from the point of view of stakeholders anchors the second section of an effectively developed strategy implementation plan using the value-driver-action model. Within each key value driver there will be a set of statements that the company aspires to hear from its stakeholders, which would indicate that the company has sincerely met its goals. It is relatively easy to develop a set of statements relating to a particular value. Done well, the statements capture the value driver's overall concept. These might include such statements as "I really like drinking Dasani water because it tastes so clean" (retail customer), or "I get the best prices without ever going out of stock on a product that sells quickly through my stores" (retail store owner), or "We love investing in Coca-Cola because of the environmental efforts they have initiated" (shareholders). Again, there is no right or wrong with these statements; they are a reflection of the way we want to see the value drivers manifest themselves with our stakeholders. In effect, they tell a story that we want to hear about our company, product, or service.

Translating experience to position. Having established the statements we are looking to achieve from our stakeholders, the company must translate each statement into a particular business or market position. These translations identify the key areas that the company must move to from where it currently exists. In 2007, the Associated Press released an article detailing how all bottled water is not the same. They found that "potassium…may give water a sweet taste. Silica may impart silkiness. Calcium can give the water a lactic taste some people find refreshing. Others enjoy the cleansing quality of water with high sodium content."[10] If Coca-Cola would like to achieve the desired stakeholder statement "I really like drinking Dasani water because it tastes so clean," then its laboratory scientists may need to develop new techniques for purifying and fortifying bottled water, which in fact they did. Similarly, the desired shareholder experience of wanting to invest in the company because of its environmental efforts might prompt management to establish a goal of becoming the leading beverage company in the recycling of plastic containers.

This latter example points out the possible disconnect between a targeted business or market position (based upon desired stakeholder experiences) and a company's existing resources and capabilities. Which resources, capabilities, structures, or programs must we have to increase the chances that our stakeholders will make the desired statements related to each value driver? Of course, it is not possible for a company to instantly become a leader in recycling, because of the significant investments required in science, infrastructure, manufacturing, customer relations, and other important value chain dimensions. Thus, part of the benefit of translating desired experiences to targeted business positions is examining what can be done immediately and what will require long-term investment.

Actions list. Implementation is often driven by the earliest of actions. An effective and motivating plan allows everyone in the company to get started on their efforts immediately. The third piece of the value-driver-actions model consists of distilling the desired stakeholder perspective goals down into specific sets of actions. Starting with each statement listed in the stakeholder experience section, the next step is to develop a list of actions that must be started. There are two kinds of actions that are identified in this phase: 1) actions that immediately address stakeholder experiences taking advantage of existing resources, and 2) actions to build new resources to address stakeholder experiences and long-term aspirations.

If Coca-Cola wishes to develop water that has a "clean, refreshing taste," then a plausible immediate action might consist of a series of lab-developed examples along with a series of customer-focused tasting sessions. The effort to achieve a clean, refreshing taste is one that the organization will constantly be trying achieve. Individuals have different tastes and what constitutes clean and refreshing might change as new competitors enter a market.

Metrics. Finally, we come back to developing metrics that afford the opportunity to monitor and control progress toward strategic goals. Each metric should tie directly to the stakeholder statement made for that value driver. Companies often have crossover metrics that align several value drivers. The initial effort will most likely lead to a long list of metrics. Prior to publishing a chart for everyone in the company, the metrics will need to be consolidated to make them universally understandable. The core of the plan is the ability to drive everyone in the organization toward the same set of measurable goals.

Coke might consider a qualitative metric comparing the refreshing taste of Dasani as compared to their competitor offerings where the desire is to have Dasani score well above their competitors. Another effective metric for the shareholder statement might be a quantitative assessment of the five- and ten-year stock performance of Coke relative to other companies with equivalent risk portfolios. Again, since this is an important statement for Coke, they would want to see this metric be substantially above their competition.

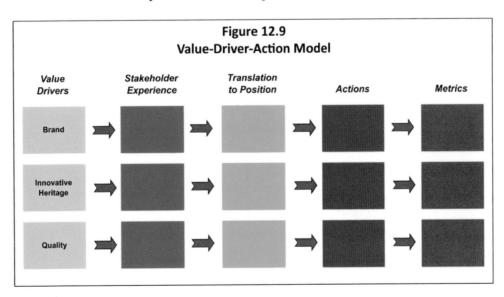

Putting all of this together is the final step. Ideally, this entire plan can be seen on a single page that can be shared with everyone in the company. The chart might look something like the one in Figure 12.9. The science of strategy implementation is the development of a set of metrics and immediate plans that are all focused on the value drivers for the organization. The art of strategy implementation is the actual terms used and the focus desired by management.

	Figure 12.10 Ford Motor Company Value-Driver-Action Model			
Value Drivers	Stakeholder Experience	Translation to Position	Actions To Take Now	Metrics
Consumer Economic Value	1. I always feel like I'm getting most bang for my buck with Ford. 2. Buying a Ford is straightforward, no haggling, no cash on the hood rebates. 3. When I sell my Ford, it feels like I'm getting a good return.	1. List price = sales price. 2. No haggle sales process. 3. Develop classic popular designs to ensure high retained value. 4. Reduce cost structure significantly to best in class.	1. Reduce management & employees as a result of efficiencies below to achieve best in class cost. 2. Change incentive structure & sales process. 3. Revamp designs where needed to classic timeless designs.	1. # of cash on the hood rebates lowest in industry 2. Avg discount off list/Industry Avg discount off list 3. Residual prices highest in peer group 4. # Consumers Choice awards for value 5. Production cost/model compared to peer group
Brand Focus	1. My family has always owned Fords and we believe in buying American Ford vehicles...it's a tradition. 2. My job is to produce the best new Ford-Back to the Future truck or car on the road. 3. Ford's repositioning strategy has combined the best of brand loyalty and preference. 4. People understand what we stand for – simply a Ford with the focus on consistency and reliability.	1. The Company immediately divests itself of other competing or distracting brands (Lincoln and Mercury). 2. Narrow Ford's selection to typify its heritage: Ford F-Series, mid-sized SUV (combining the best of the Explorer and Expedition), sporty Mustang and smaller, entry-level sedan (combining the best of the Escape and the Fusion). 3. Ford offers only four colors: Ford Black, Ford Blue, Ford Red and Ford White. Develop each of the four colors as a distinct new color only offered on Fords. 4. Develop a unique Back to the Future integrated marketing campaign that creates the 'buzz' and 'call to action' to compel consumers to buy a new Ford!	1. Locate a buyer for non-Ford brands. 2. Develop a timeline for selling down the existing Ford inventory. 3. Hire a new advertising and public relations firm to begin developing the message and planning the marketing/advertising campaign. 4. Plan an Analysts' Day to introduce Wall Street analysts to the new 'Ford – Back to the Future' strategy.	1. Survey consumers to determine the orthodox and unorthodox for a new Ford vehicle, interior and exterior. 2. Ratio of customer complaints to total customer touch points (i.e. online feedback, service questionnaires, post-purchase surveys, car show customer research). 3. Number of Ford's purchased in the U.S./Total number of cars/trucks purchased in the U.S. 4. Number of Ford trucks purchased in the U.S./Total number of Trucks purchased in the U.S. (Same metrics for SUVs, sports cars that compete with the Mustang and smaller sedans at entry price points).

Earlier in this chapter was presented a vignette about Ford Motor Company's travails in the mid-2000s, leading to their plan "The Way Forward." Figure 12.10 presents a partial picture of the value-driver-action model for Ford, based upon two of its core value drivers of consumer economic value and brand focus.

McDonald's – The Rest of the Story[11]

McDonald's illustrates excellence in strategy implementation, utilizing everything discussed in this chapter to create their "Plan to Win." The plan put the implementation effort onto a single page, in a format allowing every employee to understand the keys to success and how they will be measured. First, they established their Key Value Drivers and what those drivers meant:

Key Value Driver	Meaning
Our People	Well-trained, friendly people are key to providing I'm Loving It Service
Our Products	Our menu features the choice and variety that consumers enjoy eating often
Our Places	The comfort and convenience of our restaurants attract customers
Our Prices	Through our products and restaurant experience, we deliver value to customers
Our Promotions	"Forever Young" and engaging, our Brand connects with people around the world

Each of these drivers was then converted into stakeholder statements such as:

Key Value Driver	Stakeholder Statement
Our People	"A simple smile makes me feel welcome... it's the perfect start to my meal... it's the reason I love McDonalds."
Our Products	"What do I want from a Restaurant? Good food and good choices. That's why I go to McDonalds."
Our Places	"McDonald's is a cool place where everyone can relax. I'm comfortable here, and my friends and I know we're always welcome."
Our Prices	"Whether I have a lot or a little to spend, McDonald's always offers great taste at a great value."
Our Promotions	"I love McDonald's. I can eat great food, play and get a fun toy. I guess that's why my mom loves McDonald's too."

The company listed their critical success factors and "must do now" actions before designing a set of metrics so that they could measure success. We illustrate metrics from the first value driver as an example:

Key Value Driver	Metrics
Our People	Training & Development - $$ Investment, number of graduates from Hamburger University, New platforms for career development.
	Great Place to Work – Rated in 100 Best companies to work for.
	Diversity Initiatives – McDonald's trains more minorities and women than any other U.S. employer. 40% of Owner/Operators and more than 50% of workforce is women and minorities.
	McPassport – a program of employee training and certification that allows free movement throughout the E.U.

Overarching metrics included items such as return to shareholders, new product launches, store growth, dividend growth, etc. By virtually any measure available – whether sales, same-store sales, stock price, returns, etc. – McDonald's has executed with precision.

The 7-S Framework

The third tool available for turning strategy into action is one of the most popular and consistently-used frameworks over time. The 7-S framework was developed four decades ago by McKinsey & Co.[12] Intentionally using alliteration to help aid memory, the technique helps us align the functions of an organization. Most strategists split the seven S's into the hard S's (so called because they are relatively easy to identify and articulate in a written document) and the soft S's (named because they are more difficult to pin down in a precise manner). The entire framework (Figure 12.11) is oriented around the concept of fit. The better each of the seven fit together, the better the organization performs.

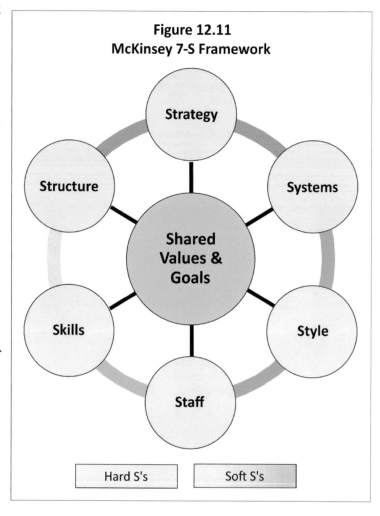

Figure 12.11
McKinsey 7-S Framework

Strategy. This is the written set of statements that constitutes the strategic direction of the company. This formulation is the compilation of most of what we have discussed in this text. It is the examination of the value chain, capabilities, resource-based advantages, and business level strategy of the organization such that it can compete effectively. The strategy is the means by which the company intends to be successful.

Structure. Most people often seen this as the written organization chart, but readers of this text should view this as the *design* of the organization, which was discussed in detail in Chapter 11. That design is a combination of knowing: 1) what constitutes the core, techno structure, and support staff of the organization; 2) how you will coordinate their activities; and 3) what organizational structures you will use. The structure should be designed to support the strategy, because "structure follows strategy."

Systems. While often thought of as the information technology systems of the company, this just scratches the surface of what constitutes the systems of the company. Having designed an effective strategy and aligned the structure such that it supports the strategy, it is incumbent upon senior management to align the systems of the company so they support both the strategy and the structure. Quality control systems, performance review systems, human resources systems, and policies and procedures are all amongst the systems that need to be considered. Aligning the systems so they support the new structure is a critical step in implementation. Little will happen if the systems do not provide the information needs of the company. Changing the systems of an organization can be quite traumatic as they have usually been developed over a long period of time, and employees are accustomed to them. That said, a new strategy and structure demands a reevaluation of all the systems of the organization. What can be eliminated? What needs to be done to support the new core functions? What new metrics must be gathered? Systems support the organization and its goals, providing the critical link between a strategy that is desired and a structure that is trying to implement that strategy.

Style. The symbolic behavior of the organization starts at the top of the organization. The way that employees treat each other, the dress code, and the approach to the work day are all elements of the organization's style. The CEO and the top management team of the company set the style that constitutes acceptable behavior. This element is based in action and often has little to do with what is actually said. An organization that is fundamentally built upon freedom of expression, creativity, and taking chances can be enhanced by a CEO like Steve Jobs who embodied those style elements and can be crushed by a CEO like John Scully whose style was corporate control and formality-oriented. In the previous chapter we mentioned the free-wheeling Zappos company, which has implemented an adhocracy structure. How strange it would be if they also instituted a coat-and-tie dress rule or required people to communicate through written memoranda! The alignment of style with the desired strategy, structure, and systems of a company has the ability to propel the organization forward.

Staff. Staffing is an examination of the means and processes for bringing in new employees as well as the processes inherent in getting them to be productive for the company. New employees take time to start really providing value to the organization. Staffing is about shortening that time and aligning the process with the rest of the company.

Too often employees are brought in with no formal means of incorporating their efforts into the organization. They learn the nomenclature, practices, and people via an informal, ad hoc system that makes early contribution to success virtually impossible. Arthur Andersen & Co. was the storied accounting firm that had this process down to a science. Every employee started their career at the Andersen school in Illinois. They learned about the processes, practices, and expectations in a high-pressure, fast-paced program that made them quickly valuable to the organization.

Skills. These are the dominant skills of the organization, and dictate what is most important in creating value for that particular organization. These are similar to what we referred to as capabilities in Chapter 6. Within the same industry, we often see a wide variety of skill sets depending upon the overarching goals of the company. One insurance company might determine that deep knowledge of insurance is a core skill for their company. They might require everyone to study insurance and be certified in the area. Another insurance company might decide that the core set of skills is customer service. They would set their training program up to establish customer service skills as those that should permeate the entire organization. Another insurance company, such as Geico, might decide it is all about sales and marketing skills. They would organize around the salespeople and emphasize sales and marketing skills as the critical capabilities set of the organization.

Superordinate Goal (Shared Values). These are the overarching goals of the organization. In practice this is usually manifested in the vision and mission of the company, representing the focus of the company and its reason for existence. Aligning the vision and mission of the company with the strategy would seem to be obvious. As we discussed extensively in Chapter 3, this is an important element in guiding the practices of every employee, every day of the week.

Art, Science, Balance, Continuity

Putting together the balanced scorecard, the value-driver-action model, or the 7-S framework for a company is as much art as it is science. With any of these implementation frameworks it is important to consider all of the elements when designing the plan and the appropriate metrics.

Balance across the company is always important. One interesting approach for incorporating the 7-S framework into the implementation plan is to require that at least several metrics touch each of the seven areas of the company. The other significant advantage of a balanced implementation effort is the benefit that it has on the speed with which the business can move in new directions. Well-designed metrics allow for an early warning system. This enhances agility to meet emerging challenges, and can provide a key source of competitive advantage in dynamic markets. The strategic management model that we outlined in Chapter 1 (Figure 1.6) is a dynamic model that has continual feedback for the decision makers in an organization. Designing and implementing strategy is an ongoing process, not an event.

The effort at aligning the organization provides the information flow necessary to create a learning organization. Company-designed metrics can provide information on the resource-based advantages of the business and feedback to initiate a review of the process all over again with new insight. Insight is provided not only on the true capabilities of the company, but also exposes new opportunities for the organization. And as we have emphasized, opportunity recognition is critical for achieving sustainable competitive advantage.

FedEx had long viewed itself as an overnight delivery service that specialized in the process of package movement. The company received continual praise for its operation and the service that it provided to business. Over the years, more and more competitors were able to approach their service levels causing the key value drivers for FedEx to start changing. The process of continually formulating and implementing strategy allowed them to see that one of their key value drivers was providing services to people for whom speed and last-minute quality handling were a priority worth paying for. FedEx acquired Kinkos and dramatically expanded their hours, service offerings, and its ties to the FedEx operation.

STRATEGIC LEADERSHIP

As a conclusion to our discussion of effective strategy implementation, we briefly mention the critical role played by strategic leadership. In fact, every step along the way in this textbook we have been highlighting points where strategic leadership is important. It is the responsibility of the senior management team to bring together all of the strategic management functions so that the business can develop sustainable competitive advantages and earn superior returns. These core responsibilities of strategic leadership can be summed up in the following list:

- **Establish vision, mission, goals**. Leadership is at its core about guiding the total business forward in a manner that has the potential to be extraordinary. Designing an appropriate vision and mission is at the heart of this effort.

- **Build senior management team**. Identifying, recruiting, and hiring the best people to lead a particular company and a particular point in time is crucial for success.

- **Establish structure for communication, coordination, and control**. The structure of the organization is wholly dependent upon the strategy that has been designed.

- **Exert control over direction**. Using a performance monitoring system ensures effective strategy implementation.

- **Establish a code of ethics for conduct and decision making.**

- **Evaluate, decide, act**. Decision making about value chain, resources allocation, type of strategy, growth, and implementation are the province of successful leaders.

- **Rational decision making**. Strategic moves are not decided on a whim or based upon personal egos or desires. Effective strategy requires excellence in deep, revealing analysis. This can then be married to intuition and perspective that comes from personal experience.

- **Establish top-management team process that challenges assumptions, surfaces alternatives**. The strategic imperatives of opportunity recognition and value creation demand nothing less.

- **Establish a match between the culture and personal leadership style**. A culture that matches the values of the leader and is in harmony with the leader's actions will prove to be a powerful driving force for the organization. Sometimes this means the culture might change to reflect a leader's style, and in other cases it may mean the leader's style must match the existing culture.

- **Motivate through incentives and rewards aligned with goals**. Establish a system that rewards employees when their individual accomplishments contribute to organizational goals.

Strategic leadership is most often the province of senior management, as the preceding list of bullet point ideas attests. But let us return to the initial idea about strategic leadership that we presented in the very first chapter of this book (on the fifth page of Chapter 1, in fact). Since strategy by definition involves all functions in a company and crosses all levels, everyone in the organization is exposed to it, affects its success, and can offer critical input on its formulation and its implementation. This includes you. Some of the ideas you have read about in this book are newer ideas that many others in your future employers won't be aware of. Not only does this VRIST strategy understanding present you with your own potential for sustainable competitive advantage in your career, it also presents you with an organizational responsibility to serve as a strategic leader within your own sphere of influence!

Guiding an organization through the combination of dynamic challenges from the general environment, aggressive competitors, demanding customers, and other stakeholders is a complex process. It is a process that demands the application of both science and art. A deep understanding of the science of strategy and its application has been the goal of this book. The art of strategy is the art of strategic leadership. You will become the strategic leaders of tomorrow, and we hope this book helps you to succeed.

CHAPTER SUMMARY

This chapter focused on the issues involved in internal control and performance, which is a challenging part of strategy implementation. We began the chapter by discussing five keys to control and performance systems:

1. Fit

2. Clear and Compelling Objectives

3. A Single Company Currency

4. Top-Management Involvement

5. Resource Allocation

We reviewed the development of different types of metrics, because any system of control and performance must be based on definable dimensions that can be measured. The set of metrics must exhibit five conditions:

1. Are tied to the overall mission/vision of the organization.

2. Are translated appropriately to all functions and levels of employees.

3. Are balanced across all functions.

4. Are composed of both quantitative and qualitative measures.

5. Are connected to a unifying incentives system.

Next we reviewed three frameworks for monitoring and evaluating performance. These systems allow management to evaluate whether short-term progress toward long-term strategic goals is positive, or if corrective actions are called for:

1. Balanced scorecard model, which examines execution through four perspectives:

   - Learning and Growth
   - Internal Process
   - Customer
   - Financial

2. Value-driver-action model, which is directly translatable to an individual organization's strategic direction and consists of five parts:

   - Value Drivers
   - Stakeholder Experience
   - Translation to Position
   - Action

- Metrics

3. The McKinsey 7-S framework, which consists of three hard S's and four soft S's:

- Strategy
- Structure
- Systems
- Skills
- Style
- Staff
- Superordinate Goals (shared values)

Learning Objectives Review

1. *Translate strategy into functional area goals and activities using the keys to implementation control.*

- There are five keys to success against which strategy implementation should be evaluated: Fit; Clear and compelling objectives; Single company currency for incentives; Top management involvement; Resource allocations to support direction and commitments.

- Implementation begins with mission and vision. The strategic approach which will accomplish the mission leads to specific strategic initiatives. Value chain activities relevant to these initiatives are conducted. Metrics evaluating value-creating activities can monitor progress on the accomplishment of strategy.

2. *Develop effective metrics for the control and growth of the organization.*

- Are tied to the overall mission/vision of the organization.

- Are translated appropriately to all functions and levels of employees.

- Are balanced across all functions.

- Are composed of both quantitative and qualitative measures.

- Are connected to a unifying incentives system.

3. *Describe the differences between the models used for implementing a strategic plan.*

- The balanced scorecard connects long term competitive and financial performance to short term actions. It relies on a cause-effect logic that requires lead and lag metrics on activities engaged in by a wide variety of stakeholders.

- The value-drive-action model builds more directly on strategy formulation efforts. Value creation goals drive actions to enable the company to move from its present position to a desired future position.

- The 7-S framework seeks to align seven important dimensions of the organization.

404

4. *List and describe the core responsibilities of strategic leadership.*

- Establish vision, mission, goals.

- Build senior management team.

- Establish structure for communication, coordination, and control.

- Exert control over direction.

- Establish a code of ethics for conduct and decision making.

- Evaluate, decide, act.

- Rational decision making.

- Establish top-management team process that challenges assumptions, surfaces alternatives.

- Establish a match between the culture and personal leadership style.

- Motivate through incentives and rewards aligned with goals.

Key Terms

7-S framework – A method for examining the various aspects of the organization in such a way that alignment can be achieved. Elements include strategy, structure, systems, style, skills, staff and superordinate goals (shared values).

Balanced scorecard – An implementation method that considers a wide variety of stakeholders in the performance of the company.

Casual logic – An cause-effect statement of belief about how and why things work the way they do.

Characteristics of effective metrics – There are five elements to high-quality metrics. They are: 1) tied to the mission and vision; 2) appropriate for the function or level; 3) balanced across functions; 4) both quantitative and qualitative; and 5) connected to incentives.

Key value drivers – Those elements of the organization that provide the company with the best opportunity for success in their industry.

Lag metrics – Represent the results that we expect to observe for each sub-dimension in a balanced scorecard.

Lead metrics – Represent the observable actions of employees that will lead to the results we are trying to achieve.

Qualitative metrics – Measures of success that are descriptive and relative rather than analytic.

Quantitative metrics – Numerically based measures of firm success.

Short Answer Review Questions

1. Why is strategy implementation so important to a company?

2. What elements would you consider to be critical for effective implementation?

3. What is a balanced scorecard?

4. How do the elements in the balanced scorecard work with each other?

5. Why do we start with the learning and growth part of the model?

6. How does the value-driver-action method differ from the balanced scorecard method?

7. How do we determine the key value drivers for an organization?

8. What types of statements constitute good stakeholder statements?

9. What criteria should you use when designing good metrics?

10. How do metrics guide the organization?

11. How would you recommend corporate metrics be translated to individual employee metrics?

12. What is a qualitative metric and how should it be used in the organization?

13. How are key stakeholder statements translated into action plans?

14. What issues should be addressed in the alignment of style?

Group Exercises

1. Select a large, well-known consumer company that is of interest to you and your group members.

    a. What are the key value drivers for this company?

    b. Given those drivers, what statements would you like to hear from stakeholders for each of the value drivers?

    c. How might you measure whether the company was successfully achieving those stakeholder statements?

2. Take a look at one of the package delivery companies such as FedEx, UPS, or the U.S. Postal Service. They each need a balanced scorecard for their organization and each of those scorecards should be quite different. Select one of those organizations and develop a balanced scorecard for the company based upon publicly available information.

3. A new salon has approached you about their business. The mission of this organization is: "Everything for the body." They plan to be the largest salon in the state of Colorado, with hairstylists, manicurists, massage therapists, tanning facilities, a huge 50 foot by 120 foot saltwater

warm bathing area, sauna facilities, yoga facilitation, meditation classes, and Pilates. There will be a personal attendant for each customer and the customer will be truly pampered. A large office staff will be required, a day care facility for the children, a high-end artsy restaurant will be on-site for the patrons, and everything will be cutting edge with each patron only having to press their thumbprint to gain access to an area or pay for their purchases! The owner would like help in designing a 7-S framework for this new business idea. Design a 7-S for this business.

References

[1] Grainger, David. 2003. "Can McDonald's cook again?" Fortune. April 14, 147(7): 40–47; Horovitz, Bruce. 2003. It's back to basics for McDonald's. USA Today. May 20

[2] Welch, Jack, and John Byrne. 2001. Jack: Straight from the gut. Warner Books. New York.

[3] Mankins, M. C. and Steele, R. 2005. Turning great strategy into great performance. Harvard Business Review, July-August, 123-131.

[4] Bossidy, L., and R. Charan. 2002. Execution: The discipline of getting things done. New York: Crown Business.

[5] www.thecoca-colacompany.com.

[6] Ford Company 2006 Annual Report.

[7] Kaplan, R. S., and D. P. Norton. 1992. Balanced scorecard: Measures that drive performance. Harvard Business Review 70(1): 71–80; Kaplan, R. S., and D. P. Norton. 1996. Linking the balanced scorecard to strategy. California Management Review 39(1): 53–79.

[8] Adapted from BS Designer, www.bscdesigner.com.

[9] Adapted from Balanced Scorecard Institute, www.balancedscorecard.org.

[10] Kayal, Michele. 2007. Top beverage. The Associated Press in The Winston-Salem Journal. November 5: D1.

[11] McDonald's Corporation – 2006 Annual Report.

[12] Waterman, Robert H., Thomas J. Peters, and Julien R. Phillips. 1980. Structure is not organization. Business Horizons. June: 14–26; Waterman, Robert H. 1982. The seven elements of strategic fit. Journal of Business Strategy 2(3): 69–73.

Made in the USA
Columbia, SC
03 January 2018